D1590814

Text and History

Text and History

Historiography and the Study of the Biblical Text

Jens Bruun Kofoed

Winona Lake, Indiana
Eisenbrauns
2005

BS
480
.K53
2005

© Copyright 2005 by Eisenbrauns.
All rights reserved.
Printed in the United States of America.

Library of Congress Cataloging-in-Publication Data

Kofoed, Jens Bruun, 1963–
  Text and history : historiography and the study of the biblical
  text / Jens Bruun Kofoed.
      p.   cm.
  Includes bibliographical references and index.
  ISBN 1-57506-094-9 (hardback : alk. paper)
  1. Bible. O.T.—Evidences, authority, etc. 2. Bible. O.T.—
Historiography. 3. Bible. O.T.—Language, style. 4. Bible. O.T.
Kings—Criticism, interpretation, etc. I. Title.
BS480.K53   2005
221.9′5—dc22
                                                    2004017732

The paper used in this publication meets the minimum requirements of the American
National Standard for Information Sciences—Permanence of Paper for Printed Library
Materials, ANSI Z39.48-1984. ♾ ™

For my wife, Vivi,
and my children, Line, Ditte, Nicolai, Mikkel, and Emil

Contents

Preface

The starting point of my research on ancient Israelite history writing began in Copenhagen in more than one sense. I grew up, academically speaking, with the half-century-long consensus of the Alt-Noth and Albright-Bright schools, and it was quite a surprise to discover, therefore, that consensus was fading when I moved to a teaching position at the Copenhagen Lutheran School of Theology in 1992 after three years outside the academy. I was fully aware that a growing number of Old Testament scholars more or less independently had begun to question the methodological assumptions underlying both the Alt-Noth school and the Albright school reconstructions of the history of Israel as early as the 1960s, but what had happened after I left the academy was that two of the leading opponents of the older schools, Niels Peter Lemche and Thomas L. Thompson, had moved to the department of Biblical Studies at the University of Copenhagen. By the time I was teaching my first course on ancient Israel's history, they had established what has been called the Copenhagen School.

In a retrospective assessment, one must admit that both Thompson and Lemche were avant-garde in drawing the logical conclusions from the methodological collapse of the older schools; this first and mainly deconstructive phase of their efforts was both inevitable and necessary. Following this initial and partially successful phase, they have been concentrating on reconstructing (the history of) Israel using a new method that is characterized by its heuristic preferences for so-called "hard data" and "material remains" as historical correctives to the textual evidence, specifically, the biblical texts. The results of this approach, however, are highly dependent on the validity of its assumptions, and it was the questionable character of these assumptions that set me onto the research trail and led me to apply the question that Nathanael once asked Philip about Jesus (John 1:45) to the situation in Copenhagen: "Can anything good come out of Copenhagen?" It is my conviction that the question must be answered in the affirmative. Though I argue in what follows that neither textual nor artifactual data are being treated fairly in the reconstructions proposed by Lemche, Thompson, and other nonresident sympathizers of the Copenhagen School, I do find—as already mentioned—their deconstruction of the prior consensus's methodological foundations both inevitable and necessary. For the same reason, it has been of immense importance for my research to participate in the senior seminars led by Niels Peter Lemche and Thomas Thompson at the department of Biblical Studies, University of Copenhagen, and (without making any participants responsible for the outcome of my research!) I appreciate the opportunities provided there to discuss the matters dealt with in the present monograph.

This study is a revised version of the Ph.D. thesis I submitted to the University of Aarhus, Denmark, in June 2002. Wonderland would probably have been much less adventurous for Alice had nobody bothered to guide her in the right direction! Like Alice, I owe a number of "Cheshire Cats," "Caterpillars," "White Rabbits," and "Duchesses" for having guided me through unknown territory—that is, for having made the submission of the present thesis possible and the foregoing research much like an "academic adventure."

It is no doubt my wife, *Vivi*, and my children, *Line*, *Ditte*, *Nicolai*, *Mikkel*, and *Emil*, who have borne the most profound sacrifices over the last three years. And without their enduring love, understanding, patience, and encouragement, I would probably still be writing the introduction!

Academic guidance has been provided by a number of people who need to be given special thanks. First of all, I want to mention Professors Alan Millard and Kenneth Kitchen, who were of immense help during my studies at the University of Liverpool in the academic year 1999–2000 and have continued to offer their assistance since I returned to Copenhagen. I also owe my supervisors at the University of Aarhus, Professor Kirsten Nielsen and former Assistant Professor Knud Jeppesen (now vice-rector at Tantur Ecumenical Institute for Theological Studies, Jerusalem). Professor Thomas Thompson also offered me guidance, especially in the initial phase of my research. Apart from my colleagues Henrik Bartholdy, Torben Kjær, Nicolai Winther-Nielsen (Copenhagen Lutheran School of Theology), Carsten Vang (Lutheran School of Theology in Aarhus), I also want to thank the historians Jon Gissel, University of Copenhagen, and Carsten Selch Jensen, University of Southern Denmark, for having shared their insights and discussed the thesis with me. Last but not least, I want to express my gratitude to the board of the Copenhagen Lutheran School of Theology for carrying the most substantial financial burden of my research.

All translations of quotations from non-English modern sources are mine.

Copenhagen
June 2003

Abbreviations

General

ANE	ancient Near East
BH	Biblical Hebrew
com.	common
DHW	Deuteronomic History Writer
DSS	Dead Sea Scrolls
DtrH/H(Dtr)	Deuteronomistic Historian
fem.	feminine
HB	Hebrew Bible
IH	Israelite Hebrew
LBH	Late Biblical Hebrew
MH	Mishnaic Hebrew
masc.	masculine
MMT	*Miqṣat Maʿaśê ha-Torah* (Some of the Torah Observations)
pl.	plural
PS	Proto-Semitic
QH	Qumran Hebrew
RH	Rabbinic Hebrew
SB	Standard Babylonian
SBH	Standard Biblical Hebrew
sing.	singular
SVO	subject-verb-object sentences
VSO	verb-subject-object sentences

Reference Works

ABD	*Anchor Bible Dictionary*
AJSL	*American Journal of Semitic Languages and Literatures*
ANET	*Ancient Near Eastern Texts*
ANVAO	*Avhandlinger utgitt av Det Norske Videnskaps-Akademi i Oslo*
AOAT	Alter Orient und Altes Testament
BAR	*Biblical Archaeology Review*
BASOR	*Bulletin of the American Schools of Oriental Research*
BBR	*Bulletin for Biblical Research*
BiOr	*Bibliotheca Orientalis*
BJRL	*Bulletin of the John Rylands University Library of Manchester*
BO	*Bibliotheca Orientalis*
BoTu	Die Boghazköi-Texte in Umschrift

BSOAS	*Bulletin of the School of Oriental and African Studies*
BZAW	Beiheft zum Zeitschrift für die alttestamentlichen Wissenschaft
CAH	*Cambridge Ancient History*
CBQ	*Catholic Biblical Quarterly*
CIS	Copenhagen International Seminar
CoS	*The Context of Scripture.* Edited by W. W. Hallo. 3 vols. Leiden, 1997–2003
CTH	E. Laroche. *Catalogue des textes hittites.* 2nd ed. Paris, 1971
DJD	Discoveries in the Judaean Desert
ErIsr	*Eretz Israel*
ESHM	European Seminar on Historical Methodology
HANES	History of the Ancient Near East Studies
HdO	Handbuch der Orientalistik
HSM	Harvard Semitic Monographs
HSS	Harvard Semitic Studies
HUCA	*Hebrew Union College Annual*
ICC	International Critical Commentary
IEJ	*Israel Exploration Journal*
JANES	*Journal of the Ancient Near Eastern Society*
JAOS	*Journal of the American Oriental Society*
JBL	*Journal of Biblical Literature*
JCS	*Journal of Cuneiform Studies*
JEA	*Journal of Egyptian Archaeology*
JEOL	*Jaarbericht van het Vooraziatisch-egyptisch genootschap "Ex Oriente Lux"*
JETS	*Journal of the Evangelical Theological Society*
JHS	*Journal of Hebrew Scriptures*
JNES	*Journal of Near Eastern Studies*
JNSL	*Journal of Northwest Semitic Languages*
JQR	*Jewish Quarterly Review*
JSNTSup	Journal for the Study of the New Testament Supplement Series
JSOT	*Journal for the Study of the Old Testament*
JSOTSup	Journal for the Study of the Old Testament Supplement Series
JSPSup	Journal for the Study of the Pseudepigrapha Supplement Series
JSS	*Journal of Semitic Studies*
JTS	*Journal of Theological Studies*
KAI	H. Donner and W. Röllig. *Kanaanäische und aramäische Inschriften.* 2nd ed. Wiesbaden, 1966–69
KBo	*Keilschrifttexte aus Boghazköi.* Wissenschaftliche Veröffentlichungen der deutschen Orientgesellschaft 30, 36, 68–70, 72–73, 77–80, 82–86, 89–90. Leipzig, 1916–
NEA	*Near Eastern Archaeology*

NIBC	New International Bible Commentary
NIDOTTE	*New International Dictionary of Old Testament Theology and Exegesis*. Edited by W. A. VanGemeren. 5 vols. Grand Rapids, 1997
NTT	*Norsk Teologisk Tidsskrift*
NZSTh	*Neue Zeitschrift für Systematische Theologie*
OPDNESPJSCU	Occasional Publications of the Department of Near Eastern Studies and the Program of Jewish Studies, Cornell University
OTL	Old Testament Library
PEQ	*Palestine Exploration Quarterly*
PMLA	*Proceedings of the Modern Language Association*
PThMS	Pittsburgh Theological Monograph Series
RevQ	*Revue de Qumran*
SJOT	*Scandinavian Journal for the Old Testament*
TAPS	*Transactions of the American Philosophy Society*
TynBul	*Tyndale Bulletin*
UF	*Ugarit-Forschungen*
UUÅ	*Uppsala Universitets Årsskrift*
VT	*Vetus Testamentum*
VTSup	*Vetus Testamentum Supplements*
WBC	Word Biblical Commentary
WTJ	*Westminster Theological Journal*
ZA	*Zeitschrift für Assyriologie*
ZAH	*Zeitschrift für Althebraistik*
ZAW	*Zeitschrift für die Alttestamentliche Wissenschaft*

Chapter 1

Introduction

We are not isolated objects who impose interpretations on a
mute world, but we and the world are an ontological unity,
and the world first imposes itself on us. We grow to self-
consciousness gradually through images and interpretations.
And just as we are constituted by an unconscious world or
myth, the process of becoming conscious is that of a world or
myth becoming conscious. It is impossible to isolate history
from meaning, theological, autobiographical, or otherwise. We
are history writing itself.[1]

Hal Childs

The Cheshire Cat

One of the more spectacular features of Lewis Carroll's *Alice's Adventures in Wonderland* is no doubt the Cheshire Cat's grin. Entering a
certain Duchess's house on her Wonderland journey, Alice spots a cat
sitting on the hearth and grinning from ear to ear. After she has asked
for directions and received an indifferent answer from the cat, it suddenly disappears. Having vanished and appeared for a second and
third time, the cat has the following conversation with Alice:

> "I wish you wouldn't keep appearing and vanishing so suddenly;
> you make one quite giddy!"
> "All right," said the Cat; and this time it vanished quite slowly, be-
> ginning with the end of the tail, and ending with the grin, which re-
> mained some time after the rest of it had gone.
> "Well! I've often seen a cat without a grin," thought Alice, "but a grin
> without a cat! It's the most curious thing I ever saw in my life!"[2]

---

1. Hal Childs, "The Myth of the Historical Jesus and the Evolution of Consciousness:
John Dominic Crossan's Quest in Psychological Perspective," Paper Read at the SBL 2000
Annual Meeting's Psychology and Biblical Studies Section in Orlando, Florida (2000).

2. Lewis Carroll, *The Annotated Alice: Alice's Adventures in Wonderland and Through the
Looking Glass* (New York: Wings, 1995) 90–91.

1

In a 1994 article, Robert Gordon noted that, "as modern research into the Samuel narratives has developed, the substantial figure of this man of several parts has tended to be reduced to grin-like insubstantiality."[3] Today, again with regards to Lewis Carroll's *Alice's Adventures in Wonderland*, we may say the same about ancient Israel's history. The older paradigms of Alt and Albright, for reasons that will be discussed below, have been deconstructed to such an extent that the history of Israel has been almost concealed from us, and though we perhaps know more about how to write history than some decades ago, we may very well know less about history itself! This situation is caused not so much by ground-breaking additions to the archaeological record as by a new way of interpreting roughly the same sources. Only twenty years ago, it was still considered mainstream scholarship to base a (political) history of Israel on the historical, chronological, and terminological framework outlined in the texts of the Hebrew Bible,[4] and John Bright, in the third edition of *A History of Israel*, was no doubt reflecting contemporary scholarship when he asserted that "there can really be little doubt that ancestors of Israel had been slaves in Egypt and had escaped in some marvelous way. Almost no one today would question it."[5] Two decades later, the situation has changed drastically, and though R. B. Coote, T. L. Thompson, and N. P. Lemche can hardly be said to represent the mainstream in current scholarship, their assertions are nevertheless typical of a strong tendency to (a) discard the texts of the Hebrew Bible as an unreliable source for a reconstruction of ancient Israel's history, (b) move away from political and personal history toward a focus on long-term and socioeconomic aspects of society in ancient Palestine, and (c) shift from the alleged nonverifiable *texts* to the pool of so-called *hard data* in the archaeological record as a point of departure for the historiographical enterprise:

> The writers of ancient Israel knew little or nothing about the origin of Israel, although the Scriptures can provide much information relevant to the investigation of early Israel. The period under discussion, there-

3. R. Gordon, "Who Made the Kingmaker? Reflections on Samuel and the Institution of the Monarchy," in *Faith, Tradition and History: Old Testament Historiography in Its Near Eastern Context* (ed. A. R. Millard, J. K. Hoffmeier, and D. W. Baker; Winona Lake, Ind.: Eisenbrauns, 1994) 255–69.

4. The term *Hebrew Bible* is employed for the sake of convenience and thus not used by the present author as a deliberate "Christian" term as opposed to the supposedly more Jewish *Tanakh* and *Miqra*. *Bible*, after all, is a Greek word and has originally no religious connotations to it. The New Testament, by the way, is also available in Hebrew.

5. John Bright, *A History of Israel* (Philadelphia: Westminster, 1981) 120.

fore, does not include the period of the patriarchs, exodus, conquest, or judges as devised by the writers of the Scriptures. These periods never existed.[6]

In writing about the historical developments of Palestine between 1250–586, all of the traditional answers given for the origins and development of "Israel" have had to be discarded. The patriarchs of Genesis were not historical. The assertion that "Israel" was already a people before entering Palestine whether in these stories or in those of Joshua is also not an historical assertion. No massive military campaign of invading nomadic "Israelites" ever conquered Palestine. There never was an ethnically distinct "Canaanite" population whom "Israelites" displaced. There was no "period of the Judges" in history. No empire ever ruled a "united monarchy" from Jerusalem. No ethnically coherent "Israelite" nation ever existed at all. No political, ethnical or historical bond existed between the state that was called Israel or "the house of Omri" and the town of Jerusalem and the state of Judah. In history, neither Jerusalem nor Judah ever shared an identity with Israel before the rule of the Hasmoneans in the Hellenistic Period.[7]

The biblical picture of ancient Israel does not fit in but is contrary to any image of ancient Palestinian society that can be established on the basis of ancient sources from Palestine or referring to Palestine. There is no way this image in the Bible can be reconciled with the historical past of the region. And if this is the case, we should give up the hope that we can reconstruct pre-Hellenistic history on the basis of the Old Testament. It is simply an invented history with only a few referents to things that really happened or existed. From an historian's point of view, ancient Israel is a monstrous creature. It is something sprung out of the fantasy of biblical historiographers and their modern paraphrasers, i.e., the historical-critical scholars of the last two hundred years.[8]

The pendulum has clearly shifted from a relative basic trust in the information given in the Hebrew Bible to a fundamental skepticism toward textual evidence and a positivistic quest for verification of information before it can be trusted and included in the pool of reliable data used for historical reconstruction—an interpretive strategy that Hoffmeier has labeled a "hermeneutic of suspicion,"[9] an approach that has been strongly challenged, because taken to the extreme it

6. R. B. Coote, *Early Israel: A New Horizon* (Minneapolis: Fortress, 1990).

7. Thomas L. Thompson, *The Bible in History: How Writers Create a Past* (London: Jonathan Cape, 1999).

8. Niels Peter Lemche, "On the Problem of Reconstructing Pre-Hellenistic Israelite (Palestinian) History," *JHS* 3 Article 1 (2000) 10 (http://www.arts.ualberta.ca/JHS/Articles/article_13.pdf [accessed April 30, 2003]).

9. James K. Hoffmeier, "The Evangelical Contribution to Understanding the (Early) History of Ancient Israel in Recent Scholarship," *BBR* 7 (1997) 80.

would mean a terminal "concealment" of the past, the end of historiography.[10] Or, as Barstad puts it in a slightly more modest assessment of the recent trends in the history of Israel: "If historical (verifiable) truth should be our only concern, the history of ancient Israel should not only be very short (written on ten pages or so), but it would also be utterly boring."[11]

No single factor can be held responsible for this dramatic change. A number of interactive factors in the fields of epistemology, theory of history, literary criticism, and archaeological method have made their contribution. The shift is thus far from limited to the subdiscipline of Israel's history but must be considered part of a long-observable change of perspective in historical studies and its related disciplines in general. The shift must, as will be shown below, in many ways be described as both inevitable and necessary and is thus to be welcomed, but it is my view that the above-mentioned principle of verification of the texts of the Hebrew Bible, applied so frequently nowadays, is out of step with the epistemological credit given to other ancient texts as well as modern. A full discussion of this is presented in chap. 2. Furthermore, I argue that the tendency to focus on structural and conjunctural factors needs to be balanced by a "rehabilitation" of the human factor—a renewed consciousness about the influence and importance of the individual in the course of history.

The thesis of the present study is that the texts of the Hebrew Bible contain much more reliable information than the above-mentioned "skeptics" claim—not only for the period of the extant text (i.e., the oldest known [unvocalized] Hebrew or Greek manuscripts) but also for the period it purports to describe—and, consequently, that it must

---

10. The point can be illustrated by the fact that in the famous reliefs of Sennacherib we can only identify persons when they are accompanied by texts. Persons represented without accompanying inscriptions may be of equal importance or interest as the picture of the tribute-paying representative from Lachish, but because the accompanying commentaries are lost or nonexistent they remain utterly anonymous.

11. H. M. Barstad, "History and the Hebrew Bible," in *Can a "History of Israel" Be Written?* (ed. Lester L. Grabbe; JSOTSup 245; Sheffield: Sheffield Academic Press, 1997) 64. Obviously, either Barstad must be wrong or the historians referred to must have failed to draw the logical consequences of their methodological assumptions, because their recent publications on the subject are both numerous and voluminous, e.g.: Thomas L. Thompson, *Early History of the Israelite People from the Written and Archaeological Sources: Studies in the History of the Ancient Near East* (Leiden: Brill, 1992), 423 pages; idem, *The Bible in History*, 397 pages; Niels Peter Lemche, *Die Vorgeschichte Israels: Von den Anfängen bis zum Ausgang des 13. Jahrhunderts v.Chr.* (Biblische Enzyklopädie; Stuttgart: Kohlhammer, 1996), 224 pages.

be *included in* rather than *excluded from* the pool of reliable data for a reconstruction of the origin and history of ancient Israel. After an introductory survey of important and relevant developments within general historical theory, I will seek to pin down the key problems related to the use or nonuse of the texts of the Hebrew Bible as historical sources and subsequently discuss the possible criteria for determining the epistemological and historiographical value of the texts.

Changing Perspectives

One of the main reasons for labeling the above-mentioned shift as a "paradigm shift," as has become increasingly common among Old Testament scholars,[12] is the change in perspective of historical studies in general, initiated by the so-called *Annales* School in the late 1920s. When, at the turn of the century, the social sciences had developed into independent disciplines, they immediately became a new tool for historians in their representations of ancient cultures and civilizations. Furthermore, the historicist anchoring of historical understanding in man's *ideas* at the same time began to be heavily criticized for its subjectivity and narrow choice of subject in a demand for a more positivistic–empirical-oriented history-writing.[13] Two impulses at the turn of the century converged into the syntheses of the American historians Frederick Jackson Turner and Charles A. Beard[14] and a few decades later became decisive for a new historiographical trend initiated by the French *Annales* school, with Lucien Fevre and Marc Bloch as its founders. Unlike the historicist's narrow, personal, and event-oriented perspective, the approach of the *Annales* historians was *multidisciplinary* in its broadest sense. Involving the full range of relevant disciplines, the new approach aimed to write a *histoire totale*, focusing not only (if at all) on kings, emperors, and nations but first and foremost on economic conjunctures, climatic changes, and sociological

---

12. Cf. Barstad, "History and the Hebrew Bible," 50–51.

13. Finn Collin and Bo Jacobsen, "Kritisk rationalisme og paradigmer," in *Humanistisk Videnskabsteori* (ed. Finn Collin and Bo Jacobsen; Copenhagen: Danmarks Radio Forlaget, 1995) 87–108.

14. A summary of Turner's approach is that "No satisfying understanding of evolution of this American people is possible without calling into cooperation many sciences and methods hitherto little used by the American historian. . . . The method of the statistician as well as of the critic of evidence is absolutely essential" (Robert P. Swierenga, "Social Science History: An Appreciative Critique," in *History and Historical Understanding* [ed. C. T. McIntyre and Ronald A. Wells; Grand Rapids: Eerdmans, 1984] 94).

patterns, in order to paint a much broader and more nuanced picture of a given historical period. A marked interest in what was claimed to be the fundamental structures of historical change first and foremost spread through the works of Fernand Braudel. Braudel, in his three-tier model of historical explanation, saw *la longue durée*, with its very slow-moving *structures* (e.g., climatic or geological changes) and the more mobile *la moyenne durée*, with its *conjonctures* (e.g., changes in sociological and economic patterns), as the basic levels of historical development, while the third level, *l'histoire eventiellement*, was to be seen as the immediately intelligible but very superficial explanation of a given historical event in regard to temporal and causal matters.[15]

Though the *Annales* history was not the only new trend to emerge in historical studies,[16] it has no doubt had the most profound impact on the study of Israel's history. Its multidisciplinary approach revealed the weak spot of the well-established schools in the study of Israel's history, with their use of the biblical texts as a starting point, and it provided a terminological frame of reference and an interpretive corrective for reconstructing the history of Israel; or in sum: it exposed the traditional historical schools' methodological inability to employ the nontextual, archaeological material on its own terms. In the early 1960s, scholars began to discuss—and question—the basic tenets of the established schools (i.e., Albrecht Alt's hypothesis of *Die Landnahme der Israeliten*, Martin Noth's theory of *Das System der zwölf Stämme Israels*, and the Albright school's synthesis of literary criticism and biblical archaeology) from a sociological perspective. Since then, an increasing number of scholars have questioned the usefulness of

---

15. The most important essays of Braudel have been published in Fernand Braudel, *On History* (Chicago: University of Chicago Press, 1980). Braudel's method is applied in his two magisterial volumes on the Mediterranean world in the age of Philip II, *The Mediterranean and the Mediterranean World in the Age of Philip II* (2 vols.; London: Collins, 1972). For a short but most helpful description of the terminology of the *Annales* School, cf. Peter Burke, *The French Historical Revolution: The Annales School, 1929–89* (Cambridge: Polity, 1990) 114–16. See also Thomas Levy (ed.), *The Archaeology of Society in the Holy Land* (New York: Facts On File, 1995) 2–8.

16. G. G. Iggers, *New Directions in European Historiography* (Middletown, Conn.: Wesleyan University Press, 1984) 32–33, distinguishes "three types of conceptions of history as a 'historical social science' which have recurred in nineteenth-century and twentieth-century historical thought" and identifies them as "a nomological, a hermeneutic, and a dialectical (Marxist) materialist approach." Inga Floto, *Historie i nyere og nyeste tid* (Copenhagen: Gyldendal, 1985) 241–45, in a similar way uses *social history* as a common denominator of trends in historical research since 1960 that have been influenced by quantification with its positivistic standards, Marxism with its materialistic approach to history, and modern ethnology and anthropology with their focus on human behavior.

the biblical texts as a reliable source for the reconstruction of early Israel's history.[17] This trend has found its most profound and radical expression in recent years in the so-called "Copenhagen School," with its employment of the *Annales* School's model of historical explanation and its characteristic emphasis on empirical data and multidisciplinary studies.[18]

Among the lasting achievements of the *Annales* School is no doubt its focus on historical times and levels of historical explanation (i.e., long-term and short-term developments), its broadening of the subject matters of historical research, and its emphasis on multidisciplinary research; and though a number of other approaches to historical research have existed alongside it, the overall picture is that scholarly society has welcomed the above-mentioned achievements. All those historians in the 1960s and 1970s who viewed their discipline as a social science—whether they were *Annales* historians of the interrelations of economics and demography, West German social historians of political power and social control, or Marxist analysts of social and ideological conflict—were students of culture and hence of meaning. What distinguished them from traditional historians . . . was their insistence that historical understanding was not exhausted by reexperiencing the intentions of the agents of history but required a careful analysis of collective human behavior in its social and cultural context; hence the insufficiency of narrative. The recognition that "men make their own history" was joined with the perception that "they do not make it under circumstances chosen by themselves."[19]

---

17. Cf. Jens Bruun Kofoed, *Israels historie som teologisk disciplin* (Copenhagen: Dansk Bibel-Institut, 1998) 37–57.

18. Cf. idem, "Epistemology, Historiography, and the 'Copenhagen School,'" in *Windows into Old Testament History: Evidence, Argument, and the Crisis of "Biblical Israel"* (ed. V. Philips Long, David W. Baker, and Gordon J. Wenham; Grand Rapids: Eerdmans, 2002) 23–43, for a discussion on the historiographical method of the "Copenhagen School." Thomas Thompson (*Early History*, 406) uses the term *spectrum studies approach* for his own and his colleague Niels Peter Lemche's approach to the reconstruction of Israel's history. Employment of the *Annales* School's method is, of course, also found outside the "Copenhagen School," two of the most prominent proponents recently being Israel Finkelstein, "The Rise of Early Israel: Achaeology and Long-Term History," in *The Origin of Early Israel—Current Debate: Biblical, Historical and Archaeological Perspectives. Proceedings of the 1997 Irene Levi-Sala Seminar, University of London* (Studies by the Department of Bible and Ancient Near East 12; ed. Shmuel Aḥituv and Eliezer D. Oren; London: Institute of Archaeology and Institute of Jewish Studies, University College, 1998) 7–39; and Levy, *Archaeology of Society*.

19. Iggers, *New Directions*, 176.

The *Annales* approach has, however, been criticized on a number of points, by "insiders" as well as "outsiders." Insiders, of course, tend to defend its basic principles, calling for only minor adjustments when a relevant critique has been launched.[20] Scholars who are generally sympathetic to the *Annales* approach have thus pointed to the problem of quantification in periods with few or no textual remains (i.e., a great deal of ancient and classical history),[21] and the inadequacy of the quantitative method as a tool for social and historical analysis (i.e., the relevance of statistics for establishing the *mentalité* of a given ethnic or political unity).[22] More profound criticisms, however, have been raised by "outsiders" questioning the basic (positivistic) principles of the historians' "detachment," the inability of the *Annales* historians to overcome the abyss between events and structure in their deployment of Braudel's model of historical explanation,[23] and its underplaying of the role of conscious direction in social processes. Two interesting articles by Annette Aronowicz and Patrick H. Hutton fall into this category.[24] Aronowicz, in her discussion of Charles Péguy's (1873–1914) distinction between "historian" and "chronicler," describes how Péguy favors the "chronicler" because he is "the one who touches something of true human significance in his recounting of the past," while the "historian"

> somehow manages to miss the point . . . the historian is always walking *"alongside* the cemetery, alongside its walls, alongside its monuments." In other words, the historian somehow avoids the problem of mortality

---

20. For examples of "insider" critique, see Joyce Appleby, Lynn Hunt, and Margaret Jacob, *Telling the Truth about History* (New York: Norton, 1994) 222, 229–31; John Bintliff, "The Contribution of an *Annaliste* Structural History Approach to Archaeology," in *The Annales School and Archaeology* (ed. John Bintliff; London: Leicester University Press, 1995) 1–33.

21. Roger S. Bagnall, *Reading Papyri, Writing Ancient History* (London: Routledge, 1995) 113ff.; Appleby, Hunt, and Jacob, *Telling the Truth*, 222; Barstad, "History and the Hebrew Bible," 49–50; Burke, *The French Historical Revolution*, 38–42, 51–53; Bernard Eric Jensen, "Historie- og tidsbevidsthed som forskningsfelt: Begrebsanalytiske og social-historiske overvejelser," in *Tidsopfattelse og historiebevidsthed* (Studier i historisk metode 18; Århus: Antikva, 1985) 62; Brian Stock, *Listening to the Text: On the Uses of the Past* (Baltimore: Johns Hopkins University Press, 1990) 76.

22. Floto, *Historie*, 186–88; Iggers, *New Directions*, 66; Stock, *Listening*, 84.

23. Braudel has thus been criticized for writing a rather conventional political and personal *l'histoire eventiellement* in his *Mediterranean and the Mediterranean World in the Age of Philip II*, apparently unable to benefit from his otherwise acclaimed descriptions of the structural and conjunctural levels.

24. Annette Aronowicz, "The Secret of the Man of Forty," *History and Theory* 32/2 (1993) 101–18; Patrick H. Hutton, "The Role of Memory in the Historiography of the French Revolution," *History and Theory* 30 (1989) 56–69.

(his own, for instance). Unlike the chronicler, with whom he is contrasted, he fails to place himself within the race. No voices come alive at the historian's touch as a result.[25]

Aronowicz describes this portrait of the historian who always manages to miss his mark as an attack "on the positivists in their heyday at the Sorbonne of Péguy's time. Their remaining alongside rather than within events reflects their notion of scientific detachment, their desire to accumulate 'facts,' their urge to establish laws of development," and she concludes with a reflection on two things:

> The first is that, in a sense, Péguy's attack on the historiography of his time amounts to a defense of such qualities as compassion and respect for the people one is studying. . . . Perhaps the fact that words such as compassion and respect—in the context of a discussion of method— make most of us scholars so uncomfortable is a sure sign that the positivism Péguy was combating is not as dead and gone as the currency of the term "postmodernism" might lead us to believe. The second conclusion derives from the first. Terms such as compassion and respect have a religious ring. Most of us in the academic world are profoundly allergic to our respective religious traditions, fearing that they can only narrow or taint our intellectual commitment. Could not Péguy's understanding of his religious tradition suggest that it is the positivism we think we have long overcome that is keeping us from noticing the very ground underneath our feet?[26]

Hutton, in his discussion of the French Revolution, in a similar way underlines the role of "passion" and the memory of the individual in the historian's reconstruction of the past:

> Memory must be conceived in terms of its repetitions as well as its recollections. A nation that has lost contact with its past must return to its places of memory once more in search of its identity. Places of memory are sources of inspiration. They contain the secrets of the commitments of historical actors, not to mention those of the historians who have sought to describe them. . . . Today's historians may not wish to commemorate the past. But a historiography that dismisses the significance of tradition for understanding the passions of the past is likely to lose its appeal to posterity.[27]

There is, however, nothing substantially new in this critique, since, as is evident from the above-mentioned quotes, it basically deals with issues long known from the discussion between historicist and positivist

---

25. Aronowicz, "The Secret," 107.
26. Ibid., 117.
27. Hutton, "The Role of Memory," 68–69.

historians.[28] A somewhat different kind of critique or *complaint* is the claim that it is virtually impossible to write a "total history" because it would require expertise of the historiographer in a series of academic disciplines that are cumulatively unmanageable[29] and that the historical discipline, by creating an increasing number of more-or-less inaccessible, specialized studies, is endangered by fragmentation. Allan Megill, however, in his discussion of the historical theory of the German historian Jörn Rüsen, claims that fragmentation as such is not a problem and that if used properly can help us to see the "forest" as well as the "trees":

> [F]or fragmentation—also known as "specialization"—is essential to the advance of research, and the fragments produced by that research may well enter into productive, hybrid interactions with other fields and with practical concerns. The problem, rather, is narrowness, and theory of historiography—especially if practiced as a rhetoric of inquiry carried out in ways both interrogative and analytical—can help practitioners to see beyond their specialties, opening their minds to broader issues and improving their work in the process.[30]

The Challenge from Postmodernity

Another important development in the historical discipline that is now beginning to make its impact on the study of Israel's history has taken place in hermeneutics, linguistics, and literary theory—the so-called "end of history movement." Whereas the *Annales* School, with its roots in empiricism and positivism (and its later proponents in the "Copenhagen School") must be described as a development *within* the realm of modernism[31]—"normal history" in Kuhnian terminology[32]—

28. Cf., e.g., Karsten Lehmkühler, "'Geschichte durch Geschichte überwinden': Zur verwendung eines Zitates," *Jahrbuch für Evangelikale Theologie* (1999) 115–37; Bernard Eric Jensen, "Historisme," in *Humanistisk Videnskabsteori* (ed. Finn Collin and Bo Jacobsen; Copenhagen: Danmarks Radio Forlaget, 1995).

29. Bagnall, *Reading Papyri*, 113.

30. Allan Megill, "Jörn Rüsen's Theory of Historiography between Modernism and Rhetoric of Inquiry," *History and Theory* 33 (1994) 57–58.

31. Barstad, in his most readable survey of elements leading to the "crisis" in conventional history, gets to the heart of the matter when he says that "the sources may be different, the methods may vary, but in many respects the *Annales* approach, which prospered in the 1950s, 60s, and 70s, represents nothing more than a revised and improved edition of traditional German historiography. 'Total history' has been able to recapture historical reality 'as it was' as little as traditional history" (Barstad, "History and the Hebrew Bible," 50).

32. Thomas S. Kuhn, *The Structure of Scientific Revolutions* (Chicago: The University of Chicago Press, 1970).

the end of the century witnessed a number of new, "postmodern" trends, which eventually resulted in a series of fundamental attacks on the presuppositions of conventional modernistic historiography, questioning its basic principles of "objectivity," "primary and secondary sources," "linear history," "historical truth," and "the impartiality of the historian"[33]—a development that has led to what is now generally labeled a crisis in conventional history. Postmodernist literary theory argues that a text has no absolute intrinsic meaning, that "meaning" is a fluid construct encompassing the cultural preconceptions and personal associations brought to the reading of the text by the reader. The intentions of the author are not conclusive for postmodernism and, indeed, are almost irrelevant. "Meaning" is a subjective result actively constructed by the reader.

Three important and highly influential contributions to the discussion of the hermeneutical, linguistic, and literary aspects of historical theory published by the philosopher Arthur C. Danto and the historians Hayden White and Robert F. Berkhofer may serve as an excellent illustration of the impact of this "agenda" on the concept of the "unbiased historian."[34] Danto and, not least, Berkhofer have shown that we cannot think historically without some kind of "grid," some larger narrative with all of the oversimplifications and blind spots that it entails[35]—an overarching "hypothesis" or "conception" (Danto) or "Great Story" or "Metastory" (Berkhofer) employed to give coherence and structure to past events—is intrinsic to history-writing. A hypothesis or metastory of this sort must be described as an "interpretation" (Danto) or as "creating meaning" (Berkhofer).[36] Hayden White,

---

33. On the question of objectivity, see E. H. Carr, *What Is History?* (London: Penguin, 1987) 7–30; Peter Novick, *That Noble Dream: The "Objectivity Question" and the American Historical Profession* (Cambridge: Cambridge University Press, 1988); Appleby, Hunt, and Jacob, *Telling the Truth*, especially 160–97; Robert F. Berkhofer Jr., *Beyond the Great Story: History as Text and Discourse* (Cambridge, Mass.: Belknap, 1995) 138–201. For an application to Israel's history, see Barstad, "History and the Hebrew Bible"; Ernst Axel Knauf, "From History to Interpretation," in *The Fabric of History: Text, Artifact and Israel's Past* (ed. Diana Edelman; JSOTSup 127; Sheffield: Sheffield Academic Press, 1991) 26–64.

34. Hayden White, *Metahistory: The Historical Imagination in Nineteenth-Century Europe* (Baltimore: Johns Hopkins University Press, 1973); Berkhofer, *Beyond the Great Story*.

35. Well-known examples are the shared overarching thematic conception of Thucydides, Herodotus, and Homer: namely, a great war; cf. Simon Hornblower (ed.), *Greek Historiography* (Oxford: Clarendon, 1994) 22. Hornblower also refers to John Gould's identification of "reciprocity—requital for both benefits and injuries—as Herodotus' governing principle" (idem, *Greek Historiography*, 20).

36. Arthur C. Danto, *Narration and Knowledge* (New York: Columbia University Press, 1985) especially 95; Berkhofer, *Beyond the Great Story*. Danto goes a step further and shows

in a similar way, has shown that a multiplicity of possible narratives can be generated by one set of data and that stories provide meaning by "emplotment," that is, the way by which a sequence of events fashioned into a story is gradually revealed to be of a particular kind. According to White such "plots" are seldom chosen consciously by the historian. Most often the historian subconsciously spots the plot-potential of the available sources. White claims that all historical narratives are cast in one of four stereotypical modes of emplotment: namely, *tragedy, comedy, satire,* and *romance.* With some justice he has been accused of being both anachronistic (imposing modern modes of emplotment on ancient narratives) and undifferentiated (being too narrow in his identification of possible modes of emplotment),[37] but this is not a real problem, since additions of further modes of emplot-

that this is also true for scientific reports. See also Patrick A. Heelan, "An Anti-Epistemological or Ontological Interpretation of the Quantum Theory and Theories like It," in *Continental and Postmodern Perspectives in the Philosophy of Science* (ed. I. Babich and E. Babette; Aldershot, Hampshire: Avebury, 1995) 55, who argues that the quantum theory needs to be given an ontological rather than an epistemological interpretation and that it describes phenomena as revealed through a process of empirical inquiry that is sociohistorical in character rather than objective in the traditional sense. This is, however, no new observation. In 1936, Edgar Wind noted that "the circle thus proves in science as inescapable as in history. Every instrument and every document participates in the structure which it is meant to reveal. . . . Men do not know themselves by immediate intuiton and they live and express themselves on several levels. . . . The investigator intrudes into the process that he is investigating" (idem, "Some Points of Contact between History and Natural Science," in *Philosophy and History* [ed. Raymond Klibansky and H. J. Paton; Oxford: Clarendon, 1936] 257–58). For a similar approach to the archaeology of "the holy land," see N. A. Silberman, "Power, Politics and the Past: The Social Construction of Antiquity in the Holy Land," in *The Archaeology of Society in the Holy Land* (ed. Thomas E. Levy; New York: Facts On File, 1995) 9. This seems, by the way, quite contrary to what Niels Peter Lemche has expressed: "What have your beliefs to do with scholarship? Isn't it immaterial whether you believe in the historicity or not? Or just a statement of faith like the statement of faith in Jesus, Moses, Muhammad or King Arthur and his merry knights? I always have to tell the students that they as persons are not an argument in a scholarly dispute"; and "it is not very different whether you say believe or say I am convinced. You cannot be an argument. You as a person do not carry any weight, neither do I for that matter. The correct phrase is to say: Evidence available has convinced me, or evidence available has made me believe that . . ." (reply to Donald Vance on the ANE mailing-list, December 18–19, 1999, archived at http://www-oi .uchicago.edu/OI/ANE/ANE-DIGEST/1999/).

37. Marcille G. Frederick ("Doing Justice in History: Using Narrative Frames Responsibly," in *History and the Christian Historian* [ed. Ronald A. Wells; Grand Rapids: Eerdmans, 1998] 225), for example, "does not accept White's contention that a historian is forced to write in one of these four narrative forms." In all fairness, it must be said, however, that White actually *does* mention a fifth possible mode of emplotment, the *epic,* and that he does not seem to reject the possibility of other modes.

ment will not change his overall theory. The real problems lie elsewhere. In a key statement, White claims that, "since no given set or
sequence of real events is intrinsically tragic, comic, farcical, and so on,
but can be constructed as such only by the imposition of the structure
of a given story type on the events, it is the choice of the story type and
its imposition upon the events that endow them with meaning."[38] Andrew P. Norman, in a discussion on historical narratives, has shown
how White's theory raises a number of hermeneutical, linguistic, and
literary questions that must be addressed before a more thorough-
going assessment of his (and Berkhofer's) theories can be reached.[39]

The truly controversial issues in White's theory of emplotment as
well as in Berkhofer's theory of "The Great Story" can be pinned
down to (a) whether *meaning* is already present *in* or created by imposing a mode of emplotment or "The Great Story" *on* a certain pool
of evidence; (b) whether the historical narrative refers to a reality outside itself or must be understood as an autonomous, nonreferential,
purely subjective attempt to reshape a certain interpretive community's collective *understanding* of the past; and (c) whether truth-
claims in historical narratives are of a different character from the
truth-claims of fictional literature. Norman distinguishes between
two major "postmodern" attacks on the epistemic value of the historical narrative: "philosophical impositionalism" is the idea of a nar-
rative- and meaning-creating structure imposed on a pre-narrativized
past by the historian, with Hayden White as its most prominent proponent; and "anti-referentialism" is the understanding of the historical narrative as a nonreferential, self-containing text, with R. Barthes
and J. F. Lyotard as its most prominent proponents.

While acknowledging the general idea of discursive entities such as
"The Great Story" and "emplotment," Norman rejects the "endow-
ment with meaning" part of the "radical impositionalism," arguing
that "because life, experience, and the past as lived are coherent and
intelligible *before* we begin telling stories about them, the skeptical
worries about imposing false coherence are founded-ill." Moreover,[40]
"the past is not initially or primarily given to us in the form of separate, isolated incidents that are then given a false narrative coherence

---

38. Hayden White, "The Question of Narrative in Contemporary Historical Theory,"
History and Theory 23 (1984) 20.
39. Andrew P. Norman, "Telling It like It Was: Historical Narratives on Their Own
Terms," *History and Theory* 30 (1989) 119–35.
40. Ibid., 122.

by an historian. Doing history is as much the breaking up of an initially seamless whole as it is the bringing together of initially unrelated events. World War II was no less real, nor more a fiction, than
was D-Day."[41]

Norman goes on to reject "anti-referentialism" and argues that

> to argue that narratives ought not to be evaluated on their truth-
> content *alone* is one thing, but to develop a dichotomy that places narra-
> tives in a language game wholly apart from truth is another thing
> again. The fact is, historical narratives for the most part *do* purport to
> tell us what the past was like. They consist of assertions *about* the past,
> and they attempt to tell us what actually occurred. This means pre-
> cisely that narrative histories purport to refer—that they claim truth.
> Furthermore, they are generally offered to us for critical scrutiny on the
> understanding that entitlement to assert them can be revoked for in-
> ability to defend them successfully against significant challenges. His-
> tories do belong—and properly—to language games wherein evidence
> must be given for novel claims; challenges to the truth of a given ac-
> count are often appropriate, and confirmation and disconfirmation do
> in fact occur. It is highly artificial, not to mention outright dangerous, to
> claim that the question of whether or not an historical narrative is true
> is not a good question, and at times it is of the utmost importance that it
> be answered. The recent revisionist histories that claim that the Holo-
> caust never occurred, for example, challenge the truth of received ac-
> counts, and themselves call for immediate disconfirmation. It just
> would not do to exempt such stories from "the criterion of truth."[42]

Here Norman is touching upon the so-called "genre-neutralization"
of the traditional distinction between fact and fiction. Postmodern literary theorists such as R. Barthes, H. White, and N. Davis have recently argued that such a distinction no longer can be upheld and that
the truth-claims of historical narratives cannot be more "true" than
fiction—only "different."[43] Taken to its logical conclusion, this would
mean the end of history, history being a representation of what actually *did* happen as opposed to the fictional narrative, which sometimes
uses the same formal language but is understood to render what
might have happened but did not.[44] That has, however, not been the

---

41. Ibid., 124.

42. Ibid., 130–31. Cf. Also F. R. Ankersmit, "Historical Representation," *History and Theory* 27 (1988) 209.

43. Iggers, *New Directions*, 118–19.

44. Cf. Paul Ricoeur, *Time and Narrative* (Chicago: University of Chicago Press, 1984). See also Kevin J. Vanhoozer, *Biblical Narrative in the Philosophy of Paul Ricoeur: A Study in Hermeneutics and Theology* (Cambridge: Cambridge University Press, 1990).

case, at least not for the majority of scholars. Iggers, in his description of White's theory, asserts that

> White goes far beyond a tradition of historical thought that, from He-
> rodotus to Natalie Davis, recognized both the literary aspects of his-
> torical accounts and the role of imagination in constructing them, but
> nevertheless maintained a faith that these accounts offered insights
> into a real past involving real human beings. Natalie Davis frankly ad-
> mitted that invention occupies a crucial place in the reconstruction of
> the past, but she also insisted that this invention is not the arbitrary
> creation of the historian but follows the "voices of the past" as they
> speak to us through the sources.[45]

It may be right, as has become increasingly common among historians, that "truth" on the one side and "fiction" on the other is not a
valid distinction anymore, but in the same breath that we say this we
must maintain that truth-claims in historical narratives are different
from those of fiction, in that they can be checked and discussed
against the available source material, the "voices of the past." (Much
more on this in chap. 5.) The question of historicity is still both a
necessary and a "good question."[46] Another important feature of the
development within linguistics and hermeneutics is, of course, the
movement from diachronic to synchronic readings and a shift in perspective from author-centered via text-centered to reader-oriented
approaches to texts.

To sum up: Berkhofer has shown how "The Great Story" is used
by historians to structure their narratives and how writing will
always be influenced by the environment (religious,[47] political,[48]

---

45. Iggers, *New Directions*, 119.

46. Though Ricoeur's notion of the past as a text is disputed (cf. Ankersmit, "Historical Representation," 209), he is fully in line with the above-mentioned argument that
fact can be distinguished from fiction by its reference to sources; see Vanhoozer, *Biblical
Narrative in the Philosophy of Paul Ricoeur.* See also the extensive defense of the referentiality of historiographical texts in idem, *Is There a Meaning in This Text?* (Leicester: Apollos, 1998).

47. See the discussion on "embellishment" in medieval sources for early Islamic history in Jacob Lassner, " 'Doing' Early Islamic History: Brooklyn Baseball, Arabic Historiography, and Historical Memory," *JAOS* 114 (1994) 1–10.

48. Examples are *legion*, of course, but a recent one can be found in a notice from the
publisher of a new journal, *Journal of Palestine Archaeology,* who writes that "in addition to
the specialists, JPA also addresses readers who view their interest in archaeology and history as a crucial step towards shaping Palestinian historical consciousness"; cf. http://
www.birzeit.edu/ourvoice/society/feb2k/jpa.html (accessed May 13, 2003). See also, in
a similar vein, an article on Palestinian history in the Danish curriculum, by Børge S.
Christiansen, "Palæstinahistorien i Skolen," *Palæstina Orientering* 1 (1994) with an updated

ideological,[49] etc.) *in* and *for* which they are writing. White has shown that there are a number of possible modes available for "emplotment" and that a series of (usually subconscious) factors is involved when the historian chooses his mode of emplotment. Development in literary theory and genre research has shown that fact and fiction use the same language and that their truth-claims, therefore, cannot be evaluated on the basis of formal grounds. Norman, however, has convincingly shown that employment of such grids or emplotments does not necessarily compromise the epistemic value of the historical narrative and that it is still both possible and necessary to distinguish between fact and fiction and to ask whether a historical narrative is "true." We have been "deprived a second time" of our innocence, as Polanyi notes in his discussion on the "sociology of knowledge":

> We have plucked from the Tree a second apple which has for ever imperiled our knowledge of Good and Evil, and we must learn to know these qualities henceforth in the blinding light of our new analytical powers. Humanity has been deprived a second time of its innocence, and driven out of another garden which was, at any rate, a Fool's Paradise. Innocently, we had trusted that we could be relieved of all personal responsibility for our beliefs by objective criteria of validity and our own critical powers have shattered this hope. Struck by our sudden nakedness, we may try to brazen it out by flaunting it in a profession of nihilism. But modern man's immorality is unstable. Presently his moral passions reassert themselves in objectivist disguise and the scientistic Minotaur is born.[50]

version available on the internet at http://www.danpal.dk/vidensbase/baggrund/bg-032.htm (accessed May 13, 2003). Another example can be found in a report by Yasemin Soysal of the European Sociological Association. Having examined how textbooks for 11- to 14-year-olds in Britain, France, Germany, the Netherlands, and Turkey have taught European history in the 1950s, 1970s, and 1990s, the study points to a new drive toward political correctness in which national identity as well as controversy and conflict have been wiped from secondary school textbooks (Yasemin Soysal, *Rethinking National State Identities in the New Europe for the Economic and Social Research Council*, forthcoming). For a summary of the report, see the review by Amelia Hill in *The Guardian*, published April 13, 2003. http://books.guardian.co.uk/news/articles/0,6109,936579,00 .html (accessed May 13, 2003).

49. An interesting example comes from the completely different field of accounting history, where Richard Fleischman discusses the characerics of Neoclassical, Foucauldian, and Marxist/Labor Process paradigms as they have developed in recent accounting history (Richard Fleischman, "Divergent Streams of Accounting History: A Review and Call for Confluence" [Sixth Interdisciplinary Perspectives on Accounting Conference; Manchester, England, 2000] 3; http://les.man.ac.uk/IPA/papers/2.pdf [accessed February 20, 2002]).

50. Michael Polanyi, *Personal Knowledge: Towards a Post-Critical Philosophy* (Chicago: University of Chicago Press, 1962) 268.

The solution, however, is neither to become "scientistic Minotaurs" (Polanyi) nor to relativize or subjectivize *all* knowledge to the extent that no "objective" knowledge can be obtained at all, but to employ the conceded "deprivation" in a refinement process of the criteria for objectivity in history-writing. Both Polanyi's and Norman's responses are, moreover, in perfect harmony with mainstream historical scholarship. In a highly influential and oft-quoted treatment of the problem, Appleby, Hunt, and Jacob say in their chapter on "The Future of History" that,

> although this book has argued against the contention that history, science, and all efforts at generalization truth have ended in failure as the postmodernists assert and the traditionalists fear, it did begin with the premise that a great transformation has recently occurred in Western thinking about knowledge. This transformation—accelerated by the end of the Cold War—affects Americans' understanding of national history, of standards of truth and objectivity, of the practice of history and the human sciences in general. As the twentieth century closes, it becomes obvious that new definitions of truth and objectivity are needed in every field of knowledge. People today are rightly questioning those values of nineteenth-century science that accompanied the institutionalization of history along with the facile equating of modernity with progress. Where relativists and traditionalists have both gone wrong is in their analysis of the nature of the crisis.[51]

And at the end of the chapter they maintain that "history will flourish in a revitalized public arena" if new definitions of truth and objectivity are created in an environment of "pragmatism, practical reason and public realm."[52] So, even if it is true that the above-mentioned attacks on conventional history have created a crisis in conventional history, they have *not* caused what so often has been prophesied: "the end of history."[53] Scholarly society has been able to withstand the attack from

---

51. Appleby, Hunt, and Jacob, *Telling the Truth*, 276.

52. Ibid., 282.

53. The accusation of Berkhofer and White as being proponents of "the end of history movement" must at least be qualified, since both Berkhofer and White seem to reject it. Jerry L. Summer is quite to the point in saying that "Berkhofer asserts that it's not time to relativize history or dismiss its objectivity and grasp of true facts. Regardless of one's politics or culture, one relies complicitly on the 'Great Story' principle to do history. All histories belong to a greater comprehensive history. No one view has greater intrinsic legitimacy over other positions, and no one historian can claim to know everything, although some might write as if they did. No human viewpoint exists completely separate from all other viewpoints" (Summer, "Teaching History, the Gospel, and the Postmodern Self," in *History and the Christian Historian* [ed. Ronald A. Wells; Grand Rapids: Eerdmans, 1998] 207). White, in a similar way, *does* distinguish between fact and

postmodern theorists and secure the existence of an academic-based historiography. As shown by Appleby, Hunt, and Jacob, however, history will never be as it was, since important new knowledge has been gained from the postmodern theorists and new criteria for truth and objectivity have to be established. The historian (as well as people in general) still wants to know what happened and what it means that it happened, and an essential part of the future historian's task is to figure out which among these alternative interpretations is best and to eliminate the discrepancies between "history-as-science" and "history-for-us." This involves, among other things, determining which among them is most likely to be true. A most important feature of this process of elimination is the historian's awareness of the provisional character of his choice. Historical research is a cumulative enterprise, and every interpretation must be phrased in a pragmatic way, open to common-sense criticism and open to public discussion, since a

> definitive description of the past is not to be given, not because there are and always will be lacunae in our evidence—which is banal and contingent—but because earlier events will continue to receive differing descriptions through the relations in which they stand to events later in time than themselves. In effect, so far as the future is open, the past is so as well; and insofar as we cannot tell what events will someday be seen as connected with the past, the past is always going to be differently described.[54]

The Impact on the Study of Israel's History

It is obvious from the massive production of historiographic literature in the last two decades that the above-mentioned not-so-new-anymore trends in conventional history have now made their way into the study of Israel's history. Scholars are still complaining about the reluctance, ignorance, or downright aversion of their predominantly theologically- and philologically-trained and sometimes clearly politically-biased colleagues to the "new" trends. Thus, they plead for treatments of Israel's history that are more methodologically reflective.[55]

---

fiction by means of the commitment of fact to its subject matter ("real" rather than "imaginary" events) rather than by form and still claims that history-writing is possible (White, "Historicism, History, and the Figurative Imagination," *History and Theory* Supplement 14 [1975] 21).

54. Danto, *Narration*, 341.

55. Most noticeably expressed by a group of scholars who in 1996 gathered for the inaugural meeting of "The European Seminar on Methodology in Israel's History." Papers

But, in spite of the almost-predictable *inertia* of conventional (theological, political) historiography on ancient Israel, the impact is now so clearly felt that scholars defying it must be considered a dying race. Scholars have for instance become increasingly aware of how a "Great Story" or an overarching "hypothesis" has influenced or directly governed the traditional interpretations of Israel's history and how the "sociology of knowledge" of the historians of Israel has colored their representations more or less unconsciously.[56] A number of publications have thus made it clear how, for example, the dichotomy between the Israelites and the Canaanites governed Albrecht Alt's understanding of the process of the Israelite settlement[57] and how the so-called Philistine paradigm influenced William F. Albright's understanding of the developments in the early Iron Age.

Others have pointed to the political environments (political, religious) *in* and *to* which the modern historiographies are addressed. Examples are legion, but some of the most recent "accusations" are Burke O. Long's discussion of Albright's use of archaeological discoveries in the service of demonstrating the inherent superiority of Western Christian culture[58] and Pasto's treatment of the Wettian understanding

---

read at the meeting were published in Lester L. Grabbe (ed.), *Can a "History of Israel" Be Written?* (JSOTSup 245; European Seminar in Historical Methodology 1; Sheffield: Sheffield Academic Press, 1997). Later seminar papers can be found in idem (ed.), *Leading Captivity Captive: "The Exile" as History and Ideology* (JSOTSup 278; European Seminar in Historical Methodology 2; Sheffield: Sheffield Academic Press, 1998); idem (ed.), *Did Moses Speak Attic? Jewish Historiography and Scripture in the Hellenistic Period* (JSOTSup 317; European Seminar in Historical Methodology 3; Sheffield: Sheffield Academic Press, 2001). Pleas for more methodological reflection in relation to ancient Near Eastern studies in general are expressed by Bagnall, *Reading Papyri*, 3; and in Marc van de Mieroop, "On Writing a History of the Ancient Near East," *BiOr* 54 (1997) 285–305, which also has a most illuminating discussion on how unaware many historians of the ancient Near East are of the impact of their "Great Stories"and their sociology of knowledge on their representations. Mieroop also demonstrates how and why a multidisciplinary method now must be considered a *sine qua non* for historians of the ancient Near East.

56. For a good overview, see now Niels Peter Lemche, *The Israelites in History and Tradition* (Library of Ancient Israel; London: SPCK / Louisville: Westminster John Knox, 1998) 133–56.

57. Uwe F. W. Bauer has demonstrated how a similar dichotomy between nomistic Judaism and spiritual Christianity has governed Luther's and modern German Protestants' interpretation of Psalm 1 (Uwe F. W. Bauer, "Anti-Jewish Interpretations of Psalm 1 in Luther and in Modern German Protestantism," *JHS* 2 [1998]; http://www.arts. ualberta.ca/JHS/Articles/article8.pdf [accessed April 30, 2003]).

58. In Burke O. Long, *Planting and Reaping Albright: Politics, Ideology, and Interpreting the Bible* (University Park, Penn.: Pennsylvania State University Press, 1997). But see also

of Judaism.[59] Pasto argues that

> the representation of the "Biblical" past *as a past* of post-exilic rupture
> between Hebrews and Jews was a portrayal of that past the way de
> Wette, and other majority Protestant scholars, wanted it to be. It was
> the "present" of a modern, post-Napoleonic and united, Protestant
> Germany in which all "particularisms," including Judaism were dis-
> solved and were set into a Biblical past in which Hebrews were sepa-
> rate from Jews and "Israel" found its completion in Christianity.

Furthermore, the historical reconstructions of scholars such as Bolin,
Lemche, Thompson, and Davies are but variations of

> the "de Wettian theme" of disjunction, in their case a variation that is
> also a projection of (or their understanding of) modern Zionism and
> the Israeli-Palestinian conflict.[60]

We may also mention Edward Fox's recent book, *Palestine Twilight: The
Murder of Dr. Albert Glock and the Archaeology of the Holy Land.*[61] In 1980,
Glock was appointed director of the newly founded Institute of Pales-
tinian Archaeology at Birzeit University in the Israeli-occupied West
Bank. In 1992, he was shot by unknown assassins near his campus, and

---

N. A. Silberman and and D. B. Small (eds.), *The Archaeology of Israel: Constructing the Past,
Interpreting the Present* (JSOTSup 237; Sheffield: Sheffield Academic Press, 1997).

59. James Pasto, "When the End Is the Beginning? Or When the Biblical Past Is the
Political Present: Some Thoughts on Ancient Israel, 'Post-Exilic Judaism,' and the Politics of Biblical Scholarship," *SJOT* 12 (1998) 157–202. See also Moshe Weinfeld, *Getting at
the Roots of Wellhausen's Understanding of the Law of Israel on the 100th Anniversary of the
Prolegomena* (Report No. 14; Jerusalem: The Hebrew University of Jerusalem, 1979).

60. Pasto, "When the End Is the Beginning?" 178–79. Dever, in his characteristically
provocative style, sharpens the critique and accuses the proponents of the Copenhagen
School of having a hidden "Post-Modern Agenda" with revolutionary and antiauthori-
tarian undertones (William G. Dever, "Archaeology, Ideology, and the Quest for an 'Ancient' or 'Biblical' Israel," *NEA* 61 [1998] 39–52). See now also, idem, "Histories and
Nonhistories of Ancient Israel," *BASOR* 316 (1999) 89–105; and *What Did the Biblical
Writers Know, and When Did They Know It? What Archaeology Can Tell Us about the Reality
of Ancient Israel* (Grand Rapids, Mich.: Eerdmans, 2001). See also Keith W. Whitelam,
"The Search for Early Israel: Historical Perspective," in *The Origin of Early Israel—Cur-
rent Debate: Biblical, Historical and Archaeological Perspectives. Proceedings of the 1997 Irene
Levi-Sala Seminar, University of London* (Studies by the Department of Bible and Ancient
Near East 12; ed. Shmuel Aḥituv and Eliezer D. Oren; London: Institute of Archaeology
and Institute of Jewish Studies University College, 1998) 41–64; and Niels Peter Lemche's remarks in the "Theologischer Erträg" in Lemche, *Vorgeschichte*. See also idem,
"The Origin of the Israelite State: A Copenhagen Perspective on the Emergence of Critical Historical Studies of Ancient Israel in Recent Times," *SJOT* 12/1 (1998) 44–63.

61. Edward Fox, *Palestine Twilight: The Murder of Dr. Albert Glock and the Archaeology of
the Holy Land* (London: HarperCollins, 2001).

Fox argues that he was probably murdered because of the political overtones of his ethnoarchaeological work—an illustration of Mortimer Wheeler's famous dictum that "archaeology is not a science, it is a vendetta"—at least when it is interpreted in politically explosive environments such as present-day Palestine.[62]

Hermann Niemann and Ingrid Hjelm have recently tried to demonstrate how such overarching concepts governed the shape of the *ancient* narratives—Niemann in his treatment of the rise of monarchy in Israel as we know it from the Hebrew Bible, and Hjelm in her discussion of the presentation of the Samaritans in early Judaism.[63]

In two other areas related to biblical studies, Barr has shown that *epigraphy*, often thought to be a purely empirical discipline, is a highly ideological subject, deeply dependent on the philosophical categories with which it is approached,[64] while Silberman has demonstrated how the linguistic presuppositions of Robinson and Smith affected their identification in the 1830s of modern villages and landmarks with sites mentioned in the Bible: they were deeply influenced by contemporary German and French comparative philology, which had a theoretical emphasis on linguistic "degenerationism."[65]

In regard to the feature of emplotment, Flemming Nielsen has recently tried to show how the so-called Deuteronomistic History Writer

---

62. Mortimer Wheeler, cited in H. O. Thompson, "Biblical Archaeology" (New York: Paragon, 1987) 424.

63. Hermann Michael Niemann, *Herrschaft, Königtum und Staat: Skizzen zur Soziokulturellen Entwicklung im monarchischen Israel* (Forschungen zum Alten Testament; Tübingen: Mohr, 1993); Ingrid Hjelm, *The Samaritans in Early Judaism: A Literary Analysis* (Copenhagen International Seminar 7; Sheffield: Sheffield Academic Press, 2000). Worth mentioning from the ancient sources is the battle of Kadesh in the fifth year of Ramesses II, which was cast in three different modes, namely in "The Poem" (or "The Literary Record"), "The Bulletin Text," and "The Reliefs." Each version has its own bias but all three present, nonetheless, a consistent picture of what happened. For a translation, see K. A. Kitchen, *Ramesside Inscriptions: Translated and Annotated*, vol. 2: *Ramesses II: Royal Inscriptions* (3 vols.; Oxford: Blackwell, 1993–2000) 2.2–26.

64. James Barr, *The Variable Spellings of the Hebrew Bible* (Oxford: Oxford University Press, 1986) 205, referring to F. M. Cross and D. N. Freedman, *Early Hebrew Orthography: A Study of the Epigraphic Evidence* (New Haven: Yale University Press, 1952) 24, and the critique of it in Z. Zevit, *Matres Lectionis in Ancient Hebrew Epigraphs* (Cambridge: American Schools of Oriental Research, 1980) 20.

65. Silberman, "Power, Politics and the Past," 13. Cf. also John H. Hayes and J. Maxwell Miller, *Israelite and Judean History* (OTL; ed. John H. Hayes; London: SCM, 1977) 55. For a list of Robinson's works, see Jay G. Williams, *The Times and Life of Edward Robinson: Connecticut Yankee in King Solomon's Court* (SBL Biblical Scholarship in North America 19; Atlanta: Scholars Press, 1999).

was dependent on Greek historiography and emplotted his narrative similar to the Greek tragedy.[66]

Most clearly felt, however, is the impact of the various synchronic and text-centered readings on biblical literary criticism. Whereas traditional exegesis (i.e., biblical interpretation using the conventional methods of biblical literary criticism that dominated biblical exegesis from the beginning of the last century until the end of the 1960s) focused on the *diachronic* aspect of the extant text (i.e., how the *Quellen*, *Sitz im Leben*, and *Überlieferungen* behind the extant text was decisive for the way it was shaped and came into being), biblical interpretation, in the course of the 1960s, was beginning to feel the impact of developments some decades earlier within conventional literary criticism, reacting against the traditional fragmentation of the extant text into the supposed but nonextant original sources, forms, and traditions. The focus shifted toward the *synchronic* aspects of the *extant text*—that is, its self-contained meaning-bearing structures and, as far as the biblical text is concerned, its relation to other texts in the Hebrew Bible. It is impossible to mention all of the important contributions in the field of synchronic readings, but some of the benchmarks have no doubt been set by contributors such as Muilenburg, Alter, Sternberg, and Bar-Efrat.[67] One of the natural consequences of this development could very well be a marked ignorance of the his-

---

66. Cf. Flemming A. J. Nielsen, *The Tragedy in History: Herodotus and the Deuteronomistic History* (JSOTSup 251; CIS 4; Sheffield: Sheffield Academic Press, 1997). In his attempt to show how the so-called Deuteronomistic History Writer (DHW) was dependent on Greek historiography and emplotted his narrative similar to the Greek tragedy, Nielsen has been criticized for being anachronistic: "The major part of Nielsen's case is flawed by a fundamental *petitio principii*: he seeks to demonstrate the striking similarity to Herodotus of the tragic outlook in DHW by presenting the latter, not in its own terms, but already in those derived from the milieu of Greek epic and tragedy, without any detailed justification of such a procedure. . . . Nielsen fails to make his particular case for clear dependence of DHW on a hellenistic milieu" (D. F. Murray, "Review of Flemming A. J. Nielsen, 'Tragedy in History,'" *JTS* 50/1 [April 1999] 183–87).

67. James Muilenburg, "Form Criticism and Beyond," *JBL* 88 (1969) 1–18; Robert Alter, *The Art of Biblical Narrative* (London: Allen & Unwin, 1981); Meir Sternberg, *The Poetics of Biblical Narrative: Ideological Literature and the Drama of Reading* (Bloomington: Indiana University Press, 1985). A good survey of the development within biblical literary criticism can be found in Rolf Rendtorff, "The Paradigm Is Changing: Hopes—and Fears," *Biblical Interpretation* 1 (1993) 34–53. See also in Danish, Hans J. Lundager Jensen, "Efterskrift," in *Sola Scriptura* (ed. K. M. Andersen, E. Hviid, and H. J. L. Jensen; Copenhagen: Anis, 1993); and, in Norwegian, Kristin Joachimsen, "Diakron og synkron, historisk eller litterær? Knut Holters *Second Isaiah's Idol-fabrication Passages* og nye trender i deutero-jesajansk eksegese," *NTT* 97 (1996) 246–51.

torical anchoring of the biblical texts; but, though some biblical literary critics do express very little or no interest in the diachronic aspects of the biblical texts, this is not the general picture. Just as the new insights from literary theory on genre have not caused the end of history, so the tendency to focus on the extant text as an originally coherent and meaningful text has not caused ignorance of the text's historical anchoring and possible embedded historical information. Instead, it has brought about a return to, or to be more precise a refinement of, Wellhausen's well-known dictum that the biblical texts reflect the time of the writers; the refinement is that the term *writers* is no longer understood as the various JEDP sources with their conventional datings but as the author(s) responsible for the final collection and redaction of the extant text—that is, the Hebrew Bible as a whole:[68]

> All of the narrative material in the Pentateuch is unquestionably contemporaneous with the final redaction. . . . We do need to investigate, however, the individual units of tradition from which the greater tradition has been formed, not only because such an investigation has been critical in delineating the sources of the Pentateuch, but also because a recognition of the self-sufficient units of a tradition gives us a method

---

68. One of the consequences of the development within literary criticism seems to be that an increasing number of scholars with otherwise conflicting views and interests no longer see the documentary hypothesis as a satisfactory explanation of the very complex compositions of the Hebrew Bible. Though Van Seters, for example, has tried to revive it by giving it a historiographical frame, the conventional literary criteria for discerning the different sources seem to be deeply flawed. Thompson's remark in 1987 that "the documentary hypothesis has become a creed empty of substance, something which students learn in their early years of study" and that "it is no longer a tool used by scholars to analyze or clarify a text" may no longer be wishful thinking (Thomas L. Thompson, *The Origin Tradition of Ancient Israel: The Literary Formation of Genesis and Exodus 1–23* [JSOTSup 55; Sheffield: JSOT Press, 1987] 49). See also idem, "The Intellectual Matrix of Early Biblical Narrative: Inclusive Monotheism in Persian Period Palestine," in *The Triumph of Elohim* (ed. Diana V. Edelman; Kampen: Kok Pharos, 1995) 117 n. 11; "How Yahweh Became God: Exodus 3 and 6 and the Heart of the Pentateuch," *JSOT* 68 (1995) 58, 64–65; "Some Exegetical and Theological Implications of Understanding Exodus as a Collected Tradition," in *Fra Dybet* (ed. Niels Peter Lemche and Mogens Müller; Copenhagen: Museum Tusculanum, 1994) 233–42; "Text, Context and Referent in Israelite Historiography," in *The Fabric of History* (ed. Diana V. Edelman; JSOTSup 127; Sheffield: Sheffield Academic Press, 1991) 74; Niels Peter Lemche, "Om historisk erindring i Det Gamle Testamentes historiefortællinger," in *Bibel og historieskrivning* (Forum for bibelsk eksegese 10; ed. Geert Hallbäck and John Strange; Copenhagen: Museum Tusculanum, 1999) 11–28; William W. Hallo, "Biblical History in Its Near Eastern Setting: The Contextual Approach," in *Scripture in Context: Essays on the Comparative Method* (ed. Carl D. Evans, William W. Hallo, and John B. White; PThMS 34; Pittsburgh: Pickwick, 1980) 4.

for the observation of redactional efforts which have linked smaller units into a functional, greater whole.[69]

Or as noted by Philip Davies, "In general, I would suggest that recent biblical scholarship in many respects has yet to be restored to the critical standards of the late 19th century."[70]

Another important difference is, of course, the "revolution" of the social sciences that has taken place since Wellhausen's time. The biblical traditions are no longer understood by many scholars as simple reflections of earlier historical reality but as a collection of texts that has been selected and shaped as a response to specific demands in the social world of the writers and that thus offers a valuable insight into perceptions of that reality from particular points of view. They "are seen as literary fictions, developing according to the demands of the audience, the author/narrator, or the tradition itself."[71] The complex process of composition is, as would only be expected, still a matter of intense discussion, but since the Hellenistic Period is the known and indisputable terminus ad quem of the *extant text*, the text of the Hebrew Bible is now increasingly used by scholars as a *historical source* for Hellenistic Period Palestine and of little or no use as witness to the earlier periods it purports to describe. A majority still hold the view that some of the texts may predate the Persia period, but the consensus of the Wellhausian era is gone, and an increasing number of scholars claim that the earliest possible date for the composition of the biblical texts is the late Persian period and that no continuity can be established between the Israel attested on the Mesha Stele and in the

---

69. T. L. Thompson, *The Origin Tradition of Ancient Israel*, 51, 62. Cf. Malul's assessment of Thompson's contribution to the controversy surrounding the patriarchal traditions: "This controversy has experienced during the long years since it started extreme oscillations, starting with the views of the German scholars, like Wellhausen and his followers who discredited the Massoretic view about the authenticity of the Patriarchal traditions, moving through a 'renaissance period' in the last decades in the schools of Albright, Gordon, and Speiser, and ending recently with the comprehensive studies of T. L. Thompson and J. Van Seters who have closed the circle and returned back in certain measure to the skeptical views of the last century" (M. Malul, *The Comparative Method in Ancient Near Eastern and Biblical Legal Studies* [Neukirchen-Vluyn: Neukirchener Verlag, 1990] 41). For a discussion on Wellhausen, see also Weinfeld, *Getting at the Roots*.

70. P. R. Davies, *In Search of "Ancient Israel"* (JSOTSup 148; Sheffield: JSOT Press, 1992) 25 n. 6, as already noted in 1978 by David M. Gunn, *The Story of King David: Genre and Interpretation* (JSOTSup 6; Sheffield: Sheffield Academic Press, 1978) 14.

71. T. L. Thompson, *Origin Tradition*, 49. See also Whitelam, "The Search for Early Israel."

Assyrian inscriptions of the 9th and 8th centuries B.C.E. and the Israel attested in the Hebrew Bible.[72]

New Knowledge—New Challenges

As is evident from the above survey, the developments within the fields of history and literary criticism have produced important, indispensable knowledge about the different levels of historical explanation, the interdependence of humanistic and scientific research in the understanding of historical development, and the awareness of historiographies (ancient and modern) as encoded narratives. A multidisciplinary approach and an employment of the insights of current literary criticism must therefore be considered a *sine qua non* for future studies of ancient Israel's history, and any historiography not acknowledging this must necessarily be judged highly problematic, if not downright blinkered and ignorant. The changes that have taken place, however, also present the historiographer of ancient Israel with new challenges—problems, if you like—many of these being related to the problem of how to use *texts* in the historiographical enterprise.

Thanks to the relatively extensive records, we *do* know quite a lot about *l'histoire eventiellement*, the political and eventual[73] history, of ancient Israel.[74] What we also know, however, is that this "conventional" knowledge is but a tiny bit of the overall picture and that in many ways it must be understood as the end result of the *longue durée* and *moyenne durée* structural and conjunctural changes. Intensive research in such structural and conjunctural changes in ancient Palestine has been carried out for some decades now but, though we already know a great deal more about climatic changes, settlement patterns, trading, and so on than we did some decades ago, more research needs to be done in order to describe the links between structural, conjunctural, and eventual levels of the history of ancient Palestine. Another problem is that research is often hampered by the fact that evidence relevant to such social and economic patterns has largely been overlooked by many excavators. The most pertinent problem, however, is how texts that predominantly represent the eventual

---

72. So, for example, the proponents of the Copenhagen School; see T. L. Thompson, *Early History*.

73. I use the term *eventual* in its archaic English sense ("dependent or contingent on certain conditions") and as a rough equivalent of the French neologism *eventiellement*.

74. The excavations at Tel Lachish and Sebaste (Samaria) provide good examples of such knowledge.

level, and nontextual archaeological remains that predominantly represent structural and conjunctural changes should be integrated into the otherwise profitable Braudelian model of historical explanation. Should they be deployed on equal and reciprocal terms, the texts illuminating possible interpretations of the nontextual material and the nontextual remains explaining otherwise incomprehensible features in the textual evidence? Or should preference be given to the structural and conjunctural factors evidenced in the nontextual material as decisive for *l'histoire eventiellement* attested in the written record?

The tendency of historians of Israel who use Braudel's model is clearly to endorse the second approach, the most conspicuous example being that of the Copenhagen School. I have elsewhere demonstrated this to be highly problematic, and a repetition of the main arguments will suffice here.[75] First, though Braudel's stress on the need to use empirical, quantifiable data in order to describe the structures and conjunctures underlying *l'histoire eventiellement* has proved very helpful in his own studies of medieval history, it is highly problematic in the study of the ancient world, because the sources of, for example, Israel's history are scattered, sparse, and—not least—event-oriented. And as Barstad and others have shown, we do not have enough evidence from the early Iron Age to handle, for example, statistics in the same way that they may be used for the medieval period. Applying Braudel's model too simply to the textual evidence from Iron Age Palestine could therefore easily result in an unnecessary and methodologically highly problematic dismissal of the biblical historiography.

Second, if historiographers using Braudel's model discard the human factor as decisive for historical development or deny textual evidence any possibility of adding much to an overall understanding of the historical development in Iron Age Palestine, it is not so much because of the model itself as it is because of the historiographers' own philosophical presuppositions. And any historiographer using Braudel's methods must therefore be aware of how his own philosophical presuppositions influence his understanding of the causal and epistemological relationships between the above-mentioned levels. We have to realize that we are entering nothing less than the well-known dis-

---

75. Kofoed, "Epistemology." See now also Marit Skjeggestad, *Facts in the Ground: Biblical History in Archaeological Interpretation of the Iron Age in Palestine* (Acta Theologica 3; Oslo: Unipub, 2001). Skjeggestad argues that an independent, nonbiblical, and "scientific" archaeological approach to the history of Palestine in the Iron Age is not possible.

cussion between empirically and nomothetically oriented positivism on the one hand and the idealistic and ideographical historicism on the other. For even if Braudel's three-tier model seems very useful, or even indispensable, "we need," as J. Maxwell Miller has put it, "to be reminded that methodologies are ways of examining evidence and never should be mistaken for evidence itself."[76] And methodologies are governed by philosophies. Thompson's methodology and philosophy are threefold: that structures and conjunctures are basic to the understanding of the Iron Age history of Palestine, that the event-oriented textual evidence is to be considered "secondary" or "intellectual" history, and that an analysis and interpretation of the artifactual data therefore must serve as the interpretive context for the textual data, not least the "biblical traditions." Such a weighing and use of artifactual and textual evidence is, as we have seen, not necessary within Braudel's model but is a materialistic or positivistic use of the model. There is no problem in analyzing the evidence from a nomothetical perspective, or for that matter, in using Ernst Troeltsch's principles of causality, analogy, and immanence in order to describe what, on the basis of well-known sociological patterns and the natural laws, can be said about the conditions, possibilities, and impossibilities under which the people of the past had to live and make their decisions. And there can be no doubt that artifactual remains are crucial to studies of this kind.

A problem does arise, however, when such nomothetically oriented methods (not least that of Troeltsch) are used to answer questions they are incapable of answering: namely, *what* people chose, and *why* they sometimes chose the unexpected and, according to the nomothetically thinking scholar, impossible. People (such as the Babylonian king Nabonidus, who suddenly moved from Babylon to Teima for 10 years) sometimes *do* make unexpected choices. Artifactual remains are certainly capable of indicating the possibilities and impossibilities under which the people of the past had to live and make their decisions, but they cannot and do not tell what choices people actually made, and they certainly do not explain why they made them. Texts, such as the texts of the Hebrew Bible, therefore should not a priori be dismissed as second-rate evidence. Only if they can be proved to be fiction or invented is it methodologically safe to discard them.

---

76. J. Maxwell Miller, "Is It Possible to Write a History of Israel without Relying on the Hebrew Bible?" in *The Fabric of History* (ed. Diana V. Edelman; JSOTSup 127; Sheffield: Sheffield Academic Press, 1991) 100.

A number of other problems arise from the developments within literary criticism. Helge S. Kvanvig rightly says that the turn from *history* to *story* in Old Testament scholarship has opened up a whole new world of exciting readings of well-known biblical narratives *but* that the various synchronic and intertextual analyses, however important, cannot be detached from investigation into the diachronic aspects of the texts. Why were the apparently historiographical narratives originally told, and why have they been retold ever since? In which particular sociological, religious, political, or other context was this literature produced in the first place, and which interpretive communities still need it?[77] And even more important, as far as the present study is concerned, how was the apparently historical information in the texts understood in the first place? Was it a *relecture* on a national heritage of oral/written historiographical traditions,[78] a literary invention created by authors living in the time of the extant texts, or something between? These are of course crucial questions if the relatively late texts are to be included in the pool of evidence for Iron Age Palestine. Answers given, perhaps not surprisingly, range from "totally factual" to "entirely fictional," but the tendency in current scholarship seems to be to discard the biblical texts as reliable witnesses to Early Iron, pre-Persian Palestine. The reasons given all have to do with the texts' employment of more or less elaborate literary strategies and narrative techniques, which, it is claimed, are markers that discredit the historical reliability of the apparently historical information given in the texts.[79]

We find, for instance—and again most conspicuously expressed by proponents of the Copenhagen School—the argument that the compo-

---

77. Helge S. Kvanvig, "Den hebraiske fortelling: Narrativ lesning av bibeltekster," *NTT* 97 (1996) 219–34. Cf. also idem, *Historisk bibel og bibelsk historie* (Kristianssand: Høyskoleforlaget, 1999). This is also stressed by Thompson, who emphasizes that both the literary devices of the biblical traditions and their external referents must be investigated; cf. T. L. Thompson, *Origin Tradition*; and idem, "Text, Context and Referent in Israelite Historiography."

78. As is apparently the case with the Assyrian Annals, which are normally called "editions" due to their "updating" of significant occasions in the history of Assyria; cf. Amélie Kuhrt, *The Ancient Near East c. 3000–330 BC* (2 vols.; London: Routledge, 1995) 2.474.

79. Thus, e.g., James Barr, "Story and History in Biblical Theology," *Journal of Religion* 56 (1976) 1–17; repr. in James Barr, *The Scope and Authority of the Bible* (London: SCM, 1980) 1–17. But see also Israel Finkelstein and Neil Asher Silberman, *The Bibel Unearthed: Archaeology's New Vision of Ancient Israel and the Origin of Sacred Texts* (New York: Free Press, 2001.

sition of the Hebrew Bible was governed by the "Great Story" of an
"Israel redivivus" or "the claim for the land" and that traditions available to the authors/collectors of the Hebrew Bible in the 3rd–2nd centuries B.C.E. were deployed according to their applicability to the
"Great Story." Furthermore, the authors or collectors paid little or no
attention to the question of the reliability of the historical information
of their sources.[80] But is this necessarily so? It is evident that *some* kind
of "Great Story" must have determined which traditions or sources to
deploy and how to arrange the selected material. And it is also evident that the bringing together of already existing sources with perhaps newly written material did create a new text.[81] But to argue that
the historical information present in such a literary innovation must
be considered a *literary invention* is a non sequitur. It is *possible*, of
course, that the historical information was distorted or even invented
by the authors/collectors of the extant text, but it is not *necessarily* so.

If such a claim is to be given any credit, it must be supported by
more evidence than a mere statement that such a reading of the texts
is possible. Claims of this kind need to be demonstrated as much as
their reverse. It has, after all, been shown conclusively that the deployment of literary devices and narrative strategies is not sufficient
grounds in itself for judging a narrative to be fictive or invented.[82] But
on what grounds, then, can we decide whether a narrative, for example, the account of Solomon's dream in 1 Kings 3, was a *reuse* for
present purposes of what was considered an ancient, reliable account
of what actually happened to the remote ancestors of the Jewish
people, or that it was understood from the beginning by the 3rd–2nd
centuries B.C.E. audience of the extant text as a literary invention using
common themes and motifs from the shared culture of the ancient
Near East? Of course, no simple answer can be given to these questions. It is evident that a number of questions need to be addressed
before an epistemic stance toward the biblical texts can be convincingly expressed, and the aim of the present study is to narrow down

80. Cf. T. L. Thompson, *Origin Tradition*; *Early History*; *The Bible in History*; "Lester
Grabbe and Historiography: An *Apologia*," *SJOT* 14 (2000) 140–61; Niels Peter Lemche,
The Canaanites and Their Land (Sheffield: Sheffield Academic Press, 1991); *Vorgeschichte*.
81. A distinction must be made here between "creation" as an emplotment of both
old and new material *and* a "creatio ex nihilo," that is, a more or less coherent text based
on newly invented material.
82. So, e.g., A. R. Millard, "Story, History, and Theology," in *Faith, Tradition, and History: Old Testament Historiography in Its Near Eastern Context* (ed. A. R. Millard, J. K.
Hoffmeier, and D. W. Baker; Winona Lake, Ind.: Eisenbrauns, 1994) 37–64.

and discuss the relevant questions so that the apparently historiographical texts of the Hebrew Bible can be employed properly in historiographical synthesis.

The thesis of the present study, as has already been mentioned, is
that the texts of the Hebrew Bible contain reliable information for a reconstruction of the period it purports to describe, and the purpose of
the following discussion is therefore to substantiate this claim. Or, with
a rephrasing of a recent title: *How did the biblical writers know and why do
we know it*?! The substantiation will be carried out by distinguishing
between two sets of (possible) "epistemic" or "historiographical" markers in the texts: those of *source critical-value* and those of *historical intentionality and referentiality*. That is, we must distinguish, first, markers
that can help us trace *the history of the text* beyond the date of the oldest
known manuscripts by comparison of various features with different
kinds of *extant* nonbiblical material from, second, various literary features that can help us determine the *genre* of the text. For the sake of
convenience, to make the corpus of texts under investigation more
manageable, we shall focus in this book on the books of Kings.

The first set of markers, those of source-critical value, will be discussed in chaps. 2, 3, and 4—markers that can help us determine a
possible terminus ad quem for the composition of the text(s) of the
books of Kings, thus enabling us to discuss the implications of the
closeness or remoteness of the text to the events it purports to describe. Chapter 2 will thus seek to answer a number of questions related to the lateness of the text: How can we use the relatively late
texts of the Hebrew Bible as witnesses to much earlier events? Is it at
all possible that they can bear witness to the (much earlier) events
they purport to describe? Was it at all possible for the Israelites to
write sophisticated literature, such as the texts of the Hebrew Bible, in
the 10th, 9th, or 8th centuries B.C.E.? What do we do with historical information in the text when no corroborative material is available to
verify or falsify historical information given in the texts? What are the
possibilities and limitations of the comparative method? How do we
know what we claim to know about the past? Should historical information given in the texts be subject to *verification* or *falsification* before
it can be trusted or discounted? This will be followed in chap. 3 by a
discussion on the possibility of distinguishing diachronically between
different strands in Biblical Hebrew as a means of dating texts. In
chap. 4, a selection of relevant extrabiblical material will be compared
with information found in the books of Kings in order to evaluate its
epistemic value as a historical source.

The second set of markers, those of historical intentionality and referentiality, will be discussed in chap. 5 under the heading of genre. Questions to be addressed are: Is it at all possible to determine the genre of an ancient text? Is it possible to determine how the ancient audience understood the texts? Were the texts intended to be history-writing in the first place? What standards do we demand from the texts before they, from our point of view, can be described as historiography? How does religious or ideological bias affect the reliability of the historical information given in the texts? Must the texts of the Hebrew Bible or any other ancient writing be considered story because of their deployment of literary devices? Which markers can help us to decide whether we are dealing with history-writing or not?

Before we proceed to a discussion proper, we need a few more clarifications of the limitations. As is evident from what has been argued above, this book does not question whether a "Great Story" has been operative in the selection and arrangement of available texts in the composition of the Hebrew Bible; neither does it reject the concept that both the individual "books" and the "Hebrew Bible" as such have been cast in certain modes to further the purpose of the authors or collectors. Regardless of whether Thompson and Lemche are right or not in what they see as the unifying theme or "Great Story" of the Hebrew Bible, and irrespective of whether Flemming Nielsen is correct or not in showing that the books of Kings are cast in the tragic mode, it is a matter of fact that some "Great Story" has been operative and that some mode of emplotment has been deployed in the composition and collection of the Hebrew Bible. Hurowitz, Halpern, Van Seters, and others have in a similar way shown that certain styles, which we know from other parts of the ancient Near East, were employed and that literary borrowing from the shared culture of the ancient Near East should be considered a common feature in the composition or collection of the books of Kings.[83] This study will, consequently, neither

---

83. Victor Hurowitz, *I Have Built You an Exalted House: Temple Building in the Bible in Light of Mesopotamian and Northwest Semitic Writings* (JSOTSup 115; Sheffield: Sheffield Academic Press, 1992); Baruch Halpern, "The Construction of the Davidic State," in *The Origins of the Ancient Israelite States* (ed. V. Fritz and P. R. Davies; Sheffield: Sheffield Academic Press, 1996) especially 47–48; John Van Seters, "Solomon's Temple: Fact and Ideology in Biblical and Near Eastern Historiography," *CBQ* 59 (1997) 45–57. The employment of literary strategies in the composition of the books of Kings is also stressed in Iain W. Provan, *1 and 2 Kings* (NIBC; Peabody, Mass.: Hendrickson, 1995) and *1 & 2 Kings* (Old Testament Guides; Sheffield: Sheffield Academic Press, 1997), but see also John Gray, *I & II Kings* (OTL; London: SCM, 1964) 23–24; and Marc Zvi Brettler, *The Creation of History in Ancient Israel* (London: Routledge, 1998).

question nor discuss whether such narrative strategies have been employed in the composition or collection of, for example, the books of
Kings. Other important points of departure are that the creation of the
extant text may very well have served contemporary religious and/or
sociopolitical interests (anything else would be odd) and that knowledge about the society of the authors or collectors can shed important
light on the process of selection and arranging of the texts.[84] The aim
of this book is neither to question nor to elaborate on these observations but to determine whether the picture that the texts paint of, for
example, the United Monarchy is (a) no more real than the world of
Narnia *or* (b) is, in addition to these presuppositions, a reliable witness
to the events that the texts purport to describe.[85]

A final, important prolegomenon on the purpose and limitations of
this study is that it will seek to argue for its thesis more methodologically than analytically. However, because a discussion of the epistemic
value of the biblical texts without any mentioning of the texts themselves must be deemed purely academic, in this work I focus on the
books of Kings as well as a considerable number of extrabiblical texts.

---

84. This has been most significantly noted by T. L. Thompson, e.g., in "Text, Context
and Referent in Israelite Historiography," and idem, "Intellectual Matrix."

85. So, for example, idem, *Origin Tradition*, 198: "A proper use of exegesis does not
really carry us beyond the text itself, but rather it serves to make us familiar with that
text. That is all. And this is appropriate; for narrative calls us into a world of Narnia, the
world of imagination in which we all can live and find sustenance. This is a world that
is in the texts themselves, and only in those texts. We do not need a key apart from them
to lead us back into the wardrobe of imagination—only a belief in the narrative world
which exists and reveals itself even to one today who chooses to pick it up and read."

Chapter 2

The Lateness of the Text

> Not granting the generations of a thousand years the ability to
> understand anything about themselves on the basis of their
> own reality is beyond everything worth calling wisdom.[1]
>
> Poul Hoffmann

The Extant Text

Before we can determine the epistemic value of a given biblical
text, it is necessary to point out any possible marker, "hard" or "soft,"
that can help us to assess the reliability of the various pieces of historical information in the text, in this case the books of Kings. If, for example, the text in its present form and content can be shown to be a
"creatio ex nihilo" (that is, a more or less coherent text based on newly
invented material) from the time of the oldest extant Hebrew manuscript, its referents must be sought in the Yehud of Hellenistic Period
Palestine.[2] Consequently, the text will have very little historically reliable to say about an Iron Age Israel. If, on the other hand, the text
must be understood as a late stabilization of a long-written and/or
oral tradition, we are dealing with a completely different situation.[3] In
this chapter, we will seek to determine and analyze markers of *source-
critical* value. That is, we will seek markers that can help us trace the
history of the text beyond the date of the oldest-known manuscripts by

---

1. My translation of "at man ikke vil indrømme tusind års slægter evnen til at be-
gribe noget af sig selv ud fra deres egen virkelighed, falder hinsides alt, hvad der tør
kaldes visdom" (Poul Hoffmann, *Nattetanker i arken* [Copenhagen: Frimodt, 1966] 48).

2. A point that has been made very clearly by T. L. Thompson, "Text, Context and
Referent in Israelite Historiography."

3. That the dating of the earliest manuscripts of a certain literary work to a particular period does not necessarily mean that the work was composed about this period and
is unreliable as a witness for an earlier period can be seen from the fact that nobody
would claim that Herodotus's or Thucydides' *Histories* were entirely unhistorical or
composed in the Middle Ages, even though that is the date of the earliest extant manuscripts of their works.

comparing various features of Kings with the features of different kinds of extant nonbiblical material. The oldest extant unvocalized[4] Hebrew manuscripts of Kings are a number of fragments from Qumran, dated by the editors from the last part of the 2nd century to the middle of the 1st century B.C.E.[5]

In Cave 4 seven fragments containing the text of 1 Kgs 7:20–21, 25–27, 29–42, 50; 8:1–9, and 16–18 have been found. The script is assigned by the editor to the late Hasmonean hand in the process of transition to the early Herodian and is dated to the middle of the 1st century B.C.E. The orthography is fuller than that of the Masoretic Text.[6] In Cave 5, three fragments containing 1 Kgs 1:1, 16–17, and 27–37 have been found. The script is described by the editor as "écriture 'hasmonéenne', postérieure à celle de 5QDeut, mais probablement relevant de la meme école de scribes," while the spelling reveals "a peu de *matres lectionis*, comme celle du TM."[7] In Cave 6, fragments containing 1 Kgs 3:12–14, 12:28–31, 22:28–31; 2 Kgs 5:26, 6:32, 7:8–10, 7:20–8:5, 9:1–2, and 10:19–21 were found. Again the editor describes the script as "relativement archaique: les formes de *he*, *kaph*, *samekh*, *resh* rappellent 1QIs[a] (seconde moitié du IIe siècle av. J.-C.)," while in the spelling "on relève des graphies pleines."[8] Cave 4 also revealed the parabiblical 4Q382 (also: 4Qpap paraKings et al.) consisting of no less than 154 tiny fragments. Relevant to our research are frags. 1–5, which contain a

---

4. The oldest *complete* and *vocalized* manuscript of the entire Hebrew Bible, however, is the much later Leningrad Codex from the 11th century C.E. (The older Aleppo Codex from ca. 925 C.E. was damaged in a fire in the mid–20th century and now only contains about 80% of the complete text of the Hebrew Bible.) Though the point of departure for this study is the *oldest* and thus unvocalized manuscripts of the books of Kings, the critical edition of the Masoretic Text in K. Elliger and W. Rudolph (eds.), *Biblia Hebraica Stuttgartensia* (Stuttgart: Deutsche Bibelgesellschaft, 1967) will be used for the sake of convenience. Ambiguity in the vocalization of the unpointed text will be discussed wherever relevant—for example, in the discussion on the text as witness to pre-Masoretic grammar.

5. Holloway, in his entry on the books of Kings in the *Anchor Bible Dictionary*, states that "the earliest known Heb manuscripts of Kings, some leather fragments preserved among the Dead Sea Scrolls, were copied no earlier than the 1st century B.C.E." (S. W. Holloway, "Book of 1–2 Kings," *Anchor Bible Dictionary* [ed. D. N. Freedman; New York: Doubleday, 1992] 4.70).

6. Eugene Ulrich and Frank Moore Cross, *Qumran Cave 4 IX: Deuteronomy, Joshua, Judges, Kings* (DJD 14; Oxford: Clarendon, 1995) 171–73.

7. M. Baillet, J. T Milik, and R. de Vaux, *Les 'Petites Grottes' de Qumran: Exploration de la Falaise—Les Grottes 2Q, 3Q, 5Q, 6Q, 7Q á 10Q. Le Rouleau de Cuivre* (DJD 3; Oxford: Clarendon, 1962) 171–72.

8. Ibid., 107–12.

biblical paraphrase based on 1 Kings 18–19 and a direct quotation from 1 Kgs 18:4. The script resembles the Hasmonean semiformal familiar from 1QS, while the orthography is generally unexceptional. Plene spelling predominates, but there are a number of cases in which defective orthography is employed.[9]

These are the "hard data" regarding the extant Hebrew texts. Since 4QSam[b] is dated to the late 3rd century B.C.E.,[10] it may be *assumed*, however, that the Qumran findings also testify to an earlier date for the Hebrew text of the books of Kings. Later manuscripts show that the books of Samuel and Kings were considered a coherent text and that division—or rather *divisions*—only were made for practical reasons (e.g., the size of scrolls).[11] If so, the age of the book should be set sometime before the latter part of the 3rd century B.C.E.[12] It needs to be pointed out, however, that, because they are extremely fragmentary, these extant manuscripts do not tell us anything about the shape and content of the books of Kings *as a whole*—only that *some* versions of the books were in circulation in the late 2nd century B.C.E. or, if the

---

9. Harold Attridge, *Qumran Cave 4 VIII: Parabiblical Texts, Part 1* (DJD 13; Oxford: Clarendon, 1994) 363–64.

10. Cf. Emanuel Tov, *Textual Criticism of the Hebrew Bible* (Minneapolis: Fortress / Assen: Van Gorcum, 1992) 106 n. 80; Eugene C. Ulrich, *The Qumran Text of Samuel and Josephus* (HSM 19; Missoula, Mont.: Scholars Press, 1978) 10.

11. James A. Montgomery, *A Critical and Exegetical Commentary on the Books of Kings* (ICC; Edinburgh: T. & T. Clark, 1967) 1–2. The same applies to the Septuagint translation; cf. Sidney Jellicoe, *The Septuagint and Modern Study* (Oxford: Clarendon, 1968; repr., Winona Lake, Ind.: Eisenbrauns, 1978) 285. On the question of scroll size, see M. Haran, "Book-Scrolls at the Beginning of the Second Temple Period: The Transition from Papyrus to Skins," *HUCA* 54 (1983) 111–22.

12. If an early manuscript of the books of Chronicles had been found at Qumran, it would have enabled us to push the age of the books of Kings even further back, because the latter undoubtedly was available to the author(s) of the former, but this is not the case. 4QChron (4Q118), dated about 50–25 B.C.E., has five lines corresponding to 2 Chr 28:27–29:3. It was published by J. Trebolle Barrera, "Édition Préliminaire de 4QChroniques," *Revue de Qumran* 15 (1992) 523–29. Trebolle Barrera interestingly notes that a series of letter readings visible in the column preceding the column of the readable lines in the fragment of 4Q118 corresponds to nothing known in 2 Chronicles (it is in Hebrew). It is possible, therefore, that it is an edition of the books of Kings or some other source for Chronicles, as distinguished from a relic of a full book of 1–2 Chronicles. Being a copy of 2 Chronicles or not, it does not, however, take us further back than the Hebrew manuscripts. Cf. M. Abegg Jr., P. Flint, and E. Ulrich (eds.), *The Dead Sea Scrolls Bible* (New York: HarperCollins, 1999) 632–33, who comment about the relative scarcity of Chronicles at Qumran that "it could be a matter of either chance or design, since Chronicles has a strong focus on Jerusalem and the Temple, from which the Qumran community had removed itself."

above-mentioned assumption is given credence, in the middle of the 3rd century B.C.E.[13]

As far as the Septuagint is concerned, no Greek manuscripts of the books of Kings have been found at Qumran, and apart from fragmentary quotations in Philo (early 1st century C.E.) and in Josephus (late 1st century C.E.),[14] the oldest Greek copies are the great Vatican Codex and Alexander Codex from the 4th and 5th centuries C.E.[15] Because Greek versions of the Pentateuch have been found at Qumran,[16] it may be *assumed*, however, that Greek books of Kings also existed at that time, because it is unlikely that these other books circulated without the books of Kings. Furthermore, if the conventional dating of the Septuagint translation to the middle of the 3rd century B.C.E. is accepted, the history of the text could be pushed even further back.[17]

---

13. Julio Trebolle Barrera, interestingly, comments on *Pseudo-Samuel* (4Q*Vision of Samuel*, 4Q160; 6Q*Apocryphon of Samuel–Kings*, 6Q9) that "many of these writings, generally marked by a strong eschatological accent, may have an origin previous to the existence of the Qumran community and independent from the Essene groups that could have made use of them" (Trebolle Barrera, "A 'Canon within a Canon': Two Series of Old Testament Books Differently Transmitted, Interpreted and Authorized," *Revue de Qumran* 75 [June 2000] 391–92, with reference to D. Dimant, "Apocalyptic Texts at Qumran," in *The Community of the Renewed Covenant: The Notre Dame Symposium of the Dead Sea Scrolls* [ed. E. Ulrich and J. C. VanderKam; Notre Dame, Ind.: University of Notre Dame Press, 1994] 175–91).

14. For a listing of these parallels, see most conveniently P. Vanutelli, *Libri Synoptici Veteris Testamenti Seu Librorum Regum et Chronicorum Loci Paralleli* (2 vols.; Rome, 1931).

15. A fragment rescued from the Cairo Geniza containing 1 Kgs 20:9–17 and 2 Kgs 23:12–27 in a 6th–7th-century hand testifies, however, to the existence of an earlier Greek translation by Aquila (said to have been produced about 128 C.E.); cf. F. G. Kenyon, *The Text of the Greek Bible* (revised and augmented by A. W. Adams; London: Duckworth, 1975) 19–20.

16. Leviticus 2–5; 26:2–16; Num 3:30–4:14, dated from the end of the 2nd century B.C.E. to the end of the 1st century B.C.E.; cf. Kenyon, ibid., 39.

17. That is, if credence can be given to the story of the translation of the Hebrew Bible into Greek in Alexandria at the behest of Ptolemy II (285–247 B.C.E.) as reported in the *Letter of Aristeas*. Though the letter in many respects has been shown to be incredible (that it was not written by a heathen courtier but by a Jew, that the writer did not live in the days of Ptolemy II but more than a century later, that the Jewish law was not translated to satisfy the curiosity of a royal patron of the arts but because the Egyptian Jews no longer understood Hebrew and were in need of just such a translation, and that the translators were not Palestinian Jews but members of the Alexandrinian diaspora for whom Greek was the language of daily life), most scholars still believe that a translation into Greek took place roughly at that time; cf. Kenyon, ibid., 14; Tov, *Textual Criticism of the Hebrew Bible*, 135–37. It should be noted, however, that the letter only mentions the *law* and that the other books of the Hebrew Bible apparently were translated at a somewhat later date. Another piece of evidence is the reference to 'the law itself and the prophecies and the rest of the books' (αὐτὸς ὁ νόμος καὶ αἱ προφητεῖαι καί, τὰ λοιπὰ τῶν βιβλίων), thus also the books of Kings, in the *Prologue to Ecclesiastes*, the Greek version of

Since there is no particular reason to suppose, as Alan Millard has noted,[18] that the Greek version was made soon after the Hebrew book appeared, this would push the date of the Hebrew version to perhaps as early as the 4th century B.C.E. This is based on *assumptions*, however, and the history of the text cannot, strictly speaking, be followed back beyond the date of the oldest *extant* texts, namely, the Hebrew fragments from Qumran from the end of the 2nd century B.C.E.

The obvious obstacle to the historian is, of course, how the long time-span between these oldest manuscripts and the events they purport to describe affects the epistemic value of the apparently historical information given. Much can be said (as demonstrated above) in favor of an even *earlier* dating of the Greek version, and hence the Hebrew, of the books of Kings, but a precise dating plays only a minor role here, because with any theoretical date there still remains a wide gap between the creation of the Dead Sea Scrolls from Qumran and the early Iron Age events reported in the books of Kings. Because these are our oldest extant texts, we simply do not know how the texts—still widely regarded the most important source for the history of Iron Age Israel—looked prior to the late 2nd century B.C.E., and we can by no objective means determine the extent of later arranging, modernizing, and harmonizing efforts of a redactor in the allegedly but empirically nonexistent earlier text. Gary Long, in his discussion on the feasibility of conventional higher criticism, hits the nail on the head when he asks:

> How can one be certain that a particular feature is markedness in discourse and not simply a stitch, a seam between sources? The short answer is that no one can be certain. The text of the Hebrew Bible is complex in its origin and development. This necessitates that discourse analysts hedge what is said about "final-form" phenomena. Prudence dictates acknowledging that a join or a seam may ultimately be behind what is labeled a particular discourse feature.[19]

Ben Sira, which was published by the author's grandson in 132 B.C.E., some 60 years after it allegedly had been written. On the historical value of the *Letter of Aristeas*, see Jellicoe, *The Septuagint and Modern Study*, 52–58. Cf. also Mogens Müller, *The First Bible of the Church* (Sheffield: Sheffield Academic Press, 1996).

18. A. R. Millard, "The Knowledge of Writing in Late Bronze Age Palestine," in *Languages and Cultures in Contact: At the Crossroads of Civilizations in the Syro-Mesopotamian Realm—Proceedings of the 42nd RAI* (ed. K. van Lerberghe and G. Voet; Orientalia Lovaniensia Analecta 96; Leuven: Peeters, 2001) 317–26; idem, "King Solomon in His Ancient Context," in *The Age of Solomon: Scholarship at the Turn of the Millennium* (ed. Lowell K. Handy; Leiden: Brill, 1997) 52.

19. Gary Long, "The Written Story: Toward Understanding Text as Representation and Function," *VT* 49 (1999) 184.

For the same reason Thompson is quite to the point in warning
against investing too many resources in the reconstruction of a nonexistent text.[20] It is, as Rendtorff has put it, hubris that we should have
left behind us:

> Scholars still seem to be proud of knowing things better than the final
> redactors or compilers. This is a kind of nineteenth-century hubris we
> should have left behind us. The last writers, whatever we want to call
> them, were, in any case, much closer to the original meaning of the text
> than we can ever be. From time to time we should remember what
> Franz Rosenzweig taught us: that the letter "R," as usually taken for
> the "redactor," actually should be read as "Rabbenu," "our master." For
> we receive the text from the hands of these last writers, and they are
> the ones whose voice and message we have to hear first.[21]

The starting point for our analysis must, therefore, be these extant
texts, or as Lemche suggests with reference to the neglected work of
Maurice Vernes, "the starting point for the analysis must be the time
where there can be no doubt that this biblical literature existed. When
an agreement is reached on this point, we may begin the next step and
see whether some part of the tradition has a prehistory."[22] In Malul's
discussion of the methodological aspects of the comparative method,
it is precisely this "next step" that he has in mind when he points out
the necessity for "corroboration"; that is, the justification of comparing
the late *extant* text of the Hebrew Bible with external evidence from,
for example, the early Iron Age: "The factor of time and place is the
main issue in the question of corroboration concerning the possibility
of existence of a historical connection between the Old Testament and
the ancient Near East in general, and with respect to specific phenomena in particular. One has to be aware of this question and attempt to
answer it before proceeding to carry out the full comparative process."[23] To this we will return in the following section. Anyway, we
are left, then, with a wide gap between the extant text and the events
it purports to describe, and the question is (a) whether it is possible
that these texts can *at all* have preserved reliable historical information

---

20. T. L. Thompson, *The Origin Tradition of Ancient Israel*, 196–97; but see also Lemche,
The Israelites in History and Tradition, 179–61.

21. Rendtorff, "The Paradigm Is Changing: Hopes—and Fears," 52. Cf. also Avi Hurvitz, *A Linguistic Study of the Relationship between the Priestly Source and the Book of Ezekiel*
(Paris: Gabalda, 1982) 19.

22. Lemche, *The Israelites in History and Tradition*, 159, cf. M. Vernes, *Précis d'histoire
juive depuis les origines jusqu'à l'époque persane* (Paris: Hachette, 1889) 7–9.

23. Malul, *The Comparative Method*, 77.

of events taking place centuries before the time of the last-known author/redactor; and, if the answer is affirmative, (b) whether it is possible to determine and locate any markers in the texts that can help us to relate the text chronologically to the events it purports to describe.

We find, not surprisingly, totally different answers to the question. Hans-Peter Müller on the one hand argues that, when more and more texts of the Hebrew Bible, especially with historical contents, are dated to the postexilic era and later, the traditions that biblical theology depends on must appear to be largely fictional.[24] Edwin Yamauchi on the other hand states that the very same texts are historically reliable and that they must be considered primary evidence, even when the archaeological evidence is lacking.[25] This disagreement is, admittedly, a result of the ambiguity of certain markers, and though there is little hope that we will ever find "conclusive evidence," we will nevertheless attempt to discuss what *can* be said about them. Though the markers of course must be traced within the text of the books of Kings itself, we cannot describe, let alone assess, them without reference to and comparison with similar markers in the relevant material from the shared culture of the ancient Near East, and we will therefore refer to a considerable amount of comparative literature.

Standards of Source Criticism

When claims are made today about a particular person's doings or about the course of a certain event, it is normally possible to control the claims by means of a considerable amount of direct and/or circumstantial evidence that is generally accepted as reliable and trustworthy. When neo-Nazi intellectuals claim that no Holocaust ever took place and that the picture painted of Hitler's regime by modern historians is a collective lie, they fail to convince the majority of people because the evidence available seems to indicate that it is they who are telling the lie. In the recent trial, when historian David Irving sued Professor Deborah Lipstadt for libel because, in her book *Denying the Holocaust: The Growing Assault on Truth and Memory*, she had identified him as "one of the most dangerous spokespersons for Holocaust

---

24. Hans-Peter Müller, " 'Tod' des alttestamentlichen Geschichtsgottes?" *NZSTh* 41 (1999) 1–21.

25. Edwin Yamauchi, "The Current State of Old Testament Historiography," in *Faith, Tradition, and History* (ed. A. R. Millard, J. K. Hoffmeier, and D. W. Baker; Winona Lake, Ind.: Eisenbrauns, 1994) 1–36.

denial," Irving lost his libel action because the trial "reaffirmed the fact that the Holocaust can be easily and fully documented by historians through the use of primary sources."[26] The judge's conclusions were that Irving had distorted, misrepresented, or manipulated the evidence to conform to his own preconceptions, that his activities revealed him to be a right-wing pro-Nazi polemicist, anti-Semitic racist, and one who associates with right-wing extremists who promote Neo-Nazism.

Another example is Mohammed Al-Fayed's well-known claim that a nurse told him the last words of Lady Diana inside the hospital, where she was taken before she died. Several witnesses are able to testify, however, that he cannot possibly be telling the truth, because he never entered the hospital during his short visit there. These are just two examples of how a historian writing modern history most often will have a considerable amount of primary and secondary, oral and written, evidence at his disposal, making it relatively easy for him to re-present "was eigentlich gewesen [ist]," what *essentially* happened in the course of a particular event.[27]

It is not so with ancient history. Though there are important exceptions to the rule that the further an event is removed from the historian the less material and corroborative evidence there is likely to be,[28]

---

26. Michael Horsnell, "False Witness," *The Times*, Wednesday, April 12, 2000.

27. This refers, of course, to Leopold von Ranke's famous but heavily criticized dictum (most recently in Lemche, *The Israelites in History and Tradition*). Bebbington has recently demonstrated, however, that while the adverb *eigentlich* means 'actually' in modern German, it predominantly carried the meaning 'essentially' in Ranke's times and that Ranke therefore has been wrongly accused of being a proponent of the possibility of reconstructing *accurately* what happened in the past (David Bebbington, *Patterns in History: A Christian Perspective on Historical Thought* [Leicester: Apollos, 1992]; cf. Kofoed, *Israels historie som teologisk disciplin*, 24). Danto understands the term as meaning 'significant,' and in his discussion on "pragmatic," "theoretical," "consequential," and "revelatory" significance, he states that "there are not two kinds of narratives in history, or at least not two kinds of the sort we have been discussing here. Ranke's characterization, whatever its vagueness, and whatever implausible readings of it may have been given by unsympathetic critics, is an admirable characterization of what historians seek to do" (Danto, *Narration*, 139). Bearing this in mind, this study maintains the optimism expressed by the dictum and understands the modern genre of history as an attempt to determine what *essentially* happened and to *interpret* it for the present. The full quotation of Ranke reads: "Man hat der Historie das Amt, die Vergangenheit zu richten, die Mitwelt zum Nutzen zukünftiger Jahre zu belehren, beigemessen: so hoher Ämter unterwindet sich gegenwärtiger Versuch nicht: er will bloß zeigen, wie es eigentlich gewesen" (Leopold von Ranke, *Geschichten der romanischen und germanischen Völker von 1494 bis 1514* [Leipzig: Duncker und Humblot, 1874] vii).

28. For example, the evidence from Egypt's Old, Middle, and New Kingdoms may be contrasted with the lack of evidence from the Second Intermediate Period and, in

the normal situation is that evidence from the ancient Near East—not least the textual—is sparse and scattered and thus often makes it extremely difficult to paint a representative or *differentiated* picture of a society, event, or person in a certain period.[29] In addition, due to the copying of texts, sometimes through the course of more than a thousand years, the evidence is often far removed from the events the texts purport to describe and is often described as being "secondary" in source-critical terminology.

Excursus:
Primary and Secondary Sources

In the process of validating the sources, scholars normally distinguish between "primary" and "secondary" sources. These labels are, of course, not an invention of historians writing on ancient Israel's history but are standard terminology of historical studies in general. They are not always used by historians of Israel, however, in the same meaning and with the same definitions as in their "original" context, and a few clarifications regarding the taxonomy are therefore necessary. In the following discussion, I will refer to a number of standard Danish textbooks, but the same information can be found, of course, in German, English, or other curriculums on historical theory as well.

One example of a problematic definition of these terms can be found in an article by Herbert Niehr on the weight of textual sources in the process of reconstructing the history of Israel.[30] Since Niehr seems to be representative of a number of other scholars referred to in what follows, a brief presentation of his definitions is appropriate. According to Niehr, a primary source is defined as being written at a time close to the event. It can be a report, a royal annal, a letter, or an original story. Primary sources are therefore more or less contemporary with the events they purport to describe. Secondary and tertiary sources differ primarily because of the temporal factor: they are, more or less, removed in time from the events they narrate or to which they testify. They

---

Mesopotamia, the relative abundance of tablets from the Old Babylonian period may be compared with the virtual absence of texts from Babylonia from the following period of 1600–1350 B.C.E. Vanstiphout, interestingly, suggests that this is evidence that "in the early second millennium, which was a period of great literary flowering in Mesopotamia (as it was in Egypt), literacy was more widespread than at the end of that millennium and the beginning of the next" (Herman Vanstiphout, "Memory and Literacy in Ancient Western Asia," in *Civilizations of the Ancient Near East* [4 vols.; ed. Jack M. Sasson, John Baines, and Gary Beckman; New York: Scribner's, 1995] 2188).

29. See, however, William H. Hallo's slightly more maximalistic words, "if my estimate is correct that cuneiform texts provide the most abundant archival documentation before the European Middle Ages, when or where on earth are we to go to reconstruct the society, the law, or the economy of a given culture if we cannot do it for the ancient Asiatic Near East?" (idem, "The Limits of Skepticism," *JAOS* 110 [1990] 192).

30. Herbert Niehr, "Some Aspects of Working with the Textual Sources," in *Can a "History of Israel" Be Written?* (ed. Lester L. Grabbe; Sheffield: Sheffield Academic Press, 1997) 156–65.

may be a copy of an original, an interpretive text, a rewriting, reediting, distortion, falsification, or the like.

By defining a primary source in terms of contemporaneity, Niehr fails to acknowledge another important distinction in heuristic terminology—namely, between "primary"/"secondary" and "firsthand"/"secondhand" sources, respectively.[31] According to this distinction, a source may still be secondary even if its information is taken from an earlier *extant* source. In other words, it is secondary if the author does not provide more information than we could obtain from another source. A source is primary, however, if it stems directly from an eye- or ear-witness or, importantly, a later account that relies on an earlier *nonextant* source. In other words, a primary account is the oldest *extant* source available. The distinction between "primary" and "secondary" has to do, therefore, with the value or *importance* of the witness rather than its contemporaneousness with the event it purports to describe. Secondary sources are unimportant as witnesses, since they only repeat what is already known. Primary sources will always be of importance, since they constitute the first *extant* information we have on a given event, person, or something else. It is crucial, therefore, that the terms "primary" and "secondary" sources are distinguished from the terms "firsthand" and "secondhand" witnesses. A firsthand account will always be a primary source, but the opposite does not apply, because a secondhand account may be the oldest extant witness and therefore a primary source. This is precisely what is acknowledged in the field of medieval Scandinavian history, where the *sagas* are increasingly treated as primary sources, even though the extant manuscripts are late in relation to the events they purport to describe.[32] This is contrary to Niehr, who does not take these finer discriminations into account. Consequently, he equates *late* with *secondary* and fails to acknowledge the *possible* primary character of the late extant biblical texts.

Another problem in Niehr's definitions is his preference for early—primary, in his terminology—sources. Niehr dismisses late—secondary, in his terminology—sources because "they did not undergo the censorship exercised by, for example, the Deuteronomistic theologians nor were they submitted to the process of canonization."[33] This pays too little attention to the fact that "censorship" was (and is) an operative factor in the creation of sources on all levels and that firsthand sources can be just as distorted, false, or edited as secondhand accounts. Even an eyewitness account (oral or written), often regarded as the most reliable testimony to an event, is infested with a series of

---

31. Johannes Steenstrup, *Historieskrivningen* (Copenhagen: Hagerups, 1915); Kristian Erslev, *Historisk teknik: Den historiske undersøgelse fremstillet i sine grundlinier* (1st ed. 1911; Copenhagen: Gyldendal, 1972) 29–70; Knut Kjeldstadli, *Fortida er ikke hva den en gang var—en innføring i historiefaget* (Oslo, 1994) 177–89.

32. Ólafía Einarsdóttir, "Om samtidssagaens kildeværdi belyst ved *Hákonar saga Hákonarsonar,*" *Alvíssmál* 5 (1995) 29–80.

33. Niehr, "Some Aspects," 157.

potentially distorted elements, since mediation of perception by memory and emotional state shapes an account. Memory typically selects certain features from the successive perceptions and interprets them according to expectation, previous knowledge, or the logic of "what must have happened" and fills the gaps in perception. Vansina notes that, "from the very first step, valid for all messages, oral or written, the hypercritical analyst can already deny validity to an eyewitness account" but adds that, though such an analyst according to the strictest theory would be correct,

> in practice, as we know from daily experience, he is wrong. For if our observations and their interpretation were so uncertain, we could not function at all. We would not remember nor efficiently act on remembrance for the situation we find ourselves daily involved in. Still, it is well to remember that the forces which already impinge on eyewitness accounts should always undergo scrutiny before being accepted as such.[34]

It is in this regard that Hallo suggests "finer discrimination," which he describes as "a critical sifting of the contemporaneous evidence, especially the royal monuments, in order to penetrate behind their propagandistic tendencies, on the one hand, and on the other hand a new respect for the authentic core contained in the 'historical' tradition."[35]

*   *   *   *   *

All sources, primary/secondary and firsthand/secondhand, need to be checked for ideological, propagandistic, religious, or other biases before the encoded historical information can be used for historiographical purposes. But secondhand sources, in addition, are also infested with another problem, the corrupting impact of time on both the carriers of a tradition and the tradition itself. The situation is relatively straightforward when a secondhand source can be checked against reliable primary sources. This is not the case, however, when an event, person, or whatever, referred to by a secondhand source cannot be corroborated by primary evidence. It poses a serious methodological problem to the historian, who has to decide whether to include such a secondhand source in his pool of reliable evidence or not. Is a text guilty until proven innocent or innocent until proven guilty?

Here we are joining, of course, the perennial discussion between credulity and skepticism, between maximalism and minimalism in the historical disciplines and, after a period of "credulity" (not least in

---

34. Jan Vansina, *Oral Tradition as History* (London: James Currey / Nairobi: Heinemann Kenya, 1985) 3–12. For a similar approach to "hypercritical" evaluations of testimony, see C. A. J. Coady, *Testimony: A Philosophical Study* (Oxford: Clarendon, 1992).

35. Hallo, "The Limits of Skepticism," 189.

the historical departments of biblical studies),[36] the pendulum has definitely swung in the minimalist direction, and we are again witnessing the rising tide of skepticism. Hallo, in his 1989 presidential address to the American Oriental Society, gave ample evidence of the way that leading scholars in recent Egyptology (Björkman) and Assyriology (Oppenheim, Kraus), have taken a skeptical stance toward the possibility of retrieving historically reliable and representative information from even primary texts.[37] It is no surprise that the tendency has spread to the "neighboring discipline" of biblical studies and intensified or *revived* what was already there: a skeptical approach to historical information in the extant texts. The essence of the problem is, of course, the question of *how* high are the standards we can demand from our sources? Or as Hallo puts it, "must we wait until all the evidence is in before we construct hypotheses in light of subsequent discoveries?"[38] and, in an answer to Kraus and Cooper, who want "incontrovertible proof for the survival of Sumerian beyond the 3rd millennium":

> Such proof can, in fact, be offered from a whole variety of indications. . . . But the real question here is one of methodology. Is there really a foolproof verification of the character of an ancient speech situation? How shall we proceed to prove that the Romans spoke Latin, or the Israelites Hebrew? Or how are we to date the change to Italian, or to Aramaic? Without a general methodology, it is hardly right to put the whole burden of proof on one side of the question or the other.[39]

Millard addresses the same question to Liverani,[40] who rejects the possibility that Sargon could have marched as far as Purushkhanda in west-central Anatolia as mentioned in a poem, "The King of Battle,"

---

36. Despite the differences between the so-called schools of Alt-Noth and Wright-Albright, they both shared the view that the biblical text had a detectable historical kernel reflecting not only the time of its last known authors but also the events it purported to describe.

37. Hallo, "The Limits of Skepticism." Cf. also James K. Hoffmeier, "The Problem of 'History' in Egyptian Royal Inscriptions," in *VI Congresso Internazionale di Egittologia Atti* (ed. S. Curto; Turin, 1992) 1.291–99. For a discussion of the views taken by another leading proponent of this approach, the Assyriologist Mario Liverani, see A. R. Millard, "History and Legend in Early Babylonia," in *Windows into Old Testament History: Evidence, Argument, and the Crisis of "Biblical Israel"* (ed. V. Philips Long, David W. Baker, and Gordon J. Wenham; Grand Rapids: Eerdmans, 2002) 103–10.

38. Hallo, "The Limits of Skepticism," 192.

39. Ibid., 191.

40. Millard, "History and Legend," 106–10.

which is available to us only in a copy from the 14th century B.C.E.;[41] thus, "from Sargon's extant inscriptions (or copies) we know for sure that he never reached beyond Tuttul on the Middle Euphrates, and had only indirect or mediated contacts with the lands further far-away in the north-west."[42] Liverani's main argument for doubting Sargon's claim is clearly that we have no firsthand monumental or archaeological evidence to support the secondhand source, a skeptical approach that cannot be sustained, because, as Millard notes, "there is no certainty that there would have been a series of monuments recording every one of Sargon's campaigns in the temple at Nippur.[43] Sargon built a new city at Akkad which has yet to be located. If it was completed by the time of the supposed Purushkhanda campaign, that might be the site preferred for the monumental record, rather than Nippur."[44] Furthermore,

> we have to ask what traces we might expect to find if a town opened its gates to an invader. The victorious soldiers might loot and rape, then leave a garrison within the walls. Material remains would hardly show any signs of that. Real proof of a conquest is only attainable if the conqueror's inscribed monument is found *in situ*, either in the re-occupied buildings or in his new structures.[45]

And in concluding his argument, Millard takes the same cautious yet optimistic stance as Hallo: "Liverani's objections to a possible campaign by Sargon beyond Tuttul into northwest Syria or beyond do not withstand scrutiny. Of course, it is not justifiable to affirm that Sargon did march that far; it is possible to argue that he did so."[46]

Hoffmeier, in his discussion of Garbini's approach, provides yet another example of how a skeptical view should be regarded as problematic.[47] Garbini claims that, in order for a monarch's statement in a text to be considered historically reliable, it must be corroborated by an external source; the implication is that the accuracy of the reports in 1 Kings and 2 Chronicles regarding the construction of Solomon's

---

41. For text and translation, see Joan Goodnick Westenholz, *Legends of the Kings of Akkade: The Texts* (Mesopotamian Civilizations 7; Winona Lake, Ind.: Eisenbrauns, 1997) 102–39.

42. Mario Liverani, "Model and Actualization: The Kings of Akkad in the Historical Tradition," in *Akkad: The First World Empire* (ed. M. Liverani; Padua: Sargon, 1993) 53.

43. Where most of the known texts of Sargon were originally placed.

44. Millard, "History and Legend," 4.

45. Ibid., 5.

46. Ibid., 5.

47. Hoffmeier, "The Problem."

temple must be rejected, because the annals of Tyre make no mention of the temple.[48] Hoffmeier argues, however, that, if we apply his reasoning to a similar context in Egypt, Garbini's claim would be comparable to saying that, because the Amarna Letters do not mention the temples that Amenhotep III built, as recorded on his mortuary temple stela, they probably were not built or were less impressive than stated. Similarly, the absence of any mention in the Hittite archives of temple-building during Ramesses II's era should lead one to reject his temple-building claims. Fortunately, in the cases of Amenhotep III and Ramesses II, some of the actual structures have survived, lending credibility to their written claims. If, however, the structures were not standing, the historian, according to Garbini, should not trust the reliability of the claim unless corroborated by an "external" source.[49]

The objections by Hallo, Millard, and Hoffmeier to the high demands for verification and incontrovertible proof made by "skeptical" scholars such as Oppenheim, Kraus, Liverani, and Garbini are to be taken most seriously.[50] Applying the skeptical approach rigorously to secondhand sources would in many cases mean that we would be forced to reject information only because it cannot be corroborated by external evidence, and as a result our knowledge about ancient history would be considerably reduced; history books would, as Barstad has put it, "be utterly boring."[51]

Had we not had, as Hallo notes, "the Sumerian King List, the epics, and the royal hymns," none of which qualifies as firsthand evidence, "our picture of Sumerian history would today be sadly distorted."[52]

---

48. Giovanni Garbini, *History and Ideology in Ancient Israel* (New York: Crossroad, 1988) 16, 23. Extracts of the annals are known to us from Josephus, who reproduces information taken from Menander of Ephesus's *Annals of Tyre* and another author's *Phoenician History*, with reference to Solomon's ally Hiram. How old or reliable they were cannot, however, be established; cf. G. Bunnens, "L'Histoire Événementielle Partim Orient," in *La Civilisation Phénicienne et Punique* (ed. V. Krings; Handbuch der Orientalistik 1/20; Leiden: Brill, 1995) 222–25.

49. Hoffmeier, "The Problem," 294.

50. A number of other prominent scholars could easily be added to the list. Hallo and Hoffmeier, in the cited articles, mention Malamat, Kitchen, and Hoffner, and both Amélie Kuhrt and Nicholas Postgate seem to take a similar stance on the matter (Amélie Kuhrt, *The Ancient Near East c. 3000–330 BC, Volume I* [London: Routledge, 1995]; J. N. Postgate, *Early Mesopotamia: Society and Economy at the Dawn of History* [London: Routledge, 1992]. Also noteworthy is K. Lawson Younger, *Ancient Conquest Accounts: A Study in Ancient Near Eastern and Biblical History Writing* [JSOTSup 98; Sheffield: Sheffield Academic Press, 1990]).

51. Barstad, "History and the Hebrew Bible," 64.

52. Hallo, "Biblical History," 4.

And "no one," Hoffner adds, "can properly reconstruct the historical events of the reigns of Šuppiluliuma I, if he ignores the historical retrospect found in Muršili II's plague prayers."[53] Yamauchi states that the same applies to classical history:

> But the date of a text's composition is not necessarily a warrant against the possibility that it preserves accurate memories, if it was able to use earlier sources. The Homeric epics, composed five centuries after the Mycenaean era they describe, can be shown to have preserved numerous memories of the Late Bronze Age, in the personal and place names and in artifacts mentioned. Roman historians use Livy to reconstruct the history of the Roman Republic several centuries before his lifetime. Classical historians use Plutarch (second century C.E.) for the history of Themistocles (5th century B.C.E.), and all historians of Alexander the Great (4th century B.C.E.) acknowledge as their most accurate source Arrian's *Anabasis* (second century A.D.).[54]

That the skeptical trend of seeking "incontrovertible proof" has been shown to be mistaken and too minimalistic in a number of cases, however, does not mean that the skeptics are wrong in every aspect of their skepticism. As we have seen, a series of problems is attached to the use of secondhand sources.[55] What is needed, therefore,

---

53. Harry A. Hoffner, "Histories and Historians of the Ancient Near East: The Hittites," *Orientalia* 49 (1980) 284.

54. Yamauchi, "Current State," 26. On Alexander, see also Lester L. Grabbe, "Hat die Bibel Doch Recht? A Review of T. L. Thompson's *The Bible in History*," *SJOT* 14 (2000) 127–28.

55. That Hallo is fully aware of these problems can be seen from his discussion of the "Letter-Prayer of Ninshatapada" (William W. Hallo, "Sumerian Historiography," in *History, Historiography and Interpretation* [ed. H. Tadmor and M. Weinfeld; Jerusalem: Magnes, 1984] 9–20). Referring to (his student) Piotr Michalowski, who, in his dissertation on *The Royal Correspondence of Ur* has demonstrated that the literary letters to and from the Neo-Sumerian kings of Ur constitute an essentially authentic record of the events they describe, though preserved in copies postdating these events by two to three hundred years, he states that "the general reliability of canonical texts known only in copies of the 18th century (more or less) was defended by comparing them to and integrating their data with the evidence of monumental and archival texts of the 21st century. . . . Ideally, I would like to be able to draw the conclusion that our case authenticates the literary correspondence as a primary historiographic source, i.e., as a group of documents copied with little or no change from originals on deposit in the royal archives. For it would be stretching credulity to suppose that a scribe would so accurately imitate the diction of the court if he was composing far away from it, in time or space. But in fact the letter-prayer of Ninshatapada does not warrant this conclusion . . . but we are entitled to draw another conclusion, equally important from the historiographic point of view. I submit that Ninshatapada, or whoever was the 'author' of our letter-prayer, wrote it in response to a real, historical situation, and wrote it, moreover, in full knowledge of the requirements of royal phraseology" (ibid., 17–18).

are methodologically sound principles regarding the inclusion of late sources into the pool of evidence for early events. That is, pertinent to our study, we need criteria for the use of the (late) extant text of the books of Kings as a source for the history of Iron Age Israel.

The Comparative Enterprise

Nobody questions the invaluable character of comparative material. The reconstruction of ancient history is often hindered by fragmentary data, late sources, and illegible texts. A historian, therefore, cannot but rejoice when he has access to parallel reports, comparable artifacts, and similar data that enable him to certify and interpret hitherto unsubstantiated or unintelligible information in his sources. But what constitutes and legitimizes the equation between a certain piece of historical information in, for example, the books of Kings, and the comparative nonbiblical material? And exactly how can the comparative material be brought in as evidence for or against the epistemic value of specific historical information? The rationale often seems to be *potest, ergo est*, 'it is possible; therefore it happened'. But, as Alberto Soggin phrased it, "*potest, ergo est* has always been a very poor argument in history and in court alike. *Potest* is nothing but a first step, for, if it cannot be we had better drop the argument altogether. But if it can be, the next step is obviously to find some more substantial arguments."[56] The comparative argument, therefore, has to be qualified and cannot by itself certify whether a given piece of historical information in the books of Kings is reliable or not.

Meir Malul, in a comprehensive study on the methodological problems related to the comparative method, is well aware of this need for qualification. Having described the various pitfalls of previous comparative undertakings, he nevertheless offers a convincing refinement of the comparative method and recommends it as an indispensable tool for the historian of Israel.[57] Since we will base the research of the following chapters on his synthesis, a brief summary of his arguments is in order. Having described two general comparative approaches, namely, the *historical comparison approach*[58] and the *typological compari-*

---

56. J. Alberto Soggin, "The History of Ancient Israel: A Study in Some Questions of Method," *ErIsr* 14 (Ginsberg Volume; 1978) 47.

57. Malul, *The Comparative Method*.

58. That is, comparisons between societies that belong to the same cultural context or the same "historic stream." This method is based on the assumption of a historical connection or a common tradition between the compared societies (ibid., 13).

son approach[59] and various applications of the historical comparison approach to the texts of the Hebrew Bible, Malul discusses the common criticisms of the comparative method.

First, Talmon's *holistic* approach—so called because, in Talmon's view, "the comparative scholar should first exhaust whatever he can glean from the immediate and wider biblical context for the elucidation of the problem at hand before turning to look for help in external sources"—is criticized for being too skeptical toward the usefulness of the comparative material.[60] Malul agrees that "Talmon's demand to pay close heed to the wide context and to its understanding in the effort to elucidate certain biblical matters is in principle valid and absolutely justified" but argues, however, that "his tendency to play down the value of external evidence in general does not seem fully justified, particularly in view of the factual limited extent of the biblical corpus."[61]

Another criticism launched against Talmon's approach is that it

> echoes the invalid assumption that the biblical corpus is a monolithic and unified work from the point of view of both its language and lexicon, as well as the ideologies and views reflected in it, so that one may freely resort to any biblical evidence from any genre or period for the elucidation of problems existing in other genres and periods.[62]

Malul also criticizes the *contrastive* approach—so called because it seeks to contrast various elements in the Hebrew Bible with allegedly comparable elements from the ancient Near Eastern culture—for being in danger of overstating the uniqeness of elements found in the Hebrew Bible: "If one examines the context in order to show some contrast, one should be careful to examine the context on both sides of the equation and without partiality."[63]

A second abuse in the use of external evidence for clarifying biblical phenomena that Malul mentions is the tendency to reconstruct theoretical constructs in the Hebrew Bible on the basis of external models. This, Malul holds, "reflects a fundamental problem in the

---

59. Also called the comparative method "on the grand scale," that is, "comparisons between societies and cultures which are far apart both geographically and chronologically; in such cases it is abundantly clear that no historical connection of any kind could exist between them. The similarities and parallelisms discovered between such historically unrelated cultures are then explained on the basis of the assumption of a universally underlying spiritual unity of man" (ibid., 14).

60. Ibid., 43.

61. Ibid., 45.

62. Ibid., 46.

63. Ibid., 51.

application of the comparative method in biblical research," since any "reconstruction" necessitates a certain amount of "gap-filling," just as the use of "external models" reflects problems involved in the application of the typological comparative approach and its delineation from the historical comparative approach (see above). As far as the latter is concerned, Malul notes, importantly, that

> the typological approach operated, or should operate, in the way of suggesting ideas and working hypotheses, while the historical approach is said, at least to a certain extent, to furnish proofs to such working hypotheses. Namely: a parallel from a distant culture does not constitute a proof of the existence of a similar one in the OT, but only a basis for considering such a possibility as a working hypothesis. On the other hand, a parallel taken from a cultural zone, which is in the same "historic stream," constitutes, at least *a priori*, preliminary suggestive evidence to the existence of a similar phenomenon in the OT. (This, however, should in turn be proven in each individual case on the basis of internal evidence.) The use of one approach does not necessarily exclude the use of the other, and one may apply both, as long as the distinction between them, both on the theoretical level as well as on the level of practical conclusions, is carefully kept in mind. . . . The typological evidence is perceived as proof of the existence of similar phenomena in the cultures under comparison, and not as heuristic evidence which furnished no more than an intellectual stimulus. This mistake is even more serious when it is realized that even within the framework of the historical comparison the parallel evidence is not to be taken as proof in the full sense of the word; in most cases it too only furnishes working hypotheses to be carefuly checked on the basis of clear interal evidence and objective methodological criteria.[64]

A third abuse of the comparative method mentioned by Malul is the problem of comparing incomparables—that is, "comparing ancient Near Eastern texts of one genre with biblical texts of another different genre" or "a lack of balance between the two sides of the equation in terms of the variety of sources called upon for mutual substantiation."[65] Malul adds, however, that this is not that serious

---

64. Ibid., 53–54, 64. A lucid example of the typological approach can be found in William A. Irwin, "The Orientalist as Historian," *JNES* 8 (1949) 301: "For the Orientalist there can be no doubt of the essential unity of human culture. There have been many civilizations, yet in deepest sense there is only one. Human life is one great stream that with many eddies and backwaters, with tributaries and channels, still is known primarily for its central current that flows on steadily in a direction determined by vast and mysterious forces."

65. Malul, *The Comparative Method*, 68.

if one's goal is to point to some authentic elements which may have been woven into the biblical stories. There is no reason why one should not assume that the biblical writer, even when composing a legendary or imaginative story, or when reformulating the Israelite history according to his specific historiosophic view, should have drawn upon authentic and actual phenomena and events from the world around him and used them as a background to his literary creation.[66]

Finally, Malul also points to the problem of dating—that is, "the wrong use of evidence from a certain period for assigning a certain date to the biblical evidence, when the same or similar evidence is in fact attested in other periods as well."[67] This is specifically relevant when the text of the Hebrew Bible is involved, because the extant texts in many cases are far removed both geographically and chronologically from the events they purport to describe. Discussing the heated controversy over the historicity of the patriarchal narratives, Malul argues that

> this problem poses serious obstacles in front of any attempt to draw comparisons between external evidence of this age and the Old Testament for the purpose of proving some historical tie between the latter and the ancient Near East. The factor of time and place is the main issue in the question of corroboration concerning the possibility of existence of a historical connection between the Old Testament and the ancient Near East in general, and with respect to specific phenomena in particular. One has to be aware of this question and attempt to answer it before proceeding to carry out the full comparative process.[68]

This is an extremely important point, because a comparison of, for example, the books of Kings with textual and artifactual evidence from, for example, the 9th and 8th centuries B.C.E. only can be justified by demonstrating the possibility or plausibility of a connection between the relatively late extant text and various pieces of archaeological remains from a considerably earlier period. Otherwise, it would be necessary—on methodological grounds—to search for the comparable material in the time of the extant text, namely the Hellenistic Period.[69]

---

66. Ibid., 70.

67. Ibid., 75.

68. Ibid., 77.

69. So, e.g., Morton Smith, *Palestinian Parties and Politics That Shaped the Old Testament* (London: SCM, 1987); Morton Smith and Shaye J. D. Cohen (eds.), *Studies in the Cult of Yahweh* (Religions in the Graeco-Roman World; New York: Brill, 1996).

The Need for Corroboration

Having pointed to this important caveat and discussed the other problems mentioned above, Malul offers his own synthesis by describing a set of principles for methodologically sound comparative research. Underlying all principles is the assumption of a general historical connection or a common tradition between the compared societies. Malul is well aware that this too is open to criticism and notes that, though the presupposition of a historical link between the Hebrew Bible and the ancient Near East is justified in principle, it should be proved in each individual case: "the general rule says that each case should be examined in its own right, trying to glean sufficient evidence which will prove or disprove the connection between the sources under comparison."[70]

According to Malul, the first step of the comparative process is, therefore, to determine the *type of connection*—whether we are dealing with (1) a direct connection, (2) a mediated connection, (3) a common source, or (4) a common tradition. The next step suggested by Malul is to perform *the test for coincidence versus uniqueness in determining the connection*: "are the similiarities and/or differences discovered between the sources/phenomena the result of parallel developments, independent of each other and, therefore, coincidental, or do they point to an original phenomenon unique to the sources under comparison? The answer to this will also dictate whether one upholds or rejects the assumption of connection."[71]

The last step in Malul's procedure is *corroboration*: "is it possible to prove the existence of the right conditions for the creation of a historical connection between the two cultures under comparison? Is the assumption of connection possible to begin with, or is the existing evidence of such a kind that it does not make room even for this assumption in general, and for specific cases, in particular?"[72] Here Malul touches on the most serious problem regarding the comparison of texts from the Hebrew Bible with textual remains from the pre-Persian periods.[73] Even though a general connection between, for example, the books of Kings and 8th- or 7th-century B.C.E. Syria–Palestine can be argued for, it is not enough when it comes to a comparison of details and specific cases. The time gap separating the biblical texts from

---

70. Malul, *The Comparative Method*, 83.

71. Ibid., 94.

72. Ibid., 99–100.

73. Malul's test case is the partriarchal narratives, that is, the Bronze Age, but the problems of comparison are in principle the same in the Iron Age.

pre-Persian texts is too important to be ignored and constitutes for many an insurmountable obstacle blocking the acceptance of the assumption of connection. Therefore, unless it is possible to find clear external evidence attesting to the actual cultural contacts between the culture of Iron Age Palestine, on the one hand, and the sociopolitical setting of the extant text (that is, 2nd-century B.C.E. Palestine), on the other hand, we simply cannot justify such a comparison.

Can a connection between the texts of the Hebrew Bible and the ancient Near Eastern culture of the Bronze Age be corroborated by nonbiblical evidence? Malul's answer is in the affirmative:

> such evidence exists in the form of archaeological and epigraphic finds from Israel and vicinity which, though not rich, seem to be sufficient for unequivocally proving the existence of direct cultural contacts between Canaan and the surrounding states, especially in the early 2nd millennium B.C.E. . . . . The basic postulate of the contextual approach is, then, valid.[74]

It is furthermore clear from Malul's study that he is particularly favorable toward the contextual method as developed by W. W. Hallo. We have already noted above that Hallo is highly critical of a too-pessimistic and skeptical stance toward the use of "late" texts, and Hallo's attempt to "stake out a place on the middle-ground of sweet reasonableness" is therefore both commendable and necessary. Hallo's suggestion, to "treat the ancient sources critically but without condescension,"[75] a procedure elsewhere described by Hallo and better known as "the contextual method," is probably still the most elaborate attempt to define a methodological basis for the selective process of the modern historian in reconstructing ancient history. It is a method also acknowledged by historians of Israel.[76] For the same reason a presentation of Hallo's basic ideas seems to be in order.

The Contextual Method

Two basic principles are fundamental to Hallo's method. First, Hallo calls for an *emic* approach to the texts, that is, interpretations of

---

74. Malul, *The Comparative Method*, 109–10.

75. Hallo, "The Limits of Skepticism," 187, 189.

76. J. Sasson, "On Choosing Models for Recreating Israelite Pre-Monarchic History," *JSOT* 21 (1984) 3–24; A. Malamat, "The Proto-History of Israel: A Study in Method," in *The Word of the Lord Shall Go Forth: Essays in Honor of David Noel Freedman* (ed. C. L. Meyers and M. O'Connor; Winona Lake, Ind.: Eisenbrauns, 1983) 303–13. And, of course, Malul.

the texts—and cultural explanations of the society in which they were written—that draw their criteria from the consciousness of the people in the culture being explained.[77] In order to uncover this insider's or native's perspective of reality, as it appears in the texts themselves, Hallo has worked out a classification system based on form as well as function, demarcating three broad text categories—or genres—defined as "canonical," "monumental," and "archival." An important aspect of this categorization is that without some kind of classification system it is extremely difficult to exert the necessary critical attitude when reading and interpreting the texts. Without a reasonable idea of the various literary conventions and styles of the ancient writers, we are in constant danger of imposing our own modern readings on the texts instead of understanding them on their own terms.[78] And,

> even if our modern taxonomy tallies with the native categories, it remains no more than a working hypothesis, a means to an end, or to diverse ends. . . . For, having once defined and distinguished our categories and genres, we can more safely aspire to re-unite them, in other words to draw on all of them jointly and severally in order to reconstruct the historical reality lying behind them.[79]

Within these three broad categories, Hallo (and others) has since tried to make even finer subdivisions in order to paint a fuller picture of the way the different genres developed in the literary history of Mesopotamia. And though originally based on textual remains from Mesopotamia, the classifications have, to a growing extent, now also been adopted and refined by scholars from the neighboring fields of Egyptology, Hittitology, and Syro-Palestinian History.[80]

---

77. As opposed to an *etic* perspective, namely, the outsider's perspective. This is the usual practice of social science and describes the world as others see it. Criteria for interpretation and explanation are, consequently, not derived from the people in question themselves but from a body of theory and method shared in a community of scientific observers.

78. Compare Sacks's evaluation of the different genres employed by the 1st-century B.C.E. Greek historiographer Diodorus in his *Bibliotheke*: "Certainly Diodorus commits numerous doublets and other factual errors throughout the *Bibliotheke*. But here is the critical consideration: they occur in the narrative, not in the speeches" (Kenneth S. Sacks, "Diodorus and His Sources: Conformity and Creativity," in *Greek Historiography* [ed. Simon Hornblower; Oxford: Clarendon, 1994] 229).

79. Hallo, "Sumerian Historiography," 11.

80. Historians could rightly claim that Hallo's method is nothing but a reinvention of the wheel, since similar strategies have been long deployed in other historiographical areas and periods. Hallo's credit is not the "invention," however, but the tuning and deployment of it in the reconstruction of ancient Near Eastern history.

Second, and deriving from the first principle, Hallo insists that secondhand sources are to be included in the pool of evidence for a certain period, person, or event—from the start. Hallo calls for a critical attitude that is applied to all of the textual sources, contemporary as well as later, documentary as well as literary. And it cannot be applied to the later, literary sources unless they are included in the enterprise in the first place. In Hallo's opinion, therefore, the traditional distinction between firsthand and secondhand sources is too simple, and the sources have to undergo a much "finer discrimination":

> We should not expect to know more than the ancient sources *knew*, but we can hope to know more than they chose to *tell*. In pursuit of these goals, I have carefully identified and separated the categories and genres of the sources, but combined them again to form the best available reconstruction of the past. The older or simpler judgment that contemporaneous sources are almost invariably preferable to later, literary ones, has yielded to a finer discrimination: a critical sifting of the contemporaneous evidence, especially the royal monuments, in order to penetrate behind their propagandistic tendencies, on the one hand, and on the other hand a new respect for the authentic core contained in the "historical tradition."[81]

A similar point has been made by Millard, who in a discussion on King Og's famous iron bed states that,

> in reading any ancient text, the historian accepts its testimony unless there is strong reason to be suspicious of it. Should such reason exist, he cannot reject that testimony out of hand unless it is totally unacceptable when judged by all legitimate criteria, above all, by the sum of the evidence available from the appropriate historical period. . . . Two or more witnesses are essential for proving an accusation, according to Deut. xvii 6, but that does not mean that the testimony of a single witness has no weight; it may be true, only the second or 3rd witness will confirm or disprove it. Failure to believe the single witness at all may result in the discounting or even the loss of genuine evidence about the past, evidence which later research or discovery may corroborate.[82]

Postgate, to mention another example, also seems to be in full agreement with this method when, in a discussion on the problems related to the Sumerian King List as a secondary source, he writes that,

---

81. Hallo, "The Limits of Skepticism," 189.
82. A. R. Millard, "Back to the Iron Bed: Og's or Procrustes'?" in *Congress Volume: Paris, 1992* (VTSup 61; ed. J. A. Emerton; Leiden: Brill, 1995) 200–201.

despite all these difficulties, we cannot merely leave the King List out of consideration. In part this is because Mesopotamian historians, whether they admit it or not, are influenced by this propaganda document of nearly 4000 years ago; in part because it can be checked in places with independent contemporary documents which show that there is genuine historical tradition incorporated within it. Hence, if the King List speaks of the hegemony of foreign powers like Mari, or Awan and Hamazi somewhere to the east, we cannot dismiss this as mere legend, but have to give it the benefit of the doubt even if there are no contemporary records of such a domination.[83]

In a discussion of the comparative approach to the biblical texts, Hallo grants Thompson and Van Seters that the comparative enterprise of bringing texts from Nuzi to bear on the dating (and thus historical reliability) of the patriarchal narratives was a discriminative one[84]—that is, a confrontation between two unequals, an attempted equation between two essentially incommensurable quantities. And once this incommensurability was pointed out, it was a relatively easy task for the generation of scholars that followed the "era" of E. A. Speiser and C. H. Gordon to dismiss the alleged parallels one by one. This does not, however, invalidate the comparative approach as such, and instead of conceding the method, Hallo stresses the need for a critical evaluation of the two sides of the equation:

> The biblical canon should be weighed, *not* against the archival data excavated from a distant corner of the Mittani empire, but rather, on the one hand, against the occasional scrap of archival evidence recovered from the soil of Palestine itself and, on the other hand and far more important, against the literary formulations of the surrounding Near East. Only then will one be comparing commensurate quantities, and only then will one be operating with a standard equally applicable to the other cultures of the ancient Near East.

Or, in Millard's words, "if biblical texts imply certain contexts for themselves, it is right to examine them in the light of knowledge about those contexts and to set them in other circumstances only if very strong evidence forces that move."[85] Hallo's concluding remarks

---

83. Postgate, *Early Mesopotamia*, 27.

84. Thomas L. Thompson, *The Historicity of the Patriarchal Narratives: The Quest for the Historical Abraham* (BZAW 133; Berlin: de Gruyter, 1974); John Van Seters, *Abraham in History and Tradition* (New Haven: Yale University Press, 1975).

85. A. R. Millard, "Books in the Late Bronze Age in the Levant," in *Israel Oriental Studies* 18 (ed. Shlomo Izre'el, Itamar Singer, and Ran Zadok; Winona Lake, Ind.: Eisenbrauns, 1998) 178.

on his discussion of skepticism are therefore to be endorsed. Acknowledging the limitations of the textual documentation he maintains that

> we are not to limit the inferences we extract from the evidence, but to treat the evidence, precisely because it is limited, as a precious resource—none of it to be ignored, or squandered, but every fragmentary bit of it critically sifted, so that it fits into our reconstruction of the history of antiquity—much as the archaeologist must use every surviving potsherd to reconstruct and restore a fragmentary vessel. The history so reconstructed—be it political or literary, linguistic or socio-economic, religious or Biblical—will then be true to its textual documentation. However limited that documentation may be, the only limits it imposes on us are to set reasonable limits to our own skepticism.[86]

It is interesting that Lassner, discussing the even more difficult secondhand sources for the formative period of Islamic civilization, opts for a similar optimistic approach. Though the available Medieval accounts are notoriously problematic as witnesses to the earlier events they purport to describe, because the story told has been shown to be embellished in a number of ways, Lassner rejects the (postmodern) skeptic's attitude, "to throw up our hands in despair and then declare that all of history or rather writing about history is mere language," as being "intellectually precious."[87] Acknowledging the serious problems in determining the relationship between the medieval literary texts and the actual states of the past,[88] he argues, nevertheless, that, "as a rule, apologists did not invent traditions out of whole cloth; they preferred instead to authenticate their writing by weaving strands of historical fact into a larger fabric of their own making" and suggests a more optimistic strategy than the skeptic's:

> What if we were to look upon the great religious and dynastic struggles depicted by the medieval chroniclers as historically rooted events and not merely linguistic play? Might not the broadest description of these events serve our investigation as touchstones or useful points of departure, to be combined with a literary analysis of the texts? Perhaps it requires a leap of faith, but I believe that, given the barest historical

---

86. Hallo, "The Limits of Skepticism," 199.

87. Lassner, "'Doing' Early Islamic History," 6 (the 1992 presidential address of the American Oriental Society).

88. Lassner, for example, points to the "the grievous error to accept the early sources without a method of analyzing them" and acknowledges that the "events were perceived and recorded for political purposes and therefore must be seen as predominantly representing the officially sanctioned views. The aim of the modern historian is, consequently, to ask if and how residual elements of that elusive reality can be extracted from the apologia in which they are embedded" (ibid., 4).

framework and variant sources, one may sometimes sense the basis of the apologists' intentions. What is required is educated conjecture and a sensivity to narrative strategy.[89]

Summing up this discussion on the standards of source criticism, we may conclude that a too-skeptical stance toward the use of "late" or secondhand sources cannot be sustained. Rejecting a priori the possibility of a historical connection between, for example, the late, extant texts of the books of Kings and the society of 8th-century B.C.E. Syria–Palestine denies us the ability to retrieve *possibly* reliable information on that period. The assumption of a historical connection must, on the other hand, be corroborated by nonbiblical evidence before any comparative process can be justified. The rest of this chapter will, therefore, be devoted to a discussion of whether it is possible to produce corroborative evidence for this connection and, thus, for including the books of Kings in the pool of reliable evidence for the history of an Iron Age Israel and Judah.

Creating and Preserving a Tradition

We can now return to the preliminary question raised above: Is it at all possible that the texts of the Hebrew Bible have preserved reliable historical information of events taking place centuries before the time of the last known author(s)/redactor(s)? According to common—or at least conventional—sense, the answer seems to be "Yes, of course it is! Jewish tradition, Israel's history, and modern Jewish national identity, after all, are based on it! Besides, it couldn't possibly have convinced so many people for so many generations, if it weren't true!" But the question is, of course, more complicated than this. An answer must not only take into consideration the transmission and reception history of the *written* traditions involved but (assuming that it existed) also discuss a number of questions related to the *oral* context in which the written tradition was created.

The Oral Tradition

It is not necessary, as we shall see shortly, to assume a prolonged oral tradition prior to the writing down of the books of Kings. A discussion of the *possibility* of such an oral tradition seems nevertheless to be justified, because it reveals how certain presuppositions determine

---

89. Ibid., 6.

the degree of trust we put in our sources. The most important question is, of course, how long an oral tradition can be considered reliable
in its rendering of past events. When does it have to be written down
in order to preserve its historical information in a stable, reliable way?
This is a hornet's nest! For who can tell? It may be *possible* for an oral
tradition to preserve reliable historical information throughout the
generations. Lemche, however, in a discussion of oral transmission,
has recently demonstrated that to progress from what is *possible* to
what is *factual* is a non sequitur, and though, as we shall demonstrate
shortly, his conclusion seems to be too skeptical and minimalist, he is
right in pointing out the problem of controls in oral transmission and
the serious problem it poses to the high source-critical standards of
the modern historian:

> Disregarding claims which place this literature either in the late pre-
> exilic period, in the exilic period, or in the postexilic period, be it the
> Persian Period or the Hellenistic-Roman one—after all this literature is
> removed from the 11th–10th centuries by, in the first example ten gen-
> erations or more (allowing for an average time of living in those days
> of, say 35 years) and in the second by probably more than twenty-five
> generations—we may safely conclude that the ordinary man in the
> street had little if any knowledge of what may have happened in his
> country hundreds of years ago. We could of course think of a prolonged
> period of oral tradition handed down from father and mother to son
> and daughter, and there can be no doubt that such tradition existed
> and that tales were told. We also know that oral tradition is infested
> with one, although very serious problem: it cannot be controlled. Being
> orally transmitted, it is in the American sense of the word "history" the
> moment it has been told. It will never remain stable but will always be
> changing until the moment when it is written down—accepting the
> truism that a written record of an oral tradition has already changed it
> into something different from what it was supposed to be.[90]

It has long been recognized and is a commonplace in contemporary
Old Testament research that a prolonged oral transmission existed in
preexilic Israel and that the written traditions of the Hebrew Bible to

90. Niels Peter Lemche, "The Origin of the Israelite State: A Copenhagen Perspective
on the Emergence of Critical Historical Studies of Ancient Israel in Recent Times," *SJOT*
12 (1998) 45–46. An example of how Lemche applies this to the Hebrew Bible, *in casu*
2 Kings, can be found in "Om historisk erindring," 16, now also available in English as
idem, "On the Problem of Reconstructing Pre-Hellenistic Israelite (Palestinian) History," *JHS* 3 (2000) http://www.arts.ualberta.ca/JHS/Articles/article_13.htm (accessed
May 6, 2003).

some extent are based on oral traditions.[91] Already Wellhausen acknowledged the existence of an oral tradition behind the individual legends of JE,[92] but it was in the Scandinavian traditiohistorical school, which had its heydays in the 1950s, that the importance attached to oral transmission in the Old Testament was most clearly expressed. Centered in Uppsala around its most forceful leader, Ivan Engnell, it was first and foremost inspired by the Swedish orientalist H. S. Nyberg, who claimed that "the written Old Testament was created by the postexilic Jewish community; earlier material was most likely put into writing only to a smaller extent,"[93] and by H. Birkeland, who, like Nyberg, stressed that the Hebrew Bible was part of an ancient oriental culture where writing was always secondary, and oral tradition was primary.[94] Thus, the hypothesis that the text had largely existed in its collected form at the oral stage prior to its being written down was of crucial importance for Engnell's understanding of the historical context of the Hebrew Bible. The oral tradition was, according to Engnell, extremely reliable, and the late, written, fixed texts therefore did not include anything new.

Consequently, the more general characteristics of the Scandinavian traditiohistorical school were a passionate conflict with conventional German literary criticism (described by Engnell as an anachronistic *interpretatio europeica moderna*),[95] a devaluation of the importance attached to the written tradition, and an extremely conservative attitude toward the Masoretic Text.[96] While the major contributions of

---

91. As evidenced by Robert C. Culley (ed.), *Oral Tradition and Old Testament Research* (Missoula, Mont.: Scholars Press, 1976); D. A. Knight (ed.), *Tradition and Theology in the Old Testament* (Sheffield: JSOT Press, 1990); and most recently Susan Niditch, *Oral World and Written Word* (Louisville: Westminster John Knox, 1996). Cf. also Henry Wansbrough (ed.), *Jesus and the Oral Gospel Tradition* (JSNTSup 64; Sheffield: Sheffield Academic Press, 1991).

92. Julius Wellhausen, *Die Composition des Hexateuchs* (Berlin, 1889) 9.

93. H. S. Nyberg, *Studien zum Hoseabuche: Zugleich ein Beitrag zur Klärung des Problems des Alttestamentlichen Textkritik* (UUÅ 6; Uppsala: Almqvist & Wiksell, 1935) 8. My translation of "das schriftliche AT ist eine Schöpfung der jüdischen Gemeinde nach dem Exil; was dem vorausging, war sicher nur zum kleineren Teil schriftlich fixiert."

94. H. Birkeland, *Zum Hebräischen Traditionswesen: Die Komposition der Prophetischen Bücher des Alten Testaments* (ANVAO 2; Oslo: Det norske videnskapsakademi, 1938).

95. Ivan Engnell, "Methodological Aspects of Old Testament Study," in *Congress Volume: Oxford, 1959* (VTSup 7; Leiden: Brill, 1960) 17, 21.

96. For a more thorough presentation of the Scandinavian traditiohistorical school, not least the differences between Engnell and other adherents (contemporary as well as later) of the school, see Eduard Nielsen, *Oral Tradition* (Studies in Biblical Theology 11; London: SCM, 1955) 11–17; and the various articles included in Knud Jeppesen and

the school were published in German (in addition to the Scandinavian languages) and subsequently generated some debate on the continent, they remained largely unknown in the Anglo-American world.[97] Furthermore, from the beginning, the school was criticized for over-emphasizing the importance of a prolonged and extremely reliable oral tradition by (1) adherents of the German traditiohistorical school[98] and (2) scholars subscribing to traditional Wellhausian literary criticism. Both emphasized the existence and importance of a written transmission predating the final redaction of the Hebrew Bible, though on different grounds.

Of equal importance was the publication of Albert B. Lord's *Singer of Tales* in 1960. Through his and Milman Parry's study of tradents in the Balkans and their literature, Lord was able to show that the bards did not memorize their traditional poems but created them anew in each performance;[99] perhaps even more pertinent to this discussion, Lord and Parry showed that *something* happened when oral traditions were fixed in a written form. Imported into new situations (i.e., literary contexts) and used for other purposes, the original emphasis and interpretation of a specific tradition was often changed. A transformation took place, as Eduard Nielsen had explained a little more cautiously some years earlier.

> It is not only a purely technical matter, the inauguration of a different method of transmission, which clearly shows its departure from the usual one by the appearance of a series of different text-variants, but an impersonal intermediary link has been introduced between the bearer of tradition and the receiver. Where the oral form of education was the predominating one, and where great emphasis was laid on the personal contact between teacher and pupil, this inanimate intermediary link in a living tradition can hardly have had immediate consequences of any importance. But if one imagines the living chain of tradition weakened, even cut off, so that only the documents are left, then the interpretation first and foremost becomes a problem, when the

---

Benedikt Otzen (eds.), *The Productions of Time: Tradition History in Old Testament Scholarship* (Sheffield: Almond, 1984).

97. A noteworthy exception being the already-mentioned translation of a number of articles orginally written in Danish and published in *Dansk Teologisk Tidsskrift* (see Eduard Nielsen, *Oral Tradition*).

98. German traditiohistorical research, inaugurated by Gerhard von Rad and M. Noth in the 1930s, preferred to speak of *Überlieferung* and *Überlieferungsgeschichte* and was more concerned with the examination of large complexes of tradition.

99. A. B. Lord, *The Singer of Tales* (Harvard Studies in Comparative Literature 24; Cambridge: Harvard University Press, 1960) 13.

tradition is to be resurrected. Prose and poetry that has achieved a stable, concise mode of expression, either from the very beginning from the hand of the master or from generations of traditionists, falls into the hands of novices. In the most favourable circumstances these will be uncertain as to a whole series of details in the texts; in the least favourable they will force their own interpretation on the material and, as they say, "arrange" the text.[100]

Engnell defended his view that nothing essential had happened to the oral tradition when it was fixed in its written form by asserting that the prophetic traditions, for example, were not popular traditions and that the transmission process of the biblical texts, due to their sacral-religious *Sitz im Leben des Volkes*, was unique. Engnell's protests, in Kapelrud's words, did "not reach the scholarly world at large," and "in Germany the stress on oral tradition and the attendant rejection of literary criticism simply made no headway."[101] And though Nielsen, as evidenced above, was much more sensitive to the criticism raised by the German scholars than Engnell was, the school never became as influential as its German counterpart. It was no surprise, therefore, when Nielsen thirty years later, in an otherwise appreciative review of H. H. Schmid's *Der sogenannte Jahwist*[102] and Rolf Rendtorff's *Das Über-lieferungsgeschichtliche Problem des Pentateuch*,[103] wrote,

> my satisfaction with these two new initiatives from Germanic scholars is mixed with one regret: the only Scandinavian work mentioned by H. H. Schmid is my own little book on the Ten Commandments; otherwise he refers only to an article by Magnus Ottosson and a lecture by A. Lauha. The rest is German, German, German. Rendtorff is only slightly better in this respect, but of Johs. Pedersen's production he refers only to "Passah-legende" (ZAW 1934), and to *Israel* I–IV not at all. Oh dear, who would have thought that Germany could be so provincial?[104]

What was rejected by mainstream continental scholarship, however, was not the possibility of a prolonged oral tradition preceding the

---

100. Nielsen, *Oral Tradition*, 33–34.

101. A. S. Kapelrud, "The Traditio-Historical Study of the Prophets," in *The Productions of Time: Tradition History in Old Testament Scholarship* (ed. Knud Jeppesen and Benedikt Otzen; Sheffield: Almond, 1984) 60.

102. H. H. Schmid, *Der Sogenannte Jahwist: Beobachtungen und Fragen zur Pentateuchforschung* (Zurich: Theologischer Verlag, 1976).

103. Rolf Rendtorff, *Das überlieferungsgeschichtliche Problem des Pentateuch* (BZAW 147; Berlin: de Gruyter, 1977).

104. Eduard Nielsen, "The Traditio-Historical Study of the Pentateuch," in *The Productions of Time: Tradition History in the Old Testament* (ed. Knud Jeppesen and Benedikt Otzen; Sheffield: Almond, 1984) 28.

written form of the Hebrew Bible as such but Engnell's and others' radical, one-sided hypothesis that the text had largely existed in its collected form at the oral stage prior to its being written down, that the oral tradition was extremely reliable, and that its late written form had virtually no negative impact on its reliability. Scholars were still convinced that oral transmission had played an important, tradition-preserving role prior to the written fixing of the Old Testament texts, and the struggle for a better understanding of oral tradition in ancient Israel has therefore continued unabated.

Recent research has not changed the overall picture, and there is still consensus that a prolonged oral transmission existed in preexilic Israel and that the written traditions of the Hebrew Bible *to some extent* are based on oral traditions. Of course, the problem of qualifying and quantifying this "extent" persists. Insights from recent research into mnemonic techniques, oral genres, and performative settings of modern oral societies has, however, given us a much more differentiated and refined understanding of *how, where,* and *by whom* oral traditions are transmitted, and we thus have much firmer ground to stand on in a discussion of oral tradition in ancient societies. Before we can return to Lemche's statement about oral tradition in ancient Israel, it is necessary, therefore, to go the long way round and discuss the "how," "where," and "by whom" of oral transmission in the light of research into orality in modern societies and then work our way back from there.

Qualifying the Oral

That our Western European society is a predominantly "bookish" one becomes evident when one realizes how people in less-literate societies of the world are able to remember and handle huge bodies of "text" without recourse to written material. Bearing in mind that Muslim sheiks and the Eastern Orthodox clergy still memorize hundreds of pages of sacred texts, Engnell's aforementioned warning against anachronistic *interpretationes europeicae modernae* proves itself to be well founded. Furthermore, current research on mnemonic techniques of modern oral societies has revealed an extraordinary ability to memorize, preserve, and transmit even vast amounts of information over several generations.[105]

---

105. The classic study is Lord, *The Singer of Tales,* but other important contributions include Vansina, *Oral Tradition as History*; Paul Connerton, *How Societies Remember* (Cambridge: Cambridge University Press, 1989); and Walter J. Ong, *Orality and Literacy: The*

However fascinating all this may be, it remains difficult for many Westerners to understand how such societies can preserve information essential to the survival of a given community: historical, ancestral, cultural, legal, and so on. There are other aspects of oral tradition that deserve scholarly attention, of course, but since our main interest here is the issue of *historical reliability* and oral tradition, we will limit ourselves to this. In his 1976 bibliographic survey,[106] Culley noted that *Oral Tradition: A Study in Historical Methodology* by Jan Vansina[107] was still a basic work in this regard and that "the general consensus seems to be that, while oral tradition must by treated with great caution, it may provide useful information for the historian."[108] In his 1985 follow-up,[109] Vansina elaborated on this consensus by providing a more sophisticated categorization of oral genres and their inextricable linkage to the dynamics of setting and performance. Vansina is fully aware of the limitations of oral tradition. He mentions in this regard the precautions of Irwin, who in his study of Liptako traditions (Upper Volta) was worried about "the variability of the messages, the casualness of transmission, the possibility of feedback, the inherent biases of interpretation, and above all about the selectivity of his sources, ethnocentric and elite oriented as they were."[110]

Vansina maintains, however, that reliability cannot be rejected a priori, because certain kinds of oral transmission—due to their genre and performative setting—tend to be more stable and to preserve reliable historical information better than others: "Factual traditions or accounts are transmitted differently—with more regard to faithful reproduction of content—than are fictional narratives such as tales, proverbs, or sayings. The criterion hinges on the notion of truth, which varies from one culture to another and which must be studied."[111]

Technologizing of the Word (London: Methuen, 1982). A somewhat dated list of *fieldwork* can be found in Robert C. Culley, "Oral Tradition and the OT: Some Recent Discussion," in *Oral Tradition and Old Testament Research* (ed. Robert C. Culley; Missoula, Mont.: Scholars Press, 1976) 1–33.

106. Culley, ibid., 14.

107. Jan Vansina, *Oral Tradition: A Study in Historical Methodology* (Chicago: Aldine, 1965).

108. Culley, "Oral Tradition and the OT," 14.

109. Vansina, *Oral Tradition as History.*

110. Ibid., 186.

111. Ibid., 13–14. For a discussion of *genre* and the impact of variability on reliability, see ibid., 14–27, 48–54. On "reproduction of performance" and "mnemotechnic devices," see ibid., 39–58. For a discussion of the latter in relation to Classical and ancient Near

Vansina, importantly, also argues that oral traditions, which would otherwise die, are kept alive by various mnemonic devices,[112] since performances are not produced at random times and places: "a formal recitation of a royal list of successors to the throne or a royal genealogy is appropriate at a coronation, and perhaps the genealogy may be recited once a year when the chiefs are assembled at the capital."[113] Though in most cases the rules relating to frequency, time, and place of performance have little to do with a desire to maintain the faithfulness of the message but are inspired by the practical use of traditions, circumstances such as frequency, time, place, intent of performance, and mnemotechnic devices such as objects (figurative objects, iconography), topographical features (changes in landscape, abandoned towns, battlefields, royal gravesites, etc.), and music (melody and rhythm) often serve to preserve a tradition, which otherwise would fall into oblivion.[114]

These are important observations on and qualifications to the fact that oral tradition is often inaccurate, inventive, or altogether false, and (a circumstance often referred to by Lemche) that individual memory normally stops at the third generation, the so-called "grandfather law."[115] The first point, that genre and performative setting play an important role, is well illustrated by Finley, who, in an inter-

---

Eastern history, see Jan Assmann, *Das kulturelle Gedächtnis: Schrift, Erinnerung und politische Identität in Frühen Hochkulturen* (Munich: Beck, 1997); T. J. Cornell, *The Beginnings of Rome: Italy and Rome from the Bronze Age to the Punic Wars (c. 1000–264 BC)* (London: Routledge, 1995).

112. Vansina, *Oral Tradition as History*, 24.

113. Ibid., 39–40.

114. Ibid., 39–47. Cf. Paula M. McNutt, "Interpreting Israel's 'Folk Traditions,'" *JSOT* 39 (1987) 47–48. Also pertinent is Heleen Sancisi-Weerdenburg, "The Persian Kings and History," in *The Limits of Historiography: Genre and Narrative in Ancient Historical Texts* (ed. Christina Shuttleworth Kraus; Leiden: Brill, 1999) 101–2, who, discussing the Behistun Inscription, notes that "before Behistun, Iranian traditions about the past were cast in oral shape. The only evidence we have for the existence and the contents of this oral (nonreligious) tradition comes from the Greek sources. Strabo (15.3.18) mentioned the education of young Persians through tales of 'the famous deeds of men and gods,' and emphasized that the young people had to learn these tales by heart. The description given by Strabo makes it obvious that these stories were taught with educational aims. The past was an instructive device for present purposes."

115. Bernhard Stade as early as 1887 wrote that "it is a fact established by experience that information about ancestors based on oral tradition goes back at the most through three, usually only two generations" (*Geschichte des Volkes Israels* [2 vols.; Berlin: Grote, 1887] 1.28; English translation quoted from Eduard Nielsen, *Oral Tradition*, 18). Cf. also Patricia G. Kirkpatrick, *The Old Testament and Folklore Study* (JSOTSup 62; Sheffield: JSOT Press, 1988) 113–14; and Connerton, *How Societies Remember*, 38–39.

esting study, demonstrates that relevance to the transmitter and his or her interest in a tradition often make it more viable, stable, and historically reliable. Finley points out the fact that no Greek author before the 5th century B.C.E. tried to organize the essential stuff of history, and that the greatest achievements of Herodotus (and after him, Thucydides) were the linking of time and the past in a chronological system and the human and secular character of his historical explanations. The earlier *epic* of Homer (and Hesiod), recounting the mythic past and creating the national pan-Hellenistic or regional consciousness, was not *history*. It was "narrative, detailed and precise," and

> may even contain, buried away some kernels of historical fact—but it was not history. Like all myth, it was timeless. Dates and coherent dating schemes are as essential to history as exact measurement is to physics. Myth also presented concrete facts, but these facts were completely detached: they were linked neither with what went before nor with what came after.[116]

A "detachment" from historical time made the question of the reliability of the tradition built up and kept alive by oral tradition utterly irrelevant. As long as the tradition was accepted, it worked. But Finley points out that this is only true as long as the tradition is a myth, that is, topically rather than sequentially arranged, without a fixed chronological framework.

An illuminating example discussed by Finley is worth quoting. Shortly after the Second World War, Claud Cockburn met with three Ladino-speaking Jews in Sofia. Cockburn had approached the three men in the railway station, not knowing who or what they were. After attempting conversation in several languages without success, he tried Spanish, and, as recorded by Cockburn,

> they understood, and replied in what was certainly intelligible as a form of Spanish—though a very strange form. . . . I remarked that it was rather odd to find Spaniards here [in Sofia]. They explained. They were not Spaniards, but, one of them said, "Our family used to live in Spain before they moved to Turkey. Now we are moving to Bulgaria." Thinking that perhaps they had been "displaced" from Spain by the

---

116. Moses I. Finley, "Myth, Memory, and History," *History and Theory* 4 (1965) 285, reprinted in Moses I. Finley, "Myth, Memory, and History," in *Geschichtsbild und Geschichtsdenken im Altertum* (Wege der Forschung 631; ed. J. M. Alonso-Nunez; Darmstadt: Wissenschaftliche Buchgesellschaft, 1991) 9–38. On the Greek epic tradition, cf. also Hornblower, *Greek Historiography*, 7ff.

upheaval of the civil war, I asked how long it had been since their family had lived there. He said it was approximately five hundred years.
. . . He spoke of these events as though they had occurred a couple of
years ago.[117]

Unlike the "mythical" concept of time in pre-Herodotan Greek tradition, which made the question of historical reliability irrelevant in
regard to the oral tradition, the concept of time that governed the
answer of the Jews in Sofia made a difference, as Finley comments:

Essentially, the "historical" references of these Ladino-speaking Jews
were like the "mythical" references of most Greeks, with one difference,
the significance of which is more potential than actual. When pressed,
the former translated "our family used to live in Spain" into "it was approximately five hundred years ago." They were able to do that thanks
to the modern calendar, with its dating by years from a fixed initial
point. The Greeks eventually acquired the technique, too, when dating
by Olympiads was introduced, but that remained for them an artificial
convention, invented and used by a small number of antiquarian-
minded intellectuals, never introduced into daily life. And that brings
us back to the matter of interest. The only people in antiquity who were
somehow "modern" in this respect were the Hebrews, and the interest
which lay behind, and which provoked, their detailed account of the
past as a continuum was, of course, a religious one, the story of the un-
folding of God's will from the Creation to the final triumph in the future. The Greeks had no such interest, religious or otherwise; whatever
the function in the present of Agamemnon, it did not require locating
him along a time continuum; it did not matter whether he lived two
hundred years ago or four hundred or a thousand.[118]

The point is, of course, that sequentially arranged narratives or traditions may testify to a concept of time in which accuracy (in the sequence and description of events, persons, etc.) does matter and thus
exemplify a genre far more able to preserve a tradition in a historically
reliable way than, for example, the topically arranged myth. So, even
if it is true that certain kinds of individual memory and oral tradition
are both historically unreliable and short-lived, going no further back
than to the third generation, it is likewise true, as this example illus-
trates, that, once a concept of historical time has developed, accuracy
and reliability do matter, and that interest in and relevance of a certain tradition increase the possibility of a prolonged oral tradition.

117. Claud Cockburn, *Crossing the Line* (London: MacGibbon & Lee, 1958) 155; quotation taken from Finley, "Myth, Memory, and History," 294.
118. Finley, ibid., 295.

Taken together with Vansina's observations, we may conclude, therefore, that there are no easy answers to the question of historicity in oral tradition. A historically reliable transmission is indeed possible, but any answer must take into careful consideration how a given piece of oral tradition is linked to performer, audience, and occasion.

Poetry or Prose:
The Importance of Genre

This does not, of course, in any way *disprove* Lemche's conclusion above. But it does demonstrate that the validity of Lemche's claim depends on whether the circumstances under which an alleged oral— and eventually written—tradition was transmitted in ancient Palestine can be shown to have made a prolonged *reliable* oral transmission possible or impossible, likely or unlikely. Or in Vansina's terminology: whether or not the genre and performative setting of the traditions made them more stable and thereby more historically reliable. However, before we consider the implications of these modern examples and observations for a discussion on oral transmission in ancient Israel, two important methodological problems must be kept in mind.

First, while much research has been done on oral *poetry*, oral *prose* has received less attention.[119] This is true not only for studies in modern orality (e.g., Yugoslavian rhapsody, African poetry) but also for discussions on medieval (e.g., the Icelandic sagas, the songs of Roland and Beowulf) and ancient (e.g., Homer's epics) oral traditions. Caution is necessary, therefore, in applying the results of research on these predominantly poetic traditions to an assumed oral narrative tradition preceding the texts of, for example, the books of Kings. Being aware of the necessity for comparable genres and settings, we find it much more relevant to look at studies on kin-based oral societies in Africa and the Middle East, and it is significant how such a change of focus also changes the conclusions!

In a study of the modern Balga bedouin in the Jordan Valley, Andrew Shryock described the extraordinary ability of the ʿAdwani tribe to remember and recite tribal history:

> Among the ʿAdwani, I recorded four hours of testimony during my first week of fieldwork. Proper sources were everywhere, and they needed little inducement to speak. Their stories, though told as separate episodes, came together in a lengthy narrative called *sirat al-ʿadwan* [the

---

119. A fact also mentioned by Robert C. Culley, "Oral Tradition and the OT," 9–11.

"saga" or "epic" of the ʿAdwan]; their genealogical knowledge, which went back thirteen generations or more, was prodigious; their poetry was abundant, better remembered, and superior in quality to ʿAbadi verse.[120]

Similar conclusions have been reached in studies on modern Arab and West African tribal societies.[121]

Second, we must remember, as Lemche rightly notes, that we have for obvious reasons no direct access to oral traditions of the distant past and can only argue for a certain understanding of ancient orality by analogy.

Working Our Way Backward

With these caveats in mind, we may now attempt to apply Vansina's points on the importance of performer, audience, and occasion to earlier periods. Working our way backward, a natural first step would be to look at the role of oral tradition in the transmission history of the Synoptic Gospels, where much attention has been given to the importance of the rabbinate as a tradition-preserving institution. New Testament scholarship has long been occupied with the problem of "oral" and "written" texts, but there is general agreement that research received an important stimulus from Birger Gerhardsson's pioneering work, *Memory and Manuscript*, on the origin of the Gospel traditions.[122] Stressing the primacy of orality, Gerhardsson portrays Jesus as a rabbinic-type teacher (ῥαββί, διδάσκαλος, ἐπιστάτης, κύριος) of the Torah who linked his words and deeds closely with the Torah and required his disciples (μαθηταὶ) to memorize his sayings. Betraying his Scandinavian traditiohistorical roots, one of Gerhardsson's main points is that, because of the authority attached to the rabbinate, we should assume a high degree of continuity and reliability in the transmission of the traditions about Jesus. The written traditions, as we find them in the Gospels, are therefore in all probability reliable presentations of the historical Jesus.

---

120. Andrew Shryock, *Nationalism and the Genealogical Imagination: Oral History and Textual Authority in Tribal Jordan* (Berkeley: University of California Press, 1997) 161.

121. Judith T. Irvine, "When Is Genealogy History? Wolof Genealogies in Comparative Perspective," *American Ethnologist* 5 (November 1978) 651–74.

122. Birger Gerhardsson, *Memory and Manuscript* (Lund: C. W. K. Gleerup, 1961), but see also Harald Riesenfeld, *The Gospel Tradition Essays* (Philadelphia: Fortress, 1970). For a survey of recent research, see conveniently Wansbrough (ed.), *Jesus and the Oral Gospel Tradition*.

A similar approach can be found in a recent study by Samuel Byrskog. In his *Jesus the Only Teacher*, he tries to demonstrate that "transmission of material concerning words and deeds of an esteemed
person exhibits features that are not as evident in the transmission of
material concerned with impersonal matters,"[123] and by analyzing the
Gospel of Matthew for its setting, motives, and process of transmission, he argues that Matthew's notion of Jesus as the only teacher "is
related to broad and essential aspects of Matthew's understanding of
Jesus' active ministry and was a vital force in his transmission of the
Jesus tradition."[124] The question of the reliability of the transmission
process is, of course, an important corollary of this result:

> This issue is not only a modern quest caused by our own standards of
> historical accuracy. Matthew's persistent interest in always relying on
> the past tradition in his controlled treatment of the Jesus tradition im-
> plies that he himself was a transmitter conscious of the distinctions as
> well as interactions between preservation and elaboration. A separate
> setting of transmission may point to a technical awareness of how to
> transmit the material, but it does not say much about why it should be
> transmitted. The presence of additional factors is necessary. If the set-
> ting was also identified as the school of Jesus and exhibited an interest
> in Jesus' teaching as intimately linked with his life and person, *we have
> all the essentials for assuming the existence of transmitters highly able and
> motivated to preserve the tradition faithfully also within their own and the
> community's creative elaborations* [italics his].[125]

So, by determining the performer, audience, and occasion as, respectively, teacher, pupil, and synagogue, Gerhardsson and Byrskog assert
that the orally transmitted Jesus-traditions preserved and presented a
reliable picture of the historical Jesus and, consequently, that there is
good reason to attach a high degree of historical reliability to the *written* Jesus-traditions.

Gerhardsson (and in consequence, also Byrskog) has, however, been
criticized   for   being   both   anachronistic   and   undifferentiated.

---

123. Samuel Byrskog, *Jesus the Only Teacher: Didactic Authority and Transmission in
Ancient Israel, Ancient Judaism and the Matthean Community* (Coniectanea Biblica, New
Testament Series 24; Stockholm: Almquist & Wiksell, 1994) 21.

124. Ibid., 399.

125. Ibid., 400. Cf. also Rainer Riesner, "Jesus as Preacher and Teacher," in *Jesus and
the Oral Gospel Tradition* (ed. Henry Wansbrough; JSNTSup 64; Sheffield: Sheffield Academic Press, 1991) 185–210. For a critical yet favorable review of Byrskog's thesis, see
Peter M. Head, "The Role of Eyewitnesses in the Formation of the Gospel Tradition: A
Review Article of Samuel Byrskog, *Story as History—History as Story*," *TynBul* 52 (2001)
275–94.

Shemaryahu Talmon sums up the critique in two points. First, some scholars reject "his portrayal of Jesus as a rabbinic-type teacher of the Torah" and argue, furthermore, that "the exclusively oral transfer of the Jesus traditions was spontaneous and unchannelled, and that it could not be geared to authoritative memorization and passive transmission."[126] Second, "students of rabbinic Judaism voice objections to his theses on the ground that they are fashioned after concepts and models which crystallized in mishnaic Judaism of the 2nd century CE. The application of these models to traditions of nascent Christianity is deemed a fallacious anachronism."[127] Addressing the criticisms of Gerhardsson's thesis, Talmon points to the material from Qumran as an obvious means of control: if the same mechanisms that Gerhardsson assumes were active in the transmission process of the Jesus-traditions can be seen in the literature from Qumran, there is no reason to believe that Gerhardsson's thesis is built on anachronistic presuppositions. Talmon answers the question in the affirmative and asserts that "no other corpus of sacred traditions in the entire spread of Judaism at the end of the Second Temple period can as fruitfully serve as a model by which to gauge the behaviour of sacred traditions in the Gospels":[128]

> It seems that in the transfer of the Teacher's message from one medium to the other, the one-time oral tradition became written transmission without undergoing any spectacular changes. Nothing gives grounds for thinking that a dramatic hermeneutic shift occurred when his spoken words became written text. It would seem, quite to the contrary, that the written version retained the original wording, as much as the cadences of oral delivery, and the typical structure of a speech or an oration. I tend to presume, although this assumption cannot be proven, that already in the Teacher's lifetime or soon after his death, his spiritual *Nachlass* became part of the Torah which the Covenanters studied periodically, audibly proclaiming this message, both from memory and from manuscript (1QS 6.7–8; etc).[129]

---

126. Shemaryahu Talmon, "Oral Tradition and Written Transmission, Or the Heard and the Seen Word in Judaism of the Second Temple Period," in *Jesus and the Oral Gospel Tradition* (ed. Henry Wansbrough; Sheffield: Sheffield Academic Press, 1991) 122–23, referring to W. H. Kelber, *The Oral and the Written Gospel* (Philadelphia: Fortress, 1983) 8–14, 207–11. Cf. also Philip S. Alexander, "Orality in Pharisaic-Rabbinic Judaism at the Turn of the Eras," in *Jesus and the Oral Gospel Tradition*, 158–84.

127. Talmon, "Oral Tradition," 123, referring to Morton Smith, "A Comparison of Early Christian and Early Rabbinic Tradition," *JBL* 82 (1963) 176–79.

128. Talmon, "Oral Tradition," 158.

129. Ibid.

So, despite heavy criticism, the "Gerhardsson school" has been able to defend its view of tradition, to clarify the role of the rabbinic analogy, and to fill out the general scheme with concrete detail.[130] Closing our discussion on the Gerhardsson approach, we note, therefore, that Gerhardsson and Byrskog seem to confirm an important element of our knowledge from modern research on orality: (1) the extraordinary ability of people to memorize, and (2) the likelihood of identity-related traditions being transmitted in a stable and reliable way.

An interesting exception to the focus in New Testament research on teacher, student, and synagogue as performer, audience, and setting, respectively, is a study by Kenneth E. Bailey,[131] who offers an alternative to the position of the form-critical school of Bultmann and to the approach of the Scandinavian School of Riesenfeld and Gerhardsson. Bailey describes Bultmann's understanding of the oral traditions behind the Gospels as *informal* and *uncontrolled*. It is *uncontrolled*, because the community "was not interested in either preserving or controlling the tradition. . . . It is *informal* in the sense that there is no identifiable teacher nor student and no structure within which material is passed from one person to another. All is fluid and plastic, open to new additions and new shapes."[132] The other prevalent approach, the Scandinavian School, is characterized by understanding the oral tradition as formal and controlled. "It is *formal* in the sense that there is a clearly identified teacher, a clearly identified student, and a clearly identified block of traditional material that is being passed on from one to the other. It is *controlled* in the sense that the material is memorized (and/ or written), identified as 'tradition' and thus preserved intact."[133]

Admitting that both the Bultmannian and the Scandinavian model still exist in the modern Middle East (e.g., as "rumor transmission" and in the memorization of the entire Qurʾān by Muslim sheiks), Bailey points to a third phenomenon with a unique methodology all its own, which, in his opinion, is a far more adequate tool for describing an assumed oral transmission preceding the written fixing of the Jesus-

---

130. Ben F. Meyer, "Some Consequences of Birger Gerhardsson's Account of the Origins of the Gospel Tradition," in *Jesus and the Oral Gospel Tradition* (ed. Henry Wansbrough; Sheffield: Sheffield Academic Press, 1991) 440.

131. K. E. Bailey, "Informal Controlled Oral Tradition and the Synoptic Gospels," *Themelios* 20/2 (1991) 4–11; reprint of idem, "Informal Controlled Oral Tradition and the Synoptic Gospels," *Asia Journal of Theology* 5 (1991) 34–54. Cf. also idem, "Middle Eastern Oral Tradition and the Synoptic Gospels," *The Expository Times* 106 (1995) 363–67.

132. Idem, "Informal Controlled Oral Tradition," 4.

133. Ibid.

traditions in the Gospels. Bailey dubs it *informal, controlled oral tradition*, and sets out to discuss the setting in which it functions, the nature of the functionaries, the kinds of material retained, the controls exercised by the community, and the techniques for introducing new material.[134] As for setting, Bailey points to the *ḥaflat samar*:[135] the gathering of an extended family, perhaps together with some close friends; or an informal gathering of villagers in the evening for the telling of stories and the recitation of poetry. The setting is informal, because there is no set teacher and no specifically identified student. The performers are usually the older men, the more-gifted men, and the socially more-prominent men, but it depends on who is seated in the circle. There is no professional storyteller, and anyone in the community could in principle be the performer. Bailey distinguishes between six types of material or genres recited in a *ḥaflat samar*[136]—namely, proverbs, riddles, poetry, parables and stories, well-told accounts of the important figures in the history of the village or community, and jokes—and points to three discernible levels of flexibility. The first level is of *no* flexibility, and proverbs and poetry alone fall into this category. The second level allows for *some* flexibility. This is true for parables, entertaining stories, and historical narratives. Their recitation is to some extent colored by the reciter's individual interest and vocabulary. A third level is characterized by *total* flexibility and comprises, according to Bailey, jokes, a retelling of the casual events of the day, and, in times of war or intercommunal violence, atrocity stories.

Because of his interest in Synoptic studies, Bailey first and foremost elaborates on the middle category by defining more precisely what is meant by "some flexibility." It is important to distinguish, he argues, between "flexibility" and "change," since the storyteller could change, say, fifteen percent of the story, but not *any* fifteen percent. Taking his point of departure in a concrete example, he demonstrates how

> the proverb that appeared in the story (the punch line) had to be repeated verbatim. The three basic scenes could not be changed, but the order of the last two could be reversed without triggering the community rejection mechanism. The basic flow of the story and its conclusion

---

134. Ibid., 6–10; idem, "Middle Eastern Oral Tradition," 364–66.

135. Literally, 'a party for preservation'. *Samar* in Arabic is cognate with Hebrew *šāmar* 'to preserve'.

136. Bailey, "Informal Controlled Oral Tradition," 6–7; idem, "Middle Eastern Oral Tradition," 364–65. Cf. David E. Aune, "Oral Tradition in the Hellenistic World," in *Jesus and the Oral Gospel Tradition* (ed. Henry Wansbrough; Sheffield: Sheffield Academic Press, 1991) 65, for a similar list.

had to remain the same. The names cou ld not be changed. The summary punch line was inviolable. However, the teller could vary the
pitch of one character's emotional reaction to the other, and the dia-
logue within the flow of the story could at any point reflect the individual teller's style and interests. That is, the story-teller had a certain
freedom to tell the story in his own way as long as the central thrust of
the story was not changed.[137]

Applying this to the study on orality in the transmission process of
the Gospel narrative, Bailey suggests that, "up until the upheaval of
the Jewish-Roman war, informal controlled oral tradition was able to
function in the villages of Palestine" and concludes his study by saying that

> here we have observed a classical methodology for the preservation,
> control and transmission of tradition that provides, on the one hand,
> assurance of authenticity and, on the other hand, freedom within limits
> for various forms of that tradition. Furthermore, the types of material
> that appear in the Synoptic Gospels include primarily the same forms
> that we have found preserved by *informal controlled* oral tradition such
> as proverbs, parables, poems, dialogues, conflict stories and historical
> narratives. . . . We are convinced that the same can be affirmed regard-
> ing the Synoptic tradition. In the light of the reality described above the
> assumption that the early Christians were not interested in history be-
> comes untenable. To remember the words and deeds of Jesus of Naza-
> reth was to affirm their own unique identity. The stories had to be *told*
> and *controlled* or everything that made them who they were was lost.[138]

Bailey's study can no doubt be criticized on a number of points. His argument is not based on conventional field studies (à la Parry's and
Lord's on the Balkan traditions) but rests on more than 30 years of living, preaching, and teaching in the Middle East, and his application of
modern oral transmission techniques to Synoptic studies is based on the
premise that "life has changed but it has also remained the same."[139]

But, even if Bailey's argument must await more conventional field-
studies before it can be sustained, it is far from being ill founded.
Bailey uses the insights of recent research in modern orality, not least
Vansina's above-mentioned focus on the importance of performer, set-

---

137. Bailey, "Informal Controlled Oral Tradition," 7.
138. Ibid., 10.
139. Bailey, "Middle Eastern Oral Tradition," 363. Bailey himself seems to be well
aware of these pitfalls. He presents his understanding tentatively as a "suggestion" and
appreciates other understandings not as alternatives but as complementary approaches.
This is especially true of the Gerhardsson approach; cf. Bailey, "Informal Controlled
Oral Tradition," 10.

ting, and audience for the question of stability and reliability, and by suggesting the informal, controlled oral tradition of modern Middle East village culture as an alternative *Sitz im Leben* for the assumed oral transmission of the Gospel narratives he has, in my opinion, pointed to a more compelling and relevant modern analogy than, for example, the oft-mentioned "Singer of Tales."[140] There may have been other *Sitze im Leben* for an oral transmission of identity-related traditions in the first centuries C.E. (the rabbinate is certainly one of them), but this only serves to strengthen the argument: even though a certain Gospel tradition may have been told for generations and to a certain extent colored by the different reciters' personas, the central thrust of the story (basic flow, punch line, conclusion, names, etc.) was not changed. It remained the same.

This is important to keep in mind, when we move further back to discuss the possibility of a prolonged oral tradition in ancient Israel, because much of what has been written on the subject seems to be

---

140. It is noteworthy that James D. G. Dunn, in an essay on oral memory and the Jesus tradition presented electronically to the *XTalk: Historical Jesus and Christian Origins* discussion group on the internet, refers favorably to Bailey's study. Describing the previous paradigms offered by Bultmann and Gerhardsson as inadequate for our own understanding of the oral transmission of the Jesus tradition, Dunn states: "Of special interest is the degree to which Bailey's thesis both informs and refines the general recognition among students of the subject that oral tradition is typically flexible, with constant themes, recognizable versions of the same story, some word for word repetition, and both fixed and variable formulaic elements depending on the context of the performance. What he adds is significant; in particular the recognition of the likelihood that (1) a community would be concerned enough to exercise some control over its traditions; (2) the degree of control exercised would vary both in regard to form and in regard to the relative importance of the tradition for its own identity; and (3) the element in the story regarded as its core or key to its meaning would be its most firmly fixed element." In the remainder of the essay, Dunn seeks to answer the key question "whether we can find the marks of such 'informal, controlled oral tradition' in the Synoptic tradition itself," and concludes by saying that "in both cases (narratives and teachings) we also noted (1) a concern to remember the things Jesus had done and said. The discipleship and embryonic communities which had been formed and shaped by the impact of Jesus' life and message would naturally have celebrated that tradition as central to their own identity as disciples and churches. We noted also (2) that the memories consisted in stories and teachings whose own identity was focused in particular themes and/or particular words and phrases—usually those said by Jesus himself. And (3) that the variations and developments were not linear or cumulative in character, but the variations of oral performance. The material examined indicated neither concern to preserve some kind of literalistic historicity of detail, nor any readiness to flood the tradition with Jewish wisdom or prophetic utterance." James D. G. Dunn, "Jesus in Oral Memory: The Initial Stages of the Jesus Tradition," http://groups.yahoo.com/group/crosstalk2/files/Articles%20for%20Review/JesusInOralMemory.htm (accessed May 6, 2003).

based on inadequate or irrelevant categorizations. It is highly questionable, for example, whether Nielsen is right in asserting that

> the bearers and creators of tradition are—no less than the bearers of written transmission—specialists, whether narrators or rhapsodists, or saga-tellers, or singers and poets, or reciters of law. And the types of literature with which *these* specialists deal are not only popular stories and fairy-tales, to which children and grown-ups listen with enthusiasm "on leisurely winter evenings," but also literature as aristocratic and artificial as one could wish. Probably nobody would venture to call the homeric epics popular; on the contrary they are aristocratic, both in structure and as to content. It is the nobility that is glorified, and the singers are the professional bards, who at the banquets held at the courts of the nobility bring out their clear-sounding lyrs and celebrate the renown of the men in songs that resound to high heaven, tales of Ulysses and the Peleid Achilles.[141]

There may very well have existed professional storytellers in ancient Israel, and there can be no doubt that reciting of various types of material did take place "on leisurely winter evenings" around the campfires (see below, p. 84) and "at the banquets held at the courts of the nobility," but it is much more likely that the primary setting for the retelling and preservation of identity-related traditions was sacral (temple, synagoge, shrine, etc.) and/or the ancient counterpart of the modern *ḥaflat samar*. Admittedly, Nielsen does mention the existence of other settings—not least the sacral—and does emphasize the exercise of control and the existence of "rejection mechanisms" in the transmission process, but still he seems to focus narrowly on the professional storyteller, the bard, as far as the performer is concerned:

> one would be mistaken in asserting that the oral tradition was subject to no control. Especially in those cases where tradition is flourishing, i.e., where there are many traditionists of the same text, the individual tradition has a very small chance of carrying through a corrupt recension. His guild brothers, but first of all his listeners, have been of immeasurable importance in upholding the tradition, whether these listeners were teachers who were to examine the scholars in the canonical texts (cf. late Judaism, Parseeism, Islam), private members of the tribe who heard the exploits of their tribe celebrated in the odes of the tribal poets (as the Bedouin do to this day), or those taking part in the annual national and religious festivals (e.g., Israel). Bound to its own *milieu*, to the rhythm of the day and the year, the spoken word is heard in the situa-

---

141. Nielsen, *Oral Tradition*, 30–31.

tion intended for it; it is not dependent on "external, foreign τύποι" and thus does not run the risk of creating "δοξοφόι—ἀντὶ σοφῶν."[142]

This must be rejected in the light of what has been discussed above. The *ḥaflat samar* is—together with the rabbinate—a much better analogy as far as setting and performer are concerned, and the question of reliability cannot receive a satisfactory answer if this is not taken into careful consideration.

This is also where we find a serious flaw in Lemche's statement on oral tradition (quoted at length above, p. 59). Reading the entire paragraph from which Lemche's statement on the unreliability and uncontrollability of oral tradition is taken makes it clear that he is very sensitive to the general possibility in the ancient Near East of information being handed down through a prolonged oral tradition and that "such tradition existed and that tales were told" also in preexilic Israel. Furthermore, his comment on the written stabilization of an oral tradition as a crucial point regarding its historical reliability must be acknowledged. His conclusion, on the other hand, that the average man in the street could know little if anything at all about what happened in his country more than, say, three hundred years ago on the basis of oral transmission and that the uncontrollability of the information in the allegedly preceding chain of oral transmission is reason enough to reject the reliability of the written tradition that is making use of it seems to be based on two assumptions that cannot be sustained by the results of recent research and must—at the least—be qualified.

First, to "think of" information being handed down "from father and mother to son and daughter" in the form of "tales" as the *only* channel and genre of oral transmission is a relic of the much-too-simplistic romantic idea of "campfire orality" (see below, p. 84). Lemche is no doubt aware of this and may have considered other possibilities,[143] but since he does not mention them, he evidently chose to discard them

---

142. Ibid., 37.

143. Lemche (*Vorgeschichte*, 29, 166–68) provides a more detailed discussion of the possibility of reliable historical information on Israel's prehistory being handed down over the centuries in ancient Israel, but though he does mention that "the folk literature is divided primarily into prose narratives and poetry" (p. 166), he nevertheless continues to focus exclusively on the latter (pp. 167–68). Similarly, though stressing that "the epic literature has no social boundaries but is used everywhere," he focuses exclusively on a single category of performers with "campfire overtones": "They certainly used skilled performers. . . . One has to imagine these singers as gypsies who traveled around and offered their services to make a living" (p. 168) [my translations].

as irrelevant. But while Nielsen, who wrote on the subject in the 1950s, may be excused, it is curious that Lemche fails to consider other, more-relevant analogies for setting and performer.

Second, by asserting that the lack of external controls on oral transmission makes it impossible for the historian to regard the (late) written stabilization of the ancient Israelite traditions as reliable, he seems to base his judgment on a similar narrow understanding of oral genres and performative settings. Despite Lemche's statement, there is good reason to believe that traditions "about what happened in his country more than, say, three hundred years ago" were handed down to both the noble and the "commoner" in the Persian or Hellenistic periods in a way that preserved the "central thrust" of these traditions. Blenkinsopp has elaborated on this observation in a recent study and seems, in his application of it to the historical memory as preserved in the narratives of the Hebrew Bible, to be much more sensitive to what we have said above.[144] Discussing the reliability of the historical tradition in the Hebrew Bible, Blenkinsopp acknowledges that "the survival of memories transmitted over such a long period of time has a very low percentage of probability even in situations of cultural and political continuity, decidedly not the case in Israel," but maintains that there was no need for historians to preserve such a historical tradition, since

> historians, in any case, are not the custodians of a society's memories, least of all in a culture in which only a very small percentage of the population had the skill, leisure, or motivation to read history. Even in more literate societies than 6th century BCE Judah social memory is shaped, sustained, and transmitted to a great extent by non-inscribed practices including rituals of re-enactment, commemorative ceremonies, bodily gestures, and the like. So it was with the destruction of Jerusalem and its temple. A prophetic text from the early Persian period, one long lifetime after the fall of Jerusalem, speaks of public fasts in the 4th, 5th, 7th, and 10th months corresponding to successive stages of the unfolding disaster from the beginning of the siege to the assassination of the Babylonian-appointed governor Gedaliah after the conquest (Zech 7:5, 8:18–19). The ritual itself therefore encoded a rudimentary history of the event.[145]

---

144. J. Blenkinsopp, "Memory, Tradition, and the Construction of the Past in Ancient Israel," *Biblical Theology Bulletin* 27/3 (1997) 76–82.

145. Ibid., 77–78. A similar view on preservation of historical traditions in the ancient Near East is suggested by H. Cazelles, "Biblical and Prebiblical Historiography," in *Israel's Past in Present Research: Essays on Ancient Israelite Historiography* (Sources for Biblical and Theological Study 7; ed. V. Philips Long; Winona Lake, Ind.: Eisenbrauns, 1999) 108, trans. of H. Cazelles, "Historiographies bibliques et prébibliques," *Revue biblique* 98 (1991)

The deficiencies of mnemonic capability and limits of oral tradition under certain circumstances do not necessarily preclude the possibility that a prolonged oral transmission kept alive a tradition on Israel's early history. On the contrary. Provided that some kind of historical consciousness had developed in Israel (as it had in the neighboring regions), it is more likely that the people of Iron Age Israel and Judah had a considerable interest in preserving traditions about the past, and there is no reason to doubt that "rituals of re-enactment, commemorative ceremonies, bodily gestures, and the like" helped to keep alive and preserve relevant historical traditions in the Iron Age as they evidently did in the Persian period.

Another interesting study by Frank H. Polak is relevant to this discussion. Taking a sociolinguistic approach, Polak divides the syntax and grammar of biblical prose into three main categories: "(1) prose from the Persian era, largely characterized by the complex, nominal style; (2) a corpus that is characterized by brisk, rhythmic verbal style by and large the opposite of the first category; and (3) a transitional category, related to the redaction of kings, and characterized by a mixture of nominal and verbal tendencies."[146] Concluding his statistical survey on the noun-verb ratio in selected samples of each category, Polak remarks that

> the characteristic style of classical biblical narrative is close to spoken language, and, by implication, to oral literature. In view of the popular nature of such narratives as the Samson tale and the Elisha narratives, in many respects the most eloquent representatives of the crisp, rhythmic, verbal style of the classical stratum, this inference is highly plausible. The high extent of structuring of classical biblical narrative also supports this conclusion. We conclude, then, that classical narrative in the main adheres to the norms of oral narrative. This thesis is not intended to mean that this corpus itself was oral, only that these narratives were written in the style of oral literature by narrators for whom the norms of literary design were those of oral narrative.[147]

Polak can, of course, be criticized for circular argumentation by presupposing that the differences between these main categories are due to a diachronic development and that they for the same reason can be

---

481–512. See also Eugene H. Merrill, "Remembering: A Central Theme in Biblical Worship," *JETS* 43 (2000) 27–36.

146. Frank H. Polak, "The Oral and the Written: Syntax, Stylistics and the Development of Biblical Prose Narrative," *JANES* 26 (1998) 69.

147. Ibid., 101–2. A similar point is taken by Gunn, *The Story of King David: Genre and Interpretation*, 49–61, especially pp. 49–50.

used as a means of dating books—for example, the books of Kings. However, the point in this connection is not dating but whether biblical narrative show signs of oral transmission, and Polak has made a good case for the books of Kings' being created in a markedly oral environment.

Despite the danger of using circular reasoning, I cannot avoid mentioning that this conclusion seems to be in full accord with what we find in the texts of the Hebrew Bible itself. Recent studies have confirmed that the texts contain both direct (explicit requests for or examples of oral instruction and transmission) and indirect (import of oral expressions, signs of oral language) evidence of an oral stage prior to the written form of the texts.[148] In addition to this, we find a plethora of rituals of reenactment, commemorative ceremonies, bodily gestures, and the like that helped the Israelites to keep alive and preserve relevant historical traditions; for example:

הַקֶּשֶׁת בֶּעָנָן 'the bow in the cloud'
When the bow is in the clouds, I will look upon it and remember the everlasting covenant between God and every living creature of all flesh that is upon the earth. (Gen 9:16)

Passover as a 'day of remembrance'
This day shall be for you a memorial day, and you shall keep it as a feast to the LORD; throughout your generations you shall observe it as an ordinance for ever. (Exod 12:14)

לְאוֹת עַל־יָדְךָ 'as a sign on your hand'
And it shall be to you as a sign on your hand and as a memorial between your eyes, that the law of the LORD may be in your mouth; for with a strong hand the LORD has brought you out of Egypt. (Exod 13:9)

אֶת־שְׁתֵּי אַבְנֵי־שֹׁהַם 'two onyx stones'
And you shall take two onyx stones . . . as stones of remembrance for the sons of Israel. (Exod 28:9–12)

אֶת־כֶּסֶף הַכִּפֻּרִים 'the atonement money'
And you shall take the atonement money from the people of Israel, and shall appoint it for the service of the tent of meeting; that it may bring the people of Israel to remembrance before the LORD, so as to make atonement for yourselves. (Exod 30:16)

---

148. Cf. Roger Lapointe, "Tradition and Language: The Import of Oral Expression," in *Tradition and Theology in the Old Testament* (ed. Douglas A. Knight; Biblical Seminar 11; Sheffield: JSOT Press, 1990) 125–42; Niditch, *Oral World*; Hans-Peter Rüger, "Oral Tradition in the Old Testament," in *Jesus and the Oral Gospel Tradition* (JSNTSup 64; ed. Henry Wansbrough; Sheffield: Sheffield Academic Press, 1991) 107–20.

חֲצֹצְרוֹת 'the trumpets'
And when you go to war in your land against the adversary who op-
presses you, then you shall sound an alarm with the trumpets, that you
may be remembered before the LORD your God, and you shall be saved
from your enemies. (Num 10:9)

צִיצָת the 'fringes'
Speak to the Israelites, and tell them to make fringes on the corners of
their garments . . . so that, when you see it, you will remember all the
commandments of the LORD. (Num 15:38–39)

אֶת־מַצֶּבֶת 'the pillar'
Now Absalom in his lifetime had taken and set up for himself the pillar
which is in the King's Valley, for he said, "I have no son to keep my
name in remembrance"; he called the pillar after his own name, and it
is called Absalom's monument to this day. (2 Sam 18:18)

Regarding the more indirect evidence, features such as repetition,
paratactic style, and the constant use of formulas or "stock phrases"
have been mentioned as signs of oral language.[149] For direct examples,
just a few will suffice. Ps 78:2–8 explicitly points out how important it
is to *tell* (ספר, הודיע) the next generation about the works of God. The
fathers' retelling is based on what they have learned themselves by
listening (שמע), and the oral transmission is rooted in God's commandment to transmit the testimony "he established in Jacob" and the law
he "appointed in Israel" (v. 5).[150] The aim is that the next generation
"might know them [the testimony and the law]" (v. 6), so that they
"set their hope in God, and not forget the works of God, but keep his
commandments" (v. 7) *and*, importantly, so that they are able themselves to pass on the testimony and law to *their* children. No written
tradition is mentioned in this connection.[151]

We may also mention the example of Jeremiah 26, where vv. 17–19
inform us that "certain elders of the land" long before the fall of Jerusalem were able to recall the words of the prophet Micah more than
one hundred years earlier. By doing so they were (according to Jeremiah) able to recall a tradition several generations older than themselves, place it in its proper historical context, quote it verbatim, and
apply it to a new context (i.e., the question of whether the doomsday
prophet Jeremiah was a true prophet or not). It is a natural conclusion

---

149. Cf. Lapointe, "Tradition and Language," 129.
150. Cf. Deut 6:20–24.
151. There are other examples, of course, in which the oral transmission is performed on the basis of or supplemented by a *written* tradition. See, e.g., Deut 31:9–11;
2 Kgs 23:2; 2 Chr 17:9.

that these elders were referring to and quoting from an oral tradition and that Micah's prophecies were preserved by "certain elders of the land," even though they were not fulfilled either in Micah's lifetime or their own. There is, however, one obstacle to this interpretation. It has been suggested that, instead of being an authentic report of the events relating to the accession of Jehoiakim in 609 B.C.E., Jeremiah 26 may have been inserted by someone of the Deuteronomistic school to create a tension between chaps. 26 and 36. Jeremiah 36 would then become a Deuteronomistic critique of Jehoiakim who, in contrast to the people, rejected the word of God and did not fear him. This, however, is hardly the case, because Jeremiah 26 suggests that large groups of people gave Jeremiah active, open support. This changes dramatically in Jeremiah 36–45, where the people (and not just the king, priest, and prophets) become his enemies. The example is still intact, however, even if the theory of Jeremiah 26 as a Deuteronomistic redaction is correct. It then simply demonstrates that Deuteronomistic circles during the exile accepted an oral tradition as belonging to Micah and as authentic. The crucial point in Jer 26:17–19 is that, long before the prophecy was fulfilled (by the fall of Jerusalem), certain circles regarded it as a reliable tradition, even though it had been transmitted for several generations after it was spoken by Micah.

Having rejected the definition of performative setting underlying Lemche's argument, I would conclude, therefore, that it is indeed *possible* that historical information was handed down orally in a reliable way in ancient Israel and that Lemche's "man in the street" *probably* could know "what happened centuries ago in his village, region or country." I say *probably* because we need to keep in mind the caveat mentioned above. We cannot know whether what was possible also happened. We may point out better analogies than performative setting and thereby strengthen our thesis, but they remain, nonetheless, analogies.

Thus, since mnemonic capability is not an objection, the most serious remaining potential obstacle seems to be the so-called "dark ages" or periods of disruption. The problem of disruption, however, poses the same problems as maintaining a written tradition, and I will postpone a more-detailed discussion of this obstacle to a later section and proceed first to discussing the possibility of a prolonged written tradition.

The Great Divide

Before we discuss the possibility of a prolonged written tradition, let us take a short excursion into the field of studies on literacy. Since the early 1970s, it has generally been thought that literacy brings about a sharp divide in the nature of knowledge in any society. This approach goes back to the studies of Jack Goody, Eric A. Havelock, and Walter J. Ong, who all focus (though on different grounds) on the introduction of writing and therefore literacy as a decisive factor in historical development. None of these scholars wishes to make writing or print the sole factor in such changes, but, as Mogens Trolle Larsen writes, "it is hard to avoid the conclusion that the terminology often tends towards the slippery, with words and phrases such as 'followed,' 'implemented,' 'made possible,' 'conditioned,' or even 'caused,' 'altered,' or 'made.'"[152] This "classical" consensus has now been been challenged, however, and the new consensus seems to be that no "great divide" exists between orality and literacy. Recent research has demonstrated that there is much more continuity between the written and the oral than previously thought, that knowledge, speech, and writing are patterned differently in various cognitive systems, and that it is much too simplistic, therefore, to focus on writing and literacy as the decisive factor in the historical development of any society.[153]

Especially pertinent to our discussion of the continuity between the written and the oral is an example given by Maurice Bloch (in the collection of articles cited in n. 153). Bloch discusses the implications of literacy on Madagascar and mentions two kinds of language-use

---

152. M. T. Larsen, "Introduction," in *Literacy and Society* (ed. Karen Schousboe and Mogens Trolle Larsen; Copenhagen: Akademisk, 1989) 8. The views of Goody, Havelock, and Ong are expressed in Jack Goody, *Literacy in Traditional Societies* (Cambridge: Cambridge University Press, 1968); idem, *The Domestication of the Savage Mind* (Cambridge: Cambridge University Press, 1977); idem, *The Logic of Writing and the Organization of Society* (Cambridge: Cambridge University Press, 1986); Eric A. Havelock, *Preface to Plato* (Oxford: Blackwell, 1963); idem, *Origins of Western Literacy* (Toronto: Ontario Institute for Studies in Education, 1976); idem, "The Alphabetization of Homer," in *Communication Arts in the Ancient World* (ed. Eric A. Havelock and Jackson P. Hershbell; New York: Hastings House, 1978); idem, *The Literate Revolution in Greece and Its Cultural Consequences* (Princeton: Princeton University Press, 1982); idem, *The Muse Learns to Write: Reflections on Orality and Literacy from Antiquity to the Present* (New Haven: Yale University Press, 1986); Walter J. Ong, *Interfaces of the Word: Studies in the Evolution of Consciousness and Culture* (Ithaca: Cornell University Press, 1977); idem, *Orality and Literacy: The Technologizing of the Word* (London: Methuen, 1982).

153. See the above-mentioned book, *Literacy and Society*, edited by Mogens Trolle Larsen, for a number of representative essays on the most recent research.

fundamental to the Merina culture: ordinary talk, which is marked by
an informal style, and the formal style of oratory, which is used for
important matters, especially history. Oratorical style, the so-called
Kabary, is the mark of a person in authority, typically an elder.[154]
Having discussed the interchange between this style of oratory and
the written, Bloch concludes:

> The written word was, and by and large still is, seen as a form of ances-
> tral oratory. As a result it is largely treated in similar ways as oral *Ka-*
> *bary.* People without authority have no right to use it, and if they do
> they are ridiculous. What has been written once should be repeated in
> further writings and publications. It should be carefully transmitted
> from authoritative person to authoritative person. Written documents
> are not, any more than the words of a respected elder who uses the
> style of ancestral oratory, open to critical examination and evaluation.
> Reading written documents is exactly like listening to traditional Me-
> rina orators and what is written is by and large identical to what would
> have been said.[155]

Taking these insights into consideration in the discussion of orality
and literacy in ancient Israel, an inevitable corollary is that no such
thing as a purely oral society existed in Iron Age Palestine and that
the romantic "campfire"[156] notion of an oral period in the history of
Israel, followed by the time of literacy, must be rejected.[157] It is also
evident that, even when traditions, stories, accounts, and so on were
written down, they probably continued to function as authoritative
speech, as did the Malagasy *Kabary.*

Susan Niditch, in her treatment of orality and literacy in ancient Israel, has most recently applied the above-mentioned new consensus
to ancient Israel by demonstrating how the "oral" and "literate" ele-

154. Maurice Bloch, "Literacy and Enlightenment," in *Literacy and Society* (ed. Karen
Schousboe and Mogens Trolle Larsen; Copenhagen: Akademisk, 1989) 19.

155. Ibid., 25.

156. This refers, of course, to Gunkel's well-known words on oral transmission: "The
usual situation we have to imagine is this: on idle winter evenings, the family is en-
camped at the hearth; the adults, but especially the children, listen in suspense to the
old, beautiful, often-heard and always-requested stories from primeval times. We approach and listen in" (*Genesis* [3rd ed.; Göttinger Handkommentar zum Alten Testament 1; Göttingen: Vandenhoeck & Ruprecht, 1922] xxxi) [my translation].

157. Niditch, *Oral World*; Paul J. Achtemeier, "Omne Verbum Sonat: The New Testament and the Oral Environment of Late Western Antiquity," *JBL* 109 (1990) 3–9; cf.
Lord, *The Singer of Tales*, 134. Interesting also is Stock (*Listening*, 142–43), who describes
as "naïve" the approach that "oral" and "written" seem to mark inviolable boundaries
in the evolution of culture and argues that, in order to avoid confusion, we should use
the expression "textuality" instead of "literacy."

ments existed side by side and formed a "continuum," with writing becoming an increasingly important resource from the late monarchies of the 8th century B.C.E. onward.[158] Though the majority agree with Niditch that the texts of the Hebrew Bible must be understood as arising from a primarily oral context, it is still a matter of debate *to what extent* the concept of writing in the Hebrew Bible must be set in an oral context; in other words, *to what degree* the literate mentality should be seen as a relatively late element, being predominantly observable in the postexilic writings—for example, the books of Chronicles, as Niditch maintains.[159]

Before going into more detail, I must emphasize that our aim is not to determine the percentage of literate people in ancient Israel as such but to assess when the conditions would have allowed a written tradition to be transmitted.[160] Niditch does not seem to favor the possibility that there was such a tradition before the 8th century B.C.E.[161]

158. Niditch, *Oral World*, 78; Mary J. Carruthers, *The Book of Memory* (Cambridge: Cambridge University Press, 1990) 17. See also Vansina, *Oral Tradition as History*, 44; and Blenkinsopp, "Memory," 77–78, on the interaction between orality and literacy.

159. See especially chaps. 5 and 6 in Niditch, *Oral World*. Though it almost goes without saying that a "literate mentality" became a more and more important resource throughout Israel's history, it has to be kept in mind that spoken words were sometimes written down immediately, as evidence from Mari has shown (cf. A. R. Millard, "La prophétie et l'écriture Israël, Aram, Assyrie," *Revue de l'histoire des religions* 202 [1985] 125–44), just as ancient letters in general can be assumed to have been written from dictation and that the oral and written element, therefore, is likely to have existed side by side from the very beginning of Israel's history (for a parallel, see Lord's examples in *The Singer of Tales*, 135). Walter J. Ong has furthermore pointed out that texts that are known to be the first written form of a previous orality (e.g., Homer's texts) can be very sophisticated indeed. In other words, an advanced use of literary devices is not necessarily a late phenomenon restricted to periods of "secondary orality" (Walter J. Ong, "Literacy and Orality in Our Times," in *Oral and Traditional Literatures* [ed. Norman Simms; Hamilton: Outrigger, 1982] 8–20).

160. For a recent discussion on literacy in ancient Israel, see Ian M. Young, "Israelite Literacy: Interpreting the Evidence, Part I," *VT* 48 (1998) 239–53; idem, "Israelite Literacy: Interpreting the Evidence, Part II," *VT* 48 (1998) 408–22. Cf. also Richard S. Hess's useful survey, "Literacy in Iron Age Israel," in *Windows into Old Testament History: Evidence, Argument, and the Crisis of "Biblical Israel"* (ed. V. P. Long, David W. Baker, and Gordon J. Wenham; Grand Rapids: Eerdmans, 2002) 82–102.

161. A similar view has been taken by David W. Jamieson-Drake, *Scribes and Schools in Monarchic Judah: A Socio-Archaeological Approach* (JSOTSup 109; Sheffield: Sheffield Academic Press, 1991) from a socioarchaeological perspective. He is followed by T. L. Thompson, *Early History*; P. R. Davies, *Scribes and Schools: The Canonization of the Hebrew Scriptures* (Louisville: Westminster John Knox, 1998); and Lemche, *The Israelites in History and Tradition*, 46–47. Jamieson-Drake's conclusion, however, is based on a series of assumptions that have been seriously questioned; cf. A. Lemaire, "Review of *Scribes and Schools in Monarchic Judah: A Socio-Archaeological Approach* by D. W. Jamieson-Drake,"

Though accepting the basic idea of written texts as arising from a primarily oral context, Alan Millard has argued that Niditch underestimates the quantity of written texts in ancient Israel, as well as the argument from analogy. Millard rejects her reading of him as adumbrating a "general literacy" in ancient Israel but maintains that a literate mentality was likely to have been present much earlier than Niditch seems to suppose and that books "were not so scarce."[162]

Though the actual remnants of 9th- and 8th-century B.C.E. Hebrew writing in contexts that were not administrative, legal, or monumental are admittedly scarce, the argument from analogy is strong. Millard goes on to argue that "the absence of actual specimens is not evidence that they were not there, and present evidence can be used to suggest they were,"[163] and having mentioned the "actual specimens" from Deir ʿAlla, Arad, and Ḥorvat ʿUza, he maintains that

> the lack of other examples is something Israel shares with the Transjordanian, Phoenician, neo-Hittite and Aramaean states. From them, very little trace of any literary compositions survives, yet that need not

JAOS 112 (1992) 707–8. He links literacy closely to scribal schools which, he claims, only came into existence with the full-blown states of the 8th century B.C.E. Niditch has argued, however, that once writing was available the oral and the written interacted on a continuum and that writing was not only learned in scribal schools but most likely also in a domestic setting, thus warning us against linking literacy too closely to the question of scribal schools (Niditch, *Oral World*, 69–70). An important modifier, however, is Young's comment on W. V. Harris's research on literacy in the Greco-Roman world: "Literacy can be passed on by education in the home, but no example of majority literacy has been documented without an extensive school system" (Young, "Israelite Literacy I," 242). The criteria in determining a full-blown state have also been criticized; see William G. Dever, "The Identity of Early Israel: A Rejoinder to Keith W. Whitelam," *JSOT* 72 (1996) 3–24; John Strange, "Arkæologisk syntese og historieskrivning," in *Bibel og historie* (ed. Geert Hallbäck and John Strange; Forum for Bibelsk Eksegese 10; Copenhagen: Museum Tusculanum, 1999) 11. For a more optimistic view on the degree of literacy in ancient Israel, see A. Lemaire, *Les écoles et la formation de la Bible dans l'ancien Israël* (Fribourg: Éditions Universitaires / Göttingen: Vandenhoeck & Ruprecht, 1981); Nadav Naʾaman, "Sources and Composition in the History of Solomon," in *The Age of Solomon: Scholarship at the Turn of the Millennium* (ed. Lowell K. Handy; Leiden: Brill, 1997) 57–58, and the works referred to there.

162. A. R. Millard, "Review: Niditch, *Oral World and Written Word: Orality and Literacy in Ancient Israel*," *JTS* 49 (1998) 699–705. For a more detailed discussion, see also idem, "Books"; "The Knowledge of Writing in Iron Age Palestine," *TynBul* 46 (1995) 207–17; and "Knowledge of Writing." For a survey of the specimens of the alphabets in the Iron Age Levant, see idem, "The Uses of the Early Alphabets," in *Phoinikeia Grammata: Lire et écrire en Méditerranée: Actes du Colloque de Liège, 15–18 Novembre 1989* (ed. V. Krings, Corinne Bonnet, and Baurain Claude; Namur: Société des Études Classiques, 1991) 101–14.

163. Millard, "Oral World," 703.

lead to the supposition that writing was limited to the ephemeral or bureaucratic in them. The same situation existed; their scribes wrote on perishable materials. When, then, the Hebrew Bible reports writing for all sorts of purposes from the Book of Exodus onwards, its witness should be respected. . . . The uses of writing throughout parallel the attested uses in Egypt and Mesopotamia except in the absence of longer letters and deeds and of books; the argument from analogy is strong and implies that literary texts were to be found in some Israelite homes as they were in those in other regions. The examples of Hebrew epigraphy presented in the handbooks (notably J. Renz, W. Röllig, *Handbuch der Althebräischen Epigraphik*, Darmstadt, 1995) include the graffiti which prove a widespread knowledge of writing across the country, far beyond the major centers.[164]

A similar conclusion on the relatively sparse remnants of Phoenician writing was drawn earlier by Ap-Thomas, who states that

it is ironical that the people who apparently invented and certainly were the first to exploit the alphabet have, with the notable exception of the clay tablets from Ugarit, left us so little in the way of literature or indeed of any written material. This does not mean that the Phoenicians made little use of writing; the reverse is probably the case—the needs of commerce are still one of the most potent forces in the development of communication techniques. Presumably the normal writing substance of the Phoenicians was papyrus, which is so perishable that it needs specially dry conditions if it is to be preserved for any length of time; and these conditions do not exist along the humid coast of Phoenicia.[165]

Broadening the perspective, Amélie Kuhrt has more recently demonstrated that absence of written material in the 12th to 9th centuries B.C.E. applies not only to Israel but to the Levant and Egypt as well and that the sparse discoveries must be seen as exceptions that prove the rule, rather than the opposite. The Neo-Hittite kingdoms are a good example. The fact that we know very little about these 12th- to 10th-century B.C.E. "petty kingdoms" does not mean, Kuhrt claims, that they were disorganized, uncivilized, illiterate. In an inscription of Yariris dated to the period in question, one of the nobles and later king of Carchemish boasts of his knowledge of several languages and claims that he is able to write four different "scripts,"

in the script of the City (i.e., Carchemish, and therefore Hittite hieroglyphs), the script of Sura (perhaps Urartian or Phoenician), the script

---

164. Ibid., 703–4.

165. D. R. Ap-Thomas, "The Phoenicians," in *Peoples of Old Testament Times* (ed. D. J. Wiseman; Oxford: Clarendon, 1973) 268.

of Assyria (Akkadian cuneiform) and the script of Taiman (possibly Aramaic). I knew twelve languages, and to me my lord gathered the son of every country by (means of) travelling for (the sake of) language, and he caused me to know every wisdom.[166]

This is a claim comparable to Ashurbanipal's boast that he knew how to read cuneiform.[167] But Šulgi, the famous ruler of the 3rd dynasty of Ur, some fifteen centuries earlier, was also proud of his scholarly proficiency.[168]

On the basis of our knowledge of mnemonic capability, orality, and literacy as a *continuum*, and the attestations of literary works throughout the Levant, it is reasonable to assume that a prolonged oral tradition was indeed possible *but* that such a tradition (if it existed in ancient Israel) must be seen alongside a possible *written* tradition. There is no reason to doubt that literary works existed in Israel *to some extent* as early as the 10th century B.C.E. And though it neither *disproves* Lemche's claim that, on the basis of oral transmission, "the ordinary man in the street"[169] of Persian Period Palestine could know nothing about what happened in his country more than three hundred years before, nor *proves* the opposite, that he *could* know, we have so far demonstrated that literacy can by no means be ruled out. It depends on whether the circumstances (as far as we can tell) allowed for a written tradition to have been transmitted, thus providing the author(s) of,

---

166. Reference and quotation can be found in Kuhrt, *Ancient Near East*, 2.415–16, but see also pp. 394–95. See also the discussion by J. C. Greenfield, "Of Scribes, Scripts and Languages," in *Phoinikeia grammata: Lire et écrire en Méditerranée: Actes du Colloque de Liège, 15–18 Novembre 1989* (ed. V. Krings, Corinne Bonnet, and Baurain Claude; Namur: Société des Études Classiques, 1991) 173–85.

167. See Greenfield, ibid., 178, for references to Ashurbanipal's claim and his well-known devotion to Nabu, god of wisdom and patron of the scribes.

168. J. Klein, *The Royal Hymns of Shulgi King of Ur: Man's Quest for Immortal Fame* (TAPS 71/7; Philadelphia: American Philosophical Society, 1981) 15.

169. A comment on Lemche's notion of "the ordinary man in the street" is necessary at this point. While it is relevant to discuss whether "the ordinary man in the street" had any knowledge of what may have happened in his country hundreds of years earlier on the basis of *oral transmission*, it is nothing but a truism in regard to a possible *written tradition*, since it is also very unlikely that the predominantly illiterate "man in the street" had any direct access to possible *written* records. They were neither written by nor intended for the "ordinary man in the street." Lemche has elsewhere made this clear, and it is therefore rather curious that he seems to use the notion of "the ordinary man in the street" with reference to both a possible oral and a possible written tradition. We will continue to use Lemche's statement as a point of departure for our discussion, however, since "the ordinary man in the street"—due to the above-mentioned ritual re-enactments, commemorative ceremonies, and other mnemotechnic devices—is likely to have had at least a *mediated* access to even written records.

for example, the books of Kings with reliable historical information on Israel's early history. Lemche's other objection—the uncontrollable nature of oral tradition—has already been discussed in the introductory paragraph on standards of source criticism (p. 39) and needs no further comment here.

The Written Tradition

As we have seen, writing was possible at a relatively early time, and it is likely that written texts existed and were copied; what, then, is the possibility that a *written* tradition was handed down from, say the 9th century to the 5th century B.C.E., thus providing the author(s) of the books of Kings with reliable historical information on early Israel's history?

First, we turn to the comparative material, because we have extensive evidence that transmission of this kind was possible and indeed took place in the ancient Near East. The best examples are from Mesopotamia, where not only texts regarded as "canonical" or "normative" but also other texts continued to be copied for more than a thousand years.[170] The Nineveh version of the "Gilgamesh Epic" from the library of Ashurbanipal harks back to the Old Babylonian version of the "Gilgamesh Epic" and to the Old Babylonian "Atrahasis Epic," the latter being copied for more than a thousand years; although the original version seems to have existed in two or more variants, the texts are so similar that we are clearly dealing with a transmission of the Old Babylonian version.[171] Other examples are "The Sumerian King List," "The Royal Correspondence of Ur," and—not least—the famous "Laws of Hammurapi."[172]

---

170. On the concept of *canon* in relation to transmission, see N. Veldhuis, "TIN.TIR = Babylon, the Question of Canonization, and the Production of Meaning," *JCS* 50 (1998) 67–76.

171. The standard book on the text history of the "Gilgamesh Epic" is Jeffrey H. Tigay, *The Evolution of the Gilgamesh Epic* (Philadelphia: University of Pennsylvania Press, 1982). For translation, see now Andrew R. George, *The Epic of Gilgamesh* (London: Penguin, 1999); and for a new critical edition, idem, *The Babylonian Gilgamesh Epic: Introduction, Critical Edition, and Cuneiform Texts* (2 vols.; Oxford: Oxford University Press, 2003).

172. On the "Sumerian King List," see Kuhrt, *Ancient Near East*, 1.29. "The Royal Correspondence of Ur" is discussed by Hallo, "Sumerian Historiography," 12. For the text of the laws of Hammurapi with variant readings, see R. Borger, *Babylonish-Assyrische Lesestücke* (Rome: Pontifical Biblical Institute, 1963). For translation, see Martha T. Roth, *Law Collections from Mesopotamia and Asia Minor* (SBL Writings from the Ancient World 6; 2nd ed.; Atlanta: Scholars Press, 1997).

Fig. 1. *Cuneiform tablet with the Atrahasis Epic. Babylonian, about 17th century* B.C.E. *From Sippar, southern Iraq. Reproduced by permission of the British Museum. © Copyright The British Museum.*

From Egypt we have another, slightly more disputed, example, the so-called "Memphite Theology." It explains the relationship between Ptah, the god of Memphis and creator, and his establishment of the falcon-god, Horus, embodied by the king and an aspect of the sun-god, Re, as overall lord. It was obviously intended "to emphasise the primacy of Memphis and Ptah in the Egyptian order of things, and link all Egyptian gods to him."[173] The only extant text is written on a stone from the time of King Shabako (ca. 716–701 B.C.E.), but it purports to be a copy of an ancient papyrus. The language and orthography of the vertical columns is archaic, and Kuhrt mentions that an early Middle Kingdom ritual text, the Ramesseum dramatic papyrus, hints that the concepts expressed by the "Theology" were in existence by the beginning of the 12th Dynasty. This makes it conceivable that the claim of the preserved text to be a genuine copy of an Old Kingdom original could be true, thus providing us with an example of a text's being transmitted for hundreds of years in roughly the same period that we are discussing in relation to the Hebrew Bible.[174]

A better example from Egypt may be the "Story of Sinuhe," which is known to us from a manuscript from the 12th Dynasty (P. Berlin 3022, abbr., B), a copy from the end of the Middle Kingdom (P. Berlin 10499, abbr., R), and from a large ostracon in the Ashmolean Museum, Oxford, which dates to the 19th Dynasty.[175] Another Egyptian example is a statue of Ramesses III found at Heliopolis.[176] The spells inscribed on it were transmitted over a long period and appear on a papyrus dated 700 years later.[177] From another quarter, we may also mention the "Ugaritic King List," which has been shown to preserve accurate information reaching back more than five hundred years: "Despite the deplorable scarcity of data on the earliest phases of

---

173. Kuhrt, *Ancient Near East* 1.145.

174. Ibid., 145. Cf. Ludlow Bull, "Ancient Egypt," in *The Idea of History in the Ancient Near East* (ed. Robert C. Dentan; New Haven: American Oriental Society, 1983) 26–32. It needs to be mentioned, however, that the consensus is challenged by a number of scholars who, in Kuhrt's words, "are convinced that it should be regarded as pseudepigraphic, that its linguistic archaisms are phony and that it illuminates theological ideas current in the late period and not earlier. . . . Significantly, it was included in a British Museum exhibition of 'fakes' in 1990" (*Ancient Near East*, 1.145–46).

175. See introduction and translation by Miriam Lichtheim in William W. Hallo and K. Lawson Younger, Jr. (eds.), *The Context of Scripture, Vol. 1: Canonical Compositions from the Biblical World* (Leiden: Brill, 1997) 77–82.

176. For the statue, see *Annales Service des Antiquités Egypte* 39 (1939) 57–89.

177. Papyri Brooklyn 47.218.138; cf. J. C. Goyon, *JEA* 57 (1971) 154–57; K. A. Kitchen, *Ramesside Inscriptions: Translations* (Oxford: Blackwell, 1993) 5.261–68, esp. pp. 263–67.

Ugarit's history, the combined evidence of the dynastic seal and the
Ugaritic King List seem to indicate that the kings of 14th–13th century
Ugarit traced back the origins of their royal house to the outset of the
2nd millennium B.C.E."[178] From yet another quarter, it has been demonstrated that most Greek historiographers were reliable transmitters
of earlier writers.[179]

Using the comparative material, two important caveats must be
kept in mind, however. First, we only know that later texts are copies
if we have an earlier version (thus the dispute over the "Memphite
Theology" text). This is not the case with the Hebrew Bible. We have
no factual evidence that the Hebrew text of the books of Kings is a
copy of a text from, for example, the 6th century B.C.E. or that the information allegedly drawn from other sources is an accurate copy of
the chronicles or royal annals of the Kingdoms of Judah and Israel in
the 9th or 8th century. Second, without an earlier text, it is impossible
to confirm the accuracy of a later version or to reconstruct an earlier or
original text. The "Gilgamesh Epic" is a good example of a text with
later and earlier versions. The above examples do not, therefore, in any
way *prove* that a similar transmission or use of reliable sources took
place as far as the books of Kings is concerned, and the examples can
only be used to demonstrate that such a transmission *did* take place in
the surrounding regions during roughly the same period. In the light
of what has been demonstrated above, however, they do provide us
with yet another argument from analogy that cannot be ignored. It
was indeed possible to transmit traditions over a considerable span of
time in the ancient Near East.

The "Dark Ages"

Was it possible to transmit traditions for a long time in ancient Israel, then? As was the case with possible *oral* transmissions, the main
obstacle to possible written transmissions seems to be the "dark ages,"
or periods of disruption.[180] First, however, another caution must be

---

178. Itamar Singer, "A Political History of Ugarit," in *Handbook of Ugaritic Studies* (ed.
W. G. E. Watson and Nicolas Wyatt; Leiden: Brill, 1999) 613. See also K. A. Kitchen, "The
King List of Ugarit," *UF* 9 (1977) 131–42. The most recent discussion on the reliability of
the king list is B. Schmidt, "A Re-Evaluation of the Ugaritic King List," in *Ugarit, Religion, and Culture* (ed. N. Wyatt, W. G. E. Watson, and J. B. Lloyd; Münster: Ugarit-Verlag,
1996) 289–304. For a translation and additional literature, see Hallo and Younger, *The
Context of Scripture, Vol. 1: Canonical Compositions from the Biblical World*, 356–57.

179. Cf. Hornblower, *Greek Historiography*, 54–72, esp. pp. 63–64.

180. For example, the Parthian "Dark Age" (91–54 B.C.E.).

sounded: disruption does not equal *corruption*. Political, ethnic, or geographical discontinuity is, of course, a major reason that traditions are lost. In the 6th century B.C.E., people still knew the location of Sargon's new capital Agade, which had been founded two thousand years earlier, but eventually the information was lost.[181] The original work of the Phoenician priest Sanchuniathon,[182] allegedly written in Phoenician in the 6th century B.C.E. and containing a Phoenician creation account, has also been lost. We only know about it because Philo of Byblos (ca. 100 C.E.) and later the church historian Eusebius (265–339 C.E.) decided to include a few passages from it in their writings.[183] Examples are *legion*. Books of ancient Near Eastern history, meditating on the mantra of *ignoramus*, are full of remarks like "we simply don't know," "so far we have not recovered," "as far as we know," "we know very little indeed," not only because of the randomness of discoveries but also because information had become irrelevant, unintelligible, or even unwanted as settlements were abandoned, ethnic entities ceased to exist, people were relocated, and the political and religious landscape changed. Many disruptive factors may have silenced a tradition that for centuries had been transmitted orally or in writing.

An important caveat must be kept in mind, however. Even though the disruptions described above may very well have been a decisive factor in the silencing of, for example, the tradition about the location of Agade, not all disruptions had the same impact. Although in the 16th century B.C.E. the Kassites who took control of Babylon were a potentially serious cultural disruption, they were quickly Babylonized. Scribes continued to write in cuneiform, and inscriptions followed the patterns of earlier Babylonian kings. J. N. Postgate, in a discussion of how cities in the Ur III to Isin-Larsa *Zwischenzeit* managed to transmit their scribal culture to later generations when they were themselves

---

181. A comprehensive list of Neo- and Late-Babylonian references can be found in Ran Zadok, *Geographical Names According to New- and Late-Babylonian Texts* (Répertoire géographique des textes cunéiforms 8; Beihefte zum Tübinger Atlas des Vorderen Orients 7/8; Wiesbaden: Reichert, 1985) 4–5.

182. Or Sakkunyaton, as a more modern spelling or the original might have it. The name means '(the god) Sakkun has given'.

183. Cf. James Barr, "Philo of Byblos and His 'Phoenician History,'" *Bulletin of the John Rylands University Library of Manchester* 57 (1974) 17–68; Sergio Ribichini, "Taautos et l'invention de l'écriture chez Philon de Byblos," in *Phoinikeia grammata: Lire et écrire en Méditerranée: Actes du Colloque de Liège, 15–18 Novembre 1989* (ed. V. Krings, Corinne Bonnet, and Baurain Claude; Namur: Société des Études Classiques, 1991) 201–13. See also Doron Mendels, *Identity, Religion and Historiography* (JSPSup 24; Sheffield: Sheffield Academic Press, 1998) 139–57 on Manetho.

moribund, says that part of the answer is that not all disruptions were
the same or universal:

> The real hiatus is the consequence of total abandonment, and abandon-
> ment did not come as a result of instability alone; as we have seen, it
> might be as much the consequence of environmental factors. Eridu, to-
> day stranded deep in a sandy and rocky desert, is a case in point, the
> city of one of the principal gods, site of a shrine which has been traced
> right back into the early Ubaid period, to at least 4500 B.C.E. Yet, as far
> as we know, no one lived there after the Early Dynastic period. The re-
> ligious cults of Eridu and their maintenance could be seen as crucial to
> all Mesopotamians, since Enki/Ea had a central role in the pantheon,
> transcending his role as local god of that city. A recent study has shown
> in detail how the entire liturgy of Enki was transferred bodily to the
> nearest major city, Ur: his temple was not re-founded, but his priests
> moved, and the daily rituals were enacted in a shrine built for him
> within the complex of his host Nanna, the god of Ur. This was not
> unique. . . . While the temples had a central role in the preservation of
> the culture's ideological identity both they and the palaces gave society
> an economic buffer against the worst effects of disruption.[184]

This example, significantly, not only provides evidence that the possible *written* traditions of the Eridu society continued to be transmitted when the city was abandoned but also demonstrates that *oral*
traditions were kept alive, because a considerable amount of information (e.g., on the performance of rituals) must have been preserved in
memory and thus by oral tradition.

Furthermore, Postgate points to an important tradition-preserving
factor that would have operated in the preservation of such a transmission: the self-preserving character of identity-related information
such as religious, ideological, and ancestral traditions.[185] In an interesting discussion on the internet during the fall of 1999, a similar
point was made.[186] A message by Liz Fried brought to readers' attention a psychological experiment, performed in the 1930s, in which
subjects were shown a slide of a scene on a crowded bus. Standing in
the aisle of the bus was a black man in a suit, holding a briefcase. He
was confronted by a white man in overalls, holding a knife. The vast
majority of (white) subjects retold the story with the black man in the

---

184. Postgate, *Early Mesopotamia*, 299.
185. A fact that is also acknowledged and discussed in relation to the concept of
canon by Veldhuis, "TIN.TIR."
186. Because postings on the Miqra-list are not archived and thus not public, permission to quote has kindly been provided by the authors.

overalls, holding the knife and the white man in the suit, with the briefcase. On the basis of this, Fried argued that

> these experiments show how people work. The stories they tell are those which fit their world view. They embellish, change, add details which make the story clearer to them, and which fit that world view. ... Although these experiments involved oral retelling, I think the process would operate equally with written sources in an age where texts are more fluid than they are today. Marginal glosses will "fill in" missing details; these would then be incorporated into the next copy as part of text. Stories are embellished simply to explain what happened to the reader, to make the story clearer, but the details always correspond to the world view of the one doing the embellishing.

This would fit well with Lemche's notion of the unlikelihood that prolonged oral transmission preserved reliable historical information.

George Athas in a reply, however, pointed out that the experiment is an example of unmeaningful recollection, or the retelling of something that has very little or no meaning or impact on the teller and that we cannot divorce the event from the effect it actually has on the retelling of it:

> (1) The experiment was an academic exercise. Historiography is never purely academic—it is done because the "history" is meaningful to the historiographer (or the one who commissioned the historiographer). In the case of the experiment, the story was not vitally meaningful to the students who participated. You might say that their story perpetuation was a type of unmeaningful historiography—something which I don't think actually existed in antiquity. (2) The students were given a story to perpetuate. This says nothing about whether the events in the story actually took place in one way or another. The outcome may have been different if the events actually took place and had some kind of meaning or influential impact on the students. (3) The story chosen for the experiment was very terse, laconic, very incomplete. Can we say that what ancient historiographers dealt with was the same? In all likelihood, it probably was not. Since ancient historiographers perpetuated "history" that was meaningful to them, it probably was not terse, laconic or incomplete to them. Take, for example, the levitical laws on sacrifice. For most readers today, this is an uninteresting, dry piece of literature to read. For those who perpetuated it in antiquity it presumably was quite the opposite.

Birger Gerhardsson, in his 1961 discussion on the origins of the oral Torah, made the same point about "detachment" (on detachment, see also the introduction, p. 9):

Disinterested historiography is a late concept in history. In Antiquity, what was narrated concerning the fathers had a practical purpose: that of providing examples to be emulated, warnings, or other definite lessons. Jewish, Hellenistic, and Christian traditions in the sources are all *tendentious*, whether edifying or otherwise didactic. Those who formed the narrative traditions of Rabbinic Judaism did so with the basic intention of preserving and spreading, in one way or another, the many-faceted wisdom of the Torah in face of all the situations of life . . . The pupil had to absorb all the traditional wisdom with "eyes, ears and every member" by seeking the company of a Rabbi, by serving him (שימש), following him and imitating him (הלך אחרי), and not only by listening to him. The task of the pupil is therefore not only to hear (ראה) but also to see . . . This terminology has as a rule a distinctly legal character. The pupil/traditionist tells what he has seen and heard. The "eyewitness" character of certain sayings is occasionally directly stressed with terms as עד, עדות, העיד. . . . The value of such sayings—for the Rabbis—is entirely dependent upon their historicity.[187]

This has a direct bearing on our discussion, because it is hard to imagine anything more "related" to the transmitter than his own ancestral heritage, beliefs, and religious practices. Even if, for political or environmental reasons, an entire ethnic entity was relocated, it is highly unlikely, as Postgate has demonstrated, that its religious heritage and ancestral traditions also were left behind. Due to their identity-related character, the traditions would have been told and transmitted carefully wherever the ethnic entity or family were forced to move (so the Saxons coming to Britain brought their gods with them!), and it is obvious that the Hebrew Bible came to occupy its unique position not primarily because of its literary value but because of its religious and social message. In his discussion of a fragment of Ben Sira found at Masada (ca. 125–100 B.C.E.), Kutscher provides us with a good example of how carefully texts that were regarded as normative were transmitted.

It is interesting to realize that the text of Ben Sira underwent many changes resulting from the "corrections" of medieval (and earlier) scribes. . . . But Psalms fared differently. Except for a few cases of defective spellings, that are also common in our MSS of the Bible, there is practically no difference between the text discovered at Masada and our Masoretic text. How are we to account for this difference between the transmission of Psalms and of Ben Sira? The answer is simply that Psalms represented a sacred text and therefore the scribes made every effort to copy it faithfully, while Ben Sira was not canonised, and so it was treated less care-

---

187. Gerhardsson, *Memory and Manuscript*, 182–83.

fully. This is a clear proof of how particular the scribes were not to change anything when copying a Biblical text.[188]

Identity-Related Information

The above example is late, but in the light of our knowledge about earlier periods, we have no reason to doubt that "holy" or "normative" texts or tales were preserved just as carefully in the earlier history of Israel. So, when Lemche "safely" concludes that "the ordinary man in the street had little if any knowledge of what may have happened in his country hundreds of years ago," it is a qualified truth: it depends, as we have seen, on what *kind* of information we are dealing with and how *universal* the disruptive factors were. Bearing this in mind, it is hard to see it as an *impossibility* that the Israelites kept their religious and ancestral traditions "orally" alive for hundreds of years, even when the differences between Mesopotamia, Egypt, and Palestine are given due credit. Disruption may have had less impact on the centuries-long established culture in Babylon, as the example of the Kassites shows, than on the less-powerful culture of Syria–Palestine. There is ample evidence that agricultural techniques, architectural styles, and literary conventions from the surrounding superpowers were often borrowed by the peoples of ancient Palestine. Due to its buffer-zone position between Egypt in the south, Syria and Anatolia in the north, and Mesopotamia in the east, and its openness to sea trade from the west, Palestine was more susceptible to foreign influence than it was impervious.[189]

---

188. E. Y. Kutscher, *A History of the Hebrew Language* (Jerusalem: Magnes / Leiden: Brill, 1982) 92.

189. Louise Hitchcock, in an article on Aegean elements in Cypriot Late Bronze Age architecture, voices an important warning against a too-simplistic approach to cultural borrowing. Discussing problems related to the transmittal of ideas relating to architecture, she notes that "colonization is, I believe a simplistic historical construct too often equated with remains of pottery while neglecting other categories of evidence. Furthermore, modern notions of colonization call to mind the social and intellectual domination associated with colonialism. Other explanations that I have investigated include: mnemohistory (remembrance of the past in oral history and cultural exchange), structuration (the role of architectural remains in orchestrating daily routines, thus forming cultural identity), peer polity interaction and competition, modified diffusion (treating indigenious development and external influences as co-occurring components of cultural transformation), and evidence for itinerant builders" (Louise Hitchcock, "One Cannot Export a Palace on Board a Ship," *Backdirt* [Fall/Winter 2000]. The online version is at http://www.sscnet.ucla.edu/ioa/pubs/backdirt/Fallwinter00/cypriot.html (accessed May 6, 2003).

There is, nevertheless, no reason to think that the *beliefs, world view(s)*, and *religious practices* of the people of Iron Age Palestine were *more* vulnerable to disruptive factors than those of, for example, Mesopotamia. It was just as important for an Iron Age farmer in the vicinity of Lachish to preserve his ancestral heritage and religious practices as it was for his contemporary Mesopotamian colleague on the outskirts of Nineveh—perhaps even *more* important, because he belonged to a small and more-vulnerable community than the people of the Assyrian, Babylonian, and later, Persian heartland. It is a well-attested fact that immigrant minorities tend to be much more conscious of preserving their language and identity-related traditions than the majority population of which they have become a part. So, when Judeans were captured and deported to Babylon, they would have continued to tell their ancestral stories to their children and to practice their religious customs. Besides, if—as has been emphasized recently—the land was *not* empty during the exile,[190] there is also reason to believe that the remnant, not least the Samaritans, continued to preserve whatever important tradition they had. They may have reinterpreted it in order to address the new situation, but this does not necessarily mean (as we shall see shortly) that it became unreliable.

Thus, though we still have not shown Lemche's conclusion to be false, it is far from "safe." It is indeed possible that a prolonged oral and/or written tradition preserved the identity-related traditions of the Israelites, thus providing the author(s) of the books of Kings with reliable information on Israel's history. We cannot say for sure, admittedly, to what extent it was possible before the time that the Kingdoms of Israel and Judah of the 9th and 8th centuries B.C.E. are attested in the extrabiblical sources.[191] To argue from the same texts as the ones whose historical reliability we are seeking to determine would be circular reasoning (so far the united monarchy of David and Solomon are only attested biblically). But the argument from analogy, as mentioned above, is strong and provides for the possibility that literary works *did* exist at the time of the biblical monarchies of the 10th and 9th

---

190. H. M. Barstad, *The Myth of the Empty Land: A Study in the History and Archaeology of Judah during the "Exilic" Period* (Oslo: Oslo University Press, 1996); Hjelm, *The Samaritans*.

191. For a list of attestations of the kings of Israel and Judah in Assyrian Royal Inscriptions, see A. R. Millard, "Israelite and Aramean History in the Light of Inscriptions," *TynBul* 41 (1990) 261–75, reprinted in *Israel's Past in Present Research: Essays on Ancient Israelite Historiography* (ed. V. Philips Long; Sources for Biblical and Theological Study 7; Winona Lake, Ind.: Eisenbrauns, 1999) 129–40.

centuries B.C.E., even if a central Judean administration as described in the biblical texts is so far unattested in the extrabiblical record.

The Ravages of Time

Another relevant question is: how long would it have taken for a tradition to be created, "pro-created" and "re-created," as is obviously the case with the complex traditions preserved in the Hebrew Bible? As mentioned before, there are no objective means by which we can re-create the composition history of the Hebrew Bible beyond the extant texts. And, though Kallai's point that a "low dating of the literary complexes inevitably presupposes an extremely compressed literary process, which does not allow sufficient time between the diverse literary manifestations to be consecutively related to each other" may be very correct indeed, his argument that a relative literary chronology can be established from the "fact" that the "United Monarchy of Israel" is the basic concept from which a series of later concepts are derived seems to involve precisely the kind of circular reasoning that we have warned against.[192] Unless we rely on the biblical narrative, we cannot know that the territorial concepts employed in the biblical narratives are "normative descriptions, that reflect the conditions of the United Monarchy."[193] It may be possible to establish a relative, inner-biblical, literary chronology based on literary derivations and allusions, but we must be cautious not to confuse it with an absolute, historical chronology.

As long as this is kept in mind, however, Kallai's argument that we must allow a considerable time for the creation of the complex tradition of the Hebrew Bible is still valid, because it is highly unlikely that both the basic concepts and the derived traditions came into being at the same time. If the entire corpus of the Hebrew Bible was composed more or less in one spurt of activity in Persian and/or Hellenistic times, it would be without parallel in the entire ancient Near Eastern record. Furthermore, an event of this magnitude would have required a virtually inconceivable exercise of power by the Judean priesthood or intelligentsia to impose a new and complex tradition of this sort on

---

192. Zecharia Kallai, "Biblical Historiography and Literary History: A Programmatic Survey," *VT* 49 (1999) 339–40. See also idem, "The Patriarchal Boundaries, Canaan and the Land of Israel: Patterns and Application in Biblical Historiography," *IEJ* 47 (1997) 69–82.

193. Kallai, "Biblical Historiography," 343.

the Jews of Palestine as well as the diaspora. Unless it can be demonstrated that there was a period of total disruption in Persian or Hellenistic Palestine, it is much more likely (as has been shown above) that the identity-related traditions of the Israelites were preserved and expanded through oral—and more likely—written transmission, as the periods of Persian administration and Hellenistic suzerainty came and went. Pasto has recently demonstrated that "the separation of an early Israel from a later Judaism is not a fact given from the historical evidence, primary or secondary,"[194] and as long as there is no evidence of such a total period of disruption, the re-presentation of the biblical past by Bolin, Lemche, Thompson, and Davies is an unsubstantiated hypothesis that, in the light of the present discussion, must be rejected.[195]

Another possible obstacle to the re-creation of Israelite history is the impact that a reuse of a certain tradition may have on its content.[196] How, for example, does the reuse of various sources by the author(s) of the books of Kings affect the historical reliability of their content? We only know the alleged sources in their present *Sitz im Korpus* and cannot with certainty determine either their original form or their previous *Sitz im Leben*. It is therefore relevant to ask whether the process of selecting and rearranging various existing sources, however historically reliable *they* may have been, for new and present purposes detracts from the epistemic value of the final literary product. Reuse of traditions seems to be at the very heart of composition technique in the ancient Near East.[197] "Authorship" often consisted in

---

194. Pasto, "When the End Is the Beginning?" 159.

195. Cf. Niels Peter Lemche, "Clio is Also among the Muses: Keith W. Whitelam and the History of Palestine: A Review and a Commentary," *SJOT* 10 (1996) 88–114; P. R. Davies, "Whose History? Whose Israel? Whose Bible? Biblical Histories, Ancient and Modern," in *Can a "History of Israel" Be Written?* (JSOTSup 245; European Seminar in Historical Methodology 1; ed. Lester L. Grabbe; Sheffield: Sheffield Academic Press, 1997); Thomas L. Thompson, "Defining History and Ethnicity in the South Levant," in *Can a "History of Israel" Be Written?* 166–87; Thomas Bolin, "When the End Is the Beginning: The Persian Period and the Origins of the Biblical Tradition," *SJOT* 19 (1996) 3–15.

196. For a similar distinction between "news" and "interpretation" in oral testimony, cf. Vansina, *Oral Tradition as History*, 3–12.

197. On composition techniques, see Piotr Michalowski, "Commemoration, Writing, and Genre in Ancient Mesopotamia," in *The Limits of Historiography: Genre and Narrative in Ancient Historical Texts* (ed. Christina Shuttleworth Kraus; Leiden: Brill, 1999) 74; Michalowski gives examples on "how meaning was produced in Mesopotamian written discourse through the very act of reshaping texts and lining them with one another, that is, through transtextual processes, to use Genette's broadest term. In this perspective, literary history and the synchronic variations of individual texts can be seen as part of a

creatively adapting existing themes and plots from other literature to new purposes.[198] This is evidenced, for example, by the reuse of various motifs from other well-known Babylonian myths and epics in the "Enuma Elish," probably created to celebrate the return of Marduk to Babylon from Elam by Nebuchadnezzar I (1121–1103 B.C.E.);[199] the deployment of an existing historical tradition in both "The Proclamation of Telipinu" and "The Apology of Hattušili III" for contemporary (Old Kingdom and Empire period) Hittite political purposes;[200] and the historical introduction to the ritual designed to heal the king from hysterical aphasia in a royal prayer from the time of Muršili II.[201] In Egypt, we may also mention the reuse of the "Paean of Victory" section of Thutmosis III's "Triumph Hymn" by Amenophis III and later by Sethos I, Ramesses II, Merenptah, Ramesses III, and Ramesses VI.[202] Vanstiphout summarizes the point well in his discussion of memory and literacy in ancient western Asia:

> Intertextuality takes different forms, starting with somewhat straightforward copying and adaptation, such as the way in which huge chunks

larger set of cultural changes and adaptations to cultural practices. At the same time, these changes were themselves a form of cultural practice and had their own resonance beyond the confines of the written word." Cf. also Sancisi-Weerdenburg, "Persian Kings," 99–100; and Maureen Gallery Kovacs, *The Epic of Gilgamesh* (Stanford: Stanford University Press, 1989) xxi–xxii. For the most recent translation of the Gilgamesh Epic, see now George, *The Epic of Gilgamesh.*

198. New creations of course also appeared, for example, "The Babylonian Wisdom Poem," "The Babylonian Theodicy" belonging to the Kassite period, and from Assyria "The Tukulti Ninurta Epic"; cf. Benjamin R. Foster, *From Distant Days: Myths, Tales, and Poetry of Ancient Mesopotamia* (Bethesda, Md.: CDL, 1999).

199. Cf. also Eckart Frahm, "Nabû-Zuqup-Kēnu, das Gilgameš-Epos und der Tod Sargons II," *JCS* 51 (1999) 73–90, for a discussion on the use and reuse of the "Gilgamesh Epic" by the learned Nabû-Zuqup-Kēnu in 705 B.C.E. Frahm concludes his article by saying that "the learned Assyrian Nabû-Zuqup-Kēnu tried to understand the death of the king [Sargon II] by studying an outstanding piece of literature, namely, the Gilgameš Epic" (p. 87) [my translation].

200. Cf. Hoffner, "Histories and Historians," 307; Hans G. Güterbock, "Hittite Historiography: A Survey," in *History, Historiography and Interpretation* (ed. H. Tadmor and M. Weinfeld; Jerusalem: Magnes, 1984) 28–29. On Hittite historiography, see also Alexander Uchitel, "Local versus General History in Old Hittite Historiography," in *The Limits of Historiography: Genre and Narrative in Ancient Historical Texts* (ed. Christina Shuttleworth Kraus; Leiden: Brill, 1999) 55–68.

201. CTH 486; cf. Hoffner, "Histories and Historians," 284. Hoffner gives ample evidence that "the Hittites very early had learned to employ not only historical but legendary narrative to introduce and provide a rationale for the main subject matter of the text" (p. 300).

202. K. A. Kitchen, *Poetry of Ancient Egypt* (Documenta Mundi: Aegyptiaca 1; Jonsered: Åströms, 1999) 165–82.

of older material rightly belonging to compositions about the gods Enlil, Enki, and Ninurta are incorporated into the new creed expressed in *Enuma Elish*. Many compositions contain allusions to others, and in a few cases, a composition can only be fully understood when we become familiar with other members of a group or cycle of texts. Thus, the Akkadian poem about Sargon of Akkad known as *Šar tamḫari* makes little sense unless other parts of this wonderful cycle are also known. . . . Furthermore, works reflecting historical ideology or theory, such as the historical laments and in a way the *Curse of Agade*, are based on the system presented in the Sumerian king list—a literary work if ever there was one.[203]

The Hebrew Bible reveals the same features. If the *toledot*-formulas in Genesis are introducing originally distinct sources, a similar situation may apply to their present position in the composition of Genesis. If the "Book of the Chronicles of the Kings of Israel" existed as an originally independent composition, (parts of) it has obviously been given a new and different function in the books of Kings. Recent research in the book of Psalms has demonstrated that the biblical psalms had different functions and may have served a number of purposes before they eventually were given a new—literary and/or liturgical—function by being included as a part of *Sefer Tehillim*,[204] and there is no reason to doubt that this is also the case with the more historiographically oriented texts of the Hebrew Bible.[205] Commenting on Israel's re-use of its psalmodic tradition, Ackroyd sums it up by saying that

> we must recognize that from a very early date such religous poetry was used and reused, and in the process came to be charged with new meanings corresponding to the current trends of thought and practice.

203. Vanstiphout, "Memory and Literacy in Ancient Western Asia," 2193.

204. As suggested by the various psalm titles and the various positions that individual psalms occupy in various manuscripts (e.g., Qumran and MT) as well as within the Hebrew Bible itself (e.g., 2 Samuel 22 and Psalm 18). See J. Clinton McCann (ed.), *The Shape and Shaping of the Psalter* (JSOTSup 159; Sheffield: JSOT Press, 1993).

205. Well illustrated by recent studies; cf. Lloyd M. Barré, *The Rhetoric of Political Persuasion: The Narrative Artistry and Political Intentions of 2 Kings 9–11* (Catholic Biblical Quarterly Monograph Series; Washington, D.C.: Catholic Biblical Association, 1988); Gary N. Knoppers, "History and Historiography: The Royal Reforms," in *The Chronicler as Historian* (ed. M. Patrick Graham, Kenneth G. Hoglund, and Steven L. McKenzie; Sheffield: Sheffield Academic Press, 1997) 178–203; K. L. Noll, "Is There a Text in This Tradition? Readers' Response and the Taming of Samuel's God," *JSOT* 83 (1999) 31–51. Cf. also Knud Jeppesen, *Græder ikke saa saare: Studier i Mikabogens sigte* (Aarhus: Aarhus Universitetsforlag, 1987) 1.94–109; and Walther Zimmerli, "Prophetic Proclamation and Reinterpretation," in *Tradition and Theology in the Old Testament* (ed. Douglas A. Knight; Sheffield: JSOT Press, 1990) 69–100, on the prophetic literature.

It is a matter of debate how far such changing use produced modifications in wording; at some points, where precise allusions appear to be
made, we may naturally suppose a particular adjustment. More often
we may see the reuse itself providing a reinterpretation, not in itself
necessitating change of wording, or requiring only such relatively
small adjustments as might better fit contemporary usage. Where this
becomes clearest is, of course, in psalms which refer to the king. It is no
longer necessary for commentators, set on a post-exilic date for all
psalmody, to argue for a late Maccabean, Hasmonean date for such royal
psalms; but equally while a pre-exilic date may rightly be claimed, it
must also be observed that use extends beyond the boundary imposed
by the end of the monarchy. Whatever adjustments of wording took
place, the references to the king remained, and in one way or another
were reinterpreted.[206]

Reuse of existing material, motifs, plot traditions, and so on for
present political, religious, literary, or other purposes, then, is well
attested throughout the written record of the ancient Near East. It
would be wrong, however, to deduce from this well-attested composition technique that such a reuse of existing traditions, narratives, or
motifs *necessarily* detracts from their historical reliability, given, of
course, that they were intended to be historically reliable in the first
place (on historical intention, see below, pp. 190ff.). It may do so. We
have evidence that this could be the case.[207] But even a parade example

206. Peter R. Ackroyd, "Continuity and Discontinuity: Rehabilitation and Authentication," in *Tradition and Theology in the Old Testament* (ed. Douglas A. Knight; Sheffield:
JSOT Press, 1990) 228–29. Cf. also Michael Fishbane, "Torah and Tradition," in *Tradition
and Theology in the Old Testament*, 275–300, on diverse modes of innerbiblical midrash.

207. Doron Mendels gives some illuminating examples of Greek "historians" (e.g.,
Hecataeus) who referred to canonical histories but reworked the data to the extent of
distortion (Mendels, *Identity*, 357–64). Westenholz has recently drawn attention to another example, the differences between the parallel traditions in the Old Babylonian so-
called "London text of the Insurrection against Naram-Sin" and the "Hittite tale of the
seventeen kings who confronted Naram-Sin" (CTH 311,1 = KBo III 13 = BoTu 3). The
latter is a New Hittite text retaining old Hittite archaisms, and its original can thus be
postulated as coming from the Old Hittite period. Though both texts clearly go back to
Old Akkadian sources, they seem to have added and subtracted from the original
material to serve contemporary Old Babylonian and Old Hittite purposes. While some
undoubtedly would describe these "reworkings" or "rescensions" as *distortions*, Westenholz's conclusion is rather optimistic: "These two traditional lists may contain a large
element of historicity, despite poetic liberties" (Joan Goodnick Westenholz, "Relations
between Mesopotamia and Anatolia in the Age of the Sargonic Kings," in *XXXIV^éme
Rencontre Assyriologique Internationale 6–10/VII/1987 — Istanbul* [Ankara: Türk Tarih Kurumu Basimevi, 1998] 16). Another example is given by Steve Tinney, who, in a discussion of three different versions of the so-called "Ur-Namma Hymn" (referred to as
"Nippur," "Yale," and "Ur," respectively), concludes that "it is clear that Aba munbale

such as the so-called birth-legend of Sargon of Akkad (2340–2285 B.C.E.)[208] is not as clear-cut an example as it appears to be and warns us that reuse is not equivalent to distortion.[209] Kuhrt, in her discussion of *"narû* literature,"[210] includes the legend in what she calls the "later stories about some of the Agade kings, which purport to be copies of royal votive inscriptions, but are clearly later compositions with a didactic purpose."[211] There is no reason to doubt that the late copies found in the library of Ashurbanipal and dating to the late Assyrian Period (760–610 B.C.E.) "illustrate, dramatically, the ideological and symbolic importance of the Agade kings" in the late Assyrian period, but it is far from safe to conclude that "they cannot be considered

---

['who will dig it?' the incipit of the text] and its motifs were subject to significant differences in meaning both by reuse in new contexts and as a result of textual alterations. One can only speculate on the existence of a hymn concerned with the digging of an actual canal, but one can demonstrate the existence of a text that in one version is associated with the Dumuzi-Inanna literature and focuses primarily on aquatic fertility (Nippur); another that combines this with some increase of emphasis on Nanna and the inclusion of coronation and royal rhetoric (Yale); and a third that excises the references to Enki with the resultant focus having the character of a royal praise of Nanna (Ur). The narrower implication of this is clear: The poetic accounts of Ur-Namma's canal-digging activities cannot simply be used as independent sources for the history of the Ur III period. Even if some form of the text were originally composed in honor of an actual Ur-Namma canal-opening or coronation, we would have no way of proving this without contemporary inscriptions: Aba munbale, historically speaking, adds nothing" (Steve Tinney, "Ur-Namma the Canal-Digger: Context, Continuity and Change in Sumerian Literature," *JCS* 51 [1999] 45). See also Michael Schwarz, "Can We Rely on Later Authorities for the Views of Earlier Thinkers?" *Israel Oriental Studies* 1 (1971) 241–48 on transmission of Arabic sources in Medieval commentaries. The question of *intentional* distortion or *fakes* will be discussed in detail in the chap. 3.

208. Kuhrt, *Ancient Near East*, 1.11–12, 44–45. For the text of the "Sargon Birth Legend," see Westenholz, *Legends of the Kings of Akkade*, 36–49, who has the slightly lower dates of 2310–2273 B.C.E. for the reign of Sargon.

209. This seems to be the assumption underlying Thompson's "lego-block hypothesis" approach to the composition technique of the biblical authors; see Thomas L. Thompson, "4Q Testimonia og Bibelens affattelse: En københavnsk legohypotese," in *Dødehavsteksterne og Bibelen* (ed. Niels Hyldahl and Thomas L. Thompson; Copenhagen: Museum Tusculanum, 1996) 233–41, or—as indicated by the title—in idem, *The Bible in History: How Writers Create a Past*.

210. Originally introduced as a *Literaturgattung* by Hans Güterbock to characterize compositions having the form of a royal inscription and often purporting to be inscribed on a stone monument. Akkadian *narû* is a stela on which a royal inscription is engraved (Hans G. Güterbock, "Die historische Tradition und ihre literarische Gestaltung bei Babyloniern und Hethitern bis 1200," *ZA* 42 [1934] 1–91 and 44 [1938] 45–149), but now used in the meaning "poetic autobiography" or most recently "pseudoautobiography."

211. Kuhrt, *Ancient Near East*, 1.47.

reliable historical sources for the period," that is, of the dynasty of Akkad, as suggested by the various definitions and subgroups of the term "*narû* literature."

Significantly, Westenholz, in a discussion on the concept of *genre* in the corpus of the legends of the kings of Akkad, has shown how scholars disagree on whether the so-called "autobiographical" or "pseudo-autobiographical" texts, that is, first-person narrations by kings of their experiences (to which the "Sargon Birth Legend" belongs), should be categorized as historical or legendary.[212] Interestingly, and highly relevant to our discussion, one of the reasons for the disagreement[213] is that some of the texts of the corpus (from the 18th century B.C.E.) have been shown to be very much in accordance with the archaeological material from the time of the kings of Akkad, just as linguistic study has demonstrated that the scribes, who allegedly were copying them from inscriptions, tried to preserve various grammatical features of the 23rd century B.C.E.[214] Being inclined herself to regard it as legendary, Westenholz nevertheless warns that "if the literary application of the term *narû* or pseudo-autobiography is limited to a false poetic royal inscription written in the first person with didactic intent, it hardly applies in is entirety to a single text in the corpus."[215] This, of course, neither precludes the possibility that the much later "Sargon Birth Legend" *was* a legend in the first place nor proves—assuming that it was *not*—that the continuing reuse of the tradition *did* preserve in an accurate way the facts about Sargon's birth (since original and other copies are lost). And even if the tradition, factual or legendary, should turn out to be accurately transmitted, we need to keep in mind what Mario Liverani has said, that the document is first and foremost "*a source for the knowledge of itself*—i.e., as a source of knowledge about the author of the document, whom we know from the document itself [italics his]." A nonliving document cannot, as is the case with a living informant, be subject to cross-examination, and asking such a

---

212. Westenholz, *Legends of the Kings of Akkade*, 16–24.

213. Other reasons are disagreement on the significance of their didactic character and writing in first person.

214. A. R. Millard, "How Reliable Is Exodus?" *BAR* 26/4 (1999) 52. Cf. also Westenholz, *Legends of the Kings of Akkade*, 27; idem, "Relations," where she discusses the reliability of the traditions about Sargon and Naram-Sin in the light of our present knowledge of philology, artifacts, and settlement and destruction patterns.

215. Westenholz, *Legends of the Kings of Akkade*, 19. A similar conclusion can be found in Brian Lewis, *The Sargon Legend* (American School of Oriental Research Dissertation Series 4; Cambridge, Mass.: American School of Oriental Research, 1980) 107–9.

document "historical" questions entails two serious difficulties: "(1) if the textual information is wrong (or in particular, internally contradictory), the error passes inevitably into the historical reconstruction; and (2) the type of information in the texts does not always satisfy the needs of the scholar, who has different scopes and interests from the ones of the writers of the documents, and who would like to obtain certain information for which the texts, to his dismay, are uncommunicative or altogether silent."[216]

A more clear-cut example, also from Mesopotamia, is the well-attested practice of divination in Assyria, where the interpreters of omens, the *narû*, could reapply old omens without changing their content. In a discussion of this practice, Millard mentions a collection of reports to the king about events of an ominous nature, with advice on their significance and action to be taken to avoid unhappy consequences. One example referred to announces, "Tonight Saturn approached the Moon," with the comment, "Saturn is the star of the Sun. Its interpretation is as follows: it is good fortune for the king; Saturn is the star of the king."[217] Millard notes that "the writers of these letters and reports were encyclopedists whose duty was to answer every problem presented. They could discover from their store of knowledge a text that was exactly or nearly appropriate, then show how it suited the incident by means of their comments."[218]

Despite all the caveats mentioned above, the examples given thus warn us that we cannot discard a late tradition per se as unreliable and that it is indeed possible for an old tradition or canonical historical text to be reused with a digressive, regressive, proleptic, or other function

216. Mario Liverani, "Memorandum on the Approach to Historiographic Texts," in *Approaches to the Study of the Ancient Near East* (ed. G. Buccellati; *Or* 42 [1973]) 179.

217. Reedited by S. Parpola, *Letters from Assyrian Scholars to the Kings Esarhaddon and Assurbanipal* (AOAT 5/1; Neukirchen-Vluyn: Neukirchener Verlag, 1970) no. 326. The comments of the scholiasts are introduced by the word *piš[ir]šu* 'its interpretation', from *pišru* 'interpretation' (or by *pišaršu* from *pašaru* 'to solve') and thus are clearly distinguishable from the quotation of the omen itself (cf. nos. 108.4; 109.9; 278.3; 326.6). On omens as an expression of the past, see the provocative essay by Jacob J. Finkelstein, "Mesopotamian Historiography," *Proceedings of the American Philosphical Society* 107 (1963) 462, where, in search of historiography, he argues that "what we must seek is that form or genre in which the Mesopotamian thinker confronts his experience of the past, with detachment as well as involvement, with the sense of urgency of immediacy as well as with the spirit of an objective quest; in short, in precisely those attitudes that we expect of any inquiry in the western world that would claim the dignity of serious historiography." For a critique of Finkelstein, see Michalowski, "Commemoration," 74–75.

218. A. R. Millard, "Text and Comment," in *Biblical and Near Eastern Studies in Honour of William Sanford LaSor* (ed. Gary A. Tuttle; Grand Rapids: Eerdmans, 1978) 248.

in a new literary creation for political, religious, didactic, or other purposes without distorting it, thus making it possible for the historian to "decode" the embedded historical information and use it for present historiographical purposes. It takes a careful literary-critical analysis of the way that various traditions have been deployed and a meticulous comparison of the text in question with any comparable material to attempt to determine the extent of reliability or distortion, and the problem must therefore be resolved on a case-by-case basis.[219]

But, just as we have demonstrated that identity-related, "canonical" information can be transmitted very carefully, it is likely that the "editors," "authors," and so on in a more selective, rearranging reuse of such material consciously intended to preserve what was *meaningful* to them. This is precisely what Gerhardsson has in mind when he writes:

> It would scarcely be an over-simplification to say that the typical Rabbi had in general no wish to be creative in his teaching. He wanted to seek out (דרש) what God had already given in the sacred Torah tradition handed down from the fathers; he worked in the desire that God might reveal (גלה) to him what was already there—though more or less hidden—in the words he had taken over. The most common idea was that of reconstructing what the ancients themselves meant. But we also encounter the idea that God allows the favored Rabbi to rediscover more than the ancients themselves found in their own sayings.[220]

Furthermore, as also noted above, it is very unlikely that a "twisting" of a canonical tradition would have been accepted universally. It would have required almost superhuman—or at least "Stalinistic"—powers of the priesthood or "intelligentsia" in Jerusalem to impose successfully on their fellow Jews and keep alive such a tradition.

We must restrict ourselves to saying "unlikely," however, since we do not know with certainty what triggered the rewriting of Israel's

---

219. A good, cautious, and convincing example of how this can be done is James Barr's study on Philo of Byblos's use of the allegedly much-older Phoenician History of Sanchuniathon. Barr warns that "we have every reason to take seriously the possibility that different local traditions have been cemented together into a unity which did not originally belong to them" and concludes his analysis, stating that "this quick survey has not been able to give a clear and universally applicable answer to the basic question posed by Philo: is the material early, and therefore a good example of the myths of early Phoenicia, or late, and therefore a good example of Hellenistic syncretism? It looks as if some elements are one, and some the other; or as if an element, taken quite formally, belongs to the one, but in content and in present function belongs to the other" ("Philo of Byblos and His 'Phoenician History,'" 45, 61).

220. Gerhardsson, *Memory and Manuscript*, 174.

history, for example, in the books of Chronicles. Neither do we know who the intended readers or listeners were in the first place or how they initially responded to it.[221] Steven Shapin, in a most interesting study of the so-called truth-warrants from seventeenth-century England, has recently demonstrated the importance of *trust* in establishing empirical knowledge about the natural world. He shows how individual scientists have arrived at their beliefs in much the same way that people have always arrived at their fundamental beliefs about the world, not through moving by various stages of experimentation from skepticism to certainty but through much more traditional means, such as reliance on trust in the community and reliance on the character of one's colleagues.[222] Though our knowledge of ancient history (unlike the 17th-century "gentleman's" knowledge of the history of England) includes virtually no evidence of how and by whom truth-claims were validated in Hellenistic Period Palestine, it requires an assumption of quite a change in human behavior to invalidate the comparison. Shapin is well aware that members of each generation would have to seek their own guarantees for each item of knowledge transmitted to them. And, though it is admittedly very difficult to determine what the truth-warrants of, for example, 3rd-century B.C.E. Jerusalem were or who validated them, it is nevertheless hard to imagine either that the truth-guarantors themselves could have successfully imposed a whole new religious tradition on their fellow Jews

---

221. Contrast the rewriting of Israel's history by Josephus, who in his *Jewish Antiquities* tells us about his authorial intent, ἐκδιηγήσασθαι διὰ τοὺς ἐν τῷ γράφειν λυμαινομένους τὴν ἀλήθειαν 'in order to refute those who in their writings were doing outrage to the truth', and intended readers, ταύτην δὲ τὴν ἐνεστῶσαν ἐγκεχείρισμαι πραγματείαν νομίζων ἅπασι φανεῖσθαι τοῖς ῞Ελλησιν ἀξίαν σπουδῆς· μέλλει γὰρ περιέξειν ἅπασαν τὴν παρ᾿ ἡμῖν ἀρχαιολογίαν καὶ τὴν διάταξιν τοῦ πολιτεύματος ἐκ τῶν Ἑβραϊκῶν μεθηρμηνευμένην γραμμάτων 'and now I have undertaken this present work in the belief that the whole Greek-speaking world will find it worthy of attention; for it will embrace our entire ancient history and political constitution translated from the Hebrew records' (H. St. J. Thackeray [trans.], *Josephus: Jewish Antiquities* [The Loeb Classical Library 242; London: Heineman / Cambridge: Harvard University Press, 1998] 2–5). Cf. also Shaye J. D. Cohen, *Josephus in Galilee and Rome: His Vita and Development as a Historian* (Columbia Studies in the Classical Tradition 8; Leiden: Brill, 1979) 232–42; ibid., "History and Historiography in the *Against Apion* of Josephus," *History and Theory* Beiheft 27 (1988) 1–11.

222. Stephen Shapin, *A Social History of Truth: Civility and Science in Seventeenth-Century England* (Chicago: University of Chicago Press, 1994); cf. also Shirley A. Mullen, "Between 'Romance' and 'True History': Historical Narrative and Truth Telling in a Postmodern Age," in *History and the Christian Historian* (ed. Ronald A. Wells; Grand Rapids: Eerdmans, 1998) 23–40.

(in and, not least, outside Palestine) or that an ideological breakaway group could have managed to oust the existing truth-warrants and to superimpose a new Jewish identity on a traditionalist ancient Near Eastern Jewish society—especially in the short time available.

In Sum

Taking sides with Hallo, Hoffmeier, Millard, Younger, and Lassner (as cited in the introduction on standards of source-criticism), I can now, as promised, return to Lemche's statement about the uncontrollable nature of oral testimony. Though the discussion from which the quotation is taken admittedly deals exclusively with the uncontrollability of oral tradition, Lemche has elsewhere argued that the same principle of excluding late evidence, which cannot be "controlled" or corroborated by contemporary evidence, should be applied to the textual sources of the Hebrew Bible,[223] and we are therefore justified in applying the above-mentioned insights to the principle underlying his statement on oral transmission.

The first thing to be concluded from the discussion above is that different, even mutually contradictory, histories can be right on their own terms. Accusations by maximalists that minimalist histories are distorted, racist, dangerous, a threat to the entire Western civilization, and so on, and by minimalists that maximalist histories are naïve, outdated, ignorant, nothing but a paraphrase of the biblical narrative, fundamentalist, and so on often show a lack of awareness of how "paradigmatic" (and thus potentially fragile) their own histories are.[224] As

---

223. For example, "it is true that here and there in the Old Testament we find historical recollections going a long way back in time. Here the Old Testament hardly distinguishes itself in comparison to comparable bodies of historical narrative in the ancient Near East or in the classical world. The historians, however, never display that kind of critical control of their sources which is required in modern historical research. This lack of control means that historical information will be placed in the context where it is required because of ideological and literary reasons, not because it really happened at a certain point in, say, Israel's history" (Lemche, *The Israelites in History and Tradition*, 129). See also idem, "Om historisk erindring," 7. Because a similar approach is taken by other "members" of the Copenhagen School, the principle of excluding late evidence may rightfully be described as one of its most significant characteristics; cf. P. R. Davies, *In Search*; T. L. Thompson, *Early History*.

224. Recent examples of such rhetorical or polemical accusations are legion, but a short list would include Dever, *What Did the Biblical Writers Know, and When Did They Know It? What Archaeology Can Tell Us About the Reality of Ancient Israel*, "Histories and Nonhistories of Ancient Israel, and "Archaeology, Ideology"; Iain W. Provan, "In the Stable with the Dwarves: Testimony, Interpretation, Faith and the History of Israel," in *International*

demonstrated in the introductory chapter (chap. 1), there is no such thing as an "impartial historian." No history is written without some kind of "grid," some larger narrative with all the oversimplifications and blind spots that entails, and either "camp" in the battle between maximalists and minimalists needs to recognize the "path-dependent" (see p. 15 above) character of their results. Lemche (and the Copenhagen School) are right in discarding the possibility of a united monarchy centered in Jerusalem, led by the great kings David and Solomon, as long as they are building on the premise that the late evidence of the biblical narratives cannot be considered reliable witnesses to the history of 11th- and 10th-century Judah when they cannot be corroborated by contemporary evidence. If we allow the possibility that the biblical narrative of Samuel–Kings is unreliable, and if we also try to ignore the culturally deep-rooted understanding of ancient Israel,[225] the interpretation of the 11th- and 10th-century B.C.E. (extensive) archaeological and (sparse) textual evidence from southern Palestine put forward by Lemche and other "Copenhageners" becomes very plausible, perhaps even convincing. The picture painted by the author(s) of Samuel–Kings, admittedly, would not immediately spring to mind as the most obvious interpretation of the evidence, had we not known and been influenced by the biblical narratives.

In building their conclusions, these scholars and their "histories" are nothing but consistent—that is, applying the above-mentioned criteria in a consistent manner to the available sources. Lemche, consequently, is "path-dependently" right in saying that "the ordinary man in the street had little if any knowledge of what may have happened in his country hundreds of years ago." The points to be made, of course, are that maximalists are equally right in their interpretation and likewise consistent in applying their method to the very same pool of

---

Organization for the Study of the Old Testament: Congress Volume, Oslo 1998 (ed. André Lemaire and M. Sæbø; VTSup 80; Leiden: Brill, 1998) 281–319, "Ideologies, Literary and Critical: Reflections on Recent Writing on the History of Israel," *JBL* 114 (1995) 585–606; Thomas L. Thompson, "A Neo-Albrightean School in History and Biblical Scholarship?" *JBL* 114 (1995) 683–98; P. R. Davies, "Method and Madness: Some Remarks on Doing History with the Bible," *JBL* 114 (1995) 699–705; Baruch Halpern, "Erasing History: The Miminalist Assault on Ancient Israel," *Bible Review* 11/6 (1995) 26–35, 47, reprinted in Baruch Halpern, "Erasing History: The Miminalist Assault on Ancient Israel," in *Israel's Past in Present Research* (Sources for Biblical and Theological Study 7; Winona Lake, Ind.: Eisenbrauns, 1999) 415–26; Niels Peter Lemche and Thomas L. Thompson, "Did Biran Kill David? The Bible in the Light of Archaeology," *JSOT* 64 (1994) 3–22.

225. As pointed out by Lemche in the *Theologischer Ertrag* of his *Vorgeschichte*. See also idem, "The Origin."

available evidence; that the comparativist's "leap of faith"[226] is no bigger than the skeptic's. Their histories are not for that reason creating "bogus" histories, as implied by Carroll.[227] The issue is not, therefore, whether either the "maximalist" or "minimalist" version is correct but what kind of history we want to write (or read) and which presuppositions we want to guide the selection and interpretation of the sources.

Historiography is not a "tyranny of evidence." The evidence will, of course, always put a limit on the number of possible and plausible interpretations, but the evidence itself is limited in that it has to be interpreted. And in interpreting it, the historian is not only relying on the pool of available evidence but also—and in this regard, significantly—on his presuppositions, "grid," or whatever we choose to call it. History-writing is therefore very much a democratic process, in which historians move toward a consensus, or rather *consensii*, on the question of method, for pragmatic reasons;[228] for methodological consensus, in the "singular" meaning of the word, is impossible (and perhaps even undesirable) to achieve in the guild of historians.

To sum up, the discussion on Lemche's "path-dependently" safe conclusions is therefore not so much about his conclusions as it is about his premises. Furthermore, these premises, considering the corroborative arguments outlined in this chapter, are to be seriously questioned. It is certainly possible to argue for a historical connection between the late, extant text of the books of Kings and the society of Iron Age Syria–Palestine Though we have not *disproved* Lemche's claim that the ordinary man in the street of Persian Period Palestine, on the basis of either oral or written transmission, could not have known anything about what happened in his country more than three hundred years before, we have nevertheless presented evidence to question seriously his *grounds* for saying so. Lemche may be right on other grounds, of course, but given the corroborating arguments presented above and the unsustainability of the skeptical approach to secondhand sources that is fundamental to his and the other Copenhageners' interpretation of the contemporary evidence, it is more likely that he is wrong. We *may*, therefore, reject the picture he paints of Iron Age Israel, because we cannot from the outset exclude the

---

226. See Lassner, " 'Doing' Early Islamic History," 6.

227. Robert P. Carroll, "Madonna of Silences: Clio and the Bible," in *Can a "History of Israel" Be Written?* (ed. Lester L. Grabbe; JSOTSup 245; Sheffield: Sheffield Academic Press, 1997) 84–103.

228. See Appleby, Hunt, and Jacob, *Telling the Truth*.

admittedly late[229] biblical narratives from the pool of reliable evidence. The word *may* is deliberately chosen, however, because only subsequent analysis of the text will show whether it seems to have preserved historically reliable information in the same way that certain other sources from the ancient Near East have. As Hallo remarks: "The Biblical record must be, for this purpose, scrutinized like other historiographical traditions of the ancient Near East, neither exempted from the standards demanded of those other traditions, nor subjected to severer ones than they are."[230]

Barstad is no doubt right when he predicts the future for biblical historiography as "a history characterized by a multiplicity of methods."[231] And Davies' plea that what we need in the future are "multiple histories" so that we "may learn in how many different ways 'history' may be represented" may be a good one.[232] We do need a multiplicity of new histories with different perspectives on, for example, Israel's history that deal fairly, of course, with the facts of the ancient Near East. They are only to be welcomed. What we do *not* need, however, are histories that do not present to the readers a full discussion of the philosophical and epistemological assumptions that have determined their choice of methods and the basis for their assertions. Repeating Davies' call for good historiographies may therefore serve as an appropriate conclusion to this chapter: "One is not to discourage the production of good historiographies, and encourage people to read many of them, so that they may learn in how many different ways 'history' may be represented, and perhaps even ask themselves why these stories differ."[233]

---

229. That is, late in date of attestation (i.e., DSS MSS), not necessarily late in date of composition.

230. Hallo, "The Limits of Skepticism," 193.

231. Barstad, "History and the Hebrew Bible," 51–52.

232. P. R. Davies, "Whose History?" 121–22.

233. Ibid., 122.

Chapter 3

Linguistic Differentiation

> The information in the early sources does not reflect a single language as it developed and changed over time, but rather different types of Hebrew at different stages of development. All attempts to fit the surviving fragments of early Hebrew into a single historical sequence are misguided and misleading.[1]
>
> Elisha Qimron

Linguistic Differentiations

Now that we have answered the preliminary question—is it possible *at all* that the books of Kings have preserved reliable historical information?—in the affirmative, we can ask whether it is possible to identify and locate markers in the texts that can help us to relate the books of Kings chronologically to the events they purport to describe. In this chapter, we shall discuss possible linguistic markers; in the following chapter, we will take up the usefulness of the comparative material.

Language becomes marked by changes that can be traced, and Hebrew is no exception. It has long been recognized that Biblical Hebrew (BH) is a conglomerate of different *types* of Hebrew.[2] Whereas it is

---

1. E. Qimron, "Observations on the History of Early Hebrew (1000 B.C.E.–200 C.E.) in the Light of the Dead Sea Documents," in *The Dead Sea Scrolls: Forty Years of Research* (Studies on the Texts of the Desert of Judah 10; ed. Devorah Dimant and Uriel Rappaport; Leiden: Brill, 1992) 360.

2. As far as typological terminology is concerned, *Late Biblical Hebrew* (LBH) will be used for the type(s) of Hebrew found in biblical books known to be written in the Persian period—that is, the writings of Ezra, Nehemiah, Chronicles, Daniel, and—to a certain extent—books such as Esther and Ezekiel. *Standard Biblical Hebrew* (SBH) will be used for the type(s) of Hebrew *assumed* to be earlier—that is, the written Hebrew of the pre-Persian Period. The point of intersection, admittedly, is somewhat arbitrarily chosen. We have no Hebrew inscriptions from the Persian Period and cannot with certainty establish exactly when and at what pace a change from SBH to LBH took place, but because the national disaster of 597/587 is likely to have had a major impact on the language, I am

113

relatively easy to write a "consensus list" of demonstrable syntactical, orthographical, and lexicographical differences between, say, the books of Kings and Chronicles, consensus soon comes to an end when these differences are to be explained. Do they reflect a diachronic development within the Hebrew language that, on linguistic grounds, enables us to establish a relative chronology among the texts? Or are they instead to be explained along synchronic lines as different dialects, sociolects, and idiolects, thus being of rather limited usefulness in dating the texts?

As mentioned above, there can be no doubt that Hebrew has changed through time and, we may add, that Aramaic has had a considerable influence on Hebrew. The once-favored *Mischsprache* hypothesis[3]—which assumed that it is possible to distinguish in BH between an early Canaanite layer, very close to Akkadian, and another more-recent layer, closer to Aramaic and Southern Semitic—has now been discarded. The new consensus is that "Aramaic might have influenced Hebrew very strongly, not when Hebrew first emerged but many centuries later, in the second half of the 1st millennium B.C.E. up to the beginnings of the Common Era. Thus, it is generally accepted that in the phonology, morphology, and lexicon of LBH as well as RH, there is a significant Aramaic component."[4] Hurvitz has thus demonstrated that the Aramaic Papyri from Elephantine "display numerous linguistic features which, within BH, are exclusively attested in books like Chronicles, Ezra or Esther—that is, in compositions written in

---

choosing to use these labels as provisional terminology. Polak, for example, argues for this date by saying that "LBH forms a stratum *sui generis*, conditioned by the domination by the Babylonian and Persian administration and the lack of a royal chancellery in which a uniform lexical, morphological, syntactic and orthographic standard could be maintained ("The Oral and the Written," 62; cf. Avi Hurvitz, "The Historical Quest for 'Ancient Israel' and the Linguistic Evidence of the Hebrew Bible: Some Methodological Observations," *VT* 47 [1997] 301–15). Other abbreviations used in this chapter include Proto-Semitic (PS), Israelite Hebrew (IH), Qumran Hebrew (QH), Mishnaic Hebrew (MH) and Rabbinic Hebrew (RH). Cf. Sverrir Olafsson, "Late Biblical Hebrew: Fact or Fiction?" in *Intertestamental Essays in Honour of Jozef Tadeusz Milik* (ed. J. Zdzislaw Kapera; Cracow: Enigma, 1992) 135–47, for further comments on terminology.

3. Formulated by H. P. Bauer in the beginning of the 20th century and developed most clearly in H. P. Bauer and P. Leander, *Historische Grammatik der hebräischen Sprache des Alten Testaments* (Halle: Max Niemeyer, 1922) 16.

4. Angel Sáenz-Badillos, *A History of the Hebrew Language* (Cambridge: Cambridge University Press, 1993) 55. The classic comprehensive works on Aramaisms in the Bible are E. Kautzsch, *Die Aramäismen im AT* (Halle, 1902); and M. Wagner, *Die lexikalischen und grammatikalischen Aramäismen im alttestamentlichen Hebräisch* (BZAW 96; Berlin: de Gruyter, 1966).

'Late Biblical Hebrew'"[5] and that the influence of Aramaic on Hebrew was something that increased with time.[6]

The possible implications are, of course, that biblical texts with no demonstrable traces of Aramaic influence are likely to be earlier than texts written *after* Aramaic began to influence Hebrew, that is, when it became the lingua franca of the ancient Near East, beginning around the 6th century B.C.E.[7] We need to exercise great caution, however, in utilizing Aramaisms as criteria for dating a biblical text when the age of the text is still uncertain, because the diachronic study of Aramaisms is beset with some of the same problems as Hebrew. A useful summary of the works of Kutscher and Hurvitz[8] by Polzin may serve to illustrate the problem:

> Aramaisms can be useful as evidence for a possible late date of a text but can say nothing for early dating of chronologically problematical texts. For the late dating of problematic texts there must be considerable evidence that these Aramaisms appear widely in *certainly late* Hebrew sources. Moreover, these Aramaisms must be shown to be related to the Aramaic of the Persian period or later. Reference to early Aramaic is irrelevant to the discussion. Since, however, it is often difficult to establish what is early and late within Aramaic itself, we must be extremely cautious in utilizing the evidence of Aramaisms, making sure that we employ as much discrimination as possible in determining what is an Aramaism in the first place and, secondly, how this or that specific Aramaism chronologically affects a Hebrew text. For example, the particular nature of the Books of Job, Proverbs, and Song of Songs makes it particularly difficult to establish any chronological judgments resulting from the incidence of Aramaisms found within them. . . . In

5. Avi Hurvitz, "The Relevance of Biblical Hebrew Linguistics for the Historical Study of Ancient Israel," in *Proceedings of the Twelfth World Congress of Jewish Studies* (Jerusalem: World Union of Jewish Studies, 1999) 27.

6. Cf. Hurvitz, "Historical Quest," 304, and the literature listed there.

7. Aramaic was, of course, present in Palestine before the 6th century B.C.E., but scholars agree that it had little impact on Hebrew until the Achaemenids made it the lingua franca of the ancient Near East. It is thus representative when, defining *althebräisch* [early Hebrew] in contrast to Aramaic as the administrative language of the Assyrian Empire after the middle of the 8th century B.C.E., Andreas Schüle states that "compared with later stages in the history of the Hebrew language, *Althebräisch* was not influenced by Aramaic" (Andreas Schüle, *Die Syntax der Althebräischen Inschriften: Ein Beitrag zur historischen Grammatik des Hebräischen* [Münster: Ugarit-Verlag, 2000] 21) [my translation].

8. E. Y. Kutscher, *The Language and Linguistic Background of the Isaiah Scroll (1QIsᵃ)* (Leiden: Brill, 1974), but see also idem, *History*, 71–76; Avi Hurvitz, *The Transition Period in Biblical Hebrew: A Study in Post-Exilic Hebrew and Its Implications for the Dating of Psalms* (Jerusalem, 1972) [Hebrew]; cf. also idem, "The Chronological Significance of 'Aramaisms' in Biblical Hebrew," *IEJ* 18 (1968) 234–40.

other words, the utilization of Aramaisms as a criterion for lateness is valuable if each late Aramaism has a linguistic Hebraic counterpart in the earlier language, and if there is a heavy concentration of Aramaisms *and other late elements* in the text under discussion. Moreover, there must not be any other plausible circumstances (apart from lateness) that readily explain the Aramaic influence of a particular text, e.g., northern dialect (Song of Songs) or wisdom phraseology (Job, Proverbs).[9]

With these cautions in mind, we may use Aramaisms to help us date texts, but, importantly, only late texts. A text with no trace of Aramaic influence may be *earlier* than texts with clear Aramaic traits (i.e., earlier than 5th–4th century B.C.E.), but since we cannot say how much earlier, the existence or nonexistence of Aramaisms is a criterion of rather limited value as far as our study is concerned. A demonstrable nonexistence of Aramaisms in the books of Kings could, of course, be an indicator that they were written before Aramaic began to influence Hebrew in the 6th century, but it would indicate nothing about a possible earlier date for texts that presumably already existed (and were quoted or referred to) when the composite text was created—for example, the information drawn from the sources mentioned in the books of Kings.

Before we proceed to analyze other possible criteria for describing a linguistic stratigraphy of BH, a more serious obstacle needs to be addressed: the attack by a number of scholars on what can be labeled the "standard theory" of diachronic development within BH. A useful description of the "hypothesis in vogue" that has been challenged by a "new approach"[10] is presented by Ehrensvärd:

> What has been labelled Standard Biblical Hebrew was the current literary language of Jerusalem (and Judah) before the exile, where it was

---

9. R. Polzin, *Late Biblical Hebrew: Toward An Historical Typology of Biblical Hebrew Prose* (HSM 12; Missoula, Mont.: Scholars Press, 1976) 10–12. Kutscher, with the above-mentioned caveats in mind, points to possible Aramaisms both in morphology and syntax but claims that "it is in the field of vocabulary that we are on the firmest ground in establishing Aramaic influence upon Hebrew" (Kutscher, *History*, 71–76, quotation from p. 75).

10. I am deliberately choosing to avoid the usual labels "minimalistic," "skeptical," and "nonconformist" (so, e.g., Hurvitz, "Historical Quest"; "Relevance of Biblical Hebrew"), because they are highly charged and, more important, tend to divert the attention away from purely linguistic arguments toward a marked *historical* interest in using linguistic arguments *heuristically* to support a specific hypothesis—for example, that parts of the Hebrew Bible are *early*, that is, preexilic. Though my interest, admittedly, is historical, I shall nevertheless try to restrict myself to linguistic arguments before employing them for a broader purpose.

probably also the spoken language. It changed character after the exile, when the spoken language is presumed to have changed to a kind of pre-Mishnaic Hebrew; Standard Biblical Hebrew continued to be used as the written language, but knowledge of it was in decline, and therefore words and expressions from the spoken vernacular(s) gained a footing. Thus a new phase in the history of the language was brought about, namely Late Biblical Hebrew.[11]

Challenging the standard theory, Knauf has suggested that BH was never a spoken language but an artificial literary construct, *ein Bildungssprache,*[12] that shows evidence of linguistic development only to a limited degree. Others, most radically exemplified by Davies[13] and Cryer,[14] have gone even further and theorized that BH for this and other reasons must be considered devoid of any chronological dimension and that the entire Hebrew Bible was probably written within a short time span.

Because Knauf's work is often referred to by others, a few quotations from the above-mentioned article are in order. In a key paragraph on the character of BH, Knauf states that

> Biblical Hebrew came into existence as the language of biblical literature in the exilic–postexilic period and was transmitted and used as a *Bildungssprache* [language in formation]. It is not even, therefore, to be understood as a "linguistic fragment" and does not represent a section of the life of the Early Hebrew language(s). . . . Biblical Hebrew is much more to be understood as an important stage in the Early Hebrew literature's *Wirkungsgeschichte* [history of impact] as it was received, edited, and immortalized in the biblical canon.[15]

Knauf's implications are that the orthography of the so-called Classical Hebrew of Genesis–Kings belongs to the 5th century B.C.E. and its syntax and morphology presuppose the epigraphically attested language of 8th–6th century B.C.E. Judah but that it is likely that the early

---

11. Martin Ehrensvärd, "Once Again: The Problem of Dating Biblical Hebrew," *SJOT* 11 (1997) 34; and see also Hurvitz, "Relevance of Biblical Hebrew," for extensive bibliographical references to proponents of the "standard theory."

12. Ernst Axel Knauf, "War 'Biblisch-Hebräisch' eine Sprache?" *ZAH* 3 (1990) 11–23; followed by P. R. Davies, *In Search*; and T. L. Thompson, *Early History*, 413–14. Cf. also ibid., "How Yahweh Became God," 60.

13. P. R. Davies, *In Search.*

14. F. H. Cryer, "The Problem of Dating Biblical Hebrew and the Hebrew of Daniel," *In The Last Days: On Jewish and Christian Apocalyptic and Its Period* (ed. K. Jeppesen et al; Århus: Åarhus Universitetsforlag, 1994) 185–98.

15. Knauf, "War 'Biblisch-Hebräisch' eine Sprache?" 11–12 [my translation].

texts were orthographically "updated" in connection with the final re-daction in the 4th century B.C.E.[16] Before discussing the implications drawn by others, however, we should note that Knauf seems more sensitive to the possibility of determining earlier linguistic strata (and thereby earlier texts) in the *extant* version of the Hebrew Bible than are the people who quote him and take up his work. In the concluding paragraph of his article, Knauf states that

> On the basis of syntax, morphology, and a number of remaining ortho-graphic archaisms, we must assume that the final redaction of the "Deuteronomistic History" (Genesis–Kings) and the books of Isaiah and Jeremiah was based on more or less extensive written Judean sources from the late 8th to 6th centuries B.C.E. Israelite sources from the (9th and) 8th century B.C.E. are only demonstrable with regard to the Song of Deborah and parts of the book of Hosea. Only a few short poetic texts (e.g., Exod 15:21; Num 21:14f.) lead us to the 10th century or still earlier periods. The fact that it is possible to identify such texts at all makes it very difficult to insist that extensive texts from these periods should have lost all traces of their origin in the process of transmission.[17]

Though Knauf may be considerably more cautious and pessimistic than others about the possibility of distinguishing different linguistic strata in the Hebrew Bible, he does not seem to draw the same far-reaching conclusions as Davies, who quotes him positively, and Cryer, who works from the same basis. Though Knauf explains the relatively homogeneous character of BH orthography, syntax, and morphology along diachronic lines (as being a result of "linguistic updating"), Davies and Cryer theorize that the lack of linguistic diversity reflects a relatively short—and late—time of composition and that the occur-rence of variable spellings and differences in vocabulary should in-stead be explained along synchronic lines. Cryer states that, because of its lack of linguistic diversity, the Hebrew Bible must have been writ-ten "more or less at one go, or at least over a relatively short period of

---

16. Ibid., 21–22. On the discussion of "Israelitisch" and "Judäisch" it should be noted, however, that Knauf's description of the language of the Gezer Calendar and Tell Deir ʿAlla Inscription ("den Sukkoth-Inschriften" in Knauf's terminology) as Israelite He-brew dialects is disputed. It is still a matter of debate whether the script and language of the Gezer Calendar are Phoenician or Hebrew (see, for example, Sandra Landis Go-gel, *A Grammar of Epigraphic Hebrew* [SBL Resources for Biblical Study 23; Atlanta: Soci-ety of Biblical Literature, 1998] 8–10), and though the language of the Tell Deir ʿAlla Inscription may show certain affinities with Hebrew, its language has by no means been established as Hebrew or "Israelite" (it is omitted by Gogel); cf. J. Hoftijzer and G. van der Kooij, *The Balaam Text from Deir ʿAlla Re-Evaluated* (Leiden: Brill, 1991).

17. Knauf, "War 'Biblisch-Hebräisch' eine Sprache?" 22.

time,"[18] during Persian and/or Hellenistic times. Cryer, examining possible explanations of this linguistic homogeneity, argues that, while "it is possible that a fair amount of both phonological and morphological development of the Hebrew language has simply gone unrecorded in the consonantal text,"[19] the lack of syntactical and lexical variation remains unexplained: there is no sign of a development in the verb-subject-object (VSO) word order within Biblical Hebrew toward Mishnaic subject-verb-object (SVO) word order, and there is no significant development in vocabulary. Both are, according to Cryer, to be expected if BH reflects a language that was used over several centuries. The main obstacle to his hypothesis, that certain texts are virtually devoid of Aramaisms, Cryer explains by the fact that the Hebrew Bible is "a work that attempts quintessentially to define the Jewish religio-national consciousness." It is therefore only natural for the authors to avoid a language that "enjoyed the status of an international *lingua franca.*"[20] Cryer does not deny that certain differences *are* discernible within BH but maintains that we do not have sufficient "baselines" to describe an "early" and a "late" stratum within Biblical Hebrew. He instead chooses the synchronic and allegedly simpler explanation, that the bulk of the biblical texts were composed over a relatively short period of time.

Davies, taking a similar stance, states that the Hebrew Bible "was at best largely compiled into its present form, and at most entirely written ... during the rule of the Persians and then the Hellenistic monarchies,"[21] in chronological terms, "between the 6th and 3rd centuries B.C.E., during which ... the biblical literature was composed."[22] Davies, like Cryer, also maintains that "there is extraordinarily little by way of external control on the dating of 'classical Hebrew'" and that "we have very few non-biblical texts by which to date the evolution of the language in which the biblical literature is written."[23] Instead of diachronic explanations, Davies points to various synchronic factors (dialect,

---

18. Cryer, "The Problem," 192. Cf. also T. L. Thompson ("Intellectual Matrix," 110), who does recognize the existence of earlier strata in the tradition but nevertheless states that the rededication of the temple in 164 B.C.E. triggered a revision or redaction of the tradition that substantially affects access to earlier strata of the tradition. Thompson concludes that "this renders an *a quo*, not an *ad quem* dating to the extant tradition."

19. Cryer, "The Problem," 189.

20. Ibid., 191.

21. P. R. Davies, *In Search*, 24.

22. Ibid., 105.

23. Ibid., 102.

idiolect, sociolect, archaizing language, etc.) as responsible for the linguistic variation indisputably found in the corpus of BH. The new approach has been vehemently attacked by proponents of the "standard theory," especially Hurvitz, and a short presentation of his and others' rebuttals therefore is appropriate.

As far as a relationship between literary language and spoken vernacular(s) is concerned, it is now generally held that BH, though now and then betraying various colloquialisms and probably also dialects, was never a *spoken* language.[24] The approximately 8,000 lexical items preserved in BH would simply not have been enough to meet the needs of a living language, and BH can therefore also be described as a "fragment of language," that is, only a part of the Hebrew spoken by the Israelites at a certain point of time.[25] The crucial point, however—at least as far as the present study is concerned—is not whether BH was ever a spoken language but whether it reflects different types of a written language and, if answered in the affirmative, whether it is possible to describe a diachronic development of *written* Hebrew that enables us to explain the typological differences in BH along diachronic lines. Hurvitz's comment on the relationship between literary languages and spoken vernaculars is pertinent:

> Even if the assumption that BH was largely literary in nature is correct, it by no means allows us to reject *a priori* the possibility that it was subject to a process of linguistic change during the biblical period. . . . Therefore, the whole question whether or not BH was "literary" is totally irrelevant to our chronological debate; raising this argument in the present context simply diverts our attention in the wrong direction.[26]

Cryer's main argument, that a language cannot be in use for as long as a thousand years without changing drastically and that the lack of diversity displayed by the Hebrew Bible therefore points to a relatively short period of composition, has been criticized by Ehrensvärd, who has argued that Cryer's choice of modern Germanic languages as comparative linguistic material is a bit odd, because written Standard Arabic seems to provide a closer and methodologically sounder parallel:

---

24. A notable exception to the rule is Gary A. Rendsburg, *Diglossia in Ancient Hebrew* (New Haven: American Oriental Society, 1990), who argues that the written language represented by LBH reflects the colloquial language of preexilic Judah.

25. E. Ullendorf, "Is Biblical Hebrew a Language?" *BSOAS* 34 (1971) 241–55. Cf. also Sáenz-Badillos, *History*, 53.

26. Hurvitz, "Historical Quest," 303; cf. idem, "Relevance of Biblical Hebrew," 29 n. 24.

"It has changed remarkably little over—roughly—the last millennium and a half, even though Arabic vernaculars have changed drastically. Indeed, the vernaculars have had a certain influence on the written language; nevertheless, it remains broadly similar."[27]

Another good comparison would be the Babylonian "literary" language or "Standard Babylonian" (SB),[28] which remained so stable that even distinguished scholars erroneously dated compositions late that later were proved to stem from Old Babylonian times. Von Soden, for example, in his analysis of the Neo-Babylonian copy of "The Great Prayer to Ištar" written in this dialect, dated it to Neo-Babylonian times, that is, after 1,000 B.C.E.,[29] while the discovery of an exact duplicate of the late Neo-Babylonian copy of the hymn in the Boğazköy archives invalidated his "guess" and indicated a much earlier date of composition, around the middle of the 2nd millennium—that is, the late Old Babylonian period.[30] So, even if Cryer's description of BH as "lacking diversity" (a description contested by Ehrensvärd and others) should be right, there is clear evidence from comparative linguistic studies that lack of diversity cannot by itself be used as an argument for dating texts to a relatively short period.

In regard to syntactical development, Ehrensvärd points to two recent studies that provide evidence of development from VSO to SVO word order[31] and of development in the appearance of the *waw*-consecutive[32] within BH. These studies provide important information, and, as a result, Ehrensvärd criticizes Cryer for neglecting them

---

27. Ehrensvärd ("Once Again," 31–32), where references to the relevant studies also can be found.

28. John Huehnergard, *A Grammar of Akkadian* (HSM 45; Atlanta: Scholars Press, 1997) xii–xvii.

29. A. Falkenstein and Wolfram von Soden, *Sumerische und Akkadische Hymnen und Gebete* (Zurich: Artemis, 1953) 401.

30. E. Reiner and H. G. Güterbock, "The Great Prayer to Ishtar and Its Two Versions from Boğazköy," *JCS* 21 (1967) 256.

31. Talmy Givón, "The Drift from VSO to SVO in Biblical Hebrew: The Pragmatics of Tense-Aspect," in *Symposium on the Mechanisms of Syntactic Change* (ed. C. Li; Austin: University of Texas Press, 1977) 181–254. See, however, the critique of Givón by William James Adams, Jr., *An Investigation into the Diachronic Distribution of Morphological Forms and Semantic Features of Extra-Biblical Hebrew Sources* (Ph.D. diss.; The University of Utah, 1987) 19, 142, 166. For a treatment of word order in the Northwest Semitic epigraphic material, see W. Randall Garr, *Dialect Geography of Syria–Palestine, 1000–586 B.C.E.* (Philadelphia: University of Pennsylvania Press, 1985; reprinted, Winona Lake, Ind.: Eisenbrauns, 2004) 189–91.

32. Mats Eskhult, *Studies in Verbal Aspect and Narrative Technique in Biblical Hebrew Prose* (Uppsala: Almqvist & Wiksell, 1990). See also Adams, "An Investigation."

and for making no reference to any book or article written in Modern
Hebrew, because studies in Modern Hebrew together with the above-
mentioned works make it clear that "the matter may be more complicated than Cryer presents."[33]

Regarding vocabulary, there can be no doubt that "different vocab-
ularies" exist among the various texts that constitute the pool of BH.
Hurvitz has demonstrated the lexicographical differences among biblical books known to be late—for example, Esther and Chronicles—
and books with an uncertain date—for example, the texts of Samuel
and Kings.[34] The crux of the matter is not, however, whether such a
difference between, say the books of Kings and Chronicles, exists (not
even Cryer would deny this) but whether it is to be explained diachronically as a *development* in vocabulary or *synchronically* as idiolects
or sociolects. Cryer is correct to point out this clarification. Whether he
is right in preferring synchronic explanations (see above, p. 119, on
Aramaisms) we will pursue in due course.

Cryer's final "obstacle" (a problem stressed even more by Davies) is
the alleged lack of external controls for describing diachronic development within Hebrew.[35] This is perhaps the most serious problem,
because an insufficient pool of external controls would make impossible any attempt to describe a stratigraphy within BH. With so much
at stake, Hurvitz's zeal in defending the "pool" as sufficient is under-
standable.[36] Hurvitz began his work and took his position long before
the rise of the current discussion, and though he has been backed by
others in his maintaining of his position,[37] due credit must nevertheless be given to scholars, such as Cryer, who have pointed out (1) the
temporary and fragile character of our present understanding of how
the Hebrew language developed in the period allegedly covered by
the biblical texts, (2) how often scholars use circular reasoning in their
descriptions of various phases in the Hebrew language by following
innerbiblical chronology to date the various "types" of Hebrew within
BH,[38] and (3) that the extent of synchronic factors responsible for

33. Ehrensvärd, "Once Again," 32.
34. Hurvitz, "Historical Quest," 311–14, and references given there.
35. Cryer, "The Problem," 197; P. R. Davies, *In Search*, 102.
36. Most recently in Hurvitz, "Historical Quest," 307–11; idem, "Relevance of Biblical Hebrew," 28–31.
37. E.g., Kutscher, *History*; Adams, "An Investigation"; Qimron, "Observations";
Garr, *Dialect Geography of Syria–Palestine, 1000–586 B.C.E.*, 9–13.
38. This is, for example, the main point of criticism in Vincent DeCaen, "Hebrew
Linguistics and Biblical Criticism: A Minimalist Programme," *JHS* 3 (2001) Article 6 (accessed online May 7, 2003, at http://www.purl.org/jhs).

differences within BH has been grossly underestimated.[39] The crucial point as far as *diversity* is concerned is not, however, the provisional character of our present understanding of development within the Hebrew language or the likelihood of other factors being responsible for differences within BH (issues that will be discussed below) but whether it is possible to consider diachronic explanations for these acknowledged differences at all.

As mentioned above, Hurvitz finds support from other scholars in maintaining that the available pool of epigraphical data is sufficient to make a comparison with the "strand" in BH usually labeled SBH. Discussing the above-mentioned claim of Davies that "we have very few nonbiblical texts by which to date the evolution of the language in which the biblical literature is written," Hurvitz states that

> The number of Hebrew inscriptions dated to the First Temple period is indeed relatively small; yet these epigraphical remains, few as they may be, are by no means negligible. These texts provide us with a "substantial corpus," which—although limited in size—is diversified in terms of the linguistic cross-section it reflects. It is through a comparative study of this epigraphical data and our transmitted biblical corpus that the linguistic profile of pre-exilic Hebrew—as preserved in the available written sources—may be adequately established.[40]

We do have enough data, therefore, to make *a* description of this early phase of Hebrew. That is, not *the* ultimate description, but a provisional and incomplete description that is open to the modifications made necessary by further research on existing and future findings. Two studies, an unpublished 1987 dissertation by Willam J. Adams[41] and the recently published *Grammar of Epigraphic Hebrew* by Gogel,[42] provide important data and will be used in the following pages to check a "consensus list" of LBH features against the epigraphical control material (see tables 1 and 2).[43]

---

39. See Adams, "An Investigation," 3–10, for similar points of criticism.

40. Hurvitz, "Historical Quest," 308. Cf. Ehrensvärd, "Once Again," 36–39; and also the extensive references to other scholars in Hurvitz's article.

41. Adams, "An Investigation. "

42. Gogel, *A Grammar of Epigraphic Hebrew.*

43. Ibid., 23–25. Gogel's list should now be supplemented with an ostracon found at Tell el-Farʿah (Area 1, Square 12, Locus 11002, Basket 1027) bearing one word: לאדננ 'To our lord'. Gunnar Lehman and Tammi J. Schneider, in a preliminary report, note that "according to E. A. Knauf and H. M. Niemann (forthcoming in *Ugarit Forschungen*), this ostracon—which dates from the late 10th–early 9th century B.C.E.—may be one of the oldest exemplars of alphabetic writing found in Israel of the Iron Age, dating from approximately the 9th century B.C.E." (Gunnar Lehman and Tammi Schneider, "Tell el-Farʿah

Table 1: Adams's External Controls

Number	Inscription	Median Suggested Date
1	Gezer Calendar (GC)	925 B.C.E.
2	Mesha Stone (MS)[a]	850 B.C.E.
3	Samaria Ostracon C1101 (SO)	786 B.C.E.
5	Grotte de Muraba'at (GM)	750 B.C.E.
6	Siloam Inscription (SI)	700 B.C.E.
7	Royal Steward (RS)	700 B.C.E.
8	Khirbet el-Kom (KK)	700 B.C.E.
9	Cave Inscriptions (CI)	650 B.C.E.
10	Meṣad Ḥashavyahu (HL)	620 B.C.E.
11	Arad Letters (A)	593 B.C.E.
12	Lachish Letters (L)	587 B.C.E.
13	Qumran (LBH)	83 B.C.E.
14	Bar-Kokhba Letters (K)	100 C.E.[b]

a. Adams is well aware that some, if not most, scholars consider the language of the Mesha Stone to be Moabite rather than Hebrew. He justifies his inclusion of the inscription in the pool of external controls, however, by saying that the theory put forward by Stanislav Segert that the Mesha inscription was written in Hebrew by an Israelite scribe who had been taken prisoner seems to be quite well accepted and that "MS does not display 'unexpected' data. In other words, as a graph line is drawn from ABH to SBH2, the data for MS (= SBH1) are 'on the line.' Thus, in one sense, the results of this study would not be different if MS would not have been included. But the inclusion of MS gives additional data for the study" ("An Investigation," 164–65). This procedure cannot be sustained. Though the language of the Mesha Stone displays clear affinities with Hebrew (e.g., the use of the relative particle and the consecutive imperfect; cf. Garr, *Dialect Geography of Syria–Palestine, 1000–586 B.C.E.*, 85–86, 137–39) there are also considerable differences. The *t*-stem of the *Qal*, attested in Mesha 11.15; 19, and 32, has no counterpart in epigraphic Hebrew; cf. Garr, ibid., 119–20. We follow Garr, therefore, by placing Moabite on the dialect continuum between the Hebrew and the Deir 'Alla dialects (ibid., 229).

b. The date should be corrected to 120 C.E.

[South], 1999 and 2000," *IEJ* 50 [2000] 260). See also Johannes Renz, "Dokumentation neuer Texte," *ZAH* 13 (2000) 106–20. The so-called "Jehoash Inscription" that recently appeared on the antiquities market should not be added to the list until further investigation has established that it is *not* a fake.

Table 2: Gogel's External Controls for Standard Biblical Hebrew

Number	Inscription	Century
1	Gezer	Late 10th
2–6	Arad 76–79, 98	Late 10th
7–10	Hazor 1–4	Mid-9th
11–20	Arad 67–70, 80, 95, 100–103	9th
21	Beth-Shean	9th/8th
22–37	Kuntillet Ajrud	Late 9th/early 8th
38–125	Samaria	Early 8th
126–27	Qasile	Early 8th
128	Ivory Pomegranate from Jerusalem	Late 8th
129–34	Khirbet el-Kom	Late 8th
135	Nahal Yishai	Late 8th
136–38	"Royal Steward Inscription" from Silwan	Late 8th
139–42	Hazor 5–8	Late 8th
143–55	Arad 59–66, 87, 92–94, 99	Late 8th
156	Sam C1101: "Barley Letter"	Late 8th
157–62	Beersheba	Late 8th
163	Wadi Muraba'at (papMur)	Late 8th/early 7th
164	Ophel 2	Late 8th
165–67	Ophel a, b, c	Late 8th/early 7th
168–70	Jerusalem Jar	Late 8th/early 7th
171	Ramat Raḥel	Late 8th/early 7th
172–91	Arad 40–46, 49–57, 89–91, 107	Late 8th/early 7th
192–93	Ketef Hinnom	Mid-7th
194	Ophel 3	7th
195	Khirbet el-Meshash (Tel Masos)	7th
196–201	Meṣad Hashavyahu (Yavneh Yam)	Late 7th/2nd half of 7th
202–3	Moussaïeff Ostraca[a]	2nd half of 7th
204–47	Arad[b]	Late 7th/early 6th
248–50	Ḥorvat 'Uza	Late 7th/early 6th
251	Ophel 1	Late 7th
252	Ophel no. 675b	Early 6th
253–312	Gibeon	6th/early 6th
313–41	Lachish	Early 6th
342–48	Khirbet Beit Lei	6th

a. Note, however, that Israel Eph'al and Joseph Naveh have questioned the authenticity of these ostraca ("Remarks on the Recently Published Moussaieff Ostraca," *IEJ* 48 [1998] 269–73). See also the remarks by Oscar White Muscarella: *The Lie Became Great: The Forgery of Ancient Near Eastern Cultures* (Groningen: Styx, 2000) 200–201.

b. Stratum VII: 31–37, 47, 86, 97, 105–8; Stratum VI: 1–24, 30, 84, 85, 110–12.

On the basis of this evidence, we must dispute Cryer's claim that, because of its lack of linguistic diversity, the Hebrew Bible must have been written "more or less at one go, or at least over a relatively short period of time." I agree with Hurvitz's criticisms of the position taken by Cryer and Davies. Recent research has demonstrated that the picture is considerably more complicated than they allow. Having said this, I have so far only acknowledged that there is a marked diversity in BH and that it is justifiable to speak of a typology of Hebrew within the corpus of BH, in regard to both syntax and vocabulary. In order to address the second part of Cryer's argument—that differences in syntax and vocabulary within BH have synchronic rather than diachronic explanations—we still need to decide whether, or to what extent, so-called SBH conforms to the type of Hebrew found in the nonbiblical control material. If, for example, so-called LBH features also show up in the 9th–6th-century B.C.E. epigraphic control material, differences between biblical texts written in this type of Hebrew and texts written in so-called SBH are likely to have other than diachronic explanations. In this case, Cryer's and Davies's assertions, despite their understatements on diversity within BH, may be *possible*. Furthermore, statements like Yeivin's on the Yavneh Yam Inscription, that "for all its uncouth wording, the document is couched in good classical Hebrew,"[44] and Sarfatti's on the Lachish Letters, that "passages from the Lachish Letters could be interpolated into the Book of Jeremiah with no noticeable difference,"[45] are unwarranted. Before we proceed to making and comparing a "consensus list" of LBH features with Gogel's *Grammar of Epigraphic Hebrew*, a number of caveats must be noted, however, not least the fact that the various synchronic factors mentioned by Cryer and Davies are likely to be responsible for at least some of the differences in syntax and vocabulary within BH.

Synchronic Explanations

That linguistic differentiation *may* have other, and sometimes more obvious, explanations that are not diachronic can be illustrated with an example from Gen 17:16, where the pronominal object in "I will bless *her*" is expressed in two different ways, with the independent pronoun and with the verbal suffix:

44. S. Yeivin, "The Juridical Petition from Mezad Hashavyahu," *BO* 19 (1962) 8.
45. G. B. Sarfatti, "Hebrew Inscriptions of the First Temple Period: A Survey and Some Linguistic Comments," *Maarav* 3 (1982) 58.

וּבֵרַכְתִּי אֹתָהּ וְגַם נָתַתִּי מִמֶּנָּה לְךָ בֵּן
וּבֵרַכְתִּיהָ וְהָיְתָה לְגוֹיִם מַלְכֵי עַמִּים מִמֶּנָּה יִהְיוּ

I will bless her, and moreover I will give you a son by her;
I will bless her, and she shall be a mother of nations; kings of peoples
shall come from her. (Gen 17:26, RSV)

Three basic approaches are normally put forward to explain differences of this kind: (1) the diachronic approach—for example, Polzin on LBH–who notes statistical deviance in this feature between SBH and LBH (see below, p. 143); (2) the textlinguistic approach—for example, Longacre on the cliticized object as more fully processed, more assumed, or less-actively thematic;[46] and (3) the literary approach, in which such differences are explained as devices for literary variation or poetic balance/weight.[47] Polzin may be *generally* right, but in many cases it seems more obvious that the author simply chose different ways of expression for literary reasons, to make the text more sophisticated and thus readable. A more-detailed discussion of other possible synchronic explanations is necessary.

Apart from literary devices of this kind and the fact that new epigraphic discoveries continue to extend our knowledge of the linguistic development of the Hebrew language, a number of other circumstances must be kept in mind when we try to describe Biblical Hebrew diachronically. First of all, we have no autographs, only copies of copies of copies. This is the normal situation with literature, but it is important to keep it in mind anyway, because it creates some obvious obstacles to the historical linguist, some of them surmountable and others clearly insurmountable. Texts were often very carefully copied, as we have seen in the preceding chapter, but careful copying does not necessarily mean that language (i.e., grammar, orthography, vocabulary) was not updated in the copying process. In fact, we have to assume that updating often took place, not least in cases where texts were copied for centuries. Second, therefore, because of linguistic "updating" we have no "pure" texts. We very seldom, if ever, find an "early" Hebrew text totally devoid of "late" elements, and "late" texts

---

46. Cf. Robert E. Longacre, *Joseph: A Story of Divine Providence—A Text Theoretical and Textlinguistic Analysis of Genesis 37 and 39–48* (Winona Lake, Ind.: Eisenbrauns, 1989) 155–57.

47. See, for example, Barr (*Variant Spellings*, 200), who states with regard to variable spelling and literary variation that "one cannot really make these correlations with a historical point, because all books, as we have insisted, have a mixture of spellings of very different kinds."

do not necessarily lack "early" features. If, therefore, biblical texts, which we cannot date with certainty, were copied for centuries, they would most likely contain both "early" and "late" features, and the historical linguist must keep in mind that no sharp distinction exists between the two strata.[48]

However, an important point in this connection is that, although we must allow for linguistic updating throughout the copying process, it is very unlikely that the language was *backdated* (on the problem of archaizing language, see below, p. 138), and occurrences of apparently "early" features—or, even better, clusters of early features—therefore still testify to an early date of the text. Unfortunately, having no autographs also creates an insurmountable obstacle, because we have no recourse to paleographical information on them, which would allow us to confirm that the texts that *appear* old were not written in a deliberately archaic fashion by a later hand.

Finally, there is the problem of applying a theory of a simple linear development to the Hebrew language. Even if we can identify "early" linguistic features in a text, it can sometimes be difficult to date them more precisely. It is impossible to predict precisely how a certain language would have developed, because languages are highly influenced by (unknown and likewise unpredictable) social and historical change. What we can do, however, is to "postdict"—that is, we can develop a theory for language change that could account for observations over a period for which we have detailed (dated) records. Then we can test the theory against the assumed developments and changes by collecting the observations and analyzing them statistically.

We now turn to a more detailed discussion of a series of problems—or caveats—in describing diachronic development within BH.

Dialect

The possibility of dialects or geographic variation as an explanation for linguistic difference or orthographical inconsistency in BH has long been recognized.[49] More than a century ago, S. R. Driver remarked

---

48. Cf. Ehrensvärd, "Once Again," 34–36.

49. See Garr, *Dialect Geography of Syria–Palestine, 1000–586 B.C.E.*, 1–21, for bibliographical references. Garr defines "dialect geography" as "the study of linguistic differentiation and interrelation in a given area at a given time. It seeks a planar layout of all linguistic features which differentiate speech areas. Dialect geography seeks an aerial view of linguistic differentiation by plotting all dialectically significant linguistic features on a map" (p. 3).

with regard to the narratives of the books of Kings that "these narratives are written mostly in a bright and chaste Hebrew style, though some of them exhibit slight peculiarities of diction, due doubtless (in part) to their North Israelite origin." Giving a more detailed list of "peculiarities," his "disciple" C. F. Burney noted a few years later that "certain peculiarities of diction probably belong to the dialect of North Palestine."[50] In current scholarship, however, there is no consensus on the issue. Most scholars would probably agree with Knauf, one of the most recent proponents of Driver's and Burney's observations, that a number of orthographical and morphological differences in the epigraphic material make it impossible to talk about a standardized or *koinē* Hebrew in the 8th century B.C.E. and that, for the same reasons, it is even more untenable to speak of *einer hebräischen Hochsprache* ('a "high" Hebrew') in the 10th century B.C.E.

The parade example of these variations is the spelling *yn* [*yēn*] for 'wine' and *št* (*šat*[*t*]) for 'year' in the Samaria Ostraca of the 8th century B.C.E., in contrast with the alleged "Judahite" *yyn* (*yayn*) and *šnh* (*šana*[*t*]),[51] but we could also point to a number of other differences in orthography, morphology, and vocabulary in the epigraphic material.[52] Consensus ends, however, when it comes to an explanation for these variations. Having rejected the existence of a *Hochsprache*, Knauf asserts that the linguistic variation in the epigraphic material testifies to a number of dialects. Discussing the Gezer Calendar, the Samaria Ostraca, and the Tell Deir ʿAlla Inscription (or the *Sukkoth Inskription*, as Knauf dubs it), he argues that "there existed at least two written

---

50. S. R. Driver, *An Introduction to the Literature of the Old Testament* (New York: Scribner's, 1913) 188; C. F. Burney, *Notes on the Hebrew Text of the Book of Kings* (Oxford: Clarendon, 1903) 208. Burney acknowledges his dependence on Driver in the preface (p. vi): "It is a special pleasure to me to express my gratitude to Dr. Driver. To his teaching and example is due most of what may be of value in this book; and I have never been without his kindly encouragement and ready suggestion upon points of difficulty."

51. A BibleWorks search of the MT produced 427 examples of *šnh* and 58 examples of *yyn*.

52. Knauf, "War 'Biblisch-Hebräisch' eine Sprache?"; B. S. J. Isserlin, "Language, Writing and Texts," *The Israelites* (London: Thames and Hudson, 1998) 217; Kutscher, *History*, §94. We may also mention Arad Ostracon 24, where we find *p* twice replaced by *b*, a feature otherwise unknown in Hebrew but occurring a couple of times in Phoenician and Aramaic: *whbqydm* (line 14) and *nbškm* (line 18). Knauf regards the latter as "ein Indiz. daß 'Schlund, Seele' im Judäischen noch **napš* lautete und nicht *nepeš*" ("War 'Biblisch-Hebräisch' eine Sprache?," 19 n. 33). Yet another example is the *ʾašer/še-* variation, where *še-* is thought to be a feature of northern Hebrew; see, e.g., Kutscher, *History*, §45; and Shlomo Morag, "Review: Die lexikalischen und grammatikalischen Aramäismen im Alttestamentlichen Hebräisch," *JAOS* 92 (1972) 299.

languages in 8th-century B.C.E. Israel,"[53] while he concludes regarding
the southern epigraphic material that

> As far as orthography, morphology, and syntax are concerned, Judean—
> i.e., the written language of Jerusalem and Judah from the end of the
> 8th to the beginning of the 6th centuries B.C.E.—is so close to Biblical
> Hebrew that it needs no further comment. Unlike the situation in Israel,
> dialectal differences can only be deduced from occasional orthographic
> errors. The higher degree of consistency in Judean is first and foremost
> due to the smallness of the state, which basically consisted only of Jeru-
> salem and its hinterland. The consistency of the language becomes even
> more striking in that it stretches from a fragment of the royal annals
> [the Siloam Inscription] to a harvester's petition, which indeed was
> composed by a professional scribe.[54]

One of Knauf's points is that these dialects are likely to be discernible
in the Hebrew Bible as well, thus enabling us, with great caution, to
identify "old" texts. Having discussed a number of possible "northernisms" (e.g., in the Song of Deborah and in the language of Hosea),[55]
Knauf concludes that

> it is indeed possible, therefore, to identify texts in the Old Testament
> with an Israelite origin, not only on the basis of assumptions but on lin-
> guistic indication. They are indeed not many or extensive, and for all of
> them this rule applies: what the Masoretes and their predecessors did
> not understand is possibly very old.[56]

Kutscher and Isserlin give the same explanation for these variations.
Taking the request by Eliakim ben Hilkiah, Shebnah, and Joah to the
Assyrian Rab-Shakeh in 2 Kgs 18:26 to speak in *yĕhûdît* 'Judahite'[57] as
an indication of the existence of a particular Jerusalemite or Judahite
dialect, Kutscher points to a number of linguistic features in BH,
which, from his point of view, are likely to be explained as dialectal

---

53. "Namely, the Westjordanian versus Eastjordanian or official versus colloquial language" (Knauf, "War 'Biblisch-Hebräisch' eine Sprache?" 17) [my translation].

54. Ibid., 19–20 [my translation].

55. See ibid., 18–19 for details.

56. Ibid., 19 [my translation].

57. דַּבֶּר־נָא אֶל־עֲבָדֶיךָ אֲרָמִית כִּי שֹׁמְעִים אֲנָחְנוּ וְאַל־תְּדַבֵּר עִמָּנוּ יְהוּדִית בְּאָזְנֵי הָעָם אֲשֶׁר עַל־הַחֹמָה 'Pray, speak to your servants in the Aramaic language, for we understand it; do not speak to us in the language of Judah within the hearing of the people who are on the wall' (2 Kgs 11:26 RSV). Jerusalemite speech is referred to as "Judean" in Isa 36:12–13, while the language of Judah is referred to as the "language of Canaan" in Isa 19:18. We may also add that the language spoken by the Israelites is not known to have been called Hebrew before the use of the term in the prologue to *Ecclesiasticus* (ca. 130 B.C.E.).

differences.[58] Both Isserlin and Kutscher seem to be a little more cautious than Knauf, however, in explaining these differences along dialectal lines. Commenting on the *yn/yyn* variation, Isserlin thus restricts himself to saying that the Samaria Ostraca show us that "in that city at least diphthongs became simple vowels, differing from Jerusalemitic standards,"[59] while Kutscher calls the *št* spelling found in the Samaria Ostraca "suspiciously Aramaic."[60] In his treatment of topographical terms, he states that "it is also possible that the richness of the vocabulary sometimes derives from dialectal differences. Take, for instance, the words הַר, רָמָה, גִּבְעָה, and גֶּבַע: גִּבְעָה and גֶּבַע do not occur in place names in Transjordan (with one exception), while הַר and רָמָה do. Unless this is due to mere chance, the attestation of the place names indicates that the use of the root גבע was restricted to Western Palestine,"[61] and in a more general assessment on the possibility of dialects within BH, Isserlin adds that

> some dialectal features appear in the Samaria ostraca, and where literary texts are concerned scholars have suggested the occurrence of northern Israelite peculiarities both in the narrative prose developed in the northern kingdom (such as the pentateuchal "E" source) and in the poetic diction of Hosea in particular. There is as yet no epigraphic backing of such wider assumptions. Northern and southern "standard" Hebrew must in any case have remained close and mutually intelligible, as shown by the ministry of Amos.[62]

Garr, in his 1985 *Dialect Geography of Syria–Palestine*, also tends to see the differences between the northern and southern epigraphic material as dialectal variation. Having treated Hebrew as one dialect in his categorization of the distinctive innovations of the various Northwest Semitic dialects (Old Byblian, Standard Phoenician, Old Aramaic,

---

58. Kutscher, *History*, §44 on the demonstrative pronoun, §§79–81 on vocabulary, §99 on the object marker, and §100 for a summary. Isserlin, "Language, Writing and Texts." On the question of *yĕhûdît* as a dialect, see also Millard, "Please Speak Aramaic"; and Ehud Ben-Zvi, "Who Wrote the Speech of Rabshakeh and When?" *JBL* 109 (1990) 79–92. For counterarguments, see Robert North, "Could Hebrew Have Been a Cultic Esperanto?" *ZAH* 12 (1999) 210–12.

59. Isserlin, "Language, Writing and Texts," 217.

60. Kutscher, *History*, §94.

61. Ibid., §79.

62. Isserlin, "Language, Writing and Texts," 207 On the supposed northern dialect of Hosea, see also A. A. Macintosh, *A Critical and Exegetical Commentary on Hosea* (ICC; Edinburgh: T. & T. Clark, 1997) liii–lxi, 585–93; G. I. Davies, *Hosea* (The New Century Bible Commentary; Grand Rapids: Eerdmans, 1992) 25.

Samalian, Ammonite, Deir ʿAlla, Moabite, Edomite, Hebrew), he argues that

> the extent to which this analysis pertains to northern Hebrew, as well as the southern dialect, however, is uncertain. Most direct linguistic evidence came from texts of southern provenience, supplemented by BH data. Where direct evidence for the northern dialect was available, it did not necessarily conform to the southern speech patterns. For example, the northern dialect exhibited complete monophthongization and a formation of 'year' derived from *šan-t; the southern dialect had uncontracted diphthongs and formed 'year' from *šan-at. This analysis of Hebrew, then, essentially reflects the southern, not the northern dialect.[63]

It is probably Gary Rendsburg, however, who has argued most rigorously for the evidence of a northern dialect, Israelian Hebrew, in Biblical Hebrew. In a recent monograph, Rendsburg attempted to prove by linguistic arguments that a group of psalms is northern in origin,[64] but, though Rendsburg may have isolated certain linguistic peculiarities in supposedly "northern" biblical texts and thereby pointed to a number of *possible* dialectal traits, the criticisms raised by Dennis Pardee in a review of his monograph, seem apropos. Pardee recognizes Rendsburg's isolation of certain peculiarities but goes on, nevertheless, to criticize his conclusions:

> he has not first provided a detailed linguistic definition of the northern dialect(s). I have no doubt that he would have done so had the data existed, but they do not; he nonetheless forged ahead with his project. In order for such a definition to be possible, texts written in the northern dialect would have to exist, either primary ancient texts, such as the Samaria Ostraca already mentioned (insufficient for the purpose), or else traditional texts of which the northern origin is certain (although certain biblical texts may have originated in the north, their present form is essentially that of the texts of Judean origin). Such data are not

---

63. Garr, *Dialect Geography of Syria–Palestine, 1000–586* B.C.E., 227.
64. Gary A. Rendsburg, *Linguistic Evidence for the Northern Origin of Selected Psalms* (Atlanta: Scholars Press, 1990). Cf. also idem, "Notes on Israelian Hebrew (I)," in *Michael: Historical, Epigraphical and Biblical Studies in Honor of Prof. Michael Heltzer* (ed. Y. Avishur and R. Deutsch; Tel-Aviv: Archaeological Center Publications, 1999) 255–58; "Notes on Israelian Hebrew (II)," *JNSL* 26 (2000) 33–45; and *Israelian Hebrew in the Book of Kings* (OPDNESPJSCU 5; Bethesda, Md.: CDL, 2002); in the latter work, Rendsburg identifies as northernisms 122 features from 25 chapters, which have 807 verses. A similar approach to the book of Hosea can be found in a dissertation by one of Rendsburg's students at Cornell University: Yoo Jong Yoo, *Israelian Hebrew in the Book of Hosea* (Ph.D. diss., Cornell University, 1999).

present, however, and Rendsburg's claim to adopt the procedures used for chronological differentiation is therefore unacceptable.[65]

One of the possible implications of Rendsburg's thesis is that these supposedly "northern" biblical texts reflect the situation in the north *before* the Assyrian conquest of Samaria in 721 B.C.E.; texts, in other words, that antedate the "southern" text or context in which they are found, providing the historian with important and trustworthy information on the Israelite Kingdom of the 8th and even 9th centuries B.C.E. The argument rests, of course, on two premises: (1) that literature ceased to be written in the (official) Israelite dialect and (2) that somebody transmitted the text, for example, the book of Hosea or the so-called "northern cycle" in the books of Kings, in Jerusalem after the fall of Samaria in 721/720—and not just "anyone," because nobody in 6th-century let alone Hellenistic Jerusalem would or could have transmitted or written a text in a northern dialect without being an ex-northerner or without otherwise being connected to the old Israelite Kingdom. We need, in other words, a continuum between the old Israelite Kingdom defeated by Assyria and northern survivors fleeing to Judah in order to postulate a "southern" interest in "northern" material, producing a prolonged transmission and preservation process from 8th-century B.C.E. to 6th-century B.C.E. Jerusalem (or later).

We do have indications of a royal political interest in accepting (or even inviting) some Samaritan refugees into the South (2 Chronicles 29–31). This reading could, of course, be rejected because it runs contrary to the later open hostility between Samaritans and Judahites.[66] But then we would still need to explain why someone bothered to reinterpret "northern" traditions if no ex-northerners were present in the Jerusalemite circles that were responsible for preserving and reinterpreting, for example, the book of Hosea and the Elijah–Elisha narratives of the books of Kings. This question becomes even more pressing if one postulates a late, Hellenistic date for the composition of, for example, the books of Kings.[67] Dialect, if it is attested in BH, in this application is used not as a synchronic but as a diachronic

---

65. Dennis Pardee, "Review of *Linguistic Evidence for the Northern Origin of Selected Psalms* by Gary A. Rendsburg," *JAOS* 112 (1992) 703.

66. Cf. Hjelm, *The Samaritans*.

67. It is also noteworthy that the markedly "southern" text of Chronicles is aware that "the rest of the acts of Manasseh, and his prayer to his God, and the words of the seers who spoke to him in the name of the LORD, the God of Israel, behold, they are in the chronicles of the kings of Israel" (2 Chr 33:18) and not, as Kings has it, "in the book of the chronicles of the kings of Judah" (2 Kgs 21:17). It could be explained by the Chronicler's

explanation of linguistic variation in BH by asserting that the alleged "northernisms" are chronologically earlier than the Standard Hebrew of the MT. It is highly questionable, however, whether the premises hold. If northern Hebrew continued to be used not only as a spoken but also as a written dialect, Davies may be right in appealing to a synchronic explanation of northernisms in, for example, the books of Kings (see above, p. 119).

Davies may find support for his perspective from a third area, however, because a number of recent studies—primarily on orthography—have questioned these diachronic explanations on other grounds. Instead of taking them as evidence of *different* dialects, the orthographic, morphological, and lexicographical variation found in BH is understood as "colloquialisms," "stylistic variation," or "normal inconsistencies" within the same dialect. James Barr, in his 1986 monograph on variable spelling in Hebrew, makes precisely this argument: spelling variations found within BH can just as well be described as normal spelling variation within a single dialect. Addressing the question of dialects, he admits that dialectal variations probably existed at the time the books originated but nevertheless concludes:

> I find no serious evidence of them in the spellings of the Masoretic text. . . . The spelling of the northern Hosea belongs with that of the southern Micah to the same general grouping of the Book of the Twelve Prophets. The same *kinds* of spelling variations are found in all books and all sources. The attempt of Freedman to show that spellings within Job could be explained by correlation with North Israelite dialect, and could thus determine the date and provenance of the book, was a conspicuous failure. So far as I can see, the spellings of the Masoretic text show no indication of anything other than one single dialect. . . . The whole idea that the idea of dialect should be invoked to help explain spelling variations should be judged to have been mistaken, and discarded.[68]

Barr is backed by Alan Millard, Ian Young, and Daniel C. Fredericks, who in different ways reject the attempt to explain linguistic "peculiarities" along dialectal lines. Millard, concluding a review of Barr's book, finds that Barr's work answers two important questions:

> First, is the Masoretic Text peculiar in respect to variable spellings, or is it an example of an *insouciance* in these matters common to the ancient Near East (and to English before the labors of Samuel Johnson and his

---

different use of the term "Israel" compared to the usage in Kings, of course, but could also be evidence of the preservation of a northern text.

68. Barr, *Variant Spellings*, 201.

heirs)? This question can be answered quite easily, and the answer—which is Yes—places the biblical phenomenon in its proper context. Secondly, if variation was a familiar feature of the culture, how far does it extend? If stylistic preferences were a cause of it, may not variations in vocabulary, in the divine names, be susceptible to the same explanation, and with what repercussions for literary analysis of the Torah?[69]

Young, in his 1993 monograph on *Diversity in Pre-exilic Hebrew*,[70] also rejects the dialectal explanation and understands the variations as the type of inconsistencies we would only expect to find,[71] while Fredericks hits Rendsburg's blind spot when he concludes that

> the methodologies used so far to identify a North Israelite dialect in biblical Hebrew cannot answer the questions about the inconsistent and uneven appearance of "North Israelite" features throughout the Hebrew Bible and within supposed North Israelite texts themselves. However, these anomalous grammatical traits may be, and indeed have been, explained more along the lines of the vernacular. If the North (and late biblical Hebrew?) loosened literary standards, thereby inadvertently allowing colloquialisms to slip in more frequently than did Judean and united monarchic scribes, this hypothesis would present a better explanation for all the evidence cited to support any North Israelite dialect.[72]

So, however tempting the theories of Knauf and Rendsburg may be, the material is too inconclusive to see the orthographical and morphological variations found in both the epigraphic material and BH as traces of dialects. There can be no doubt that a northern dialect existed. Peculiarities found in the book of Hosea and other biblical texts *may* testify to the existence of such a dialect. However, because the control material (at least for the time being) is insufficient to construct a detailed linguistic description of a northern dialect, we are also prevented from using these peculiarities to date the allegedly "northern" texts as being earlier than the text or context in which they are embedded.

---

69. A. R. Millard, "Review of James Barr, *The Variant Spellings of the Hebrew Bible*," *JTS* 41 (1990) 575. See also his follow-up article, "Variable Spelling in Hebrew and Other Ancient Texts," *JTS* 42 (1991) 106–15.

70. Ian M. Young, *Diversity in Pre-Exilic Hebrew* (Forschungen zum Alten Testament 5; Tübingen: Mohr [Siebeck], 1993).

71. "Both the language of the inscriptions and [classical] Biblical prose reflect offshoots of the same tradition. . . . The differences represented in the two standard languages are due to difference in genre and origin"; "They ought to be accounted for in terms of 'nuances of style'" (Young, *Diversity in Pre-exilic Hebrew*, 104, 109).

72. Daniel C. Fredericks, "A North Israelite Dialect in the Hebrew Bible? Questions of Methodology," *Hebrew Studies* 37 (1996) 20.

Sociolect, Idiolect, Colloquialisms,
and Technical Language

Another nondiachronic explanation of linguistic variation that has
been put forward is that a sociolect or group-idiolect is at work—that
is, the idea that linguistic change is not so much of a linguistic phenomenon as a sociological one. William M. Schniedewind, in a recent
discussion of the anomalous character of Qumran Hebrew (spelling,
vocabulary, orthography, and paleography), points to a number of
cases in which it is difficult to uphold the usual explanations (e.g., אחיהו
in contrast with classical אחיו as "historical spelling"[73] or the linguistic
diversity among the scrolls as *Dialektmischung*[74]). Taking a sociolinguistic approach, Schniedewind suggests instead that "these peculiar forms
result from the ideological creation of an idiolect for the community"
and are "the outcome of ideological manipulation of linguistic form."[75]
Describing QH as an "anti language" Schniedewind continues:

> these sociolinguistic observations seem especially apt for understand-
> ing the language of the Qumran community. Applying these observa-
> tions to QH, we should expect that this phase of the language was at
> the same time a continuation of Late Biblical Hebrew and a reaction
> against the colloquial languages spoken in Palestine—both Aramaic
> and Mishnaic Hebrew. The attempt to form an antilanguage is most
> apparent in the surface structures of language (e.g., lexicon), while the
> deep structure (e.g., syntax) is less affected. Anti languages both relexi-
> calize and overlexicalize. Conversely, anti languages nevertheless be-
> tray a familiarity with the native and colloquial languages through
> grammar—in the present case reflected by Aramaic and Mishnaic He-
> brew. M. A. K. Halliday writes, "The principle is that of same grammar,
> different vocabulary; but different vocabulary only in certain areas,
> typically those that are central to the activities of the subculture and
> that set it off most sharply from the established society." Group ideol-
> ogy finds its reflex in a linguistic ideology. This, I believe, is the situa-
> tion we confront in Qumran literature.[76]

---

73. E. Qimron, *The Hebrew of the Dead Sea Scrolls* (HSS 29; Atlanta: Scholars Press,
1986) 60.

74. R. Meyer, "Das Problem der Dialektmischung in den hebräischen Texten von
Chirbet Qumrân," *VT* 7 (1957) 139–48; idem, "Bemerkungen zu den hebräischen Aussprachetraditionen von Chirbet Qumrân," *ZAW* 70 (1958) 39–48.

75. William M. Schniedewind, "Qumran Hebrew as an Antilanguage," *JBL* 118
(1999) 238.

76. Ibid., 239. Halliday quotation from M. A. K. Halliday, "Anti-Languages," *American Anthropologist* 78 (1976) 571. Cf. also Qimron, "Observations," who argues that the
morphology of the DSS does not reflect the transition from BH to MH but rather a particular colloquial dialect.

Sáenz-Badillos points to a similar possibility in the Lachish Letters, saying that "the formulas of greeting which begin the Lachish Letters do not occur in the Bible and seem to derive from a different social environment."[77] Isserlin mentions signs of different "styles of speech" that find no representation in biblical vocabulary:

- The (Samaritan) ostraca offer mainly educated scribal style with a bureaucratic slant (Gogel nos. 38–125, 156).
- Clipped military speech. 2 Kgs 1:9–11; 9:27 paralleled in Arad ostracon 24, lines 18–19 (Gogel no. 241).
- Lower-class Hebrew is perhaps illustrated by a so far unique ostracon from 7th-century Meṣad Hashavyahu (Yavneh-Yam). It contains the petition of a harvest-worker for the return of an impounded garment (Gogel no. 196).[78]

In addition to the possible antilanguage and idiolect of a group, we may also mention the same feature on a personal level, namely, the use of an idiosyncratic, technical, or personal language. An example often referred to is the language of Job,[79] but we may also mention a couple of other examples. Blenkinsopp, in his ongoing refutation of Hurvitz's dating of P on linguistic grounds, mentions that, though the noun *'iššeh* 'fire offering' is common in "P" but never occurs in Ezekiel, this says nothing about its diachronic use. It might well be a technical term that is the lengthened form of the one deployed by "P" but, for some synchronic reason, not by Ezekiel.[80] Another example is the use of the lengthened forms of the 1st com. sing. imperfect (also referred to as the volitive or cohortative form) and of the imperfect consecutive as a characteristic feature of LBH. In Chronicles, Polzin has been able to find only one lengthened imperfect form and no lengthened consecutive forms, and he argues that Chronicles in this way is a special case, an exception to the rule followed in Ezra, Nehemiah, and Daniel,

---

77. Sáenz-Badillos, *History*, 68; Dennis Pardee, *Handbook of Ancient Hebrew Letters* (Chico, Calif.: Scholars Press, 1982); Sarfatti, "Hebrew Inscriptions," 74.

78. Isserlin, "Language, Writing and Texts."

79. Knauf, "War 'Biblisch-Hebräisch' eine Sprache?" 12 n. 4. See, however, North ("Cultic Esperanto," 204 n. 8), who points to studies discussing Job as a translation from an original Aramaic or Arabic.

80. J. Blenkinsopp, "An Assessment of the Alleged Pre-Exilic Date of the Priestly Material in the Pentateuch," *ZAW* 108 (1996) 513. See now also Avi Hurvitz, "Once Again: The Linguistic Profile of the Priestly Material in the Pentateuch and Its Historical Age. A Response to J. Blenkinsopp," *ZAW* 112 (2000) 180–91. Driver, whose method was similar to the method now used by Hurvitz, used the *'ănōkî / 'ănî* variation to distinguish between "P" and "JED" (*An Introduction to the Literature of the Old Testament*, 135).

which have these forms. Henrik Bartholdy, in a discussion on LBH features, mentions that Polzin clearly has a problem with the criteria of distribution and that it seems best, therefore, to call these features an idiosyncrasy of Chronicles.[81] This is shared by Kropat, who remarks that "these forms were clearly a part of Hebrew from the beginning and were deliberately used archaically by Nehemiah and Daniel."[82]

Finally, we may also mention the possibility that a number of features in the prose style of BH relate to the differences between oral and written language.[83] In light of these observations, we must be open to the possibility of an antilanguage, sociolect, idiolect, or colloquial language as being responsible for at least some of the linguistic variation in BH.

Archaisms

A final complication to be considered, before proceeding to an analysis proper of possible LBH features and the use of them in dating texts, is the use of archaic language. Once a language dies as a spoken language (i.e., it no longer has any native speakers but is used solely for liturgical or literary purposes), it is no longer subject to the same pressure to change that is true of living languages. This is a feature well known to the historical linguist, who must be trained to recognize situations or contexts in which archaisms are likely to occur (poetry, religious or legal texts, monumental inscriptions, etc.) in order to compensate for them when dating the texts. Before discussing the possibility of identifying such archaisms, we must first make an important distinction between "archaic" and "archaizing" language, "archaic" being the predominantly *unconscious* employment of older spelling, orthography, and so on, and "archaizing" being the *deliberate* attempt to give a text an old, and presumably more authoritative, appearance. Second, we must distinguish between script and language.[84]

---

81. Henrik Bartholdy, "Syntactical Criteria for Determining Late Biblical Hebrew—and an Appendix on Esther," in a paper submitted to Dr. Robert Hubbard at Trinity Evangelical Divinity School (1997) 11; published in Danish as "Syntaktiske kriterier til bestemmelse af sent bibelsk hebraisk—med et appendiks om Ester," *Nemalah* 16/3–4 (1997) 96–112. On the language of Chronicles, see also Zipora Talshir, "The Three Deaths of Josiah and the Strata of Biblical Historiography (2 Kings XXIII 28–30; 2 Chronicles XXXV 20–5; 1 Esdras I 23–31)," *VT* 46 (1996) 213–36.

82. A. Kropat, *Die Syntax des Autors der Chronik* (BZAW 16; Giessen: Alfred Töpelmann, 1909) 75 [my translation].

83. Polak, "The Oral and the Written."

84. An even finer distinction, between "honest" and "fraudulent" archaizing, could be made: "honest" being the attempt to use archaic language in an attempt to make the

As mentioned above, historical linguists are used to compensating for archaisms in dating linguistic phenomena and linguistic change. Identifying them is not an easy task, however. First, it is sometimes more than difficult to judge whether a particular form is archaic or has been reintroduced as a so-called "mirage-form" and therefore must be considered part of normal language. Kutscher, referring to the *skip/ ship* variants in English, thus states:

> Had we not known that these forms entered English at a relatively late date, we might have assumed that they are archaic English forms that had somehow managed to defy the sound change [sk] → [sh] and to survive in their ancient form. We shall assume that the same process was operative in Hebrew. The suffix [-ti:] was still in existence in Archaic Hebrew but became [-t] in SBH. When Aramaic influence started transforming SBH, this was one of the forms which it brought back, which had survived in Standard Aramaic. Thus it creates the "mirage" of the reappearance of an archaic form.[85]

Second, because we have no autographs, we cannot have recourse to paleographical information, which would otherwise allow us to confirm that texts that appear old were not written in deliberately archaic fashion by a later hand. Without recourse to comparative paleographic data or the motives of the scribe(s), it is often impossible to judge whether a given feature is "archaic" or "archaizing." The latter is usually argued on the basis of the content and context of a given text and therefore depends heavily on a given interpretation of the text. If we allow for some variability within the same dialect in, for example, orthography (see below, pp. 151ff.), Barr's comment makes sense:

> Since "consistency is at a discount, and variation at a premium" as far as spelling is concerned, it follows that terms like "archaizing" or "archaism" have no meaning. Nowhere in my studies of variable spelling

---

text more authoritative; "fraudulent" being the attempt to make the text appear older than it is. We shall limit ourselves to discussing "honest" archaizing here, however, because the problem of fraud (factual and fictive language) will be discussed in a later chapter. Suffice it to say that Hurvitz has pointed out that the (late) biblical writers were not able to write archaic Classical Hebrew without slips and that labeling biblical texts that are normally dated early as "fraudulent" archaizing must be rejected (Avi Hurvitz, "Can Biblical Texts Be Dated Linguistically? Chronological Perspectives in the Historical Study of Biblical Hebrew," in *IOSOT Congress Volume: Oslo, 1998* [ed. A. Lemaire and M. Sæbø; Leiden: Brill, 2000] 154–57). Cf. also Kutscher, *History*, §161.

85. Kutscher, *History*, 38–39 The same applies to 3rd fem. sing. [-at], which, in Kutscher's view, was replaced by the Aramaic mirage-form [a:] (Ezek 46:17). The latter is already apparent in Aramaic, however, in the 8th century B.C.E. See, however, A. R. Millard, "A Lexical Illusion," *JSS* 31 (1986) 1–3, for caution.

have I seen evidence that requires or even suggests an understanding of this kind. "Archaizing" implies some kind of deliberate choice of the older, some intentional preference that led to spelling in styles of an earlier time. I see no reason whatever to believe that this had a part in the matter. . . . They are old spellings which, because of the haphazard character of the change in spelling, had never been altered.[86]

Having said that, we must also admit that there are a number of extrabiblical cases in which archaic/archaizing script and/or language clearly have been employed. Take, for example, the Ekron Inscription and the Tell Fakhariyeh Statue. Francis I. Andersen, in a discussion of the Ekron Inscription, mentions that "the conservatism of the city's religion is matched by the archaic nature of the inscription itself. The letter shapes are very old-fashioned, the spelling likewise. If it were not for the firm stratigraphical and documentary controls, one might suspect that this slab of stone came from a much older building."[87] Indicating just how problematic it can be for the historical linguist to distinguish between "archaic" and "archaizing," Andersen proceeds to write that "the paleographic, orthographic, and linguistic features of the text of the inscription remain to be explained. As with the notorious problem of the archaic letter shapes [i.e., the script only] in the Aramaic portion of the Tell Fekhariyeh bilingual, where palaeography by itself would point to a date earlier than the strictly historical analysis, it could be that letters incised in stone would be given their aura of antiquity."[88]

An example perhaps closer to the biblical texts is the Qumran Scrolls, in which the square script is used, except for the divine name YHWH and both ʾēl and ʾēlî, in *Pesher Habakkuk*, the *Hodayot*, and the *Psalms Scroll* from Cave 11.[89] Even more interesting are perhaps the so-called classicizing tendencies in the syntax and orthography of QH. Kutscher writes that "the writers of the sectarian scrolls tried to imi-

---

86. Barr, *Variant Spellings*, 203.

87. Andersen, in a footnote, mentions that "Sasson cautiously opened this possibility, but then rightly discarded it. The position of the stone in the ruins, and its similarity to the stones used in the building itself indicate with near certainty that the inscription commemorates the 7th century building. The date is established by the stratigraphic history of the site and the evidence for its rulers found in Assyrian sources" (Francis I. Andersen, "The Dedicatory Philistine Inscription from Eqron," *Buried History: Quarterly Journal of the Australian Institute of Archaeology* 35/1 [1999] 7–22).

88. Andersen, "The Dedicatory Philistine Inscription from Eqron," 11. Other examples often referred to are the inscriptions of Nebuchadnezzar: it is generally held that they are written in Babylonian in a very archaic style, presumably emulating Hammurapi.

89. Cf. Tov, *Textual Criticism of the Hebrew Bible*, 110, 216, 220.

tate SBH, but lapses in the use of the *waw* conversive indicate that they were not completely at ease with this usage. Some characteristics indicate that their language should be in some respect considered as an offshoot of LBH, especially Chronicles. A case in point is the employment of the infinitive construct plus *lo'* for the prohibitive."[90] Examples of similar "lapses" can be found in the *Isaiah Scroll,* where the scribe obviously had problems in copying the presumably older SBH relative clause (without the relative particle) and therefore used the presumably younger and current form (with the relative particle).

From another time and quarter, we may mention the Šulgi hymns, all stemming from the Old Babylonian period but exhibiting a considerable number of deviations from contemporary Old Babylonian orthographical and grammatical practices. Jakob Klein, in an article on the royal hymns of Šulgi, notes that "a preliminary study of these orthographical and grammatical irregularities revealed that the majority of them correspond to standard Ur III practices, and therefore they can be considered as archaic survivals from the Ur III period."[91]

Determining "Late" and "Early" in Biblical Hebrew

Aware of the above-mentioned pitfalls, we may now proceed to a discussion of how to determine a true diachronic development within BH. First, the normal procedure of the historical linguist would be to trace the development from one linguistic layer to another, later linguistic layer on the basis of securely datable texts (e.g., from Old Akkadian to Middle Babylonian and then to Neo-Assyrian/Babylonian; or in English, from Beowulf to Shakespeare). It is imperative to follow this procedure in an investigation of Hebrew as well if we want to avoid circular reasoning, in which earlier layers of BH are reconstructed on the basis of the extant texts (i.e., biblical texts from Hellenistic times).

Second, if linguistic change is used for dating texts, it is necessary to subscribe to a method that involves the execution of two principles:

---

90. Kutscher, *History,* §161.

91. Klein, *The Royal Hymns of Shulgi,* 27. Klein's study is a good example of how historical linguistics can be applied to the discussion of transmission history, and this makes his work pertinent to our study. Summing up his observations on the above-mentioned "orthographical and grammatical irregularities," he states (among other things) that "these archaic orthographical and grammatical survivals seem to support the theory that at least a great part of the Šulgi hymns were transmitted by a quite accurate literary (written), rather than oral, tradition" (ibid.).

(1) linguistic contrast or opposition; and (2) linguistic distribution or penetration. The first principle seeks to identify early linguistic forms that have been replaced by later ones. The second principle aims to determine the frequency or penetration of the latter in literature known to be late.[92] We may note that Hurvitz, who subscribes to these principles in his implementation of historical linguistics with regard to BH, adds a another *principle of accumulation*: a text "will not be considered late unless it manifests numerous late elements—one or two isolated examples can always be interpreted as a coincidence."[93] As far as the first principle is concerned, we have already argued that the available pool of epigraphic data is sufficient to make a comparison between different linguistic strands in the Hebrew Bible (see above, p. 123), and the *Grammar of Epigraphic Hebrew* by Gogel confirms this.[94] Regarding the remaining principles, we have already noted that Hurvitz uses them, and in the following discussion on various linguistic features we shall try to determine to what extent these principles can be used to transfer a feature from the category of "probable" to the category of "true" LBH features.

92. A useful discussion on method can be found in Avi Hurvitz, "Linguistic Criteria for Dating Problematic Biblical Texts," *Hebrew Abstracts* 14 (1973) 74–79; and Mark F. Rooker, "Dating Isaiah 40–66: What Does the Linguistic Evidence Say?" *WTJ* 58 (1996) 303–12.

93. Hurvitz, "Linguistic Criteria," 77. A comment on Hurvitz's use of historical linguistics may be in order at this point. While historical linguists normally seek to date linguistic *phenomena*, Hurvitz's aim is to date the *texts* in which these linguistic phenomena occur. Though Hurvitz's procedure may be both logical and methodologically defendable, a comment by Søren Holst (*Verbs and War Scroll: Studies in the Hebrew Verbal System and the Qumran War Scroll* [Ph.D. diss., University of Copenhagen, 2003] n. 84) is pertinent: "An accurate and absolute dating of texts by their language alone is in fact a far from usual procedure in historical and literary studies (cf. the statement on Sanskrit literature in Winternitz 1909, where only a vague relative dating is attempted: 'Vor allem ist die Chronologie der indischen Litteraturgeschichte in ein geradezu beängstigendes Dunkel gehüllt . . . in diesem Meer von Unsicherheit gibt es nur wenige feste Punkte. . . . Da ist vor allem das Zeugnis der Sprache, welches beweist, das die Lieder und Gesänge, Gebete und Zauberformeln der Veda unstreitig das Älteste sind, was wir vom indischen Literatur besitzen), and practically unheard of in linguistics: Cf. e.g., Lass 1997: 242: 'Absolute chronology (if it can be established at all) is an archival, not reconstructive matter.' Just about the closest one gets is a short article by Mario Alinei (1991). However, both Lass and Alinei deal with dating linguistic *phenomena* rather than texts." The bibliographical data for the texts referred to are: M. Winternitz, *Geschichte indischen Litteratur* (Die Litteraturen des Ostens 9; Leipzig, 1909); R. Lass, *Historical Linguistics and Language Change* (Cambridge Studies in Linguistics 81; Cambridge: Cambridge University Press, 1997); and M. Alinei, "The Problem of Dating in Historical Linguistics," *Folia Linguistica Historica* 12 (1991) 107–26.

94. So does Adams, "An Investigation."

Evidence for diachronic Hebrew dialects is to be sought in three areas: (1) grammar (morphology, phonology, syntax), (2) orthography (variable spellings), and (3) vocabulary (lexicographical variation). We shall now proceed to discuss samples from each of these areas.

Grammar

Henrik Bartholdy has recently worked out a "consensus list" of LBH grammatical features, taking up the features suggested by Polzin in light of recent research.[95] It is important to note, however, that Polzin is heavily influenced by innerbiblical chronology, and because this is also the case with, for example, Rooker, the list remains tentative until it can be checked against and confirmed by the extrabiblical control material. Only if a feature in the above-mentioned "consensus list" is absent from (or at least occurs with considerably less frequency in) the securely datable *earlier* control material *and* conforms to the likewise securely datable *contemporaneous* control material can it be confirmed as a genuine LBH grammatical feature. Because space and time prevent us from checking all features against the control material, we will restrict ourselves to a comparison of a (random) selection of them with Gogel's *Grammar of Epigraphic Hebrew*: features #1, #2, #3, and #8 on the above-mentioned "consensus list"[96] (see table 3, p. 144).

#1 *Radically Reduced Use of* את *with Pronomial Suffix*

Hebrew has two ways of expressing pronominal objects: (1) a verbal pronominal suffix and (2) a pronominal suffix on the "object marker" את.

---

95. Bartholdy, "Syntactical Criteria," published in Danish as "Syntaktiske Kriterier." Bartholdy uses the following works: Hurvitz, "The Chronological Significance of 'Aramaisms' in Biblical Hebrew"; Polzin, "Late Biblical Hebrew"; Gary A. Rendsburg, "Late Biblical Hebrew and the Date of 'P,'" *JANES* 12 (1980) 5–80; Kutscher, *History*; Ronald L. Bergey, "Late Linguistic Features in Esther," *JQR* 75 (1984) 66–78; Qimron, *The Hebrew*; Mark F. Rooker, "The Diachronic Study of Biblical Hebrew," *JNSL* 14 (1988) 199–214; Sáenz-Badillos, *History*.

96. The list is, of course, not comprehensive and is only chosen for the sake of convenience. For additional syntactical features, see Polak ("The Oral and the Written," 70–76), who demonstrates how, in the Persian era, narrators tended to use long strings, to express the various arguments of the predicate explicitly, and that the prose of this period was characterized by a low frequency of verbal predicates that are not accompanied by nominal arguments and by a clear predilection for subordination of clauses (embedding, hypotaxis). Cf. also F. W. Dobbs-Allsopp, "Linguistic Evidence for the Date of Lamentations," *JANES* 26 (1998) 1–36; and Martin Ehrensvärd, *Studies in the Syntax and the Dating of Biblical Hebrew* (Ph.D. diss., University of Aarhus, 2002) 60–63.

Table 3: "Consensus List" of LBH Features

#1   Radically reduced use of את with pronomial suffix[a]

#2   Expression of possession by prospective pronominal suffix[b]

#3   Collectives construed as plurals[c]

#4   Preference for plural forms of words and phrases[d]

#5   Absence of infinitive absolute as imperative[e]

#6   Repetition of singular word + כל = 'every'[f]

#7   Merging of 3rd-fem. pl. suffix with the 3rd-masc. pl. suffix[g]

#8   Use of verbal consecutive forms recede[h]

#9   Change in order of dimension and measurement or measurement classifier and measurement[i]

#10   Frequent use of ל as object marker[j]

#11   מן not assimilated before noun without article[k]

#12   The use of בין...ל[l]

#13   Increased use of the *Piel* form קים[m]

#14   היה + participle as periphrastic verb form[n]

#15   Object clauses introduced by אשר[o]

#16   Asyndetical imperfect apodosis[p]

#17   Initial ביום in calendar expressions[q]

#18   Development in the verb-subject word order (VSO) toward Mishnaic subject-verb-object (SVO)[r]

#19   Passive *Qal* replaced by *Niphal*[s]

#20   Active constructions preferred to passive[t]

a. Polzin, "Late Biblical Hebrew," 28–31; Rendsburg, "Late Biblical Hebrew," 66; Qimron, *The Hebrew*, 76; Mark F. Rooker, *Biblical Hebrew in Transition: The Language of the Book of Ezekiel* (JSOTSup 90; Sheffield: JSOT Press, 1990) 86–87. Cf. also Ehrensvärd, "Studies," 64 n. 21; Kropat, *Syntax*, 73.

b. Polzin, "Late Biblical Hebrew," 38–40; Rooker, *Transition*, 91–93.

c. Polzin, "Late Biblical Hebrew," 40–42; Rooker, *Transition*, 94–96.

d. Kropat, *Syntax*, §2; Polzin, "Late Biblical Hebrew," 42–43; Rendsburg, "Late Biblical Hebrew," 67; Qimron, *The Hebrew*, 74; Sáenz-Badillos, *History*, 118; Dobbs-Allsopp, "Date of Lamentations," 14–16.

e. Kropat, *Syntax*, §7; Kutscher, *History*, §122; Polzin, "Late Biblical Hebrew," 43–44; Qimron, *The Hebrew*, 47. Ehrensvärd ("Studies," 62) notes that "as far as I can see only one syntactic feature of any frequency in one group is absent from the other: the infinitive absolute used as a command is found about forty times in the biblical texts, and I have found no instances in the five central books of the first group." For the epigraphic material, see Garr, *Dialect Geography of Syria–Palestine, 1000–586 b.c.e.*, 181.

f. Polzin, "Late Biblical Hebrew," 47–51; Qimron, *The Hebrew*, 81; Rendsburg, "Late Biblical Hebrew," 68–69.

g. Polzin, "Late Biblical Hebrew," 52–54; Kutscher, *History*, §59; Rooker, *Transition*, 78–81. See also Qimron (*The Hebrew*, 63), who cautiously notes that if some of the suffixes are in fact fem. dual forms this would reduce the number of occurrences.

h. Kropat, *Syntax*, §§5–6; Kutscher, *History*, §§66–67; Polzin, "Late Biblical Hebrew," 56–68; Sáenz-Badillos, *History*, 120; Eskhult, *Studies in Verbal Aspect and Narrative Technique in Biblical Hebrew Prose*, 119. Cf. also Eskhult 1998.

i. Kropat, *Syntax*, §§2, 18; Polzin, "Late Biblical Hebrew," 60–61. See, however, the refinement of the criteria in Rooker, *Transition*, 113–14; and Bergey, "Late," 74–75.

j. Kropat, *Syntax*, §14; Kutscher, *History*, §122; Polzin, "Late Biblical Hebrew," 64–66; Rendsburg, "Late Biblical Hebrew," 72; Rooker, *Transition*, 97–99.

k. Polzin, "Late Biblical Hebrew," 66; Rendsburg, "Late Biblical Hebrew," 72.

l. Qimron, *The Hebrew*, 83; Rooker, *Transition*, 117–19.

m. Rooker, *Transition*, 83–85; Rooker, "Dating Isaiah," 307; Dobbs-Allsopp, "Date of Lamentations," 19. See, however, the critique in Blenkinsopp, "An Assessment," 511–12.

n. B. K. Waltke and M. O'Connor, *An Introduction to Biblical Hebrew Syntax* (Winona Lake, Ind.: Eisenbrauns, 1990) §37.7.1c; P. Joüon, *Grammaire de l'Hébreu Biblique* (Rome: Pontifical Biblical Institute, 1923) §121g; Qimron, *The Hebrew*, 70; Sáenz-Badillos, *History*, 127; Rooker, *Transition*, 108–10. See, however, the refinement of this criterion by Eskhult, *Studies in Verbal Aspect and Narrative Technique in Biblical Hebrew Prose*. For the epigraphic material, see Garr, *Dialect Geography of Syria–Palestine, 1000–586 B.C.E.*, 187.

o. Kropat, *Syntax*, 75; Rooker, *Transition*, 111–12; Sáenz-Badillos, *History*, 127.

p. Kropat, *Syntax*, §32; Rooker, *Transition*, 120–22.

q. Bergey, "Late," 73.

r. Kropat, *Syntax*, §8; Ehrensvärd, "Once Again," 32–33; Givón, "The Drift."

s. Kutscher, *History*, §§48, 122; Rendsburg, *Diglossia in Ancient Hebrew*, 181–82.

t. Kropat, *Syntax*, §4; Kutscher, *History*, §122.

When the object is pre-verbal, אֵת is mandatory, but after the verb the object can be expressed in either of the two described ways.[97]

Ezra 1:4

יְנַשְּׂאוּהוּ אַנְשֵׁי מְקֹמוֹ בְּכֶסֶף וּבְזָהָב וּבִרְכוּשׁ וּבִבְהֵמָה

the men of his place shall help him with silver and gold and goods and cattle

Ezra 4:2

אֵסַר־חַדֹּן מֶלֶךְ אַשּׁוּר הַמַּעֲלֶה אֹתָנוּ פֹּה

Esarhaddon, king of Assyria, who brought us here

Both forms are widely used in BH, but Polzin has argued that, though the verbal suffix quite substantially predominates over אֵת with pronominal suffix throughout BH, it is a feature of books known to be late "to avoid, even more so than earlier Hebrew, the use of אֵת with suffix."

---

97. Bartholdy, "Syntactical Criteria," 5, with reference to Frederic Bush, *Ruth/Esther* (WBC 9; Dallas: Word, 1996) 25.

His sampling of 216 verses of JE in Exodus and Numbers shows a 12 : 7 ratio in favor of verbal suffixes, while his analyses of the so-called Court History and Deuteronomistic History show a similar ratio. In contrast, the Chronicler's language exhibits at least a 10 : 1 ratio in favor of the verbal suffix.[98] The "descriptive" part of Polzin's argument, that the verbal suffix is preferred by books known to be late (in comparison with books that cannot be dated with certainty), must be accepted, but the conclusion implied by the "diachronic" aspect of his argument, that books with a more-even distribution of the two forms reflect an "earlier" form of Hebrew and therefore must be dated "earlier," is more controversial and must be corroborated by evidence from nonbiblical texts before it can be sustained. Polzin acknowledges the sparseness of epigraphical Hebrew evidence but maintains that it is "consonant with the evidence from the biblical texts."[99] More evidence has come to light since Polzin first published his study, and the most recent list of occurrences in the convenient study by Gogel seems to support the conclusion reached by Polzin: "The relative frequency of verbs with the direct object marker אֵת and verb plus the object suffix is more than two to one in favor of the latter in epigraphic Hebrew."[100]

Polzin's conclusion in 1976 was based on six occurrences of the verbal suffix and three of אֵת with pronominal suffix in the epigraphic material, but Gogel's 1998 list includes seven attestations of the verb plus object marker in contrast with twenty of the verbal suffix. The extrabiblical control material remains very sparse, however, and relatively little weight can be given to this criterion. Future epigraphic discoveries may alter the picture. Furthermore, employment of this criterion to date a biblical text is not very precise. We have no epigraphic Hebrew evidence from the Persian period and cannot, therefore, trace the chronological development from the supposedly frequent use of אֵת with pronominal suffix in the 9th–6th-century B.C.E. inscriptions to the well-attested, radically reduced use in the corpus of LBH texts. In sum, there is good reason to believe that a text that frequently uses אֵת with pronominal suffix is "earlier" than books known to be late, but we cannot say how much earlier.

98. Polzin, "Late Biblical Hebrew," 28–31; Rendsburg, "Late Biblical Hebrew," 66; Qimron, *The Hebrew*, 76; Rooker, *Transition*, 86–87.

99. Polzin, "Late Biblical Hebrew," 31.

100. Gogel, *A Grammar of Epigraphic Hebrew*, 162–64, 282–84, 308.

#2 *Expression of Possession by Prospective Pronominal Suffix*

Compare an example from

1 Chr 7:9

וְהִתְיַחְשָׂם לְתֹלְדוֹתָם רָאשֵׁי בֵּית אֲבוֹתָם

and their enrollment by genealogies, according to their generations as heads of their ancestral houses

with the usual construction as it appears in two other texts:

Gen 29:9

עִם־הַצֹּאן אֲשֶׁר לְאָבִיהָ

with her father's sheep

Gen 41:12

עֶבֶד לְשַׂר הַטַּבָּחִים

a servant of the captain of the guard

Polzin argues that it follows from the occurrences of this phenomenon in Phoenician, Aramaic, Akkadian, and Ethiopic that

> this is probably not of Aramaic provenance. Its renewed late popularity may simply be due to an inner Hebrew development. The occurrences of this phenomenon both at Karatepe and at Gezer, and in BH only in late texts, means that, although it was a feature of Old Canaanite and therefore available to the writers of classical Hebrew (a rare dialectal possibility), it was in fact not utilized until quite late in BH . . . it may, therefore, be characterized (with these restrictions) as a proto-mishnaic feature.[101]

Again the epigraphic control material appears to support Polzin's conclusion. And again we are warned that the picture may change: "With regard to pronominal suffixes, the actual number of attested forms is limited, and while possessive suffixes outnumber object suffixes, future discoveries of both suffix types are needed."[102]

---

101. Polzin, "Late Biblical Hebrew," 38–40; Rooker, *Transition*, 91–93. Polzin's conclusion is rejected by Rendsburg ("Late Biblical Hebrew," 67), but the argumentation accompanying his list of 10 occurrences in preexilic books is, as Bartholdy has shown, not convincing: "3 of them do not apply; 4 of them have another construction (verb + suff. + את); 3 of them seem to fit one of Polzin's categories, but they are found in poetic texts, i.e., in the Bileam oracles with a possible influence from other semitic languages. All together Rendsburg's criticism does not stand, and the construction may be seen as a LBH feature" (Bartholdy, "Syntactical Criteria," 7).

102. Gogel, *A Grammar of Epigraphic Hebrew*, 175–76. For a list of attested possessive suffixes, see pp. 154–62.

#3 *Collectives Construed as Plurals*

Compare these parallel passages:

1 Chr 11:13

וְהָעָם נָסוּ

and the people fled

2 Sam 23:11b

וְהָעָם נָס

and the people fled

Polzin, following Kropat and others, argues that this phenomenon is much more common in LBH than earlier.[103] This has been disputed by Rendsburg and (therefore) refined by Rooker, who states that in SBH one may choose either a singular or plural form of a verb that has a collective noun as its subject, but the plural is preferred.[104] Bartholdy rightly notes that "the usefulness of this criteria, then, depends on the number of occurrences in a particular book."[105] Kropat, Polzin, and Rooker do not discuss the epigraphic material, but a glance through Gogel's list of (the very few) attestations of plural verb forms reveals no examples of this phenomenon; thus, for the time being, we can neither support nor reject the view that #3 is a LBH feature.

#8 *Use of Verbal Consecutive Forms Recedes*

It is universally held that use of the complicated *waw*-consecutive constructions decreased over time. It was already noted by Kropat,[106] and it has been confirmed by recent research (cf. note e to table 3, p. 144 above). Verheij seems to be representative of scholarly opinion, therefore, when he concludes his study on the frequencies of the Hebrew verbal tense forms in the books of Samuel, Kings, and Chronicles by saying that

> speaking of the language of Chronicles specifically, the first remarkable thing about it is its relatively sparse use of verbs. I have tentatively connected this feature with a greater average length of the clauses in this book. Secondly, the book shows a more frequent occurrence of the forms of qatal, qetol and qotel. The increase of qatal forms is in the narrative material. It is partly at the expense of the Wa-yiqtol form and it

---

103. Kropat, *Syntax*, §2; Polzin, "Late Biblical Hebrew," 40–42.
104. Rendsburg, "Late Biblical Hebrew," 67; Rooker, *Transition*, 94–96.
105. Bartholdy, "Syntactical Criteria," 8.
106. Kropat, *Syntax*, 22.

can therefore probably be seen as heralding the replacement of Wa-yiqtol by qatal in post-biblical and modern Hebrew.[107]

The same tendency exists in the epigraphic material.[108] After reminding us once again that "the limitations placed on the analysis of epigraphic Hebrew syntax are severe, namely: the short time span for the inscriptions (most texts date to between the mid–9th and early 6th centuries), the lack of royal monumental inscriptions (as were common in Mesopotamia and Egypt), the scarcity of narrative prose, the large proportion of name lists/seals, the absence of poetry, the brevity of individual texts, and the fragmentary state of preservation of many texts,"[109] Gogel concludes that "the documents in prose indicate that epigraphic Hebrew narrative syntax, which is attested from at least the 7th century B.C.E., has important parallels with biblical prose."[110] And if we include the disputed (with regard to language) Tell Deir ʿAlla inscription and the Mesha Stele, a consistent picture emerges, with extensive use of *waw*-consecutive constructions, whereas the Judean ostraca, for example, do not use them very often.[111] This makes it likely, therefore, that the verbal usage of, for example, Samuel and Kings is early compared to the usage of, for example, Esther and Chronicles.[112]

We must once again stress the tentativeness of the features included in the above-mentioned "consensus list." As far as #1, #2, #3, and #8 are concerned, the available epigraphic material seems to support their status as characteristic LBH features. Only further study of the other features will reveal whether they also can be safely counted as genuine LBH features, just as new epigraphic discoveries may change the picture in all cases. We also need to be aware that, in some of the cases mentioned above, the decision to include them on the list is based on a relatively small number of biblical occurrences and that in most cases we are dealing with differences in frequency between two groups of texts, not just one syntactic feature that is frequently used in one group and absent from the other. Ehrensvärd's warning is pertinent, therefore: "it is easy to blow them [the differences] out of proportion, and this is probably useful sometimes for matters of clarity. However,

---

107. Arian J. C. Verheij, *Verbs and Numbers: A Study of the Frequencies of the Hebrew Verbal Tense Forms in the Books of Samuel, Kings, and Chronicles* (Assen: Van Gorcum, 1990) 119–20.

108. Kutscher, *History*, §66.

109. Gogel, *A Grammar of Epigraphic Hebrew*, 233.

110. Ibid., 292.

111. Cf. Garr, *Dialect Geography of Syria–Palestine, 1000–586 B.C.E.*, 185–86.

112. This is also the conclusion reached by Adams, "An Investigation."

it is important to keep in mind that we are dealing with relatively slight differences in frequency."[113]

Nevertheless, the differences do exist, and even when due attention is given to the sparseness of material, tentativeness of the criteria, and so on, there is good reason to distinguish between different linguistic strata and to reckon with diachronic dialects in BH. However, because no Hebrew inscription has survived from the Persian era, it is still impossible to date more precisely the development of these syntactical features. Adams is well aware of the problems related to sparse (pre-Persian period) or nonexistent (Persian period) inscriptional material but postulates an even finer division of diachronic Hebrew dialects on the basis of statistics. Determining (a) the level of confidence,[114] (b) the degree of relationship between variables,[115] and (c) the linear regression analysis[116] enables him to divide Hebrew into no less than eight diachronic dialects from Archaic Biblical Hebrew (ca. 925–900 B.C.E.) to Mishnaic Hebrew (ca. 100 C.E.).[117] Even though employment of these statistical tools on the very brief Hebrew inscriptions must be questioned (and this of course calls into question his results), Adams's analysis nonetheless confirms the view expressed by Hurvitz, Ehrensvärd, and others that enough Hebrew inscriptions exist to distinguish an early linguistic layer within BH from a later layer, with the national disaster in 597/587 being the dividing point.[118] This view is backed by Knauf, who states that "their [the inscriptions'] syntax and morphology testify to a time when the Judean language spoken in 8th–6th-century B.C.E. Jerusalem had begun to metamorphize into the later *Mittelhebräisch*."[119]

---

113. Ehrensvärd, "Studies," 64–65.

114. By using a specific area of statistics, "confidence interval for the proportion," Adams seeks to answer the question "How much confidence can we place in any one percentage?'" ("An Investigation," 42–44).

115. Determining the level of confidence gives us an upper and lower limit of confidence, and by using the statistical tool "degree of relationship between variables," Adams seeks to answer the next question, "Are these numbers [the upper and lower limits of confidence] the result of chance or are they truly interrelated?" (ibid., 44–48).

116. This third statistical tool aims to answer the question "Does the data taken together form a pattern? Can this pattern be used to predict what future discoveries should reveal?" It should be noted that it is by using this third tool that Adams is able to overcome the classical problem of the lack of Hebrew inscriptions from the Persian period (ibid., 48–52).

117. Ibid., 41–52.

118. See n. 2 (p. 113).

119. Knauf, "War 'Biblisch-Hebräisch' eine Sprache?" 21 [my translation].

Ehrensvärd's cautious statement may therefore serve as a fitting conclusion to this section:

> As mentioned, the inscriptions offer a certain confirmation of the differences between the two biblical corpora. The Hebrew of the first group [i.e., the corpus of assuredly late biblical texts] has more features in common with Qumran Hebrew and Mishnaic Hebrew: when there is a difference, these forms of Hebrew tend to use features shared by the first group more often than features shared by the second group [i.e., biblical texts that cannot be dated with certainty]. The opposite holds true of pre-exilic inscriptions: they tend to use features more often shared by the second group than by the first group. We would not expect the inscriptional evidence to be identical with biblical Hebrew, and it is not; still, the tendencies are clear enough.[120]

Orthography

No one denies that varied spellings exist within the corpus of BH. It is therefore not the existence but the *significance* of these varied spellings that has been the subject of discussion in recent years. Are they to be explained along diachronic or synchronic lines—that is, as evidence of different strata in development of a language or as normal stylistic variation within the same language?

One of the parade examples is the use of *matres lectionis*. It has long been recognized that plene spelling dominates in books known to be late, while defective spelling is particularly evident in the key corpus of the Torah and in verb forms, and since the publication of F. M. Cross and D. N. Freedman's pioneering study, *Early Hebrew Orthography*, there has been a consensus that later texts tend to exhibit fuller spellings.[121] Kutscher mentions that ירושלם is spelled without a *yod* in the final syllable more than 600 times but only spelled with a *yod* 5 times—3 times in Chronicles and once in Esther.[122] An even clearer example is the name *David*. In contrast to the defective orthography

---

120. Ehrensvärd, "Studies," 65.

121. Cross and Freedman, *Early Hebrew Orthography: A Study of the Epigraphic Evidence*. Dobbs-Allsopp ("Date of Lamentations," 31) notes that "all later studies, even those generally critical of Cross and Freedman's approach, confirm these broad conclusions," with reference to Kutscher, *History*, §118; Z. Zevit, *Matres Lectionis*; F. I. Andersen and A. D. Forbes, *Spelling in the Hebrew Bible* (Rome: Pontifical Biblical Institute, 1986); Barr, *Variant Spellings*; and D. N. Freedman, A. Dean Forbes, and F. I. Andersen, *Studies in Hebrew and Aramaic Orthography* (Winona Lake, Ind.: Eisenbrauns, 1992).

122. Kutscher, *History*, §118; e.g., בִּירוּשָׁלָיִם (1 Chr 3:5).

employed in the books of Samuel and Kings,[123] Chronicles insists on
writing דויד, the plene spelling.[124] Because the development from defective to plene spelling continues in the DSS and MH, it is generally
held that the difference between the books of Samuel and Kings, on
the one hand, and the book of Chronicles on the other, should be explained along diachronic lines.[125]

It is important to note, however, that this does not enable us accurately to date texts that make little or no use of plene spellings. It is
one thing to endorse a broad conclusion such as the one phrased by
Cross and Freedman—that is, that the tendency was for later texts to
exhibit fuller spellings—but another thing to determine exactly when
plene spellings became a part of normal orthography, thereby enabling
us to date texts (for example, the books of Kings). Furthermore, as
mentioned above, we need to consider to what extent orthographical
variation was acceptable. However, before discussing these matters,
we should mention a few additional examples.[126]

#1 *The Third-Person Suffix -ô, Spelled with* <u>Waw</u>,
    Replacing the Earlier Spelling with <u>He</u>

In Gen 49:11 the Kethiv form of עירה with *he* is altered to the usual
form with *waw*, עירו, in the Qere.[127] The point being made, of course, is
that the Kethiv form is old and points to an early date of copying. Barr,
however, points out that the spelling with ה is attested right down to
exilic times and that the occurrence of it in Genesis 49 *may* take us
back in time (i.e., to the time of Nehemiah) but not far enough (e.g.,
the 10th or 9th century B.C.E., when this chapter of Genesis may have

---

123. Plene spelling is completely absent in Samuel and appears in Kings only on
three occasions: 1 Kgs 3:14; 11:4, and 36.

124. See Rooker, *Transition*, 68–71; idem, "Dating Isaiah," 305–7; Bush, *Ruth/Esther*,
23–24, for statistics on this. It has to be kept in mind, however, that place names and
personal names tend to preserve older spellings. Barr (*Variant Spellings*, 197), for example, describes the differences in terms of lexicalized convention.

125. Kutscher, *History*, §118; Rooker, *Transition*, 68–71; idem, "Dating Isaiah," 305–7;
Knauf, "War 'Biblisch-Hebräisch' eine Sprache?" 20–21. See also the magisterial work of
Kutscher, *The Language and Linguistic Background of the Isaiah Scroll (1QIsᵃ)*, where spelling plays a significant role in his dating of the *Isaiah Scroll*. On the extremely sparse use
of *matres lectionis* in Ugaritic, see Daniel Sivan, *A Grammar of the Ugaritic Language* (Leiden: Brill, 1997) 11–15.

126. Again, this is only a selection. Other examples can be found in Barr, *Variant
Spellings*; Young, *Diversity in Pre-Exilic Hebrew*; Kutscher, *History*.

127. Barr, *Variant Spellings*, 208.

been written).[128] Kutscher, commenting on the variation between *lh* and *lw* ('to him'), argues that

> while we know that PS had an /h/ in this suffix, which also appears in the early Phoenician inscriptions of Byblos, this /h/ disappeared from Canaanite dialects at a very early date and does not appear in the El-Amarna glosses or in the early Phoenician inscriptions outside Byblos. In later inscriptions from Byblos this suffix is spelled as in the Bible, namely with *waw*, e.g., אדתו.[129] Therefore the occurrence of this suffix *he* in the Lachish letters (early 6th century B.C.E.) is worthy of study, the more so because רעו 'his fellow' in the Siloam inscription does seem to have the spelling with *waw*.[130]

This change, however demonstrable it may be, seems then to be of limited help in dating texts.

#2 *The Evidence from Place-Names and Personal Names*

By comparing MH and BH, Kutscher has found a number of phonological, morphological, and orthographical changes in place-names and personal names.[131] An example pertinent to our discussion is illustrated by the tendency, known from MH, to add [-n] to the final /-o:/ of place-names. Kutscher asserts that this diachronic development is also traceable in BH: the usual spelling of the place-name Megiddo is מגדו (9 occurrences in Genesis–Kings, 2 in Chronicles), but it appears in the form מגדון in Zech 12:11.[132] Another example comes from the tendency to drop the final *waw* of the theophoric element יהו in personal names.[133] Compare, for example, עֲזִיָּהוּ in 2 Kgs 15:32 with עֲזִיָה in 1 Chr 6:9 and Neh 11:4. The trend is confirmed by Hebrew and Aramaic inscriptions as well as by Akkadian transliterations of proper names. In the Lachish Letters (6th century B.C.E.), only the longer forms with *waw* appear, while in the Aramaic documents from Elephantine (5th century B.C.E.), the names formed according to this pattern nearly always lack the final *waw*.

---

128. Barr is supported by Knauf ("War 'Biblisch-Hebräisch' eine Sprache?"). Another example is the זו/זה variation.

129. By "later," Kutscher means 10th century, but note that Johannes Renz and Wolfgang Röllig (*Handbuch der althebräischen Epigraphik I* [Darmstadt: Wissenschaftliche, 1995]) mention two attestations of /h/ from about 1000 B.C.E. (KAI 6.2 and 7.4).

130. Kutscher, *History*, §95.

131. Ibid., §§84–93.

132. Ibid., §86. Cf. also Ἁρμαγεδών in Rev 16:16.

133. Kutscher, *History*, §89.

We need to be cautious, however, in interpreting these examples exclusively along diachronic lines. The very small number of occurrences makes the first example very vulnerable. The second example, while based on more occurrences, may be susceptible to explanations other than diachronic. The shorter form עֻזִּיָּה also occurs in 2 Kgs 15:30, just as two seals, contemporary with or slightly later than Hezekiah (727–698 B.C.E.), bear the names הודיה and מעשׁיה without a final *waw*.[134]

So, though it is relatively easy, as can be seen from these examples, to point out certain orthographical inconsistencies in the corpus of BH, there is no consensus when it comes to an *explanation* for these differences. Do they inform us about different stages of development in Hebrew orthography? Or are they to be taken as normal variation within the same stage of the language? Two questions are involved. First, the various features need to be checked against securely datable nonbiblical material in order to determine whether they are peculiar to BH or are to be explained along synchronic lines. Second, if we *do* find a similar pattern in the nonbiblical material (e.g., a tendency toward plene spelling in late texts), we need to consider whether these differences are the kind of differences we would expect to find in a given linguistic stratum.

With regard to the first point, we have already noted the consensus that certain orthographical changes *did* take place over time (e.g., that there *was* a tendency for later texts to exhibit fuller spellings), and a more precise chronology of this development would thus enable us to date a given text. In regard to the second point, the consensus brought about by the work of Cross, Freedman, Andersen, and Forbes,[135] that it is possible to distinguish sharply between different orthographic standards in BH, has been challenged recently by a number of scholars, notably James Barr.[136] Against Cross and Freedman's assertion that a single orthographic tradition was systematically imposed, deliberately designed, and given official support by the Masoretes, combining the best features of the different orthographies current in the

---

134. Cf. ibid., §89. Kutscher points to the difference between personal names in the Lachish Letters and the letters from Elephantine as a parallel to similar differences between Kings and Chronicles but warns (§§89–90) that personal names have a tendency to preserve archaic forms and therefore should be used with great caution as a means of dating texts. For the seals, see N. Avigad and B. Sass, *Corpus of West Semitic Stamp Seals* (Jerusalem: Israel Academy, 1997) 132, no. 280; and 183–84, no. 438, respectively.

135. Freedman, Forbes, and Andersen, *Orthography*, 3–15; Cross and Freedman, *Early Hebrew Orthography: A Study of the Epigraphic Evidence.*

136. Barr, *Variant Spellings.*

4th–3rd centuries B.C.E.,[137] Barr maintains that "the obvious character of biblical spelling is its *haphazardness* [italics Barr's]. Consistency is at a discount, and variation at a premium. As we have repeatedly observed and insisted, the variations run across all books, all sources, all periods. Exceptions are not exceptional, but are the normal thing."[138]

Instead of explaining orthographic differences as due to orthographic reforms, Barr suggests that "the Masoretic text has the spellings that it has because one particular manuscript, or one small group of manuscripts, was decreed to be authoritative, and the spellings that happened to be within that manuscript or this manuscript thereby became more or less normative."[139] For the same reason Barr refuses to speak of different orthographies in BH:

> there are not really a variety of "orthographies" embedded in the Masoretic text. Strictly speaking, there is only one orthography, which is the same for the entire Bible. But it divides into two zones. The first is the zone of non-varying spellings: it is of this zone that the term "orthography" is really meaningful. . . . The other zone, the zone of variable spellings, is quite different. In it there is not an "orthography," strictly understood: choices are not between right and wrong. For a particular form there are options, at least two, often three or four.[140]

It is important to notice that Barr does not deny that orthographic change took place and that some of the differences in the zone of variable spellings *may* testify to an early versus late orthographic convention—not least the use of *matres lectionis*. His point is that "when the text, which became ancestor of our own, became decisive, it was caught in the middle of a long process of change" and that "much of this change took place haphazardly: as texts were copied, a *waw* was added here, a *yod* there, and in many cases not methodically; what was done in one verse was not done in the next. The probable understanding of this is that much of it was unconscious."[141] And because "the variations run across all books, all sources, all periods" and go in opposite directions (sometimes from the shorter to the longer, sometimes the opposite), we are unable to distinguish between different orthographies, diachronically speaking.

---

137. Ibid., 187.
138. Ibid., 202–3.
139. Ibid., 202.
140. Ibid., 204.
141. Ibid., 203.

How old, then, is this "orthography, which is the same for the entire Bible?" Barr first warns that

> it must be considered unlikely that any book, perhaps that any passage, still retains the spelling of the original composition, or even the spelling of moderately ancient time like the last century of the Judean kingdom. Characteristic spellings of the times of Isaiah and Jeremiah are never found in the Masoretic text. If a prophet wrote *ym* 'day' or *nb>* 'prophet', as is quite likely, then his original spelling has been revised out of existence,[142]

and that "we are skeptical, then, of all attempts to correlate the spellings, and the dates of spellings (if they could be known), with the dates, early or late, when books originated."[143] Second, Barr admits that one feature, the use of *matres lectionis* in the extant text—that is, the spelling preserved by the Masoretic Text—indicates an era from 400 to 100 B.C.E. as the period of formation:

> For the latter limit, first of all, we would put this point: spellings of a common Dead Sea Scroll type . . . do appear in the Masoretic text, but only very marginally: this could well suggest that the text was already well formed before these spellings became influential. This does not prove that these spellings were not yet in existence at all, but if they were the Masoretic text paid little attention to them and only few found entrance, so that in that sense, whatever its date, it reaches back to a stage anterior to them. In addition, it is well known that the second major Isaiah Scroll is quite close to the Masoretic text, and this confirms the existence of something close to our text by (say) the first century A.D. . . . For the starting point as named above, 400 B.C., I would think that the agreement of Nehemiah with many characteristic spellings of the Torah must be significant. The transliterations of place names in the LXX might also be significant; so might the view, often expressed by experts in the subject, that the LXX was translated from a text that had fewer vowel letters than the Masoretic.[144]

---

142. Ibid., 206.

143. Ibid., 199. So, even if, for example, the book of Judges was written in the 10th century B.C.E., it is unthinkable that PS forms like *Akka* and *Magidda*, attested in the Amarna Letters for *Akko* and *Megiddo*, could have survived. The shift from from /a:/ → /o:/ must have taken place sometime before the late 9th century B.C.E., because Assyrian inscriptions from the 7th century B.C.E. have *Akku* and *Magiddu*. But such forms, if they existed in the original manuscript, would no doubt have been updated.

144. Ibid., 200. Cf. also his remarks on pp. 206–7. This is supported by Knauf, "War 'Biblisch-Hebräisch' eine Sprache?" and Young, *Diversity in Pre-Exilic Hebrew*. On the *matres lectiones*, see also Schüle (*Syntax*, 38–40), who states that "dass Vokalbuchstaben für inlautendes /-_-/ und /-ū-/ erst ab dem Ende des 8. Jh.s parallel aufkommen, wobei deren Einsatz lokal verschieden ist" (quotation from p. 40).

A. R. Millard, in a review of Barr's monograph and a subsequent article on the same subject,[145] accepts Barr's conclusions but also points to a question unanswered by Barr's work: Was the Bible unique in this phenomenon? He maintains that "the answer to the question can only be discovered through a survey of other texts from the world in which the Bible was created. Placing the Bible in its ancient environment is essential to a full understanding of its creation and history, and at the end of the twentieth century, biblical scholarship has to undertake this exercise thoroughly and objectively."[146] Analyzing, first, the early Hebrew inscriptions, Millard suggests that,

> while Barr's date for the peak of the process is reasonable, the epigraphic sources indicate a far earlier period for its commencement. Isaiah of Jerusalem could have used some *matres lectionis* in writing his oracles about 700 B.C. The question remains, Would such a writer have mixed *plene* and defective spellings in the first manuscript of his work? In the absence of extensive Hebrew manuscripts older than the Dead Sea Scrolls, little more can be said about early Hebrew spelling. An indirect answer to the question may be sought through the writings of nearby cultures where scribes applied the same alphabet to their own languages.[147]

After a survey of early Aramaic texts[148] and other ancient writing systems (Ugaritic, Babylonian, and Egyptian), Millard concludes that

> the arbitrary element in biblical Hebrew spelling, the inconsistency in the inclusion or exclusion of vowel-letters to which James Barr has drawn attention, can now be seen to be part of a common feature of ancient Near Eastern scribal practice. This does not mean there were no conventions controlling the writing of vowel-letters. Barr has shown some of them, and the parallel work of F. I. Andersen and A. D. Forbes—with which Barr is often in disagreement—emphasizes some of them. It is clear, however, that there were no rigid rules, variable spelling was permissible, as it was in English until the nineteenth century. On this matter there is nothing peculiar in the Bible, nothing which makes it different from other ancient writings.[149]

---

145. Millard, "Review of James Barr"; idem, "Variable Spelling. "

146. Millard, "Variable Spelling," 106–7.

147. Ibid., 108.

148. Demonstrating, for example, that the word 'barley' is written both *plene* and *defectively* in the same text on the Tell Fakhariyeh Statue: š‘ryn (line 19) and š‘rn (line 22). Cf. Ali Abou-Assaf, Pierre Bordreuil, and A. R. Millard, *La Statue de Tell Fekherye et son inscription bilingue Assyro-Araméenne* (Cahier/Editions Recherche sur les Civilisations 7; Paris: Editions Recherche sur les civilisations, 1982) for the text.

149. Millard, "Variable Spelling," 114–15.

We may conclude, therefore, that orthographic differences are of little help in dating texts. Barr and Millard have convincingly demonstrated that variable spellings existed side by side in the same texts and that variations run across all books, all sources, and all periods and go in opposite directions. No conclusive evidence—with the probable exception of the use of *matres lectionis*—can be found, therefore, of different orthographical strata within BH. Taking Millard's refinement of Barr's conclusion into consideration, we are left, then, with a period from about 700 to 100 B.C.E. as the time of the formation of the present spelling found in the Masoretic Text. So, even if it is *likely* that (parts of) the books of Kings, due to its predominantly defective spellings, originated sometime near the earlier limit, the direct and indirect orthographic evidence cannot *in itself* preclude that this spelling originated in a later period (near the lower limit).

Vocabulary

A final area of interest for the historical linguist is vocabulary. Lexicographical variation also exists on a synchronic level, of course, but if it can be ascertained that an early linguistic form has been replaced by another form, the latter may be described as a late linguistic feature, in this case a LBH feature. It must be noted, however, that even where this can be demonstrated, the nonoccurrence of the presumably later form in earlier texts may be a matter of "chance." Kutscher, for example, warns that, although the word for *carob* does not occur in BH, "there is little doubt that it was known in Biblical times."[150] The list of suggested features is long, and we limit our discussion to but a few, frequently mentioned candidates.[151]

#1 אני *Displaces* אנכי

Two forms of the 1st-person sing. independent pronoun exist in BH, but they are not used interchangeably in all texts. Apart from Neh 1:6 (אנכי and אני), 1 Chr 17:1 (אנכי), and Dan 10:11 (אנכי), the assuredly postexilic books of Ezra, Nehemiah, Esther, Daniel, and Chronicles

150. Kutscher, *History*, §85.
151. For additional examples, see Hurvitz, "Can Biblical Texts Be Dated?" See also Blenkinsopp, "An Assessment," and the literature by Hurvitz cited there. Talshir, "Three Deaths of Josiah," also mentions a number of examples but does not discuss them in light of epigraphic material.

always use אֲנִי.[152] Since אָנֹכִי disappears in MH, it is likely, as Kutscher puts it, that "this is a clear indication that during that period—about the 5th century B.C.E.—אָנֹכִי was on its way out of colloquial Hebrew and being replaced by אֲנִי."[153] The same is true for the 1st-person pl. independent pronoun אֲנַחְנוּ (BH), which was being replaced by אָנוּ (MH).[154]

However, the example is not as clear-cut as it seems. According to Gogel, the "later" form, אֲנִי, is attested once in the early epigraphic material, on one of the late-8th-century B.C.E. Arad ostraca. As far as the "older" forms are concerned, Gogel lists one occurrence each of אָנֹכִי and נֵחְנוּ in the late-7th- and early-6th-century B.C.E. ostraca from Lachish, respectively.[155] Qimron, on the other hand, points out that at least one of the presumably *older* forms continued to be used, because the MT uses only אֲנַחְנוּ.[156]

Due to these attestations, it is dubious, therefore, that we can use occurrences of the presumably older forms אָנֹכִי and אֲנַחְנוּ/נֵחְנוּ as a means of dating the biblical texts in which they occur. Though there is a demonstrable *tendency* to use the shorter forms from the 5th century onward, the very existence of the short form in early epigraphic material makes it possible that they existed side by side at a very early time, perhaps as a written versus a vernacular form. It is also worth noting that in Ugaritic the comparable forms *'ank* and *'an* exist side by side. Daniel Sivan notes that "from the standpoint of usage there is no difference in Ugaritic between *'an* and *'ank*. As for distribution, it would appear that *'an* is more typical of literary texts while *'ank* is characteristic of all kinds of texts. In some texts both pronouns are used together, especially in literary passages."[157]

---

152. A search using BibleWorks software revealed the following results: Ezra (2×), Nehemiah (14), Esther (6), Daniel (22), 1–2 Chronicles (27). Chronicles, significantly, wherever the parallel texts in 2 Samuel and the books of Kings have אָנֹכִי, uses אֲנִי. Compare, for example, 2 Sam 24:12, 17 with 1 Chr 21:10, 17.

153. Kropat, *Syntax*, 75; Kutscher, *History*, §40; Driver, *An Introduction to the Literature of the Old Testament*, 135.

154. Rendsburg, *Diglossia in Ancient Hebrew*, 139–40; Kutscher, *History*, §42. Note, however, that the MH form אָנוּ is also attested in Jer 42:6 (Kethiv).

155. A 88:1, L 6:8 (as reconstructed by Pardee), and L 4:10–11: Gogel, *A Grammar of Epigraphic Hebrew*, 153. Because Gogel seems to have missed Arad 88 in her list, see Renz and Röllig, *Handbuch der Althebräischen Epigraphik I*, 302. See also the short notice in A. R. Millard, "Epigraphic Notes, Aramaic and Hebrew," *PEQ* 110 (1978) 26.

156. Qimron, "Observations," 358.

157. Sivan, *A Grammar of the Ugaritic Language*, 49–50.

#2 *Replacement of* אֲשֶׁר *by* -שֶׁ

In MH, -שֶׁ has replaced אֲשֶׁר entirely as the relative particle, and though it appears in Genesis (1×), Judges (4×), and the books of Kings (1×), Kutscher sees its frequent occurrence in allegedly later compositions—especially Ecclesiastes (51×)—as an indicator of the process of replacement within the Hebrew Bible.[158] The distribution pattern, however, does not reveal a completely clear picture, and Kutscher himself mentions that the difference may be due to dialectical rather than diachronic reasons (see the discussion on dialects above, pp. 128ff.).[159] This is confirmed by Rendsburg, who favors a combination of the two standard theories: (a) אֲשֶׁר was the literary form while -שֶׁ was the colloquial (probably independent of geographic distribution), and (b) אֲשֶׁר belonged to Judean Hebrew, while -שֶׁ was a characteristic of northern (i.e., Israelite) Hebrew.[160] Because the distribution pattern suggests that both forms existed side by side, it is difficult—dialect or not—to use this feature to date texts. The same is true, according to Rendsburg, with regard to the shift from אֲשֶׁר לְ- in BH to שֶׁל in LBH/MH.[161]

#3 מַלְכוּת *instead of* מַמְלָכָה *or* מְלוּכָה

It is an established fact that the noun pattern with the derivational suffix -וּת became more and more prevalent in the course of the change from BH to MH. Because nearly all of the occurrences of מַלְכוּת are in books known to be late (compare the only three instances in Genesis–Kings: Num 24:7; 1 Sam 20:31; 1 Kgs 2:12), many interpret this difference within BH in diachronic terms.[162] Note, however, the more cautious approach of W. J. Martin. Discussing S. R. Driver's list of probable LBH expressions, Martin commented that "in the light of Hebrew usage it is difficult to see why this word [*malkût*] was included. . . . It is not only well attested but it is a pattern of noun widely used in all periods of Hebrew."[163] Thus, even though there *is* an increased use of the

---

158. Kutscher, *History*, §45. Other occurrences are Ezra (1×), Chronicles (2×), Song of Songs (24×), Lamentations (4×), Jonah (2×), and Psalms—all from the last book (19×).

159. No help can be found in the ephigraphic material, because there are no occurrences of -שֶׁ. For attestations of אֲשֶׁר, see Gogel, *A Grammar of Epigraphic Hebrew*, 168–72.

160. Rendsburg, *Diglossia in Ancient Hebrew*, 113–18.

161. Ibid., 120. See also Qimron, "Observations," 355–56, on both features.

162. Kutscher, *History*, §§65, 123; Rooker, "Dating Isaiah," 304–5. Rooker mentions that the trend continues in the Dead Sea Scrolls, where מלוכה occurs 14 times while the earlier term, ממלכה, occurs only once.

163. W. J. Martin, "The Hebrew of Daniel," in *Notes On Some Problems in the Book of Daniel* (ed. D. J. Wiseman et al.; London: Tyndale, 1965) 28. Gogel lists no attestation of the specific form *malkût* or any other *-ut* forms in the epigraphic material.

derivational suffix וּת- toward the period of MH, the occurrence of
מַלְכוּת cannot be taken as conclusive evidence against an early date of
composition.

#4 *אגרת Replaces ספר*

Hurvitz has demonstrated that within the Hebrew Bible the lexeme
אגרת 'letter' is attested ten times, all in the corpus of assuredly late
books,[164] while outside the Bible it is frequently employed in the Aramaic correspondence of the Persian Period—that is, in sources contemporary with the corpus of assuredly late biblical books. In other
biblical books, in books of uncertain chronological origin, the function
of 'letter' is performed by the classical counterpart סֵפֶר, and Hurvitz
therefore concludes that in LBH אגרת replaces סֵפֶר.[165] This is confirmed
by Millard, who writes that "the vocabulary of books and writing in
the Pentateuch is simple, comprising a few common West Semitic
words, some attested in the Late Bronze Age. . . . This contrasts strik-
ingly with the biblical texts of the Persian era which show Hebrew
adopted several terms then current in Aramaic, among them *'iggeret*
'document, letter,' *patšegen* 'copy,' and, of Persian origin, *pitgam* 'de-
cree,' *ništᵉwan* 'letter.'"[166] Texts using demonstrably *earlier* counterparts (especially in the case of *'iggeret*) may therefore be ascribed to a
date before Imperial Aramaic became influential—that is, sometime
before the 6th century B.C.E.

#5 *The Idea of 'Gathering' Expressed by Different Verbs*

In BH the idea of gathering or collecting is expressed by two verbs
קבץ/אסף. In books known to be late, however, this idea is also expressed by the verb כנס in the Qal and Piel stems.[167] Because the latter
is not found outside books known to be late, it is often taken as a true
LBH lexeme. Accordingly, should it occur in a text that cannot be
dated with certainty, this text is likely to be of late origin.[168]

---

164. Esther (2×), Nehemiah (6×), and Chronicles (2×), Hurvitz, "Can Biblical Texts Be
Dated?" 150.

165. Ibid., 149–50; Hurvitz, "Historical Quest," 311–14; idem, "The Origins and Development of the Expression מְגִלַּת סֵפֶר: A Study in the History of Writing-Related Terminology in Biblical Times," in *Texts, Temples, and Traditions: A Tribute to Menahem Haran*
(ed. M. V. Fox et al.; Winona Lake, Ind.: Eisenbrauns, 1996) 37*–46* [Hebrew]. For attestations of ספר in the epigraphic material, see Gogel, *A Grammar of Epigraphic Hebrew*, 358.

166. Millard, "Books," 178. Cf. also idem, "Writing," in *NIDOTTE* (ed. W. A. VanGemeren; Grand Rapids: Zondervan, 1997) 1293.

167. The word כנס occurs in 1 Chr 22:2; Neh 12:44; Esth 4:16; Ps 33:7, 147:2; Qoh 2:8,
2:26, 3:5; Isa 28:20; Ezek 22:21, 39:28.

168. Rooker, "Dating Isaiah"; Hurvitz, "Linguistic Criteria," 77.

Implications

Having discussed the possibility of determining early and late linguistic elements in the areas of grammar, orthography, and vocabulary, we may now try to draw some conclusions.

The occurrence of *Aramaisms* in a text points to a relatively late date of composition—that is, after Imperial Aramaic began to influence literature written in Palestine during the 6th and 5th centuries B.C.E. On the other hand, though the *absence* of Aramaisms in a given text may point to an *earlier* date of composition, we cannot say *how much earlier*, because the absence of extrabiblical Hebrew documents from the Persian Period makes it impossible to predict precisely when, and at what pace, Aramaisms began to find their way into Hebrew texts. The absence of Aramaisms in the books of Kings, therefore, *may* take us back in time before, say, the 6th century B.C. but cannot be used to determine a possible earlier date for various texts *within* the books of Kings.

With regard to *dialect*, the peculiarities found in the Elijah/Elisha cycle and in Hosea in all likelihood reflect a northern dialect and, accordingly, an early northern provenance of these texts. Again, however, because no texts have survived from the Persian Period, it is impossible to follow the life (and perhaps decline) of this northern dialect; and though these passages probably antedate their inclusion in the books of Kings, we still are unable to go further back than *before* the 6th century B.C.E.

We found that differences *do* exist between the Hebrew *grammar* of definitely late texts and the Hebrew of the preexilic epigraphic material. We also noted, however, that we are dealing with differences in *frequency* between two groups of texts, not the *absence* in one group of a syntactical feature frequently used in the other. This and the fact that no Hebrew inscription has survived from the Persian era again prevents us from using these features to more precisely date, for example, the books of Kings. All we can say, therefore, is that the differences *do* exist and that the Hebrew of the books of Kings has more features in common with the Hebrew of the preexilic inscriptions. That is, the book of Kings was composed at a date closer to the preexilic inscriptions of 8th–7th century B.C.E. than to the extant LBH texts of the 3rd–2nd century B.C.E.

Orthographic differences have perhaps turned out to be the most disappointing area of investigation. Following Barr's and Millard's conclusions, we are left with a broad span from the 6th to the 2nd century B.C.E. as the time of the formation of the spelling we observe. Even if it is *likely* that (parts of) the book of Kings, due to its predominantly defective spellings, originated sometime near the earlier limit, the direct and indirect orthographic evidence cannot *in itself* preclude that this spelling could have originated in a later period. Orthographical differences are therefore of little help in dating texts.

Many examples from Hebrew *vocabulary* have proved inconclusive. A few lexemes seem promising, however, and may reveal some diachronic change. Hurvitz's demonstration that אגרת is a LBH feature is especially convincing, and Millard's conclusion confirms the broad results reached in the areas of Aramaisms and syntax that the book of Kings is likely to have been composed during the 6th and 5th century B.C.E. (see quotation above, p. 161).[169]

On the positive side, therefore, there is a difference between the Hebrew of definitely late biblical books such as Ezra and Nehemiah and the Hebrew of other books such as Kings that cannot be dated with certainty. Moreover, this difference *does* conform to the difference between the preexilic Hebrew inscriptions and the Hebrew of the texts dated to the 2nd century B.C.E. through 2nd century C.E.[170] We are justified, then, in speaking of preexilic versus postexilic Hebrew or, in more neutral terms, Hebrew A and B. On the negative side, it is impossible to make any finer distinction that would enable us to date more precisely *when* during the Persian Period the transition from Hebrew A to B took place. In other words, though the linguistic data place the composition of the books of Kings closer to preexilic epigraphic Hebrew than to the texts of the 2nd–1st centuries B.C.E., we cannot use linguistic features to determine how much earlier the texts are that were embedded in the composite work of the books of Kings. Linguistic change has proved itself to be a relatively "soft" yardstick for dating texts.

---

169. Millard, "Books," 178. Cf. also idem, "Writing."

170. Hurvitz mentions as the most prominent later texts the Dead Sea Scrolls, the fragments of Ben Sira, the letters of Bar Kokhba, and Mishnaic Hebrew ("Historical Quest," 310).

Chapter 4

The Comparative Material

> If the books of Kings were wholly, or even largely, a product of
> the Persian era and written without access to pre-exilic sources
> (as the "minimalists" claim with regard to the United monarchy
> of David and Solomon), we should expect multiple errors both
> in chronology and in the names of major public figures, such as
> kings. Herodotus, writing at the very time Davies, Thompson
> and Van Seters posit the activity of our biblical authors,
> commits such errors with obstinate regularity, despite the fact
> that he traveled extensively in the lands on which he reports. He
> relied, it would seem, primarily on oral sources. . . . Yet the
> books of Kings do in fact preserve a very large assortment of
> accurate information on international affairs.[1]
>
> Baruch Halpern

Checking for Anachronisms

Now that we have provided arguments corroborating the relationship of the Hebrew language of Kings with the languages of the comparative sources (see chap. 3 above), we proceed to a comparison of
the contents of the books of Kings with the contents of extrabiblical
material from the period that Kings purports to describe. The ultimate
goal of a comparison of this sort is, of course, to determine whether or
not the historical information reported in the books of Kings, either
wholly or partly, is in line with the information provided by contemporary, nonbiblical sources. There are both a positive and a negative
side to comparisons. Comparisons, on the one hand, allow us to check
relatively late biblical texts for anachronisms, errors, corruption, and
even possible forgeries. In other words: a comparison can *falsify* a specific piece of historical information, thus calling into question the
epistemic value of the text as a whole. Though it is very unlikely,
as we have seen in chap. 2 (see p. 107), that a canonical tradition

---

1. Halpern, "Erasing History," 418.

would have been accepted universally if it twisted or tampered with identity-related information, we need at least to be open to the possibility of an "inventive" or "creative" hand in the composition of texts, because we know from other parts of the ancient world that forgeries did exist.[2]

One well-known example of an ancient forgery is the Cruciform Monument of Maništušu (2269–2255 B.C.E., son of Sargon the Great).[3] Ostensibly written in Maništušu's own lifetime, the inscription purports to be autobiographical and asserts that Maništušu has donated such and such an amount to the Ebabbar temple in Sippar, conspicuously assuring the reader that "this is no lie; it is the truth" (XII 14–16). Scholars have long held that the text is a late forgery, but it was I. J. Gelb who established the inauthenticity of the inscription on empirical grounds by demonstrating that (a) the forms of the signs are not typical of the Old Akkadian period; (b) the monument employs some signs with syllabic values that are not otherwise attested in the Old Akkadian period; (c) there are some unusual representations of both consonantal and vocalic quality; and (d) there are linguistic forms that are not attested until after the Old Akkadian period.[4] Gelb also rejects the possibility that it is a late copy of an Old Akkadian original. Examples of other late copies simply do not match the Cruciform Monument. In contrast, they show that scribes normally attempted "to reproduce rather faithfully the Old Akkadian dialect and system of writing" when they were copying ancient inscriptions and that the copying "scribes had no interest in trying to enhance the importance of their compositions by concealing points which could betray their late and secondary origins."[5] Gelb concludes:

---

2. Cf. http://www.parthia.com/parthia_forgery.htm (accessed May 8, 2003) for examples of contemporary forgeries of ancient coins. Though the focus in Muscarella, *The Lie Became Great*, is on *modern* forgeries, Muscarella also lists a few *ancient* forgeries.

3. The monument is called "cruciform" because, viewed from above, it has the shape of a (Greek) cross. For the text, see L. W. King, "The Cruciform Monument of Manishtusu," *Revue d'Assyriologie et d'Archeologie Orientale* 9 (1912) 91–105; J. D. Prince, "An Akkadian Cruciform Monument," *AJSL* 29 (1912–13) 95–110; G. A. Barton, "The Cruciform Monument of Maništušu," in *The Royal Inscriptions of Sumer and Akkad* (New Haven: Yale University Press, 1929) 130–35; E. Sollberger, "The Cruciform Monument," *JEOL* 20 (1968) 50–70. For a treatment of its genre, see Tremper Longman III, *Fictional Akkadian Autobiography: A Generic and Comparative Study* (Winona Lake, Ind.: Eisenbrauns, 1991) 79–83.

4. Ignace J. Gelb, "The Date of the Cruciform Monument of Maništušu," *JNES* 8 (1949) 346–48.

5. Ibid., 348.

Fig. 2. Cruciform Monument of Man-ištušu. From Sippar, southern Mesopotamia (Iraq). Reproduced by permission of the British Museum. © Copyright The British Museum.

All the points listed above make it clear that the Cruciform Monument was written after the Old Akkadian period. The use of the sign DI for *di* and of SA for *sa* and the regular expression of quantity speak in favor of a date after the Ur III period. On the other side, the consistent use of the mimation calls for a date not later than the Old Babylonian period. Thus the Old Babylonian period remains the most probable date of the composition of the Cruciform Monument.[6]

In his treatment of the inscription in *Fictional Akkadian Autobiography*, Tremper Longman adds:

Of course, in the case of the Cruciform Monument the most obvious argument against its being a copy is that it was written on a stone monument; scribes used clay tablets to copy inscriptions from stone monuments. Gelb believed that the monument was composed in the Old Babylonian period because mimation was present in the text. Since the beneficiary of the donation was the Ebabbar temple, he identified that institution's priesthood as the pious forgers.[7]

On the other hand, comparisons also enable us to *verify* pieces of historical information and thereby render probable the historical reliability of a text as a whole. If, for example, we can point to information in the books of Kings on political conditions in 9th-century B.C.E. Judah

6. Ibid., 347–48. Cf. Sollberger, "The Cruciform Monument."
7. Longman, *Fictional Akkadian Autobiography*, 81–82.

that can be confirmed by contemporary evidence but that would have been impossible for an author writing in the Persian or Hellenistic Period to invent, we may deduce either that the information survived through a prolonged, reliable oral/written transmission or that a late "Persian" or "Hellenistic" author had access to reliable sources. And the more examples we are able point to, the more plausible it is that an account is also reliable in details that we are unable to check against nonbiblical, contemporary sources.

Fig. 3. Cuneiform tablet with part of the Babylonian Chronicle describing Nebuchadnezzar II's campaign in the west (605–594 B.C.E.). Neo-Babylonian, about 550–544 B.C.E. From Babylon, southern Iraq. Reproduced by permission of the British Museum. © Copyright The British Museum.

Cases

The most obvious places to search for comparative material that can either corroborate or invalidate the apparently historical information given in the books of Kings are the Assyrian Royal Inscriptions and the Babylonian Chronicle. As contemporary sources of historical information, they provide the first, best, and in many cases also the only extrabiblical attestations of a number of kings and events mentioned in the biblical account. Lester Grabbe recently argued that, while "the [biblical] text is reasonably accurate about the framework," we "can have little *prima facie* confidence in the details. . . . [S]ometimes they seem accurate, but at other times they are demonstrably misleading or wholly inaccurate and perhaps even completely invented."[8] V. Philips Long has demonstrated, however, that it is Grabbe who is "misleading" or "wholly inaccurate"

---

8. Grabbe, "Fellow Creatures," 24.

Table 4: The Books of Kings and Ancient Near Eastern Texts

The Books of Kings	*Ancient Near Eastern Texts*
Ahab	*Ahab* at the Battle of Qarqar (ca. 853 B.C.E.) ^{1}*a-ḫa-ab-bu* ^{māt}*sir-ʾi-la-a-a* 'Ahab the Israelite' Shalmaneser III (ca. 858–824 B.C.E.), Kurkh Stele III R 8 ii 92
Ahab fights the Arameans Assyrians not mentioned Ahab weak	Ahab allied with the Arameans Enemies are the Assyrians Ahab strong
Mesha	*Mesha* Inscription (ca. 830 B.C.E.) *ʾnk mšʿ* 'I am Mesha'
King of Moab and vassal of Ahab	King of Moab and vassal of Omri and Ahab Mesha rebelled during Ahab's lifetime
Jehu	*Jehu* a tributary (ca. 841 B.C.E.) ^{1}*ya-ú-a mār* ^{1}*ḫu-um-ri-i* 'Jehu the Omride' Shalmaneser III (ca. 858–824 B.C.E.), Black Obelisk
Nothing about the Assyrians	Jehu submits to Shalmaneser III
Jehoash/Joash (of Israel)	*Joash* a tributary (ca. 796 B.C.E.) ^{1}*ya-ʾa-su* ^{māt}*sa-me-ri-na-a-a* 'Joash the Samarian' Adad-nerari III (ca. 810–783 B.C.E.) Tell al-Rimah Stele
No reference to Assyrians	Pays tribute to Adad-nerari III
Menahem	*Menahem* a tributary (ca. 738 B.C.E.) ^{1}*me-ni-ḫi-im-me* ^{al}*sa-me-ri-na-a-a* 'Menahem the Samarian' Tiglath-pileser III (ca. 744–727 B.C.E.), 'Annals' III R 9.3 50
Pays tribute to Pul (Tiglath- pileser III)	Pays tribute to Tiglath-pileser III
Jehoahaz/Ahaz (of Judah)	*Ahaz* a tributary (ca. 732 B.C.E.) ^{1}*ya-ú-ḫa-zi* ^{māt}*ya-ú-da-a-a* 'Jehoahaz the Judean' Tiglath-pileser III, Nimrud Slab II R 67 rev. 11
Becomes Assyrian vassal to gain aid against Israel and Damascus	Pays tribute to Tiglath-pileser III
Pekah and Hoshea	*Pekah and Hoshea* (ca. 732 B.C.E.) [The people of Beth-Omri] *pa-qa-ḫa šarru-šú-nu is-ki-pu- ma* ^{1}*a-ú-si-ʾ* [*ana šarrūti ina muḫḫi*]-*šú-nu áš-kun* 'They overthrew their king Peqah, and I set Hoshea as king over them', Tiglath-pileser III, Nimrud Tablet III R 10.2 28, 29
Pekah overthrown by Hoshea	Pekah overthrown by internal revolt
Hoshea takes throne in internal coup	Tiglath-pileser III puts Hoshea on throne
Samaria conquered by Shalmaneser V	Samaria conquered by Sargon II according to Sargon's inscriptions
	Conquered by Shalmaneser V according to the Babylonian Chronicle ^{uru}*š-ma/ba-ra-ʾ-in iḫ-te-pi* 'he [Shalmaneser V] ravaged Samaria' Shalmaneser V (ca. 726–722 B.C.E.), Babylonian Chronicle I i 28

Table 4: The Books of Kings and Ancient Near Eastern Texts (cont.)

The Books of Kings	Ancient Near Eastern Texts
Hezekiah	Hezekiah a tributary (ca. 701 B.C.E.) ^{1}ḫa-za-qí-ya-ú ^{māt}ya-ú-da-a-a 'Hezekiah the Judean' Sennacherib (ca. 704–681 B.C.E.), 'annals' iii 37ff. and other texts
Pays tribute; Jerusalem delivered miraculously	Submits to Sennacherib and pays tribute, but despite a major siege Jerusalem does not fall
Sennacherib killed (by two sons)	Sennacherib killed (by one son)
Manasseh	Manasseh a tributary (ca. 674 B.C.E.) ^{1}me-na-si-i šar ^{al}ya-ú-di 'Manasseh king of Judah' Esarhaddon (ca. 680–669 B.C.E.) ^{1}mi-in-se-e šar ^{māt}ya-ú-di 'Manasseh king of Judah' Ashurbanipal (ca. 668–627 B.C.E.) Prism C ii 27
No reference to Assyrians (2 Kgs 21)	Required to send tribute to Esarhaddon and Ashurbanipal
Taken captive in Babylon (2 Chr 33)	
Jehoiachin and Zedekiah	Jehoiachin and Zedekiah
Jerusalem conquered and Jehoiachin taken captive by Nebuchadnezzar	Jerusalem conquered and its king taken captive by Nebuchadnezzar āla iṣ-ṣa-bat šarra ik-ta-šad 'he captured the city (and) seized (its) king' Nebuchadnezzar (ca. 605–562 B.C.E.), Babylonian Chronicle 5 rev. 12
Zedekiah	Zedekiah the puppet king šarra ša [libbi]-šu ina ĥbbi ip-te-qid 'a king of his own choice he appointed in the city' Nebuchadnezzar (ca. 605–562) Babylonian Chronicle 5 rev. 13
Jerusalem conquered by Nebuchadnezzar	No information after 594 B.C.E.

The list is based on information from J. B. Pritchard (ed.), *Ancient Near Eastern Texts Relating to the Old Testament* (3rd ed.; Princeton: Princeton University Press, 1969); A. K. Grayson, *Assyrian and Babylonian Chronicles* (Texts from Cuneiform Sources 5; New York: Augustin, 1975; repr. Winona Lake, Ind.: Eisenbrauns, 2000); Millard, "Israelite and Aramean History," 271–73; Grabbe, "Fellow Creatures," 25–26; and Long, "How Reliable," 369–70. For English translations, see the references given in Millard's list. Note that *Azariah/Uzziah* has been omitted from Grabbe's and Long's lists because chronological and historical difficulties make the identification of Azariah of Judah with the Azriyau of Ya'udi mentioned in the account of Tiglath-pileser III's 737 campaign unlikely.

in his use of comparisons and has suggested that he (and other participants in the inaugural meeting of the European Seminar on Methodology in Israel's History) may have "approached the evidence with certain preconceived notions of what would be found."[9]

Whether Long is right or not in his "suggestion," it is safe to say that the Assyrian Royal Inscriptions and the Babylonian Chronicle provide contemporary historical information that corroborates information in the books of Kings on a number of points (see table 4)—not just in terms of "framework" (i.e., the existence, sequence, and approximate chronological period of Israelite or Judean kings from the mid–9th century onward) but also in regard to the details, because the differences between the information given in the books of Kings and in the extrabiblical texts have other, more likely explanations than that they are "contradictions," as suggested by Grabbe.

Because it would be impossible within the limits of this book to review all of the relevant comparative material in relation to the books of Kings, I have chosen to discuss in detail only a few cases, which have all been used to date texts: (a) the speech of the *rab-šāqê* in 2 Kgs 18:19–25, 27–35, (b) the Hebrew rendering of Assyrian royal names, (c) the Hebrew personal *yw* and *yhw* names, and (d) the queen of Sheba incident in 1 Kgs 10:1–2. The cases related to name-rendering and literary style are a natural choice, because anachronisms are particularly likely to occur in such areas (see pp. 153ff.).[10]

#1 The Speech of the Rabshakeh in 2 Kings 18:19–25, 27–35
= Isaiah 36:4–10, 12–20[11]

2 Kgs 18–19 describes the high Assyrian officials whose mission was to persuade Hezekiah to surrender during Sennacherib's 701 B.C.E.

9. V. Philips Long, "How Reliable Are Biblical Reports? Repeating Lester Grabbe's Comparative Experiment," *VT* 52 (2002) 382–83.

10. Another interesting area of comparison would be the topographical information, because we know that a number of places were renamed during the Persian and Hellenistic periods. If an official document originated in the Persian or Hellenistic Period, it would probably use the current names instead of using preexilic names, while unofficial or indigenous documents would continue to use the old. In other words, if the Hasmoneans were responsible for writing or even "creating" the books of Kings (as argued by, e.g., Thomas Thompson, "Intellectual Matrix," 110), we would expect at least some "slips." That is, we would find place names or sites attested as being no earlier than the Hellenistic Period. This does not seem to be the case, however. A comparison of the topographical information in the books of Kings with preexilic place-names would need to consider, of course, the possibility of modernization and—not least—revision; cf. the name reversal from Leningrad to St. Petersburg in recent times.

11. See also 2 Chr 32:10–18.

campaign against Judah. "The king of Assyria sent the Tartan, the Rabsaris, and the Rabshakeh with a great army from Lachish to King Hezekiah at Jerusalem. They went up and came to Jerusalem. When they arrived, they came and stood by the conduit of the upper pool, which is on the highway to the Fuller's Field" (2 Kgs 18:17). When the text describes the delegation's encounter with Hezekiah's officials, however, it provides us with a puzzling piece of information, indicating that this particular Rabshakeh was able to speak to the Judeans in their own tongue. "Then Eliakim son of Hilkiah, and Shebnah, and Joah said to the Rabshakeh, 'Please speak to your servants in the Aramaic language, for we understand it; do not speak to us in the language of Judah within the hearing of the people who are on the wall'" (2 Kgs 18:26). But just how likely is it that this Rabshakeh (the name given to the chief cupbearer or the vizier of the Assyrian court) would be able to address Hezekiah and his officials in *yĕhûdît* 'Judahite' and have a fairly good knowledge of Judean customs, as he allegedly does according to 2 Kings 18? The majority of commentators are skeptical and suggest, instead, that the speeches of the biblical Rabshakeh must be considered a late literary creation. The implications for our study are, of course, that if this speech is either re-created on the basis of Isaiah's prophecies or entirely an invention of the author(s) or redactor(s) of the books of Kings, we should expect other pieces of information in Kings to be fictional as well, thus detracting from the books' value as a historical source.

Chaim Cohen has questioned the consensus, however, and maintains that a "historical" reading is just as likely as an understanding of the speech as a late literary creation.[12] Cohen takes as his point of departure Tadmor's "revolutionary" theory—that the major role played by the biblical Rabshakeh in the Assyrian delegation was not allotted to him by virtue of his prominent administrative status but because of his special knowledge of Judean customs and his proficiency in the Judean dialect.[13] Tadmor suggests that the Rabshakeh's skills may have been due to the fact that he was of Aramean or even Israelite ethnic origin. One of the sources Tadmor refers to is the Aramean Aḥiqar, who is known to have been the *ummānu* 'wise sage and adviser' of Esarhaddon. In order to substantiate Tadmor's theory, Cohen set out to investigate whether "the extant words of the Biblical רב־שקה are indeed not a

---

12. Chaim Cohen, "Neo-Assyrian Elements in the First Speech of the Biblical Rab-Šaqê," *Israel Oriental Studies* 9 (1979) 32–48.
13. Ibid., 32.

late literary creation based wholly on Biblical parallels, but rather contain Neo-Assyrian reflexes which demonstrate that they are based on an authentic oral or written tradition which was at least partially influenced by the actual words of the biblical רב־שׁקה."[14] By isolating all major elements in the first speech of the biblical Rabshakeh that have parallels in the Neo-Assyrian annals and organizing and presenting them together with their parallels in three categories,[15] he is able to demonstrate that many of the major elements in the first speech of the Rabshakeh have parallels in the Neo-Assyrian annals. It is therefore quite likely that a substantial part of the extant first speech was based on the actual words of the Assyrian official. Tadmor's theory concerning the possible Aramean or perhaps even Israelite ethnic origin of this particular Rabshakeh thus becomes even more credible and the assertion of the rabbis in *b. Sanh.* 60a, that רבשקה ישׂראל רמום היה 'Rabshakeh was an apostate Israelite' may now be seen to have been based on more than fanciful midrash.[16]

Peter Machinist, in an article on "Assyria and Its Image in the First Isaiah,"[17] reaches a similar conclusion. The purpose of his study is to ascertain (1) the picture of the Assyrian state presented in Isaiah and (2) the origin of that picture. Machinist analyzes six different motifs occurring in Isaiah and their parallels in the Neo-Assyrian inscriptions and concludes that they "all reveal connections between the First Isaiah and the Neo-Assyrian royal inscriptions"[18] and that "what we have found in the way of a general image and specific motifs is enough to raise the distinct possibility that Isaiah's knowledge of Assyria was gained not merely from actual experience of the Assyrians in Palestine, but from official Assyrian literature, especially of the court. . . . In other words, in Isaiah we are evidently dealing with the effects of Assyrian propaganda."[19] Machinist goes on to adduce the Rabshakeh incident as evidence of this royal propaganda and says that, "however one may evaluate the present form of these speeches, the historical reality behind the tactic they represent is confirmed by the report of similar embassies in Assyrian sources, such as that during Tiglath-

---

14. Ibid., 34.

15. Cohen's 3 categories are: (1) the setting, (2) specific reflexes of Neo-Assyrian style, and (3) general parallels to the argumentation of the biblical Rabshakeh.

16. Chaim Cohen, "Neo-Assyrian Elements," 47.

17. Peter Machinist, "Assyria and Its Image in the First Isaiah," *JAOS* 103 (1983) 729.

18. Ibid., 728.

19. Ibid., 729.

pileser III's siege of Babylon in 729 B.C.E."[20] Ziony Zevit, in a review of Van Seters's *In Search of History,* adopts the same conclusion:

> The speech of the Assyrian officer to the men on the walls of Jerusalem, reported in 2 Kgs 18 and Isa 36, contains Neo-Assyrian elements. Their presence indicates that the speech cannot be the late creation of someone living in a period when the Assyrian dialect could not have laced Hebrew, but rather that it was recorded in 701 B.C.E. by a scribe and eventually made its way into a document that came into the hands of the Deuteronomistic historian.[21]

This neither proves, as implied by Zevit, that 2 Kings 18–19 was composed in or shortly after 701 B.C.E. nor that it reports what was actually said. It does demonstrate, however, that the report in 2 Kings 18 is in accordance with Neo-Assyrian language and customs and that the *source* of 2 Kings 18—if not 2 Kings 18 itself—was recorded contemporaneous with or shortly after the event it describes. There is no trace of anachronisms.

#2 *Hebrew Renderings of Assyrian Royal Names*

One important aspect of modern study of Aramaic is that it has shed light on Akkadian phonetics. In contrast to cuneiform texts, which were written in accordance with scribal convention and therefore exhibit historical spelling rather than reflecting current pronunciation, Aramaic transcriptions of Akkadian names probably reflect what the scribes *heard*.[22] Analyzing transcription practices provides us, therefore, with valuable insight into Akkadian phonetics and enables us also to describe the differences in phonology between the dialects of Assyria and Babylonia. One of the interesting implications for our study is that, because Hebrew transcriptions of Assyrian names in the books of Kings reveal the Akkadian forms underlying them, our knowledge of the Assyrian and Babylonian dialects enables us to determine whether the Hebrew transcriptions were transcribed from the original Neo-Assyrian forms or from later Babylonian or Aramaic renderings. In an article published in 1976, Alan Millard set out to investigate "how well or ill the handful of Assyrian royal names relevant to its narrative

---

20. Ibid., 729.

21. Ziony Zevit, "Clio, I Presume," *BASOR* 260 (1985) 76.

22. The most complete study of Aramaic renderings of Assyrian words is Frederick Mario Fales, *Aramaic Epigraphs on Clay Tablets of the Neo-Assyrian Period* (Studi Semitici n.s. 2; Rome: Università degli studi "La Sapienza," 1986).

have been preserved in the Hebrew text of the Old Testament."[23] Having discussed the Hebrew renderings of Assyrian royal names in chronological order,[24] Millard concludes that "this examination has shown how closely the Hebrew writings of Assyrian royal names conform to their contemporary appearance in Assyria and Babylonia in conformity with ancient orthographic custom. Tiglath-pileser, Sargon, and Esarhaddon mirror distinctively Assyrian forms, and so does Shalmaneser, whatever our doubt over the first sibilant."[25] Millard draws a number of conclusions from these data:

> The distinctively Assyrian forms may be assumed to derive from Hebrew sources set down in writing at or near the times of the various episodes, a conclusion reached on other grounds by many commentators who assign the passages in Kings containing them to some official annalistic compilation. Nevertheless, we may remark upon their remaining unchanged by any compiler or editor of Kings or Isaiah during the exile in Babylonia, or later, when the Assyrian forms had become obsolete. For Sennacherib and Sharezer we might posit a Babylonian source of information, if the sibilants cannot be accommodated to Assyrian usage.[26]

In his overall conclusion, Millard states:

> The remarkably accurate preservation of these Assyrian names for a couple of centuries in the case of the Ahiqar papyrus and for far longer in the case of the Hebrew texts, is striking testimony to the care of the ancient Semitic scribe faced with incomprehensible forms. That care is

---

23. A. R. Millard, "Assyrian Royal Names in Biblical Hebrew," *JSS* 21 (1976) 1–14. One of the things Millard's article argues is that Montgomery and Gehman's conclusions in their commentary are in error (see p. 12 for references).

24. (1) Tiglath-pileser III, Akkadian *Tukultī-apil-ešarra* 'my help is the son of Esharra', occurs in 2 Kgs 15:29 and 16:10 as תגלת פלאסר, in 1 Chr 5:6 and 2 Chr 28:20 as תגלת פלנאסר, in 2 Kgs 16:7 as תגלת פלסר, and in 1 Chr 5:26 as תגלת פלנסר. Tiglath-pileser III also appears under the name פול *Pūl* in 2 Kgs 15:19 and 1 Chr 5:26. (2) Shalmaneser V, Akkadian *Šulmānu-ašarēd* 'Shulaman is preeminent', is attested in 2 Kgs 17:3 and 18:9 as שלמנאסר. (3) Sargon II, Akkadian *Šarru-kēn* 'the king is legitimate', occurs in Isa 20:1 as סרגן. (4) Sennacherib, Akkadian *Sîn-aḫḫē-erība* 'Sin has supplied brothers', appears a dozen times in the Hebrew Bible. All passages have the transcription סנחריב except 2 Kgs 19:20, which has סנחרב. (5) Esarhaddon, Akkadian *Aššur-aḫ-iddin* 'Ashur has given a brother', is attested in 2 Kgs 19:37, Isa 37:38, and Ezra 4:2 as אסר־חדן. (6) The names of the two sons who according to 2 Kgs 19:37 and Isa 37:38 murdered Sennacherib are given as אדרמלך and שׁראצר. (7) The last transcribed Assyrian name is Asnapper, אסנפר, in Ezra 4:10. The list can be found in Millard, "Assyrian Royal Names in Biblical Hebrew," 7–11.

25. Ibid., 12.

26. Ibid., 12–13.

highlighted when the wide range of variation in the Greek manuscripts of the Septuagint and the various Hellenistic historians is set out for comparison. There, however, aspects of Greek orthography, phonetics, and scribal habits are involved that fall beyond the present essay. Suffice it to say they differed from their Semitic counterparts in many ways.[27]

The important observation, as far as our study is concerned, is that it is highly unlikely that a Persian- or Hellenistic-era writer could have rendered these names correctly, that is, in accordance with their contemporary Assyrian forms, at a time when these Assyrian forms had become obsolete. Instead of pure chance, we should assume either that the texts in which they occur were written shortly after the events they describe or that a later author had access to reliable (i.e., orthographically correct) information on these names.

#3 The Hebrew Personal *yw* and *yhw* Names

Stig Norin has suggested that Hebrew personal names beginning with the divine name in the longer abbreviated form *yhw* are a sign of the Deuteronomistic hand and that texts in which this "hand" occurs, consequently, should be dated later than texts in which names beginning with the shorter variant form, *yw*, occurs.[28] Norin bases his argument on the observation that there is no evidence of the longer form in the earlier prophetic books, whereas it appears frequently in Jeremiah and the historical writings. Norin also claims that the attestation of these names in the nonbiblical material supports his case.[29]

> The analysis demonstrates that the form Jo- must be the older one. The form Jeho- was apparently used by the Deuteronomist to add a more sacred ring to certain names. The more well-known figures are the ones who have these Jeho- names. The extrabiblical material shows that the form Jo- prevails in the preexilic period, while the longer form dominates the postexilic period. This can be seen in the names Jo'aš, Joram, and Jonathan. These names begin in the Deuteronomistic History partly with Jo-, partly with Jeho-, and it turns out that texts with the

---

27. Ibid., 14. Cf. idem, "Judith, Tobit, Ahiqar and History," in *New Heaven and New Earth: Prophecy and the Millenium* (ed. P. J. Harland and C. T. R. Hayward; Leiden: Brill, 1999) 195–203.

28. Stig Norin, "*Jô*-Namen und *Jehô*-Namen," *VT* 29 (1979) 87–97. See also his update in Stig Norin, "Onomastik zwischen Linguistik und Geschichte," in *International Organization for the Study of the Old Testament: Congress Volume, Oslo 1998* (ed. André Lemaire and M. Sæbø; Leiden: Brill, 2000) 161–78.

29. Ibid., 93.

shorter form must be the earlier ones, while the forms with Jeho- appear to be the more conventional ones.[30]

If Norin is right, we would be able to date texts in which the *yw* names occur to the period before the so-called Deuteronomistic History allegedly was written, that is, at the time of Josiah in the 7th century B.C.E. Norin's thesis is based on two premises: (a) the assumption of a Deuteronomistic circle responsible for the writing of the so-called Deuteronomistic History sometime in the 7th century B.C.E., and (b) the assumption that the longer *yhw* forms are later than the shorter *yw* forms. Instead of venturing into a long and tiresome discussion of these premises, we will take a "shortcut" and cite a short study by Alan Millard, who has pointed out that "unfortunately, the external control which Norin has drawn upon does not support his case when examined carefully." [31] Providing an updated list of extrabiblical attestations of *yhw* and *yw* names, Millard refers to a seal impression of *yhwzrḥ*, son of *ḥlqyhw*, an officer (*ʿbd*) of Hezekiah, and comments:

> The identity of the father's name with that of the minister of Hezekiah, king of Judah (2 Kings xviii 18; Is. xxxvi 3) is surely too great to allow anyone to argue that this impression was not made by a seal in use in the time of Hezekiah the king. This impression alone can be held sufficient to establish the currency of the *yhw*-element well before Josiah's reform and the rise of any "Deuteronomist," but it does not stand alone. Among the ostraca from Arad, two bearing the names *yhwʾb* and *yhwʿz* lay in a stratum assigned by the excavator, the late Y. Aharoni, to the late 8th century B.C.E. These examples in particular, and all the others in our list, ought to satisfy any doubt that the *yhw*-names were popular in Judah prior to the Exile. To challenge their testimony would necessitate a total re-evaluation of Hebrew epigraphy, including the date of the Siloam Tunnel inscription, the Silwan tomb notices, the ostraca from Arad and Lachish, and the seals attributed to the pre-exilic period, for paleography has traced lines of development from one point to the next. Re-dating the ostraca would involve re-examination of the stratigraphy and the pottery sequences at Arad and Lachish, and at all the sites with which archaeological correlations are made. To place all the seals in our lists after the reform of Josiah or in the exilic and post-exilic periods seems to be quite impossible.[32]

---

30. Ibid., 97 [my translation].

31. A. R. Millard, "*YW* and *YHW* Names," *VT* 30 (1980) 208–12.

32. Ibid., 211. See also the "update" (in idem, "The Corpus of West Semitic Stamp Seals: Review Article," *IEJ* 51 [2001] 85), where Millard states that "The Hebrew divine name occurs as a name element as *yw*, *yh* and *yhw*. (It is found once in its full form on a seal, that of *mqnyw ʿbd yhwh*, now in Harvard, No. 27.) The initial position is never taken

Thus, without discussing the premises as such, we may nevertheless conclude that the occurrence of *yw* and *yhw* theophoric names unfortunately turned out to be of no use for dating the texts in which they are found. This does not, of course, disprove the Deuteronomistic hypothesis, nor does it say anything in general about the chronological order of shorter and longer linguistic forms. But it does show us that the presence of *yhw* names does not point to a Deuteronomistic hand, that both forms (*yw* and *yhw*) seem to exist side by side in the early extrabiblical material, and that the existence of the shorter form in certain texts cannot be taken as evidence of an "untouched" early text embedded in the extant text of the books of Kings.

#4 *King Solomon and the Queen of Sheba*

1 Kgs 10:1–2 reports that, "when the queen of Sheba heard about the fame of Solomon and his relation to the name of the LORD, she came to test him with hard questions. Arriving at Jerusalem with a very great caravan—with camels carrying spices, large quantities of gold, and precious stones—she came to Solomon and talked with him about all that she had on her mind."[33]

Legends about the queen of Sheba are common throughout Arabia, Persia, Ethiopia, and Israel. The legend of King Solomon, the queen of Sheba, named Makeda,[34] and their son Menelik is of supreme importance in the Ethiopian national consciousness, and it is recorded in the *Kebra Nagast* (*The Glory of Kings*), the Ethiopian national epic.[35] The

---

by *yh* and it is the least common form, but there are sufficient cases to establish its existence beyond doubt, that is, there is no confusion with names ending with *yhw*, although the same name may be written with either (e.g. *hwdyh, hwdyhw, ʾzryh, ʿzryhw*). As the first or last element, *yw* stands in some twenty-five names. While Israelite seals regularly have this form, as in *zkryw* on jars from Tel Dan and Bethsaida (No. 669) and *ʿmdyw* from Tel Dan (No. 692), it is by no means restricted to the northern kingdom, as often supposed, for we may instance *ʿzyw*, doubtless Uzziah king of Judah (Nos. 3, 4) and *ywkn* on jar handles from Tell Beit Mirsim, Beth Shemesh and Ramat Raḥel (No. 663) and most remarkably *ywbnh, yhwbnh* and *ybnh*, son of *mnhm*, Nos. 676–678. The difference may be chronological rather than regional, *yw* being used in the 8th century." This suggests, of course, that *yw* was older, 8th century B.C.E., with *yhw* overlapping and continuing into later times; the implication for Norin's "Deuteronomistic History" is, consequently, that it stems from the 8th century B.C.E.!

33. See the parallel account in 2 Chr 9:1–12. Other biblical references to the queen of Sheba are Ps 72:15 and, in the New Testament, Matt 12:42 and Luke 11:31.

34. Also Magda, Maqda, and Makera, meaning 'Greatness'.

35. The *Kebra Nagast* probably was composed between the 6th and 9th centuries C.E. It received definitive form in the 14th century, during the reign of King Amda Seyon (1314–44 C.E.); served as the "charter legend" for Yekuno Amlak's foundation of the new

legend is based on the biblical accounts of the visit of the queen of Sheba to King Solomon, as found in 1 Kgs 10:1–13 and 2 Chr 9:1–12. In addition, Arabian folklore and the Qurʾān present fanciful stories of the queen of Sheba, who is called Bilqus or Balkis. The stories involve magic carpets, talking birds, and teleportation, and the miraculous transfer of Balkis's throne in Sheba to Solomon's palace. One notable tale involves the hoopoe bird, who tells Solomon about Balkis and delivers a demand from him to her: unless she visits him, he will annihilate her people. In one story, her foot which is shaped like an ass's foot, is transformed into a human foot when she steps on Solomon's glass floor; in another story, Solomon invents a depilatory to remove goat hair from her legs. Several Jewish legends that developed in postbiblical times also present dubious accounts of the queen and Solomon.[36]

Solomonic Dynasty in 1270 C.E., claiming descent of the new rulers from the ancient rulers of Axum and the king of Israel; cf. Steven Kaplan, *The Beta Israel (Falasha) in Ethiopia: From Earliest Times to the Twentieth Century* (New York: New York University Press, 1992) 22–23. On its origin and redaction, see also Basil Lourié, "From Jerusalem to Aksum through the Temple of Solomon: Archaic Traditions Related to the Ark of Covenant and Sion in the Kebra Nagast and Their Translation through Constantinople," *Xristianskij Vostok* 2/8 (2000) [publ. 2001] 137–207 (in Russian, with a detailed English summary); Irfan Shahid, "The Martyrs of Najran: New Documents," *Subsidia Hagiographica* 49 (1971). For a translation of the *Kebra Nagast*, the standard works in English are Edward Ullendorf, *The Ethiopians: An Introduction to Country and People* (London: Oxford University Press, 1973); idem, *Ethiopia and the Bible* (The Schweich Lectures; London: Oxford University Press, 1968). See also E. A. W. Budge, *The Queen of Sheba and Her Only Son Menylek: Being the History of the Departure of God and His Ark of the Covenant from Jerusalem to Ethiopia, and the Establishment of the Religion of the Hebrews and the Solomonic Line of Kings in That Country* (London: Medici Society, 1922), which is a translation from the Coptic version of the 12th century C.E. According to the *Kebra Negast*, the queen of Sheba, known as Makeda, was born in 1020 B.C.E. in Ophir and educated in Ethiopia. Her mother was Queen Ismenie; her father, chief minister to Za Sebado, succeeded him as king. When her father died in 1005 B.C.E., Makeda became queen at the age of fifteen. Contradictory legends refer to her as ruling for forty years or reigning as a virgin queen for six years. In most accounts, she never married. The *Kebra Negast* also has it that she traveled from Aksum to visit King Solomon in Jerusalem. During her stay, Solomon not only dazzled her with his wisdom but also tricked her by a clever ruse into having sexual relations with him. The queen conceived a son, whom she bore upon her return to Aksum. When he reached maturity, this son, Menelik, journeyed to Jerusalem to meet his father. At the completion of Menelik's visit, Solomon commanded that the firstborn sons of the priests and elders of Israel accompany him to Aksum. Before setting out, however, Menelik and his companions, led by Azariah, the son of the high priest, stole the Ark of the Covenant from the Temple. Thus, the glory of Zion passed from Jerusalem and the children of Israel to the new Zion, Aksum, and the new Israel, the Ethiopian people.

36. Cf. Louis Ginzberg and Henrietta Szold, *The Legends of the Jews* (Philadelphia: Jewish Publication Society of America, 1913) 4.144.

Josephus referred to her as Nikaulis, queen of Ethiopia and Egypt (*Ant.* 8.6.5).[37]

Because of the fanciful and questionable character of many of these stories, it was common among 19th- and early-20th-century biblical commentators to reject the historicity of the biblical account and assert that the biblical version of the tradition was incorporated into the books of Kings for literary reasons, to praise the wisdom and piety of the great King Solomon and to further the religious, political, or ideological purposes of the supposedly Deuteronomistic author(s) or redactor(s).[38] The absence of contemporary textual and archaeological evidence for an incident of this kind only strengthened the case. The only attested Arabic queens outside the Hebrew Bible are those of North-Arabian tribes (Arabia and Qedar), whose names appear in Assyrian records.[39] Because the same records mention that tribute, such as spices, gold dust, and precious stones, was received from these queens, it has been suggested that the biblical narrator had access to confused traditions about Arab queens who controlled the kinds of commodities attributed to the queen of Sheba.

One of the implications of this discussion is, of course, that if the author(s) or redactor(s) of the books of Kings chose to include a legendary account in one case, he or they might well have done it in other cases as well. This in turn would force us to be much more cautious before we take at face value other information that is presented as historical. On the other hand, if we could substantiate that a queen of

---

37. Josephus, *Jewish Antiquities* (trans. H. St. J. Thackeray; Loeb Classical Library 281; Cambridge: Harvard University Press, 1998) 300–301. For an informative article on the queen of Sheba traditions, see Tracy Marks, "Makedah," at http://www.windweaver.com/sheba/Shebahome.htm (accessed May 9, 2003).

38. See, for example, I. Benzinger, *Die Bücher der Könige* (Kurzer Hand-Commentar zum Alten Testament; Freiburg i.B.: Mohr, 1899) 71: "Der legendarische Charakter der Erzählung ist augenfällig"; but also E. Meyer, *Geschichte des Altertums* (2 vols.; 2nd ed.; Stuttgart: Cotta'sche, 1928–31) 2.268; and A. T. Olmstead, *History of Palestine and Syria* (New York: Scribner, 1931) 341.

39. K. A. Kitchen (*Documentation for Ancient Arabia, Part 1* [World of Ancient Arabia Series; Liverpool: Liverpool University Press, 1994] 167, 237) gives the following references and dates: Queen Zabibe of Arabia and Qedar, ca. 750–735 B.C.E., mentioned in Annals of Tiglath-pileser III (section commonly attributed to 738 B.C.E.); Queen Samsi of Arabia, ca. 735–710 B.C.E., mentioned in Annals of Tiglath-pileser III (section commonly attributed to 733 B.C.E.); Queen Iatiʾe of Arabia, ca. 710–695 B.C.E., mentioned in Annals of Sennacherib (section from 703 B.C.E.); and Queen Teʾelkhunu of Arabia, ca. 690–676 B.C.E., mentioned in Annals of Sennacherib (691 B.C.E.). See also M. C. A. MacDonald, "North Arabia in the First Millennium BCE," in *Civilizations of the Ancient Near East* (ed. Jack M. Sasson; New York: Scribner, 1995) 1355–69.

Sheba existed at that time and that trade relations did exist between the kingdom of Saba and Israel as early as the 10th century B.C.E., the case for reading not only 1 Kings 10 but also the wider context as reliable history-writing would be strengthened. The question is, therefore: does 1 Kings 10 include a historically verifiable—and therefore reliable—memory of South-Arabian trade during the 10th century B.C.E., or is it a conflation of the above-mentioned information on other Arabian queens from Assyrian annals with legendary traditions about the queen of Sheba?

As new evidence has come to light, it has become more and more untenable to claim that the biblical account of the queen of Sheba is legendary. First of all, though many legends connect the queen of Sheba with ancient Ethiopia, we now know that it is much more likely that she resided in the country of Saba, in southwest Arabia on the eastern tip of the Red Sea, present-day Yemen. We are indebted to Kenneth Kitchen for having provided the scholarly community with the first-ever comprehensive presentation and discussion of archaeological and inscriptional material related to ancient western Arabia, and his monographs clearly demonstrate that the ancient kingdom of Saba was well established already by the 10th century, that the Sabeans had their own script, and that Sabean merchants engaged in a lucrative caravan trade.[40] It is worth quoting parts of two paragraphs. Discussing the archaeological material from Marib and a number of other ancient Sabean sites (especially their irrigation techniques and hydraulic history), he concludes that "the continuity of irrigational techniques and engineering does presuppose in some measure a continuity of population from at least the mid–2nd-millennium B.C.E. and probably much earlier. The Sabeans were not invented in 1000 B.C., nor their language nor their basic culture."[41] And, dismissing the idea of a separate Sabean state in northwestern Arabia because of lack of evidence, he concludes that "both the Sheba (and its queen) of the biblical tradition and the Sabeans of the Assyrian texts came from Saba proper in SW Arabia, and not from some imaginary second Saba in NW Arabia. The gold and incense associated with Saba(eans) in

---

40. Kitchen, *Documentation for Ancient Arabia, Part 1*; idem, *Documentation for Ancient Arabia, Part 2* (The World of Ancient Arabia Series; Liverpool: Liverpool University Press, 1999); idem, "Sheba and Arabia," in *The Age of Solomon: Scholarship at the Turn of the Millennium* (ed. Lowell K. Handy; Leiden: Brill, 1997) 127–53.

41. Kitchen, *Documentation for Ancient Arabia, Part 1*, 131. Cf. also p. 136 on the Sabean script.

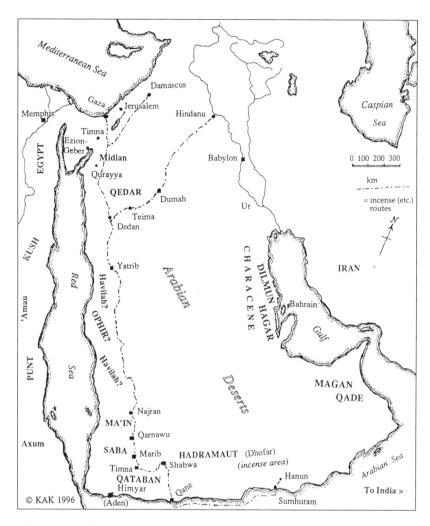

Fig. 4. Map of Ancient Arabia. Courtesy of Kenneth L. Kitchen.

both biblical and Assyrian sources also reflects the trade from south to
north along the so-called 'incense route,' from Saba to the Levant, and
across (via Dumah) to Mesopotamia."[42] This has also been noted by
Liverani, who, in an article on "Early Caravan Trade between South-
Arabia and Mesopotamia," points to the publication of new texts from

42. Ibid., 119.

the 8th century B.C.E.[43] containing the earliest information on South-Arabian trade caravans in Mesopotamia found to that time.[44] The texts were issued by a king of Suhu (the middle Euphrates Valley, downstream from the present Syria–Iraq border) and describe how a caravan with at least 200 camels coming from Sheba was plundered by Suhu troops:

> People from Teima' (^{LÚ}te-ma-'a-a-a) and Sheba (^{LÚ}ša-ba-'a-a-a), whose abode is far-away, whose messenger did not come to my presence, and who did not advance up to my presence: a caravan of theirs approached to the Martu-well and the Halatum-well, and went (even) beyond, and entered the city of Hindanu. I got the news at noon in Kar-Apladad, I harnessed my yoke, in the night I crossed over the river, and on the next day before noon I reached Azlanu. Three days I remained in Azlanu, and on the 3rd day they arrived. 100 of them I took alive, and 200 of their dromedaries with their loads: purple-wool, 'road'-wool, iron, and alabaster, all of their consignments I took away. A great booty I plundered, and I took it inside Suhu.[45]

Liverani notes that, while Teima is known to have played an important role as a junction in the caravan network between Yemen and Mesopotamia, the texts throw additional light on the role of the independent kingdom of Hindanu (mentioned in the text). The inscriptions of Ashurnasirpal II (883–859 B.C.E.) and his predecessor, Tukulti-Ninurta II (890–884 B.C.E.), inform us that they both collected tribute in the area and that, since the beginning of the 9th century B.C.E., Hindanu was the outlet of the main caravan road from Arabia to Mesopotamia. Liverani concludes, therefore, that "the analysis of tributes is effective in pushing back the information provided by the Suhu 'Annals' from ca. 750 to ca. 890 B.C.E.—by far the oldest attestation of trade relations between Yemen and Mesopotamia."[46] Liverani then tries to establish the beginning of Hindanu's function as a junction in the caravan network. Because Hindanu was neither independent (it was included in the kingdom of Suhu) nor a dispenser of

---

43. That is, "new" in 1992.

44. Mario Liverani, "Early Caravan Trade between South-Arabia and Mesopotamia," *Yemen* 1 (1992) 111–15.

45. A. Cavigneaux and B. K. Ismail, "Die Statthalter von Suhu und Mari Im 8. Jh. v. Chr," *Baghdader Mitteilungen* 21 (1990) 321–456. Here quoted from Liverani, "Early Caravan Trade," 111–12. See now William W. Hallo and K. Lawson Younger, Jr. (eds.), *The Context of Scripture, Vol. II: Monumental Inscriptions from the Biblical World* (Leiden: Brill, 1997) 281–82.

46. Liverani, "Early Caravan Trade," 112.

exotic goods at the time of Tiglath-pileser I (1114–1076 B.C.E.), Liverani concludes that

> the beginning of its function as the outlet of the caravan road, and its subsequent political fortune, is to be dated at some point in between 1075 and 890. It could hardly be pure chance, and it is worth recalling the current dates for Solomon's reign (and therefore for the queen of Sheba affair, true and proper "foundation legend" for the South-Arabic trade in the north): ca. 960–920! . . . A starting phase of the South-Arabian trade in the second half of the 10th century would perfectly agree both with the Old Testament traditions and with the Assyrian royal inscriptions— and would also fit in the technological development of the Arabian mastery of the "desert" environment and its caravan network, as it is presently reconstructed. Needless to say, a beginning of the South-Arabian trade in the (late-) 10th century, implies the existence of the Yemeni caravan cities (at least in an embryonic form) at the same time and probably even before. This is also in accordance with the results of the most recent archaeological and epigraphical research in Yemen.[47]

It is highly likely, therefore, that by 1000 B.C.E. camel caravans occasionally traveled the 1,400 miles up the "Incense Road" and along the Red Sea to Israel, bringing with them the highly prized goods of Saba. To conclude this small survey on possible extrabiblical evidence for the queen of Sheba incident, the comments and questions of the economist Morris Silver seem pertinent: "How did the much later writers of the material in Kings know that this trade should be placed back in the 10th century? Was it just a lucky stab or a lucky fake? After second thoughts it must, it seems to me, be granted that the biblical authors might well have had access to much earlier materials concerning important matters. (This is not to deny that they shaped this material to further certain ideological interests)."[48] And speaking of trade and economy, Silver adds another interesting comment:

> The Bible tells us that Solomon was reaping the riches of the caravan trade. Then something apparently went wrong. According to 1 Kgs 11.14–25, Aram and Edom began causing problems for Solomon. The biggest problem would have been, of course, the wresting of control over the King's Highway from Solomon. It is at this point in the story that the Israelites begin complaining about the burden of taxation (forced labor) and Rehoboam even strives to raise taxes (1 Kgs 12). If the Israelite state, deprived of the transit taxes, could no longer pay for the services it desired it is not surprising that it would seek to raise

---

47. Ibid., 113–14.
48. Discussion on the ANE mailing list. This e-mail and other messages in the discussion are archived at http://www.oi.uchicago.edu/OI/ANE/ANE-DIGEST/2000/.

taxes. I am not saying that this is what must have happened, only that it seems to have a logic.[49]

In sum, it is highly likely that the queen of Sheba's visit to Solomon's court served diplomatic purposes or purposes other than those explicitly mentioned in the biblical text, but the account, in addition, is perfectly in line with what we know from other sources about the Sabean kingdom and the beginning of South-Arabian trade. The information given in the wider context also makes perfect sense in a 10th-century setting.

An important caveat in relation to this discussion regarding trade must be kept in mind, however, before we jump to a conclusion: just because the picture in 1 Kings 10 is consistent with what we know from other sources about the trade relations of the kingdom of Saba in the 10th century does not mean that it actually took place. We need to ask when this trade started and when it ceased. If such trade relations continued to exist, say, until the period after the *mukarrib*s, commencing with King Yadi'ubil Bayyin, ca. 350–335 B.C.E.,[50] an author in the Persian or even the Hellenistic Period would have been able to extrapolate what took place in the 10th century B.C.E., even if he had no recollection of what happened that long ago. The possibility that we are dealing with reliable information would still exist, but the argument would be weakened.[51]

Other Examples

As mentioned above, it is impossible to review all of the comparative material relevant to the books of Kings. Suffice it to mention a

---

49. Morris Silver, March 23, 2000, on the ANE list. See also his *Prophets and Markets: The Political Economy of Ancient Israel* (Social Dimensions of Economics; Boston: Kluwer-Nijhoff, 1983) especially pp. 49 and 61–62.

50. Kitchen, *Documentation for Ancient Arabia, Part 1*, 200.

51. This is also the case with Hurowitz's discussion on similarities between the account of Solomon's temple building and other ancient Near Eastern building accounts (*I Have Built You an Exalted House*). On resemblances between Solomon's temple and other ancient Near Eastern temples, see also Volkmar Fritz, "Temple Architecture: What Can Archaeology Tell Us about Solomon's Temple?" in *Essential Papers on Israel and the Ancient Near East* (ed. Frederic Greenspahn; New York: New York University Press, 1991) 116–28; A. R. Millard, "The Doorways of Solomon's Temple," in *Eretz-Israel 20* (Yigael Yadin Volume; Jerusalem: Israel Exploration Society, 1989) 135*–39*; K. A. Kitchen, "Two Notes on the Subsidiary Rooms of Solomon's Temple?," in *Eretz-Israel* (Yigael Yadin Volume; Jerusalem: Israel Exploration Society, 1989) 107*–12*; John Monson, "The New 'Ain Dara Temple: Closest Solomonic Parallel," *BAR* 26/3 (2000) 20–35, 67. See also Halpern's discussion on the motif of the acquisition of horses and chariot as a characteristic of Middle Assyrian historiography: Baruch Halpern, *The First Historians: The Hebrew Bible and History* (San Francisco: Harper & Row, 1988) 49–51.

number of cases brought to our attention by Joe Baker, all of which seem to support the overall picture reached by the analysis of the above-mentioned examples:

1. We know from Assyrian records (long since buried by Persian or Hellenistic times) that Jehu of Israel and Hazael of Damascus were contemporaries (both attested in 841 B.C.E.). How did the Biblical writers know this—a flash in the pan?
2. We know from Assyrian records that Tiglath-pileser took Damascus in 732 B.C.E. and that around this time [Jeho]ahaz of Judah paid tribute. How did the Biblical writers know that this particular Assyrian king was responsible for taking Damascus? More importantly these same writers place the reign of Ahaz right at this time, that is between 739 and 724 B.C.E. (16+29+55+ 2+31+11 years before 597—okay a slight adjustment is made due to year counting). Is this a one in a million chance?
3. The Babylonian Chronicle records that in the middle of 609 B.C.E. a combined Assyrian and Egyptian army crossed the Euphrates. This is the only time the Chronicle mentions such a joint campaign. In this very year, that is, at least 11 years (or nearly 12 years) and 6 months before Mar 597 the Biblical writers also record that a combined Assyrian and Egyptian army operated along the Euphrates (2 Kgs. 23:29). How did they know this? You just gotta buy a lottery ticket on those odds.[52]

The Best Fit

As mentioned earlier, limited space has permitted us to review only a few representative cases. Bearing in mind the limitations, we can now return to the question we set out to answer at the beginning of this chapter: Is the historical information given in the books of Kings (either wholly or partly) in line with the information provided by the

---

52. E-mail posted on the ANE mailing list, March 27, 2000, on the subject "Does the Bible Recall the 10th Century?" The e-mail is archived at http://www-oi.uchicago.edu/ OI/ANE/ANE-DIGEST/2000/v2000.n089. The same point is made by A. Malamat ("The Aramaeans," in *Peoples of Old Testament Times* [ed. D. J. Wiseman; Oxford: Clarendon, 1973] 145), who mentions that the developments under Tiglath-pileser III and Hazael "are well reflected in the Elisha cycle." See also Nadav Naʾaman, "Sources and Composition in the History of David," in *The Origins of the Ancient Israelite States* (ed. V. Fritz and P. R. Davies; Sheffield: Sheffield Academic Press, 1996) 170–86; "Royal Inscriptions and the Histories of Joash and Ahaz, Kings of Judah," *VT* 48 (1998) 333–49; "The Contribution of Royal Inscriptions for a Re-Evaluation of the Book of Kings as a Historical Source," *JSOT* 82 (1999) 3–17.

contemporary extrabiblical sources? In other words: Where do the books of Kings "fit in," heuristically speaking? Where should we place them on the epistemic continuum? In order to answer the questions and thus conclude our analysis, we will take a brief detour to a parallel study by Alan Millard on the books of Judith and Tobit.

In Millard's study of the epistemic value of the books of Judith and Tobit, he has demonstrated that it was the availability of sources that affected the accuracy (or inaccuracy) of the information reported in these books. The author of Judith apparently confused names and events from the Assyrian, Babylonian, and Persian periods,[53] thereby painting a historically misleading picture and creating an epistemically unreliable "historiography." Though other reasons for this historical confusion have been suggested, Millard concludes that "neither supposition explains or excuses the chronological muddle. Either the author purposely constructed a setting, with the Babylonian king victorious far away to the east at the time when Jewish historians told of his attack on Jerusalem which he expected his audience, aware of their national history, would understand to be artificial, or he had little knowledge and did not anticipate others to be better educated."[54]

In contrast, the book of Tobit, which also places its story in an earlier setting, "does display a good level of historical accuracy and has the Assyrian kings in their correct sequence: Shalmaneser V, [Sargon,] Sennacherib, Esarhaddon."[55] The only error or mistake occurs in the last verse, where Tobit names the Median king who captured Nineveh in alliance with the Babylonians as Assuerus instead of the correct king, Cyaxares (ca. 623–584 B.C.E.). Millard demonstrates, furthermore, that both the spelling and the sequence of names (including the omission of Sargon) can be readily explained if "the greater part of the framework of the story is drawn from the biblical text of Kings and

---

53. The events of the book are set at a time when the Israelites "had just returned from captivity" (Jdt 4:3), and Millard notes the following points of historical confusion: "1. Nebuchadnezzar did not rule from Nineveh. . . . 2. There was no king of Media named Arphaxad. . . . 3. The general Holofernes bears a name of Old Persian type and so does his steward Bagoas, but all the known names of Nebuchadnezzar's officials are Babylonian. . . . 4. Nebuchadnezzar's twelfth year was 593–92 B.C.E., his seventeenth 588–587. Far from Israelites recently returning to Jerusalem and rebuilding the Temple, their earlier deportations to Babylon had not long taken place in 593; in 587–86, Nebuchadnezzar's eighteenth year, the final attack on Jerusalem was under way, bringing the destruction of the city and the Temple and another deportation" ("Judith, Tobit, Ahiqar and History," 195–96).

54. Ibid., 196–97.

55. Ibid., 198.

from the Aramaic narrative of Ahiqar, which, likewise, have the Assyrian kings correctly."[56] Millard finds support for this view in the fact that the book of Tobit is clearly distinguishable from other works, which, like Judith, are characterized by the same historical confusion. Broadening the analysis, Millard therefore suggests that Hellenistic texts that purport to recount ancient Near Eastern history be divided into two categories:

> The books of Judith and Tobit exemplify different opportunities for ancient writers about past times. Those in the first category had received or learnt a little which they altered and supplemented to suit their purposes, or else they deliberately selected from more extensive information the names and events they thought most appropriate, regardless of precision. Beside Judith, Ctesias and Eupolemus fall into this category. Josephus' apparent compression of the 5th and 4th centuries can be attributed to lack of clear sources. He may be put in the second category, classed with those authors who were able to refer to fuller records and tried to incorporate them into their compositions without altering their tenor. Berossus is the prime example, with the author of Tobit standing nearby, his Median Assuerus being the best he could do to supply a missing name.[57]

This conclusion finds support in an observation made by Heleen Sancisi-Weerdenburg in her discussion of the Behistun Inscription.[58] The inscription, presumably set up by Darius, the son of Hystaspes, is written in three languages: Old Persian, Elamite, and Babylonian. The Old Persian text is divided into five paragraphs (I–V), but the Elamite and Babylonian versions only contain the first four paragraphs (I–IV). Attempting to explain this difference, Sancisi-Weerdenburg argues that "the most likely explanation for the absence of Elamite and Babylonian versions of DB V seems to be that no document was available any longer. . . . The absence of written documents of the King's *faits et gestes* explains partially, but not completely, the 'vagueness' of the inscriptions later than DB V."[59]

By framing the above analysis and categorization, Millard has provided a helpful tool that permits us to assess the results of our analysis in relation to the books of Kings. As far as our analysis is concerned, there can be no doubt that the books of Kings are to be placed in the same category as Berossus's *Babyloniaca*, Josephus's *Jewish Antiquities*,

---

56. Ibid., 198.
57. Ibid., 202.
58. Sancisi-Weerdenburg, "Persian Kings."
59. Ibid., 109.

and the book of Tobit.[60] The strongest argument comes from the spelling and usage of personal names: the books of Kings evidently (a) have the foreign rulers in the right sequence, (b) have the correct historical spellings of their names, and (c) report accurately about their interactions with the Israelite and Judean kings whenever we can check them against external sources. This conclusion is supported by the weaker arguments found in our analysis of the examples of literary style (the Rabshakeh incident) and trade relations (the queen of Sheba incident). If the author of the books of Kings wrote in Hellenistic or Persian times, how did he get it so right? By what mechanisms did he succeed in getting all of the names correct and providing the "best fit," chronologically speaking, for his various accounts? The *more unlikely* answer is that it was "a flash in the pan," that he only accidentally got the information right (when we can check it in other sources) and that a basic skepticism toward information that cannot be checked should therefore be maintained. The *most likely* answer is, as in the case of Tobit, that the author/editor of Kings had access to reliable sources and that a basic trust in his historical information, therefore, is heuristically defensible and commendable—not only when we can check the information elsewhere, but *generally*.

Returning from these excursory remarks to the main road of this chapter, we are now in a position to conclude the discussion. First, the analysis has demonstrated that a clear distinction must be made between text and reality in order to clarify the possibilites and limitations of the comparative enterprise. The implication of making this distinction is, as demonstrated in case #1 (see pp. 170ff.), that, while the comparative material is incapable of proving *when* the information contained in the extant text was written down and *whether* it conforms to reality (what actually happened), it *is* capable of revealing possible anachronisms. The real importance of the comparative material is, therefore, its ability to demonstrate whether information given, for example, in the books of Kings, is in accordance with information provided by the extrabiblical, primary sources. Neither more nor less. Second, whether information that cannot be checked against external sources conforms to the same pattern can only be answered by analogy in terms of *plausibility* or *probablity*. Third, the leap from an accord

---

60. On Josephus's use of sources, see Shaye J. D. Cohen, *Josephus in Galilee and Rome.* Comparing Josephus's works, Cohen's focus is primarily on the language, sequence, and content of Josephus's sources, but the study (especially chap. 2) also testifies to the overall accuracy of Josephus's chronological framework.

between *texts* (biblical and extrabiblical sources, primary and secondary) to an accord between text and *reality* (what actually happened) must necessarily take into account both historical (corroboration with evidence) and literary aspects (*Tendenzkritik*).

Taking these observations into account, we conclude, therefore, that the information given in the books of Kings is in accord with the external sources wherever we can check it. Comparative analysis favors the view that what has been transmitted by the author of the books of Kings (wherever we can check it) paints a picture that is consistent with the information of the extrabiblical sources and that the author(s) or editor(s), irrespective of *when* the books of Kings were written or edited, based his (their) account on reliable sources. On the basis of the parallel studies referred to above, it is also my contention that a basic trust in information that cannot be checked against external sources is both defensible and commendable. The number of cases with demonstrable agreement make it too difficult, in my opinion, to uphold a skeptical stance toward uncorroborated information. Whether the information is in accord with what actually happened is outside the scope of this chapter, and an answer must be postponed to the conclusion of the next chapter, where the relevant literary aspects will be discussed.

Chapter 5

Genre

If a character in a novel is exactly like Queen Victoria—not rather like but exactly like—then it actually is Queen Victoria, and the novel, or all of it that the character touches, becomes a memoir. A memoir is history, it is based on evidence. A novel is based on evidence plus or minus x, the unknown quantity being the temperament of the novelist, and the unknown quantity always modifies the effect of the evidence, and sometimes transforms it entirely. The historian deals with actions, and with the characters of men only so far as he can deduce them from their actions. He is quite as much concerned with character as the novelist, but he can only know of its existence when it shows on the surface. . . . The hidden life is, by definition, hidden. The hidden life that appears in external signs is hidden no longer, has entered the realm of action. And it is the function of the novelist to reveal the hidden life at its source: to tell us more about Queen Victoria than could be known, and thus to produce a character who is not the Queen Victoria of history.[1]

E. M. Forster

Historical Intention

At the end of chap. 1, we distinguished two sets of markers to be sought in the books of Kings if we are to discuss the epistemic value, heuristically speaking, of the books of Kings: markers of *source-critical value* and markers of *historical intention and referentiality*. In chaps. 2, 3, and 4, the first set of markers was discussed, and it is therefore now time to address the second set.

What is the genre of the text? By what means do we delimit, describe, and interpret it? In other words: Were the books of Kings intended to be history-writing in the first place? Does the text refer to factual persons and real-time events? Is it historiography or a histori-

---

1. E. M. Forster, *Aspects of the Novel* (London: Penguin, 1970) 52–53.

cal novel? To use the terminology of the initial quotation from Forster: is it a memoir or a novel? *Memoir* is history based on evidence, and a *novel* is "evidence plus or minus x." These questions are obviously just as essential to answer as questions of a source-critical nature if we are to determine the extent to which we can rely on the text as a historical source and where we are to place it on the epistemic continuum.

The Power of Genre

In 1938, the October 31 edition of *The New York Times* reported that "a wave of mass hysteria seized thousands of radio listeners between 8:15 and 9:30 o'clock last night when a broadcast of a dramatization of H. G. Wells's fantasy, 'The War of the Worlds,' led thousands to believe that an interplanetary conflict had started with invading Martians spreading wide death and destruction in New Jersey and New York."[2] The hysteria was so massive that, according to the reporter, it "disrupted households, interrupted religious services, created traffic jams and clogged communications systems." At 8:48, while the program was still on the air, the Associated Press sent out a note that "queries to newspapers from radio listeners throughout the United States tonight, regarding a reported meteor fall which killed a number of New Jersey-ites, are the result of a studio dramatization,"[3] and, later, police agencies all over America had to assure the public that the event was imaginary. It may be, as David L. Miller recently has argued, that "in the days following the broadcast, the print media greatly exaggerated the nationwide reaction,"[4] but it remains, nevertheless, a most lucid example of the power of genre. Because the broadcast was interpreted as "news" rather than a "drama" or a "story," it triggered a totally different set of actions than it would have had people heard the announcement at the beginning of the program: "The Columbia Broadcasting System and its affiliated stations present Orson Welles and the Mercury Theatre on the Air in *The War of the Worlds* by H. G. Wells" (see n. 2). We may find the incident rather amusing and would certainly not be so easily deceived by radio dramatizations today but, as a contemporary example shows, the phenomenon of genre confusion continues to

2. "Radio Listeners in Panic, Taking War Drama as Fact," *New York Times*, 31 October 1938, p. 1. For a full script of the dramatization, cf. http://members.aol.com/jeff1070/script.html (accessed May 9, 2003).

3. "Radio Listeners," *New York Times*.

4. David L. Miller, *Introduction to Collective Behavior and Collective Action* (Prospect Heights, Ill.: Waveland, 2000).

prompt actions that, after the erroneous genre recognition is realized, cause great consternation.

An interesting contemporary parallel to the Orson Welles dramatization is the faked illness and death of a made-up 19-year-old character named Kaycee. In May 2000, Randall van der Woning "met" her in the CitizenX internet chat room,[5] and sometime in June she shared with him that she was struggling with leukemia. Through her *weblog* at *Blogger*,[6] she and her mother, Debbie, described the fight against leukemia and how she lost it in the end. It was this weblog together with private correspondence that led Randall van der Woning, who lived in Hong Kong, as well as a number of other internet users around the world to a series of sympathizing actions, including the exchange of various gifts and long conversations on the phone. And it was not until Debbie, the pretended mother of the now "deceased" Kaycee, posted her confession that he realized that the entire story was a hoax—or, rather, an example of genre confusion—and that he had been interpreting the *weblog* as "biography" or "diary" rather than "fiction." The power and extent of the deception is noted by van der Woning himself, who has described the impact it had on him when he found out that the persons he had so tenderly been interacting with, Kaycee and her mother, Debbie, did not exist:

> I'm definitely not the only person hurt by this awful, bloody mess. I know many people with serious health problems were lifted by the words they read, only to have their spirits crushed by the cruelty of the truth. I hope my story will help people understand what happened, and perhaps, if I'm fortunate, it will help us all learn to trust each other again. I won't stop caring about people. I'm not going to change who I am. I like me. I have a life to live.[7]

Examples abound; and they lead us to make at least three important observations. First, the examples show that the phenomenon of genre confusion does not occur only in periods when people are less informed and easier to manipulate (e.g., in the 1930s); and genre recognition is not always as straightforward a task as it may seem. Con-

5. http://www.citizenx.com (accessed May 9, 2003).

6. *Blogger* is a free, web-based tool in the rapidly growing arena of web-publishing known as *weblogs* or simply *blogs*, located at http://www.blogger.com (accessed May 9, 2003).

7. "The End of the Whole Mess," published at http://www.vanderwoning.com/mess.shtml/mblog.shtml (accessed September 21, 2001). Cf. also David Winer, "Faking a Death Online," posted May 20, 2001, on http://davenet.userland.com/2001/05/20/fakingADeathOnline (accessed May 9, 2003).

sequently, if readers and listeners continue to struggle with the task of genre recognition *today* and sometimes find it difficult to interpret *modern* texts, we cannot expect fewer problems with *ancient* texts. Second, the "timeless" problem of genre recognition demonstrates that genre recognition is an intrinsic part of reading and listening itself; some kind of "horizon of expectation" must be present in order to facilitate communication. This is what Christopher Pelling has in mind when he says:

> True, it may well be impossible to conceive communication without any generic expectations at all: there must be some "horizon of expectation" in the audience, even for the simplest material. If one has no prior understanding whether a note ("two pints today") is a milk-order, an invitation to the pub, or a coded love-letter, one will find oneself in difficulties, particularly if one is a milkman. But, when we move to literary rather than sub-literary texts, theorists have become increasingly wary of finding firm 'rules' which decisively mark out one genre from another.[8]

Third, and related to the previous paragraph, the examples make it clear that authorial intent *does* matter and that a radical reader-response approach is out of touch with the way readers in general approach a text (see above, p. 13). Without proper genre recognition for the books of Kings, we are in danger of experiencing the same consequences of incongruity between authorial intent and reader response as outlined above. If we interpret and promote the text as "historiography" and it turns out that the author intended it to be a "historical novel" or a "story," there will—with a rephrasing of van der Woning's words—be many people with *historical* problems who "were lifted by the words they read, only to have their spirits crushed by the cruelty of the truth." A similar reaction would result from the opposite situation, and the point here is neither to defend nor to attack a certain position with regard to genre but to demonstrate the *genre-bound* nature of any interpretive action triggered by a reading of the books of Kings, whether it is the historian's use of the text as a reliable source or the believer's use of the text for spiritual comfort. Genre recognition is paramount for any decision about whether to include or exclude the text as a historical source for the history of Iron Age Israel.

Before analyzing the genre of the books of Kings in particular, we must make a few general remarks on genre. This will include a tentative definition of *genre*, a consideration of the "cultural contingency"

---

8. Christopher Pelling, "Epilogue," in *The Limits of Historiography: Genre and Narrative in Ancient Historical Texts* (ed. Christina Shuttleworth Kraus; Leiden: Brill, 1999) 328–29.

of genre, and a discussion of the possibility of distinguishing between fact and fiction in narrative.

The Verbal Map

Because meaningful communication is impossible without at least some "horizon of expectation in the audience," it is not surprising that literary critics from Aristotle to the present have occupied themselves with the task of defining *genre*. However, because a full discussion of the history of genre analysis is clearly beyond the scope of this book, we must be satisfied with only a general summary of present research into the mechanics of generic expectation.

Defining *genre* is a complex matter, because genre can be described from a number of perspectives or, rather, on different levels. Formally, genres are classes of texts grouped according to similarities in meter, structure, subject matter, mood, or setting. But, although it is relatively easy to determine whether the setting is judicial or the meter is dactylic[9] in a given text, categorization of this kind is only a first step in determining the genre. Even after we have analyzed the internal data and determined the setting in a given text as, for example, judicial, a number of questions remain unanswered: How does the *author*'s political, social, or religious background and agenda affect his configuration of setting, mood, subject matter, and so on in a particular text? How does the *reader*'s sociology of knowledge affect his/her interaction with the text? And, especially pertinent to our research, how does one determine whether a given text is fact or fiction?

A purely formal approach to the definition of genre does not answer these questions and is, therefore, of limited help in interpreting texts and thus, for us, facilitating meaningful communication. This is what John Marincola has in mind when he states:

> Genre, according to Conte, cannot simply be based exclusively on formal characteristics—we would not, for example, consider all poems in the Aeolic dialect to be a genre—nor simply on contents and recurring *topoi*, since this would run "the danger of never indicating the boundary between the general and the particular." The value of genre lies instead in the relationship between the structures of content and the structures of expression: "A genre is not characterized as a 'stuffing' of isolated fragments of content but as a totality of reciprocal structured

---

9. A dactylic foot consists of an accented syllable followed by two unaccented syllables, as in "chronicle," "fictional," "history."

relationships. The single element must enter into constellation with others if it is to be transvalued and redefined—until it, too, is able to connote, by its presence, the presence of a whole genre."[10]

Heather Dubrow goes even further and points out that not only constellations of *formal* elements but also their interaction with *extra-textual* elements must be taken into consideration: "Despite the assertions of the Russian formalists, not only literary but also extra-literary systems—political, social, religious and so on—contribute significantly to the shaping of literary forms. We all recognize, for instance, that Queen Elizabeth I's self-conscious imitation of 'Petrarchian Mistress' enhanced the popularity of the sonnet."[11]

The term *recognition* is a key word in this second step of defining genre. Dubrow closes a longer section on recognition as a prerequisite for literary understanding with a discussion that describes the process of recognition as an interaction between a number of textual and extra-textual elements, and at least three of her observations deserve attention here.

First, one cannot re-cognize something one has never seen, read, or heard before. Re-cognizing a textual genre, therefore, presupposes the previous cognition of a similar configuration of elements. Thus, when the above-mentioned radio listeners were terrified by what they heard, it was because hitherto separate elements (a factual report and a fictional text) were blended into a new and unknown genre. It is because of this first cognition of the genre that people could now re-cognize it and react correspondingly—that is, without being horrified. The issue of re-cognition is especially pertinent to the study of ancient texts, because the risk of facing unknown "configurations" in texts from a remote past is expected to be much higher than with contemporary texts. We shall return below, therefore, to a more detailed discussion on the possibility of re-cognizing the genre of the books of Kings.

Second, it is important to note that this recognition functions on both a conscious and a subconscious level. When a literary critic *analyzes* a text in order to determine its genre, he is obviously working on

---

10. John Marincola, "Genre, Convention, and Innovation in Greco-Roman Historiography," in *The Limits of Historiography: Genre and Narrative in Ancient Historical Texts* (ed. Christina Shuttleworth Kraus; Leiden: Brill, 1999) 282, quoting G. B. Conte, *Genres and Readers: Lucretius, Love Elegy, Pliny's Encyclopedia* (Baltimore: The Johns Hopkins University Press, 1994) 106–8.

11. Heather Dubrow, *Genre* (London: Methuen, 1982) 112. A sonnet is, according to the *Oxford English Dictionary*, a poem of 14 lines with a fixed rhyme-scheme and, in English, usually 10 syllables per line.

a conscious level. But if a message from his secretary pops up on his computer monitor saying, "Your mother-in-law is here to see you," his interpretation of "your mother-in-law" and "is here" as referring to a real person, standing downstairs in the secretary's office, wanting to enter his office, will function on a subconscious level (provided he is a regular computer-user and familiar with receiving messages on-screen). He will immediately recognize the genre and respond accordingly ("Tell her I'm not in" . . .).

It is difficult, of course, to determine a ratio between conscious versus subconscious genre recognition, but there can be no doubt that the vast majority of our reading and listening activies function on the subconscious level. We immediately know how to interpret and respond to a multitude of genres, because we are familiar with them. They are part and parcel of our culture, and learning how to interpret and respond to them is an essential part of the curriculum from elementary school to university or, in the broadest sense, from cradle to grave. This is an important observation because it underlines the *cultural contingency* of genre recognition. Or, as Christopher Pelling dubs it, the "discursive exchange" into which a given text fits.[12]

This is true not only for the reader. The subconscious and cultural contingent elements of a *reader's response* to generic markers is intrinsically linked to the same subconsciousness and cultural contingency in the *author's* choice of how to write. When Dubrow writes that "established genres—whether they be popular ones like the detective novel or serious ones like the *Bildungsroman*—carry with them a whole series of prescriptions and restrictions, some codified in the pronouncements of rhetoricians and others less officially but no less forcefully established by previous writers,"[13] it follows that both the author and the reader of a text are to some extent "prescripted" and restricted in their writing and reading. The author will consciously or subconsciously be writing in and responding to a certain genre tradition, using predefined, culturally-based standards, conventions, and styles, with only minor deviations. In a similar way, the reader will be guided by a culturally-based approach to these standards, conventions, and styles. This is precisely what Christopher Pelling has in mind when he speaks of "discursive exchange." Taking his setting from an episode of *Star Trek*, in which the *Starship Enterprise* "boldly

---

12. Pelling, "Epilogue," 325.
13. Dubrow, *Genre*, 9.

came upon a strange new vessel, manned by a people called Tamarians," he explains:

> Stories typically (probably indeed universally) fit into a "discursive exchange": they communicate, and respond to earlier communications. That is true of stories told over the dinner table or in the café; it was true of the stories summoned up by the Tamarians, both as they discussed among themselves how to respond to the overtures and as they tried to communicate with the outsiders; and in a more elaborate way it is true of the narratives of written historiography. . . . The simplest sort of "discursive exchange" comes when one text continues another, picking up where the first left off. Thus within the Greco-Roman tradition various authors set out to continue Thucydides—Xenophon in *Hellenica*, Theopompus, *Hellenica Oxyrhynchia*, Cratippus; later Phylarchus continued Duris of Samos; the phenomenon is as early as Thucydides himself, picking up the narrative of the "Pentecontaetia" at the point where Herodotus finished (at Sestos, 1.89). Continuation was even more frequent on the Roman side. . . .[14]

Pelling goes on to demonstrate that such a continuation or "discursive exchange" could be much more subtle and that serial history (as evidenced in the *Hellenicas*) typically was "a contribution to a continuing exchange and debate about how history should be written" and that this "redefinition can go in different directions."[15] That Pelling also is aware of the extent to which *extra-literary* systems influence the concept of genre becomes clear when he concludes the discourse from which the above-mentioned quotation has been taken by saying that "we may believe we can tell a thoroughly recent story without the distant past, or can explain wars without women, or can leave the gods out; but if for an instant we do think that way we are swiftly drawn to think differently. And in its way that is programmatic too, intimating that in this text historical explanation will be a very provisional, elusive, and challenging business."[16]

---

14. Pelling, "Epilogue," 326. Cf. also Veldhuis, who in an article on the concept of canon in Mesopotamian literature argues that "canon is a phenomenon of reception as well as production, since new texts may be composed in conscious relation to canonical ones. In this use of the term canon, inclusion and exclusion are matters of degree or perspective, rather than an absolute characteristic of a text. We may distinguish between core and periphery, between canons of different social groups, or we may perceive changes over time in the position that a certain composition has within the canon. In this perception, the character of a canon is not solely defined by the corpus that is included, but at least as much by what is excluded and by the relations maintained between the canonical and the trivial" ("TIN.TIR," 79).

15. Pelling, "Epilogue," 327.

16. Ibid., 337.

The influence of "extra-literary systems" on this "continuation" or "redefinition" is discussed by Thomas O. Beebee, who, quoting the Prague structuralists, notes:

> When described formally rather than thematically, a genre emerges as a set of *fixed structural* elements, such as the metrical form (in the *chansons de geste*, for instance), the lexical selection (as in the heroic epic), or the technique of composition (as in the short story in contrast to the novel). In time, the particular combinations of such generic devices undergo considerable change. While some elements remain unaltered, maintaining the genre's continuity, the influx of new elements assures its freshness and elasticity. But in extreme cases even those elements with which the genre is primarily identified may disappear, whereas the secondary elements endure. Thanks to such permutations in the function of individual elements, a given genre may, over a long period, produce two almost unrecognizable evolutionary offshoots, such as the picaresque novel and the modern novel. Even for epic and lyric it appears impossible to design simple and unambiguous definitions adequate for literatures of every period. Thus genre is a historically conditioned concept, not a universally valid one.[17]

Beebee's warning against too-rigid definitions of literary genres is extremely important, because definition of genre is a key issue in any discussion of the books of Kings. To this we will return in due course. Next, however, we will take up some considerations on an equally important aspect: what this means for the *reader's* response.

The *reader's* interaction with the text is subject to precisely the same influence, and his recognition of a given text's genre will, therefore, to a great degree be determined by the approach of a consensus of contemporary culture to the concept of genre. "It is evident," Pelling writes,

> that any genre of historiography will be a shifting and cumulative thing, with the audience's expectations developing as the store of past works grew greater. As Alasdair Fowler puts it, genre is "much less of a pigeon-hole than a pigeon,"[18] not so much a set of pre-cast categories as something which itself continually moves and changes. In Greek and Roman historiography these developments sometimes simply created

---

17. F. W. Galan, "Literary System and Systemic Change: The Prague School Theory of Literary History 1928–48," *PMLA* 94 (March 1979) 279. Quoted from Thomas O. Beebee, *The Ideology of Genre* (University Park, Penn.: Pennsylvania State University Press, 1994) 270. Cf. also Ralph Cohen, "History and Genre," *New Literary History* 17 (1986) 204.

18. A. Fowler, *Kinds of Literature: An Introduction to the Theory of Genres and Modes* (Oxford: Clarendon, 1991) 34.

new norms; more often, as we shall see, they furnished a wider range of affiliations from which a new writer could select. For "history" was always an extremely broad and capacious category, so broad indeed that it is a question how far we should think of a "genre" historiography at all.[19]

Third, the foregoing observations on discursive exchange and genre as historically-conditioned concepts prompt us to avoid too-simple perceptions of the reader's response. It is precisely because of the above-mentioned, pigeon-like character of genre that Dubrow warns that "we should remind ourselves, too, that the reader's reactions to genre do not necessarily follow a pattern that might be codified as 'If/Then', as many critics have assumed ('If it is a *Bildungsroman*, then x, y and z will be present')." Instead, she and others suggest that the reader's interaction with a text should be formulated as "'What if/Then probably' ('What if the genre of this work is the *Bildungsroman*? Then probably the hero will test out a series of alternative father figures, though of course this may just be one of the few *Bildungsromane* where that pattern does not operate')."[20] Dubrow goes on to argue that "the process of reacting to generic signals is seldom a simple and linear one" and that the mechanics of genre recognition are complex:

> Admittedly, sometimes we merely start out with no idea about the work's genre, arrive at a satisfactory decision about it, and respond to the rest of the work accordingly. Often, however, even on our first reading we will reach a preliminary hypothesis about genre, bear it in mind as we glance back over earlier passages, and re-read the whole work in the thought of our assumptions about its literary form. In doing so we will typically note both further evidence of the work's relationship to that type and previous deviations from the model.[21]

Summing up this tour of modern genre theory, we may conclude that, if there is one word we *cannot* use in a definition of genre and in describing the mechanics of genre recognition, it is *rigid*. This, of course, does not make genre recognition impossible per se, but it does warn us that the impact of time on ancient genres is a complicating factor in our attempt to re-cognize them. Genre definition and genre recognition are subject to cultural change and consequently must be seen as historically-conditioned concepts. Genre is, therefore, not merely "a group of texts which display the same characteristics," as

---

19. Pelling, "Epilogue," 328.
20. Dubrow, *Genre*, 106–7.
21. Ibid., 107.

M. J. Wheeldon puts it, but "a preconception held by readers about such a group which influences in advance their reading of individual texts in or impinging upon that group; this general idea may then be revised when new texts of this kind are experienced."[22] Any attempt to determine the genre of, for example, the books of Kings must accordingly take into consideration this *influence*.[23]

Literary critics, in an effort to combine these aspects of genre recognition in a single definition, often describe genre with recourse to metaphors. E. D. Hirsch defines it in terms of the rules of a game or a code of social behavior: "Coming to understand the meaning of an utterance is like learning the rules of a game,"[24] while Vanhoozer speaks of genres as verbal maps, each with its own "key" and "scale":

> Literary genres are verbal maps, each with its own "key" and "scale." The "key" tells you what a piece of discourse is about. Just as there are different kinds of maps—of roads, of geological characteristics, of historical incidents, of the stars—so different literary genres select and attend to various features of reality more than others. Similarly, every literary genre has its own "scale" or manner of fitting words to the world. The aim of history, for instance, is to make our words fit or correspond to the world, viz., the past; the aim of utopias is to make the

---

22. Averil Cameron, "Introduction," in *History as Text: The Writing of Ancient History* (ed. Averil Cameron; London: Duckworth, 1989) 44.

23. This does not, on the other hand, render the understanding of ancient genres impossible. Danto's remark in this regard is pertinent: "There is one fatal objection against the thesis that increasing temporal distance entails decreasing intelligibility of human actions. It is that our temporal distance from the Greeks ought to make it equally difficult to write, or to understand, an account of *political* happenings in 300 B.C.E. and an account of artistic activities at that same period. But this simply is not the case. Thucydides' book is very nearly a paradigm of intelligible political history. His account, indeed, is so astute that we can apply it to our own time, and argue, if we wish, that peoples have changed very little. What it comes to, then is *not* that we are temporally more remote from the Greeks of the 3rd century B.C.E. than we are from, say, the French of the 19th century C.E.; but that we simply have a better understanding of political than of artistic behaviour. And this means that we have a more extensive and perhaps a more reliable stock of what I have termed *conceptual*, in contrast with *documentary* evidence for political constructions in contrast with artistic ones. One may then go on to suggest that our conceptual evidence, in the case of politics, will enable us to construct more complex narratives, independently of specific documentary evidence, than our corresponding conceptual evidence for artistic activity will permit us to achieve. If there should be any doubts about this, let someone imagine trying to write the history of 19th century painting on the basis only of a list of names of artists and works. I dare say that relative proximity in time will help us very little. And if we knew all about the 19th century *except* what was painted, we could hardly imagine Impressionism" (Danto, *Narration*, 125).

24. Eric Donald Hirsch, *Validity in Interpretation* (New Haven: Yale University Press, 1967) 70.

world fit or correspond to our words. The point is that words do not naturally refer to reality in uniform fashion. Rather, every genre has its own conventions and strategies for relating to the real.[25]

In addition to providing us with a good metaphor for understanding the complex interaction of the aspects of genre recognition discussed above, Vanhoozer points out another problem that needs to be discussed before we can proceed to a genre analysis proper of the books of Kings. We have already mentioned that one of the questions left unanswered by a purely formal approach to genre definition—especially as far as the genre "historiography" is concerned—is whether a text presents fact or fiction; by arguing that "every genre has its own conventions and strategies for relating to the real," Vanhoozer has actualized the question once again. To this we now turn.

Fact and Fiction

In the introductory chapter, we touched upon the so-called "genre-neutralization" of the traditional distinction between fact and fiction (see above, p. 14) and its potential implications for the writing of history. Taken to its logical conclusion, such a blurring of genres would mean the end of history, history being a representation of what actually *did* happen in contrast to fictional narrative, which sometimes uses the same formal language but is understood to render what *might* have happened but did not.

As we have noted, most scholars have rejected the attack of "philosophical impositionalism" and "antireferentialism" (see above, p. 13) on the epistemic value of the historical narrative by maintaining that truth-claims in historical narratives are different from those of fiction because they can be checked and discussed against the available source material, the "voices of the past." At this point, however, we ought to elaborate a little more on this postulate, and a speech by Paul Ricoeur at the opening ceremony for the "Humanities at the Turn of the Millennium" conference, University of Århus, Denmark (June 4, 1999) will serve as a good point of departure.[26]

---

25. Kevin J. Vanhoozer, "Introduction: Hermeneutics, Text, and Biblical Theology," in *NIDOTTE* (ed. Willem A. VanGemeren; Carlisle: Paternoster, 1997) 39.

26. Paul Ricoeur, "Humanities between Science and Art"; a transcript of Paul Ricoeur's speech (transcription by Eline Busck) can be found at http://www.hum.au.dk/ckulturf/pages/publications/pr/hbsa.htm (accessed May 9, 2003).

Ricoeur, speaking on the discipline of historiography as "a paradigmatic case of human science, which extends between the two poles of
science and arts,"[27] pointed out three distinct phases in the process of
history-writing: the documentary phase, the explanatory or comprehensive phrase, and the literary phase. The initial stage is dubbed
"documentary" because it is from written documents or "testimonies"
that the historiographer takes his departure. Ricoeur defines "testimony" as "a declaration of a witness who says three things: (1) *I was
there* (2) *believe me or not* (3) *if you don't believe my word ask somebody else*"
and stresses that "the whole structure of the linguistic community to
which I belong relies on whether the truth-claim of a given testimony
is trusted or not."[28] It is such trusted testimonies that, according to
Ricoeur, constitute the basic scientific component of truth-claims
raised by historical knowledge. The next step is the explanatory/com-
prehensive phase, in which questions about causes and reasons are
asked—or, to use the terminology of the *Annales* School, the phase in
which explanations are sought for the relationship between structures,
conjunctures, and events. In the final, literary phase, the trusted,
"raw" material of the first phase is given order, based on the explanation of the second phase, in a literary representation, the *narrative* or
historical discourse.

Ricoeur's three-tier model has several epistemological and heuristic
advantages. First, it accounts for the observation, increasingly acknowledged by scholars, that history is after all a kind of literature
and that as such it must be exposed to the same methods of criticism
and interpretation as literature in general. Historiography, in other
words, is *not* a literary genre completely isolated and different from
any other genre. It may be different with regard to its referent, but it
deploys precisely the same literary devices as a number of other literary genres: rhetoric, digression, irony, metaphor, hyperbole, and so
on. Or as Robert Berkhofer phrases it: "Although history and fiction
may have different conventions of referring to the worlds they depict,
they share narration and other modes of representation in doing so."[29]
This is new wine in old bottles, of course, because the literary or *rhetorical* character of historiography was acknowledged as early as the
classical era.

---

27. Ibid., 3–4.
28. Ibid., 7.
29. Berkhofer, *Beyond the Great Story*, 69.

Second, therefore, Ricoeur's most important, or novel, observation is not the awareness of historiography's literary character but his eye for the potential tension between the deployment of various literary devices and the referential character of historiography:

> For example narratives are not transparent structures, which would let events speak, if we may say so; narratives tend to draw the interest of the reader toward their own play; the narrative structure tends to absorb the referential tread of discourse for the sake of its game; stories become a world of their own, increasing the wealth of intertextual relationships; a narrative world is born which tends to exclude from its sphere any referential claim. Such is the paradox. Narratives do not merely channel the referential claim of historical consciousness but celebrate their story. This exclusion of the real past from the linguistic realm is still more impressive at the level of the rhetorical devices, praise and blame, metaphors and irony.[30]

What Ricoeur points out here is the heuristic importance of discerning between the different levels in the process of history-writing. The key words, as evidenced above, are *tension* and *danger*. There is no equation between literary device or *narrative*, on the one hand, and fiction on the other—only *tendentiousness*: (historical) narratives *tend* to draw the reader into a literary world without any necessary referents in the real world. Or, to use Hirsch's terminology, the reader is invited to play a game in which the rules are prescribed, not by the reader, but by the genre itself, and in which he is facing the ever present danger of *ludens*: forgetting real time. By describing this feature of historiography as a *tendentiousness* toward "exclusion of the real past from the linguistic realm," Ricoeur not only acknowledges the *dehistorizing* power of literary devices deployed in the historical narrative, he also suggests that, because this "exclusion" is a tendentiousness and *not* a necessity, we cannot tell from the literary level whether various elements in the (historical) narrative refer to the real world by analyzing the *literary* level of a given text. Whatever literary devices it contains, it may or may not refer to real events in time.

In order to discuss the epistemic value of these elements, we need to regress—Ricoeur continues—from the representational level via the explanatory/comprehensive to the documentary. Referring to revisionist historians' denial of the Holocaust, Ricoeur points to precisely this "regression" as a necessary procedure if we want to distinguish fact from fiction:

---

30. Ricoeur, "Humanities between Science and Art," 13–14.

To my mind, the reply cannot be found at the level of the literary representation where the gap between fiction and reality is bridged by the
very devices of representation, either narrative, rhetorical, or fictional;
the solution resides at the two previous stages of the historiographical
process, at the level of explanation and beyond it at that of documentary
evidence. As long as you stay at the mere level of representation you
get in the paradox of the icon of the past, which was already the paradox of the memory-image; you are never sure that an icon is not a phan-
tasm(o), that the mimesis is not an invention. You have to regress from
representation to explanation and comprehension, and from explanation to documentary evidence, and beyond documentary evidence to
the testimonies provided in the archive. Then, by chance, you will hear
the voice of the witnesses who said *I was there—believe me or not—and if
you don't believe me, ask somebody else*. The reliability of witnesses is our
ultimate resource. The confidence put in the word of somebody saying *I
was there* is our only help. We have nothing better than testimony and
the critique of testimony.[31]

By basing arguments for and against factuality in historical narratives on the explanatory (authorial intention) and documentary (testimony) levels, Ricoeur gives voice to the consensus of contemporary
historical theory and epistemology. Hayden White thus argues that
fact can be discerned from fiction by means of its commitment to
its subject matter (i.e., "real" as opposed to "imaginary" events) rather
than by form.[32] Similarly, Robert Berkhofer claims that, while fiction
allows for multiple scenarios, historical narratives allow for multiple
interpretations but *not* for multiple pasts. Discussing historical representations and truthfulness, he says that "to normal historians, then,
a plurality of interpretations in practice never implies a plurality of
(hi)stories, let alone a plurality of pasts. Multiple Great Stories and
Great Pasts are inconceivable according to normal methodological assumptions,"[33] and (quoting Peter Gay) "the objects of the historian's
inquiry are precisely that, objects, out there in a real and single past.
Historical controversy in no way compromises their ontological integ-
rity. The tree in the woods of the past fell in only one way, no matter
how fragmentary or contradictory the reports of its fall, no matter
whether there are no historians, one historian, or several contentious
historians in its future to record and debate it."[34] It is these "objects"
that make the "history" genre so different from "fiction":

---

31. Ibid., 14.
32. White, *Metahistory*, 6; "Historicism," 21.
33. Berkhofer, *Beyond the Great Story*, 49.
34. Ibid., 48, quoting Peter Gay, *Style in History* (New York: Basic Books, 1974) 210.

A novel may be praised for its verisimilitude because of its simulation of reality even as its author makes up conversations, actions, places, characters, and plots. Historians, on the other hand, claim accuracy with regard to their subjects and fidelity to the past in their texts on the grounds that they do not create persons or actions as existing without some evidence from past sources, do not allude to acts or events for which they lack documentary information, and do not put words into their character's mouths or minds without specific evidence of such (although they may imply that they know the entire climate of opinion of the times or the collective opinion of a group of people on the basis of documentation derived from only a few cases at best). When one of their guild makes up a document, as Simon Schama did in his narrative experiment, *Dead Certainties (Unwarranted Speculations),* his fellow historians castigate him severely for violating the historian's first commandment: Thou shalt not create documents and their evidence.[35]

The same stance is taken by Danto who, from an epistemological perspective, notes that "we cannot distinguish true from false sentences merely by inspecting, so to speak, the surface of the sentence. For truth has to do with a relationship between sentences and whatever it is that they are about."[36] Discussing Leonardo da Vinci's painting *The Last Supper,* Danto notes that if we only knew the date of the picture, the title of the painting, and the name of the artist, we would be able "to stretch a few facts rather a long way" and that "an imaginative appeal to our general concepts will fairly soon get us a narrative of some sort which we might then use as a guide for further research, seeing whether some further but independent evidence might be found for our narrative." Danto's point, however, is:

> Without this further evidence (and here we *are* at the mercy of the resources of history-as-record), our narrative would float on air: it would, for all we knew, be fiction. But this surely helps us to see what is the difference between narratives and the evidence we have for them (a fictive narrative is one which requires *solely* conceptual evidence). One might say that the difference between a chronicle and a proper piece of history is the difference between a well-supported, in contrast with a poorly supported, narrative. And this, in turn, would suggest a comparison between a well-confirmed and a poorly confirmed theory. But this is not a difference between kinds or genres of theories, or, for that matter, between kinds or genres of narratives: it is a wholly quantitative difference between degrees of confirmation or amounts of support.[37]

---

35. Berkhofer, *Beyond the Great Story,* 68.
36. Danto, *Narration,* 64.
37. Ibid., 123–24. Cf. also Mullen, "Between 'Romance' and 'True History,'" 35.

Third, and by implication, Ricoeur's model demonstrates that the factuality or fictionality of a given textual element must be judged not on literary grounds but on explanatory (authorial intent) and especially documentary (testimony) evidence. Or, to be more specific with regard to ancient historiography: supernatural elements, dreams, genealogies, speeches, chronology, and references to external sources may very well be literary devices that are used to further a certain explanation (emplotment), but their factuality or fictionality cannot be determined on the literary level.[38] Even if a (hi)story is "well written" or deploys a number of literary devices that are characteristic features of decidedly fictional genres such as "fantasy" or "legend, " it does not necessarily follow that it is also fiction. The (hi)story of Sargon's birth, for example, is most often referred to as Sargon's birth *legend*, and it is a commonplace among biblical scholars to interpret the account of Moses' birth as a variation on this alleged fairy-tale theme. It may be so, but not *necessarily*, as a curious modern example shows.

In 1999, the October 7 edition of *Liverpool Echo* reported that "a boy who was brought up by monkeys was due to arrive in Liverpool today for a visit with a children's choir."[39] John Ssabunnya was abandoned as a two-year-old in the jungle of Uganda, where a colony of monkeys adopted him as one of their own and raised him "monkeywise." In 1991, an astonished woman spotted the now five-year-old monkey boy. When tribesmen returned to pick up the boy, his monkey guardians put up a ferocious fight, but the naked boy was caught and ended up in an orphanage where he eventually learned human ways. "As he began to utter his first words, it was discovered he had a fine singing voice. John has now joined the 20-strong Pearl of Africa children's

---

38. Note, however, the pioneering work of my colleague Nicolai Winther-Nielsen, who argues that even though no proof, strictly speaking, of factuality can be found on the literary level, modern contextual analyses of language use and discourse situations in stories from the Hebrew Bible demonstrate that the interaction going on in the stories does not differ from natural language use in ordinary social situations. See Nicolai Winther-Nielsen, "Fact, Fiction and Language Use: Can Modern Pragmatics Improve on Halpern's Case for History in Judges?" in *Windows into Old Testament History: Evidence, Argument, and the Crisis of "Biblical Israel"* (ed. V. Philips Long, David W. Baker, and Gordon J. Wenham; Grand Rapids: Eerdmans, 2001) 44–81; and "Tracking the World of Judges: The Use of Contextual Resources in Narration and Conversation," forthcoming in *Hiphil*, a subjournal at http://www.see-j.net.

39. Rachel Tinniswood, "Choirboy Raised by Monkeys," *Liverpool Echo*, Thursday, October 7, 1999, p. 9. This is where I first read the story. When I checked the "testimony," however, I found minor disagreements as to his age and other details. Cf., e.g., BBC's version at http://news.bbc.co.uk/1/hi/uk/466616.stm (accessed May 9, 2004). The essential story, however, is the same.

choir, which is performing in the North West as part of a three-week tour of Britain."[40] The historian's advantage in the case of the report on John Ssabunnya in contrast with the Sargon/Moses case is, of course, that witnesses abound and the main character himself is alive and available for questioning. We trust the testimonies and consider it *not* to be a fictitious variation on the Tarzan or Mowgli theme. John Ssabunnya was not "invented" to raise money for the Pearl of Africa children's choir (though his membership in the choir may have helped!). He actually *was* a monkey boy.

But there are more similarities than first appear between the Sargon/Moses case and this present-day example. If all we had was the *Liverpool Echo* text, we would have just as few clues about whether we were dealing with a fairy-tale or a factual report as in the case of Sargon/Moses. Literary grounds are insufficient. It is on the explanatory level (the author's intent to tell the truth) and—especially—on the documentary level that we find the answer. Because we trust the testimony and the authorial intent of the *Liverpool Echo* reporter, we decide that the monkey boy is not a fictitious literary device but a historical person. Another implication of the John Ssabunnya example is that even when we have no "testimony" on the documentary level and/or no explicit expression of "authorial intent" on the explanatory level, the report of a fantastic event may be factual.

The same points are made in relation to ancient historiography by Simon Hornblower, who, in an article on Greek historiography, notes that

> though there are fairy-tale elements in Herodotus, particularly the early stretches, it is not likely, nor has it been demonstrated, that Herodotus is merely an ingenious teller of lies and fairy-tales—a view which surely makes too little allowance for the difficulty of using oral tradition. There is another objection. We sell the pass too cheaply if we allow that literary or rather rhetorical stylization of presentation are somehow incompatible with truthful reporting. Thucydides offers an obvious comparison. I have tried to show . . . that Thucydides uses the whole tool-box of rhetoric without, in my view, forfeiting his claim to be believed when he tells us (for instance) that there was a plague at Athens in 429 BC or—to take a still less controversial item, since even Thucydides' plague has actually been doubted in modern times—that the Peace of Nikias guaranteed free access to the common sanctuaries of Greece: 2.47–54; 5.18.2.[41]

---

40. Tinniswood, "Choirboy Raised by Monkeys," 9.
41. Hornblower, *Greek Historiography*, 18–19.

Millard, in a rebuttal to Barr's description of the texts of the Old Testament as "story" rather than "history," in a similar way stresses that, though the allegedly historical texts of the Hebrew Bible also must be acknowledged as artistic creations, this fact does not necessarily entail concluding that they are fictional. Acknowledging that "the biblical stories possess a continuing appeal that is a tribute to the skill of the narrators" and that "the setting of scenes, delineation of character and development of plot is usually done with great economy," Millard notes:

> Distinguishing *story*, as a narrative that may or may not report real events, from *history*, which is required to be factual narrative, is made more difficult since both may use the same language and relate comparable episodes. Egyptologists face this problem with the text called "The Taking of Joppa." A general, Djehuty, captured Joppa by gaining the confidence of the local ruler, then introducing his soldiers into the city hidden in baskets, a stratagem recalling the Trojan Horse. Djehuty is known to have served Thutmosis III (ca. 1479–1425 B.C.E.), who rewarded him with a golden dish now in the Louvre. Is the story history, legend, or a mixture? Egyptologists are ambivalent, the authors of a standard book saying, "it is not entirely unlikely . . . it may seem dangerous to count as historical an event, however likely, which is attested by a single story which has clear legendary inspiration." Another author remarks, "Although the details of the story . . . may be of the stuff of folklore rather than history, the central fact that the city was besieged and taken may well be true." Terms like *legendary inspiration* and *folkloristic features* flow as easily from the pen as *etiology*, and the same dangers accompany them. Skeptical or negative attitudes are adopted toward the whole of a narrative containing these elements, often without the caution just quoted, because discarding what seems less than likely can, superficially, be presented as the "scientific" way. However, discarding should be the last resort, for it risks rejecting evidence that may be the only source for an episode of history. . . . Literary, folkloristic, etiological, paradigmatic, and all other ways of studying the narratives are to be welcomed, but no one of them can take priority over any other except for the assessment of them for what they claim to be on their own terms.[42]

---

42. Millard, "Story, History, and Theology," 49–50. Cf. also Yamauchi, "Current State." For arguments for and against literary devices as markers of fiction, see the following studies. On dreams, see Jean-Marie Husser, *Dreams and Dream Narratives in the Biblical World* (Biblical Seminar 63; Sheffield: Sheffield Academic Press, 1999). On prayers, see Samuel E. Balentine, "'You Can't Pray a Lie': Truth *and* Fiction in the Prayers of Chronicles," in *The Chronicler as Historian* (ed. M. Patrick Graham, Kenneth G. Hoglund, and Steven L. McKenzie; Sheffield: Sheffield Academic Press, 1997) 246–67. On chronology, see Gerhard Larsson, "Chronology as a Structural Element in the Old Testament," *SJOT* 14 (2000) 207–18. On genealogies, see Roddy L. Braun, "1 Chronicles 1–9 and the

Having argued that deployment of various literary devices does not necessarily detract from a text's factuality, we must stress of course that the opposite also applies. Just because a text makes relatively sparse use of literary devices does not imply that it is more factual. This is exactly what Brettler has in mind when he states that "there is no internal biblical reason to distinguish between these genres; from the perspective of the Israelite, 'the waters of Noah are no less real than the waters of Shiloah.' "[43] Kitchen makes the same point when he states, with regard to the epistemic value of the account of the Exodus, that "if this body of texts is viewed on its own, to the exclusion of all other evidence (both biblical and external), then there is no way of knowing a priori whether we have here an historical account, or total fiction, or one of several possibilities between these extreme and opposite poles. If we are not content simply to remain total agnostics on the subject."[44]

The Blending of Genres

However simple Ricoeur's three-tier model may seem, the actual analysis of a text in order to determine its factuality/fictionality is nevertheless most often a "muddy" enterprise. Or as Lester Grabbe has it, "Writing history is a messy business. It is very akin to mud-wrestling or muck-spreading. If you actually get down to trying to be a historian, you are going to be dirty. You will have to make judgments, weigh evidence, and deal with problematic data. Many of your reconstructions are likely to be fragile and open to criticism. You will not be able to sit on the fence."[45]

Reconstruction of the History of Israel: Thoughts on the Use of Genealogical Data in Chronicles in the Reconstruction of the History of Israel," in *The Chronicler as Historian*, 92–105; and Mark W. Chavalas, "Genealogical History as 'Charter,' " in *Faith, Tradition, and History* (ed. A. R. Millard, J. K. Hoffmeier, and D. W. Baker; Winona Lake, Ind.: Eisenbrauns, 1994) 103–28. Cf. also the article on "lions" as a metaphor in Daniel by Karel van der Toorn, "In the Lions' Den: The Babylonian Background of a Biblical Motif," *CBQ* 60 (1998) 626–40.

43. Brettler, *The Creation*, 12.

44. K. A. Kitchen, "Egytians and Hebrews, from Ra'amses to Jericho," in *The Origin of Early Israel—Current Debate: Biblical, Historical and Archaeological Perspectives* (Irene Levi-Sala Seminar, 1997; Studies by the Department of Bible and Ancient Near East 12; ed. Shmuel and Eliezer D. Oren Ahituv; London: Institute of Archaeology and Institute of Jewish Studies University College, 1998) 65. Cf. also Whitelam, "The Search for Early Israel," 58.

45. Lester L. Grabbe, "Fellow Creatures—or Different Animals?" in *Can a "History of Israel" Be Written?* (JSOTSup 245; ESHM 1; ed. Lester L. Grabbe; Sheffield: Sheffield Academic Press, 1997) 22.

The fusion of fact and fiction, that is, the blending of genres, sometimes makes it impossible or at least extremely difficult to distinguish
between referential and nonreferential claims or information. The
problem is surmountable when, on the explanatory level, there is a
clear indication of authorial intent and/or when we find available
data on the documentary level to verify or falsify the author's information. It is much more difficult to determine the epistemic value
when there is an intentional/unintentional blending of genres. Modern examples are legion. From the present, Smelik mentions Jean-Paul
Sartre's *Les Mouches* and Berthold Brecht's *Der kaukasische Kredekreis*;[46]
from the Rennaisance, Shakespeare, who recontextualized historical
figures in fictional works, comes to mind; a lucid example from classical times is Virgil. Jens Juhl Jensen, discussing the genre of Virgil's
Eclogae, thus comments that "well-known Romans not seldom pop
up in the middle of an otherwise fictitious discourse, just as we find
transparent allusions to contemporary historical events and Italian
place names. Altogether a curious blend of fact and fiction."[47]

It is even more problematic when an author consciously aims to de-
ceive his audience/readers. One of the most recent examples is the
publication of Binjamin Wilkomirski's *Fragments* in 1996.[48] Wilkomirski describes in the book how, after his father was killed by German
soldiers, he was taken to the Majdanek death camp when he was three
or four years old. Moved from camp to camp as the years went on, in
1945 he was half-kidnapped, half-rescued from an orphanage in Cracow and hidden with a group of children traveling to Switzerland for
adoption. Once there, his new family never allowed him to talk about
his previous life. Overshadowed by terror, he saw everything unfa-
miliar as a potential instrument of death (an example is the ski-lift on
a school skiing trip). Only in adulthood did he find a way to recover
his memories. The book was warmly praised by Jewish groups and
literary critics[49] and won the 1996 National Jewish Book Award for

46. K. C. E. Smelik, *Converting the Past: Studies in Ancient Israelite and Moabite Historiography* (Oudtestamentische Studien; Leiden: Brill, 1992).

47. Jens Juhl Jensen, "Vergil ifølge ham selv," *Weekendavisen* Bøger (9 April 1999) 7,
review of Marianne Wifstrand Schiebe, *Vergil og Tityrus: Et studie i selvbiografisk læsning
af Bucolica* [in Danish; my translation]. See also Peter Heehs, "Myth, History, and Theory," *History and Theory* 33 (1994) 1–19, where Heehs demonstrates how the blending of
myth and history in an old Indian *ashram* story poses almost insurmountable problems
to the historian who wants to distinguish fact from fiction.

48. First published in 1995 by Jüdischer Verlag im Suhrkamp Verlag, Frankfurt
am Main.

49. The *Daily Mail* thus wrote that "rarely has a time of ultimate horrors been de-
picted with so searing a child's simplicity coupled with adult emotions stripped naked

Autobiography; in Britain, it was awarded the Jewish Quarterly Literary Prize, and in France the Prix Mémoire de la Shoah. By invitation, Wilkomirski toured throughout America and gave speeches to Jewish organizations as a Holocaust victim. In 1998, however, the Swiss reporter Daniel Ganzfried, researching Wilkomirski's background, published an article in the Swiss weekly *Weltwoche* (August 27, 1998), presenting legal documents and school records that contradicted the author's claim of being a Holocaust survivor. Although he claimed to have been born in Latvia in 1939 and to have arrived in Switzerland in 1947 or 1948, Swiss legal records showed that he was actually born in Switzerland in February 1941, the son of an unwed woman, Yvette Grosjean. The infant was then adopted and raised by the Doesekkers, a middle-class Zurich couple. Though the author to this day maintains that his story is true, it is now generally recognized by the public as a cunning fraud; having read and reviewed the story as an example of the genre "autobiography," literary critics the world over have found themselves licking their wounds and discussing how on earth this could happen,[50] while revisionist historians have found Wilkomirski's successful deception as a useful argument in their ongoing denial of the Holocaust.

This complexity is precisely what Berkhofer has in mind when, having referred to a number of different types of historical narratives, he notes:

> As these examples suggest, history, historical fiction, fictional history, and fiction all exist along a spectrum ranging from supposedly pure factual representation of literal, historical truth to pure non-literary, invented fictional representation of fantasy. No work of history conveys only literal truth through factuality, and few novels, even science fiction ones, depict only pure fantasy. Like histories, most historical novels have until recently tended toward invoking the authenticity of the time they describe, but both histories and historical novels employ devices of interpretation to flesh out the documentary and artifactual evidence. Similarly, novels, like historical novels, may evoke a time's

---

by experiences beyond all reason," while the *Daily Telegraph*'s Paul Bailey confessed that "I had to read it slowly, taking silent walks between chapters, so raw and powerful are the feelings it contains and inspires. . . . The bravery of his undertaking cannot be exaggerated, nor the sense of human dignity it leaves with the reader." Taken from the review at http://www.amazon.co.uk (accessed November 15, 2001).

50. See, for example, the interesting on-line article by Barbara Bauer and Waltraud Strickhausen, "Autobiographie oder Fiktion? Zum Fall Benjamin Wilkomirski," Zum Program der Tagung 'Für ein Kind War das Anders' (2001), located at http://staff-www .uni-marburg.de/tatbauerb/text_wilkom.html (accessed July 30, 2001).

reality to give context to their imaginary characters and plots. But even realistic novels, like fantasies, create the worlds their characters inhabit. Thus the issues of differences and similarities among these literary genres center upon both the actual existence of the characters and the reality of their larger contextual world, hence upon what readers expect from each genre.[51]

Distinguishing fact from fiction is no easy task, therefore, and even if Ricoeur's three-tier model is promising in terms of determining the referentiality/nonreferentiality of a given text, it is important to be aware of its limitations. Ricoeur's model may be able to link the literary presentation of explanatory arguments with "real" information on the documentary level. But, as Ricoeur himself notes, "the whole structure of the linguistic community to which I belong" relies on whether the truth-claim of a given testimony is trusted or not.[52] Furthermore, because we never face a text that can be totally verified, there is only a certain amount of information that can be cross-checked. There will always be some claims, arguments, and information the factuality of which can only be assessed as part of a verifiable context.

Now that we have reviewed the insights of current research with regard to genre recognition and referentiality, we are in a favorable position to discuss the genre of the books of Kings in the Hebrew Bible.

Balls, Pitchers, and Quarterbacks

Describing the intent of the historian(s) responsible for the books of Kings—or, in broader terms, the so-called Primary History or Deuteronomistic History—is a complex task. However, one of the most important issues in the scholarly debate, at least as far as the present study is concerned, is whether this history-writing betrays what has been labeled *antiquarian* or *historiographical* interests—not least because these characterizations of authorial intent have been linked by some scholars to matters of factuality. Before we proceed, therefore, it seems appropriate to make a few comments on these terms.

The distinction between the interest of the antiquarian and the historian (with the corresponding terms *antiquarianism* and *historiography*) goes back a long way, but probably no one has influenced the current use of the term *antiquarian* as much as the classical historian Arnaldo Momigliano. Already in his *Ancient History and the Antiquarian* (1950),

51. Berkhofer, *Beyond the Great Story*, 67.
52. Ricoeur, "Humanities between Science and Art," 7.

we find a substantial discussion of the conflict between antiquarians and historians in the early modern period. Subsequently, these views were refined and elaborated in a series of individual studies on Herodotus, Gibbon, and other writers, as well as in wider surveys—especially *The Place of Ancient Historiography in Modern Historiography* (1979) and his Sather lectures, *The Classical Foundations of Modern Historiography*, first delivered in 1961 but extensively revised and published posthumously in 1990. Mark Salber Phillips, in an article on Momigliano, writes:

> His most elegant formulation, "Historiography on Written Tradition and Historiography on Oral Tradition" (1961), sums up more than two millennia of historical writing with astonishing economy. Here Momigliano points to the combination in Herodotus of geographic and ethnographic interests derived from the non-Hellenic world with the fundamental Greek idea that the historian's primary duty is to collect and preserve traditions, particularly those concerning the events of the recent past. Thucydides, in turn, rejected parts of this Herodotean synthesis and restricted history to a linear narrative of recent politics. In imposing this more rigorous definition, Thucydides excluded other kinds of knowledge about the past. This alternate knowledge came to express itself in erudite monographs based on written traditions. It was antiquarian and systematic, and it formed a natural alliance with philosophy rather than political narrative.[53]

Though Momigliano never saw an absolute divorce between historiography and antiquarianism (or *erudite research*), he nevertheless upheld a clear distinction between the two: "Historiography from Thucydides onward was above all political in subject-matter, it set out to explain and instruct, it followed a chronological order, and was concerned with great events, with important nations or cities. Erudite research on religion, art, customs, proper names, events of obscure cities or nations and so on was excluded; usually . . . it [i.e., erudition] was hostile to chronological order."[54] Elizabeth Rawson similarly argues that, while "Roman historiography strove for 'literary elegance' and had a 'moral aim,' antiquarian writing was 'a scholarly genre' with 'a lack of literary pretention . . . a bias to religious and political

---

53. Mark Salber Phillips, "Reconsiderations on History and Antiquarianism: Arnaldo Momigliano and the Historiography of Eighteenth-Century Britain," *Journal of the History of Ideas* 57 (1996) 297–316. Quoted from the online edition, http://muse.jhu.edu/demo/journal_of_the_history_of_ideas/57.2phillips.html (accessed May 9, 2003).

54. From Arnaldo Momigliano, *Studies in Historiography* (London: Weidenfeld & Nicolson, 1966) 217.

institutions,' and emphasis on 'the giving of causes or origins.' "[55] And a quotation from Polybius demonstrates that this distinction was already acknowledged in the classical era: "The serious historians . . . were contemporary historians."[56]

Moving away from Roman and Greek historiography, we find the same terminology in discussions on ancient Israelite and early Christian history-writing. Hubert Cancik, though recasting antiquarianism as "cultural historiography," maintains the same distinction in his discussion on Luke's history-writing.[57] Knauf, in his discussion of history-writing in ancient Israel, similarly asserts that "history that does not try to arrive at generalizations (as, for example, the mechanics of state formation) would not be, in my opinion, history at all, but antiquarianism, which boils down to running an intellectual curiosity shop with no more relevance to society at large than providing entertainment for the idle, the jaded and the doomed."[58] Thompson also characterizes historiography as the critical evaluation of the past, as distinct from antiquarianism, which displays the "more ecumenically pluralistic motivations of the librarian," whose aim is "to preserve what is old."[59]

---

55. Elisabeth Rawson, *Intellectual Life in the Late Roman Republic* (London: Duckworth, 1985) 233.

56. See also Momigliano (*Studies in Historiography*, 217), who explains that "even at the beginning this antiquarian research was concerned with written sources, with collecting and reporting documents from archives, describing statues and buildings, interpreting foreign languages . . . we must emphasize that . . . the use of primary documents is in antiquity the custom not of historians but of 'archaeologists,' 'philologists,' 'grammarians,' that is, of antiquarians." Historiography, on the other hand, is characterized by an emphasis on political history with the highest priority given to eyewitness accounts and the author's firsthand investigation. Marincola ("Greco-Roman Historiography," 307) notes on antiquarianism that "this term is something of a catch-all, but it usually comprehends a type of learned research into origins, and in particular is concerned with names and etymologies, institutions, rituals, inscriptions or documents, monuments, and topography."

57. Hubert Cancik, "The History of Culture, Religion, and Institutions in Ancient Historiography: Philological Observations Concerning Luke's History," *JBL* 116 (1997) 681.

58. Knauf, "From History," 35 n. 1; cf. Thomas Bolin, "History, Historiography, and the Use of the Past in the Hebrew Bible," in *The Limits of Historiography: Genre and Narrative in Ancient Historical Texts* (ed. Christina Shuttleworth Kraus; Leiden: Brill, 1999) 131 n. 69.

59. Thomas L. Thompson, "Historiography (Israelite)," *ABD* (ed. David Noel Freedman; New York: Doubleday, 1992) 3.209. See also Bolin, "History, Historiography," 131 n. 69, for the same distinctions.

So much for terminology. We now turn to a discussion of *how this distinction is applied* in scholarly readings of the historical information in the Hebrew Bible, in particular the books of Kings. Literature on the character of history-writing in ancient Israel is both vast and multi-faceted and, because it is impossible within the limits of the present book to give a satisfactory presentation of the history of scholarly research in this regard, we will concentrate in the pages that follow on the "quarterbacks" in the study of ancient Israelite history-writing and point out other works that give a more-thorough presentation of the other "players in the league."[60]

In 1943, Martin Noth described the Deuteronomistic Historian as an *antiquarian*: "The closest parallels [to the Deuteronomistic Historian are those Hellenistic and Roman historians who use older accounts, mostly unacknowledged, to write a history not of their own time but of the more or less distant past. . . . We owe the preservation of valuable old material wholly and solely to this respect for the value of old narratives and historical accounts."[61] A year later, Gerhard von Rad, in contrast, defined ancient Israelite history-writing as being based on "a particular form of causational thinking, applied in practice to a broad succession of political events," which he contrasted with "mere antiquarian details."[62] Both agree that the texts in question—the Succession Narrative (von Rad) and the Deuteronomistic History (Noth)—are history-writing in some sense. But, while Noth describes the Deuteronomistic Historian as an antiquarian, first and foremost writing on the distant past, von Rad labels him a historian or

---

60. One of the most recent reviews can be found in Bolin, ibid., 113–33.

61. Martin Noth, *The Deuteronomistic History* (JSOTSup 15; Sheffield: JSOT Press, 1981) 11, 84. Translated from Martin Noth, *Überlieferungsgeschichtliche Studien* (Halle: Max Niemeyer, 1943).

62. Gerhard von Rad, "The Beginning of Historical Writing in Ancient Israel," in *The Problem of the Hexateuch and Other Essays* (trans. E. W. Trueman Dicken; Edinburgh: Oliver and Boyd, 1966) 166–67. See also the chapter on "Methodology" in Gerhard von Rad, *Old Testament Theology* (trans. D. M. G. Stalker; vol. 1; Edinburgh: Oliver and Boyd, 1962). On the difference between Homer and ancient Israelite history-writing, von Rad notes that "the main difference lies in the fact that in the rendering of her story Israel handled the old material much less freely than the Greeks. A later age could not venture to recast the old legends in respect of theme and thought and to combine them so as to give rise to what was in fact a new history complete in itself. They were bound in a much more conservative way to what had come down to them, and especially to the forms in which they had received it—that is, they handled it much more as if it were a document. The result of this . . . was a completely different form of theological handling of the tradition" (*Old Testament Theology*, 124).

historiographer occupied with "chronological order," "great events," and "important nations or cities," to use Momigliano's terminology.

Moving from these still-influential "quarterbacks" to the present, two other "quarterbacks" immediately spring to mind: John Van Seters and Baruch Halpern. Van Seters, *In Search of History* (1983),[63] and Halpern, in *The First Historians* (1988),[64] argue (as did Noth and von Rad) in favor of the thesis that the Former Prophets constitute history-writing. It is fair to say, however, that while Noth and von Rad never really provided systematic arguments in favor of the thesis, credit must be given to Van Seters and Halpern for providing these arguments.

In Search of History

The aim of Van Seters's study is to determine a terminus a quo for the final form of Genesis–Kings, the so-called Primary History, by comparing it with other pre-Hellenistic historical writings. Van Seters, in what must still be considered "the most significant recent synthetic work on ancient Near Eastern history-writing,"[65] begins by defining history as "the intellectual form in which a civilization renders account to itself of its past"[66] and seeks—by means of a survey of ancient Near Eastern history-writing from the pre-Hellenistic period—"to understand the origins and nature of history-writing in ancient Israel."[67] Van Seters points to "genre as the key issue"[68] and concludes his survey by asserting that no historiographic literature developed in Egypt, the Hittite Empire, or Mesopotamia. Though all of these neighbors of Israel *did* write about the past, Van Seters finds no historiographical works among them similar to those of Israel and Greece—that is, the history-writing found in the Hebrew Bible and the histories of Herodotus and Thucydides, especially the former. These texts, according

---

63. John Van Seters, *In Search of History: Historiography in the Ancient World and the Origins of Biblical History* (New Haven: Yale University Press, 1983; repr. Winona Lake, Ind.: Eisenbrauns, 1997) and the sequels *Prologue to History: The Yahwist as Historian in Genesis* (Louisville: Westminster/John Knox, 1992); idem, *The Life of Moses the Yahwist as Historian in Exodus–Numbers* (Louisville: Westminster/John Knox, 1994).

64. Halpern, *The First Historians*. See now also Baruch Halpern, *David's Secret Demons: Messiah, Murderer, Traitor, King* (Grand Rapids, Mich.: Eerdmans, 2001).

65. Brettler, *The Creation*, 11.

66. Van Seters, *In Search of History*, 1, following the classical definition of Johan Huizinga, "A Definition of the Concept of History," in *Philosophy and History: Essays Presented to Ernst Cassirer* (ed. Raymond Klibansky and H. J. Paton; Oxford: Clarendon, 1936) 9.

67. Van Seters, *In Search of History*, 6.

68. Ibid., 354.

to Van Seters, are to be distinguished from other ancient Near Eastern pre-Hellenistic writings about the past for at least two reasons.[69]

First, following M. Noth's hypothesis that Deuteronomy, Joshua, Judges, Samuel, and Kings originally were a literary entity, Van Seters postulates that an exilic author,[70] the so-called Deuteronomistic Historian, collected disparate material and arranged it paratactically[71] into a continuous history, the so-called "Deuteronomistic History." Though using existing material, he—according to Van Seters—acted more like an author than a redactor, and Van Seters finds the nearest parallel to this kind of work in Greek historiography, especially Herodotus: "On the basis of narrative style and technique alone the Old Testament and Herodotus share a great deal in common and ought to be studied together."[72] Considering content and composition techniques, Van Seters

---

69. Flemming A. J. Nielsen (*Tragedy*, 105–7) also points to another important difference: the role of the divine in history. While all deities in the ancient Near East involve themselves to some extent in human affairs, it is only in Greek and Israelite historiography that we find the deity working toward a given goal. Referring to J. Licht, Nielsen states that, "if it is not in Israel's immediate neighborhood that we find the same conception of history as that of the Old Testament, where the deity works throughout many generations in accordance with Licht's 'long-term policy,' we can indicate Hellas instead, where the said characteristic is recognizable in Herodotus, among others" (p. 107).

70. While our main interest in Van Seters's study is his treatment of genre, Van Seters is also, or perhaps first and foremost, interested in the date of the composition. Due to the similiarities between Herodotus and the Deuteronomistic History, Van Seters postulates that both histories originated in the 6th century B.C.E. and that the latter was shaped under "considerable foreign influence" (Seters, *In Search of History*, 8).

71. One of three rhetorical figures used in the ordering of textual material:

1. *Parataxis*, the placing of clauses etc. one after another, without words to indicate co-ordination or subordination or cohesion between clauses [or actions] of equivalent rank joined by simple conjunctions (for example: *and*, *but*); cf. Susan Melrose, *A Semiotics of the Dramatic Text* (New Directions in Theatre; New York: St. Martin's, 1994) 274. Parataxis has implications of sequentiality (and . . . and . . . and).

2. *Hypotaxis*, the subordination of one clause to another or cohesion through dependency of clauses [or actions], joined by relative pronouns etc. Hypotaxis has implications of simultaneity (*while . . . as . . . besides*); cf. Melrose, *A Semiotics of the Dramatic Text*, 274.

3. *Katachresis*, misapplication; originally meaning the use of metaphors for objects for which there is no name, for example, "the leg of the table"; or in the usage of G. Spivak, a process of reinscription, jarring articulations; G. Spivak, "Identity and Alterity: An Interview," *Arena* (1991) 70. Katachresis has implications of temporal discontinuity (*This. This. This.*).

(Source: The University of Wales, Aberystwyth, Performance Studies Homepage at http://www.aber.ac.uk/~psswww/pf30610/lecture4.htm [accessed December 10, 2001])

72. Van Seters, *In Search of History*, 39. With regard to the more annalistic material included in the history—that is, the information allegedly drawn from named sources—Van Seters points to the Babylonian Chronicle as the nearest parallel.

notes that both "deal with recent events, such as the Persian Wars or the Exile," and that both shape existing annalistic sources and popular traditions into a "multigenre product."[73] With regard to factuality or referentiality, Van Seters regards them both as forms of creative historiography, expressing the ideologies, perspectives, and distortions of the authors and reflecting the historical, political, religious, and other worlds of their origins and transmission. According to Van Seters, the Deuteronomistic Historian therefore is "the first known historian in Western civilization truly to deserve this designation."[74]

Second, while acknowledging that king lists, genealogies, royal inscriptions, chronicles, myths, legends, and so on *were* used outside Israel and Greece as accounts of the past, Van Seters asserts that they did not lead to *true* history-writing, for "only when the nation itself took precedence over the king, as happened in Israel, could history-writing be achieved."[75] In other words, while the accounts of the past evidenced by the above-mentioned Greek and ancient Israelite history-writing are characterized as "true history writing," the other "historiographical genres" are described by Van Seters as didactic, pragmatic, or propagandistic and therefore not to be regarded as historiography proper.

As might be expected, Van Seters's work has caused both great appreciation and controversy. Reviewers have used labels such as "important" and "praiseworthy,"[76] "stimulating,"[77] and "most significant"[78] to describe Van Seters's contribution, while at the same time heavily criticizing a number of premises underlying his thesis.

(1) Van Seters's subscription to the well-known definition of history by Johan Huizinga is problematic. By identifying true history-writing with "national histories" and arguing that this identification is in line with Huizinga's definition, it appears, in Lawson Younger's words, "that Van Seters has misunderstood Huizinga's definition and in-

---

73. Ibid., 51.

74. Ibid., 362.

75. Ibid., 355.

76. K. Lawson Younger, "Book Review: Van Seters, John. *In Search of History: Historiography in the Ancient World and the Origins of Biblical History.* New Haven and London: Yale University Press, 1983," *JSOT* 40 (1988) 110, 114.

77. Helga Weippert, "Book Reviews: Van Seters, John. *In Search of History: Historiography in the Ancient World and the Origins of Biblical History.* New Haven, Conn.: Yale University Press, 1983," *Journal of Religion* 67 (1987) 531.

78. Marc Zvi Brettler, "Book Reviews: Van Seters, John. *In Search of History: Historiography in the Ancient World and the Origins of Biblical History.* New Haven, Conn.: Yale University Press, 1983," *Journal of Religion* 70 (1990) 11.

vested it with a meaning quite different from the Dutch historian's."[79]
This same point is made by Halpern, who states that "ironically, the
author [Van Seters] appropriates J. Huizinga's definition of *history*, but
construes it so as to exclude Huizinga's own work. Huizinga also af-
firms that only texts intended to accurately depict events are history, a
qualification Van Seters violates, in silence."[80] Younger proceeds to
demonstrate that, for Huizinga, history-writing is not necessarily
"nationalistic" and that Van Seters has been influenced by the historicist's view of history as secular, unbiased, antithetic to religion, non-
pragmatic and nondidactic. Younger concludes that "Van Seters's
definition of history writing is inadequate for an investigation of ancient Near Eastern or biblical history writing (or for that matter, any
history writing)."[81]

(2) Though stating that genre is "the key issue in the discussion,"[82]
Van Seters never provides his readers with a proper definition of
genre. This forces Van Seters into circular argumentation. Because, as
Younger points out, he assumes that "there is a particular genre of history writing which is distinct from a larger genre of historiography,"[83]
namely "national histories," his genre analysis "becomes a hunt for the
point of transformation into the nationalistic form."[84] This reveals,
furthermore, that Van Seters's concept of genre is too simplistic. With
a quotation from Ralph Cohen on genres as "open categories,"[85]
Younger concludes that

> from the Renaissance and until well on into the eighteenth century
> genres were carefully distinguished, and writers were expected to fol-
> low the rules prescribed for them. This was, however, hardly the case
> in the ancient Near East. And unfortunately, many OT critics read this
> Western European genre theory into biblical literature. Thus, while

---

79. Quotation from Younger, "Book Review," 111, where the appropriate quotations
from Huizinga also can be found.

80. Baruch Halpern, *The First Historians*, 14 n. 10.

81. Younger, "Book Review," 110–12. See also Brettler's critique of Huizinga's definition as being too rigid in its distinction between history and literature: "Any understanding of history which depends on historicity cannot be profitably applied to the
biblical corpus. In sum, to the extent that Huizinga's definition of history implicitly emphasizes a correct self-understanding by the civilization, it is unsuitable for the Bible,
which typically cannot be evaluated in these terms" (*The Creation*, 11). For the latter, see
also Brettler, *The Creation*, xxxii–xxxiii.

82. Van Seters, *In Search of History*, 354.

83. Younger, "Book Review," 112.

84. Ibid., 112.

85. Ralph Cohen, "History and Genre," *New Literary Theory* 27 (1986) 204.

Van Seters's efforts at understanding the texts are praiseworthy, his generic approach cannot succeed in helping to clarify the issues confronting a study of ancient historiography.[86]

Though ancient authors *were* expected to follow the rules prescribed for them, as Pelling has pointed out in his treatment of the *Hellenica*s (see p. 197), Younger's main point—that Van Seters's concept of genre is too rigid—finds support in current genre research and remains intact.

Another problem in this regard is Van Seters's apparent confusion of the labels "antiquarianism" and "historiography." While these labels, as is evident from the above discussion, are used to designate *different* subgenres within the larger category of "history-writing" in both ancient and classical history, Van Seters has dismissed the distinction as "not easy to maintain"[87] and uses the terms almost interchangeably. He maintains that the Mesopotamian king lists reflect "antiquarian or 'historical' interest" or exhibit "antiquarian and historiographic intentions."[88] This a priori dismissal of a generally accepted genre designation indicates, as Thomas Bolin remarks, "that Van Seters's aim is more to redefine ancient historiography while still using that term in regard to the Hebrew Bible than to reassess the question whether the Hebrew Bible is any kind of historical writing at all."[89]

(3) A further point of criticism concerns Van Seters's claim that the demonstrated (and acknowledged by other scholars) similarities between Herodotus and the Deuteronomistic Historian legitimate and even necessitate a comparison of the Hebrew Bible's history-writing with Herodotus's. As Younger states,

this is true only if one accepts Van Seters's dates for the Dtr. While there can be little doubt that there was contact and subsequent influence between the Hebrews and the Greeks, one must question if Van Seters's heavy dependence on the comparison of Greek historiography with Israelite is truly justified. Van Seters argues that the issue of date cannot be used to avoid such a comparison, but he does so by redating the biblical material by means of such a comparison (p. 8). This is highly circular argumentation![90]

(4) A last criticism worth mentioning also concerns Van Seters's comparison of DtrH with Herodotus. Helga Weippert, in her review

---

86. Younger, "Book Review," 114.
87. Van Seters, *Prologue to History*, 96.
88. Van Seters, *In Search of History*, 71, 76.
89. Bolin, "History, Historiography," 130–31.
90. Younger, "Book Review," 114–15.

of Van Seters's work, states that "my skepticism concerns Van Seters' comparison between Herodotus and the Deuteronomistic Historian"[91] and asks:

> Is it sufficient to prove that both histories originated in the 6th century B.C.E. and that the Deuteronomistic history was shaped under "considerable foreign influence" (p. 8)? Typical for both works is their reshaping of traditions, dovetailing them into the concept of the whole, their creation of a chronological framework for the events, and their use of parataxis as a literary technique, thus creating "a sense of unity in a long and complex work" (p. 358). In my opinion, it was not "Dtr's unfortunate fate . . . that, unlike Herodotus, he remained anonymous, so that his work has been fractured into a number of canonical books" (p. 359). Contrary to Herodotus, he never introduces his own person, and he never speaks of himself in the first person. Instead, it is the word of Yahweh uttered mostly by prophets that shapes the Deuteronomistic history. It is true, prophets and oracles do appear in Herodotus' history, but their role is incidental and not substantial. After having introduced himself, Herodotus informs the reader of the purpose of his history: human events, manly deeds, and the reasons leading to wars should be remembered. Could such an introduction open the Deuteronomistic history?[92]

The First Historians

Baruch Halpern, on the other hand, supports his thesis by means of an exegesis of biblical texts from the Deuteronomistic History, in which he tries to discern the logic of *authorial intent*. Having acknowledged the *formal* identity of "romance" with "history," Halpern argues that, "whether a text is history, then, depends on what its author meant to do"[93]—that is, on its "author's relationship to the evidence" and its "antiquarian interest."[94] Through an extensive analysis of the themes and working techniques of the Deuteronomistic Historian, designated H(Dtr) by Halpern, he draws two conclusions. First, he asserts, the H(Dtr) had a genuine historical consciousness and historical intent:

> The historians of Deuteronomistic History could and did consciously differentiate myth and history, evidence from confection, and reconstruction from dramatization; that they set out from the conviction that history vindicated their partisan biases to set down what they could

---

91. Weippert, "Book Review," 530.
92. Ibid.
93. Halpern, *The First Historians*, 8.
94. Ibid.

learn of the events; that their antiquarian curiosity balanced the urge to censorship; that they subdued whatever was ideologically troubling more by metahistorical, editorial discourse than by falsifying concrete political developments.[95]

Second, the H(Dtr), according to Halpern, built his narratives on sources, which he only bent or supplemented with imaginary "facts" under *certain* circumstances—that is, when gaps or apparent contradictions made it necessary. While acknowledging this creativity in H(Dtr)'s composition technique, Halpern nevertheless maintains that he was a *responsible* historian: "However much he might twist contradictory detail, or press refractory fact into uneasy ideological service, H(Dtr) relied upon a fair representation of the past to prove his point."[96] By doing so, H(Dtr), according to Halpern, not only betrays a sincere historical intent but also demonstrates that he was engaged in fundamentally the same enterprise as Greek historians such as Herodotus, Thucydides, Xenophon, and Polybius.[97]

> The secret of historical method—that one must put the sources to proof—was no mystery in antiquity. Thucydides and Hecateus were conscious of it; the urge, found in Hesiod's *Theogony*, to find the literal truth probably presupposes the same principle. Whether H(Dtr) employed the method is moot. But that he attempted sincerely to analyze the past insofar as he could know it, to learn from the past as he could grasp it, should be clear. H(Dtr) saw a pattern in the transactions of Yhwh with Israel, a pattern more profound than the ones Mesopotamians refined from portents (Deut. 4:19). Because *all* human history, in his view, manifested and certified divine intent, every aspect of history was a field for collecting data. This is a start in the development of the genre of history, of antiquarian research, as we know it.[98]

Halpern, not surprisingly, has been criticized even more than Van Seters, probably due to his more provocative style.

(1) By postulating that the H(Dtr) only elaborated on the material when gaps or apparent contradictions made it necessary, Halpern begs the question (phrased rhetorically by Brettler) "How do we know if an elaboration goes beyond the evidence the author had, especially when that evidence is no longer available to us?"[99] We *don't* know! Halpern may have provided good exegetical arguments to identify the loca-

---

95. Ibid., 277.
96. Ibid., 207.
97. Ibid., 233–34, 243–44.
98. Ibid., 235.
99. Brettler, *The Creation*, 11.

tions where such elaborations and gap-fillings are *possibly* to be found, but we only have the author's—and Halpern's—word for it. Only occasionally can we verify the distinction by material external to, for example, the book of Judges and Halpern's exegesis.

(2) This methodological problem becomes even clearer when we consider Halpern's main argument. For, if it cannot be demonstrated heuristically that the H(Dtr) was loyal to his sources and responsible in his elaborations, Halpern's assertion that the H(Dtr) had a genuine historical consciousness and historical intent is flawed. Recalling Ricoeur's three-tier model cited above, we see clearly that Halpern is much too optimistic about what can be deduced from the literary and explanatory levels. Halpern has, in my opinion, made a good case for the view that the H(Dtr) had a genuine historical interest and *intended* to represent the past responsibly regardless of whatever religious, political, or other purpose he had for his narrative. What Halpern has *not* demonstrated, however, is whether he succeeded.

This is precisely what Shaye D. Cohen has in mind when, in a review of Halpern's work, he distinguishes "authorial intent" from "authorial competence" and points out that, even if the author *did* intend to write history, we still need to determine whether he succeeded in doing so.[100] Halpern, in Cohen's view, "does not devote enough attention to proving that he succeeded." Though admitting that Halpern's thesis—that "the biblical author had an antiquarian's interest in the past"[101]—is possible, Cohen's evaluation of Halpern's work comes out on the negative side: "The thesis is self-validating, and the initial assumption is questionable."[102] The same judgment can be found in Patrick M. Arnold's review: "By casting the debate largely as a question of H(Dtr)'s sincerity and competence, H[alpern] rhetorically takes the reader's eyes off the historical ball, so to speak, in order to focus on the skills and sincerity of the pitcher. Nevertheless, serious questions of the deuteronomistic history's historicity remain."[103]

This is too skeptical, however. While both Cohen and Arnold correctly note that Halpern confuses authorial intent with authorial skill

---

100. Shaye J. D. Cohen, "Book Reviews. Van Seters, John. *In Search of History: Historiography in the Ancient World and the Origins of Biblical History.* New Haven: Yale University Press, 1983," *American Historical Review* 95 (1990) 1500–1501.

101. Ibid., 1501.

102. Ibid.

103. Patrick D. Arnold, "Book Reviews: Van Seters, John. *In Search of History: Historiography in the Ancient World and the Origins of Biblical History.* New Haven: Yale University Press, 1983," *CBQ* 52 (1990) 713–14.

and that he does not devote enough attention to whether the H(Dtr) actually succeeds in what he intends to do, Halpern has argued convincingly that H(Dtr)'s work on the literary and explanatory levels bears all signs of being an intended account of a real past. What lacks in Halpern's work, then, is a clearer consciousness of the limitations of his analysis. Though Halpern is aware of the distinction between authorial intent and competence,[104] he nevertheless overstates his argument on authorial intent by asserting that the H(Dtr) not only intended to write history but also succeeded in doing so. He may have. But by failing to admit that this is impossible to "prove" from the literary and explanatory levels, he gets "sticky" hands, as James C. VanderKam puts it: "Halpern . . . writes that for John Van Seters the historian was '. . . a rogue and a fraud, a distributor of taffy' (p. 31). Yet Halpern's historian, too, seems to have had something sticky on his hands."[105]

(3) A final criticism is that Halpern, like Van Seters, seems to blend the generally accepted genre definitions of "historiography" and "antiquarianism," thus making a comparison of the Deuteronomistic History with other historical works more difficult. For example, he writes in the very beginning of his 1988 work that the "thesis of the volume is that some of these authors—those who wrote works recognizably historical—had authentic antiquarian intentions"[106] and argues that Macaulay's "Bacon" or "Clive" "remain historical because they are antiquarian."[107]

Though Halpern's study can rightly be described as a rejoinder to Van Seters, their contrasting methods are not as incompatible as they may seem, or as Halpern himself argues! Kurt L. Noll, in a message posted on the ANE mailing list, rightly notes that Halpern "has not 'refuted' Van Seters. If viewed as allies, Van Seters and Halpern generate a powerful (and almost convincing) argument that the Former Prophets were conceived by their ancient authors to be 'history.'"[108] In singling out the importance of Van Seters's and Halpern's contribu-

---

104. Cf., e.g., Halpern, *The First Historians*, 67.

105. James C. VanderKam, "Book Reviews: Van Seters, John. *In Search of History: Historiography in the Ancient World and the Origins of Biblical History.* New Haven: Yale University Press, 1983," *Interpretation* 44 (1990) 293–95.

106. Halpern, *The First Historians*, 3.

107. Ibid., 11; cf. 12, 235.

108. Posted on the ANE mailing list, March 25, 2000. Archived at http://www-oi .uchicago.edu/OI/ANE/ANE-DIGEST/2000/v2000.n087. Other e-mails on the subject are archived at http://www-oi.uchicago.edu/OI/ANE/ANE-DIGEST/2000.

tions, however, we must qualify what is meant by "a powerful argument," since both Van Seters and Halpern seem to overstate their cases and blend what can be deduced from the literary, explanatory, and documentary levels in the process of history-writing.

While Van Seters has argued convincingly that the Deuteronomistic History on a number of points resembles Greek historiography and therefore must also be regarded as true history-writing, he is less than convincing on at least two key points. (1) Contrary to the results of current research on genre recognition, he defines true history-writing much too narrowly, thus making the "true" historiographic character of the Deuteronomistic History dependent on whether (a) the Deuteronomistic History was originally an entity written by a single author at a time "when the nation had taken precedence over the king" and whether (b) it resembles the composition technique and literary style of Herodotus on all major points. But, as has been pointed out, even if Deuteronomy–Kings was written, edited, collected, and so on by different authors at different times, this does not mean that we cannot regard it as true history-writing. (2) Just because we find "substantial" similarities between Herodotus and Deuteronomy–Kings does not mean that Deuteronomy–Kings must therefore be considered just as creative as the history of Herodotus has been demonstrated to be.

Halpern is right to focus on authorial intent as an important criterion for establishing the genre of Deuteronomy–Kings, and he has convincingly shown (as pointed out above) that the author did intend to give a reliable account of a real past. However, when it comes to the question of referentiality, Halpern, like Van Seters, uses arguments from the literary/explanatory levels to answer questions that can only be answered on the explanatory/documentary levels. These are precisely the flaws or deficiencies that Noll points out in an evaluation of the scholarly response to Van Seters's and Halpern's studies:

> It is the exegetical detail in Halpern that is valued, not the thesis he derives from the exegesis (a thesis which, in Halpern's baldest formulations, is just an anachronism). For example, the recent Brettler volume directly contradicts Halpern. Halpern had claimed that H(Dtr)'s "antiquarian interest" guarantees H(Dtr)'s desire to write a reliable narrative. Brettler seems more "mainstream" when he asserts, contra Halpern, that the ancient scribe, Dtr, was more concerned with his theory of how things should have been than with what his sources actually said. . . . What has been obscured by Halpern's strongly worded and misleading rhetoric (which borders on insult) is the reality that there is almost no difference at all between Halpern's "H(Dtr)-Historians" and Van Seters's

"Dtr-Historian," with respect to ancient authorial methods. In both theories, these hypothesized ancient scribes gathered sources, sifted them carefully, then wrote "history" in accordance with the conventional ancient understanding of that genre. Both invented "facts" when it suited their purpose (as did all ancient historians), both were "biased" and permitted the bias to distort their vision of past events (also common), and both lacked accurate sources for much of what they wrote (again, not unusual). In other words, both Van Seters and Halpern have painted a plausible portrait of how an actual ancient scribe would have written a history. And both conclude that much of the history is not historical. In the more moderately expressed portions of Halpern's book, he agrees with Van Seters with respect to all these aspects of the issue. The bottom line on both the Van Seters and Halpern "Dtr" hypothesis is that neither scholar has demonstrated that the Former Prophets are works of history writing. . . . To date, Van Seters and Halpern remain the *best* two attempts to argue in favor of the idea that the Former Prophets are history writing, and they are excellent and enlightening reading, highly recommended.[109]

On the subject of determining the genre of the Former Prophets, or the books of Kings specifically, Van Seters and Halpern have provided us with two complementary approaches that must be regarded as equally valuable. We need to analyze the text in its own right, as Halpern does, *and* compare it with similar texts, as Van Seters does. While Halpern's approach is the best guard against viewing the historiographical texts in the Hebrew Bible too naïvely as sui generis, Van Seters's method convinces us not to determine the genre of the same texts exclusively from foreign (i.e., Greek) standards. Taken together, despite their confusion of "historiography" and "antiquarianism," the methods of Van Seters and Halpern must be considered important strategies for determining in what way and to what extent a certain piece of biblical literature is true history-writing.

Having reviewed these two "quarterbacks," we can see clearly that, despite the importance of their contributions, Van Seters and Halpern have left two important questions unanswered. Which specific label, if any, can we use to describe the genre of the books of Kings? Is it possible to be more specific than calling them "history-writing"? And, if it is, which conventions and strategies does this particular genre have for connecting information with reality? It is not surprising that these are the questions that have occupied a number of scholars in the aftermath of the initial reaction to Van Seters's and Halpern's studies.

---

109. See n. 108 above.

Historiography or Antiquarianism

Because Halpern's study was first and foremost valued for its exegetical details, it is not surprising that in the ongoing discussion of the
genre of the so-called historical books of the Hebrew Bible scholars
have concentrated on the unresolved issues in Van Seters's work.
Given that the biblical texts *are* "history-writing" in some sense, how
does this rather broad and general label relate to the more-specific
subgenres of antiquarianism and historiography? More than 50 years
ago Noth had already seen the DtrH as an "antiquarian" (see above,
p. 215), and recent studies clearly go in the same direction (contrast
Van Seters's use of the term "historiography"), even though they do
not always refer to a single "Deuteronomistic" author responsible for a
unified history.

Thomas Thompson rejects the label "historiography" and favors the
designation "antiquarianism," because none of the so-called historical
texts of the Hebrew Bible displays the same formal characteristics that
normally are connected with Greek historiography. Having described
the Greek genre *historia* (but also the genre of Mesopotamian and Hittite history-writing) in terms of "rational critical research and as an
evaluative science, in contrast to the more imaginative literary and poetic traditions of epic and mythology," Thompson argues that "the criterion for this discipline of historiography was historicity: the truth of
the events recounted. In sharp contrast to this extensive historiographical tradition of *Greece* from the early 5th century B.C.E. on, and to some
extent, even that of the Hittites of a much earlier age, biblical tradition
does not present us with any critical historiographical production
prior to the Hellenistic work of Jason of *Cyrene* which 2 Maccabees pro-
fesses to summarize (2 Maccabees 2:23)."[110]

Thompson acknowledges that, *if* the term "historiography" is
broadened by accepting Huizinga's definition of historiography as
"the intellectual form in which a civilization renders account to itself
of its past," that is, history *interpreted*, then it *does* allow us to "understand the documentary sources of the pentateuch, the final editions
of the 'former prophets,' and the compilations of 1–2 Chronicles,
Ezra and Nehemiah as historiographies, and to speak of their authors as historians."[111] However, he argues that such an understanding
is invalid for a number of reasons. First, by accepting "an intellectual

---

110. Thompson, *Early History*, 373–74.
111. Ibid., 374–75.

tradition of morally and religiously critical commentary on Israel's past as 'historiography,' genre is confused with 'a frame of mind.'"[112] Such a view "blurs the boundaries between genre which were of such importance to late antiquity and confounds current attempts to understand the variety of very distinctive functions that were active in the formation of ancient literature."[113] Second, Thompson argues, what distinguishes the historical narrative from the fictional is neither content nor plausibility but their referent as perceived by their author.[114] Because we have no clear indication of the author's intent in, for example, the "former prophets," such as the clear indications we have in Greek and Hittite historiography, this understanding of the biblical texts (a) "ignores the origins of Greek and Hittite historiography specifically as a critical discipline," and (b) "is dependent on a perception of the larger blocks of prose narrative as substantially unitary, historiographically motivated, productions of literary authors, and denies both the fragmentary nature (and the potentially oral and folkloric roots) of the smaller units collected within the literary contexts of the larger frameworks."[115]

In order to reach a methodologically sound definition of "historiography" as a genre, Thompson points out the necessity of paying due attention to the "considerable number of discrete formal types" in the prose narrative traditions and the redactional techniques employed in combining these types or subgenres. It is this redactional technique that, according to Thompson, reveals the antiquarian interest of the biblical authors, an interest that Thompson sees as

> specifically inimical to that of historiography. Historians ask the question of historicity and critically distinguish and evaluate their sources. They "understand" history, and therefore at times slip into tendentious ideologies and theologies. The antiquarian on the other hand shows the more ecumenically pluralistic motivations of the librarian: classifying, associating, and arranging a cultural heritage that is both greater than the compiler or any single historiographical explanation.[116]

Having discussed the "chronological progression of tradition from Genesis to 2 Kings," Thompson adds that

---

112. Ibid., 375.

113. Ibid.

114. Ibid., 376. Cf. idem, *Early History*, 168; and "Text, Context and Referent in Israelite Historiography."

115. Thompson, *Early History*, 376–77.

116. Ibid., 377. See his "scholarly bibliophiles" in "Text, Context and Referent in Israelite Historiography," 79.

this extended tradition is internally structured very loosely as a succession of heroic biographies. However, this structure, although apparent, clearly stands at a distance from the narratives themselves, and is for the greater part a very secondary ordering of stories that are individually wholly independent of this structure. Externally, Genesis–2 Kings is structured as a succession of great periods. It is extremely difficult to see in this any purpose beyond that of a general classifying or cataloguing function.[117]

Although Thompson does allow for "occasional historiographical tales,"[118] he maintains nevertheless that, due to their antiquarian outlook, "the biblical traditions are rather origin traditions than historiography,"[119] and that they, as such, refer to a "world of story" rather than to a real past:

> Historiography is a subgenre of narrative literature, and, even in the ancient world, distinguishes itself from other narrative genres by its intention to give a representation of what was perceived or traditionally held to be the real world of the past. The worlds of biblical traditions are, however, neither those of the real past, nor of its contemporary world's politics and cant. They are rather worlds of story and fragmented tradition past, worlds from which theology and self-understanding—with their future orientations—spring.[120]

Thompson is followed by Flemming Nielsen, who adopts roughly the same view in his portrait of the Deuteronomist,[121] while Thomas Bolin argues for a similar understanding in his discussion of the use of the past in the Hebrew Bible. Arguing for the importance of upholding the distinction between historiography and antiquarianism, Bolin notes that, "while not all biblical scholars have eschewed the distinction between antiquarian and historiographic writing, that the Bible is an example of ancient antiquarian writing *distinct from ancient historiography* is an option that has not been investigated."[122] Having compared a number of biblical texts with the acknowledged characteristics of historiography and antiquarianism, Bolin concludes that "it is my contention that the Hebrew Bible does not represent any kind of

---

117. Thompson, *Early History*, 378.
118. Ibid., 377.
119. Ibid., 168.
120. Ibid., with reference to Lemche, *Canaanites*, 151ff. See also T. L. Thompson, *The Bible in History: How Writers Create a Past*, 189: "The Bible isn't interested in telling us anything about the past. It is using old traditions about the past as parable."
121. Nielsen, *Tragedy*, 107–14.
122. Bolin, "History, Historiography," 131.

historiography as that genre was understood in antiquity and that the
possibility that it is an example of the equally well-attested literary
specimen of antiquarian writing is one worthy of further investigation."[123] Bolin complains that "the term 'historiography' is understood
not as a genre classification, but rather as a sort of truth claim founded
upon the assumption of equivocation between historical fact and
truth"[124] and insists that

> the historicity of biblical narratives and whether the Hebrew Bible is
> written to be historiography are distinct issues. The latter can be ad-
> dressed only by careful attention to genres as they were understood in
> antiquity, and apart from any doctrinal or philosophical presupposi-
> tions on the part of the investigator. That the biblical authors were con-
> cerned to preserve anything that smacked of antiquity tells us much
> about their motivations which, along with cultural and religious con-
> cerns, appear to be based on values treasured by scribes for millennia.
> That the Bible may not be the coherent, systematic portrayal of ancient
> Israelite history is an assertion that has long been under question. That
> it was never intended to be such by its authors, however, is a possibility
> which now requires consideration.[125]

In assessing Thompson's, Nielsen's, and Bolin's suggestion that the
so-called historical books of the Hebrew Bible manifest antiquarian
rather than historiographical interests, I must make several things
clear. First, though historicity is clearly among the defining elements
of the genre designation "historiography," Bolin is fully in line with
current genre research when he points out that it is not the only one:

> Although Thompson is correct in stressing that historicity is a criterion
> for historiography as a genre designation placed on a text by a reader,
> this criterion cannot be so rigidly maintained when looking at the au-
> thor's intent. History is a past remembered, and the latter two terms
> must be stressed equally. An author may intend to write historiogra-
> phy and instead write a partially incomplete and fictitious account for
> the reason that not everything that happened is remembered and not
> everything that is remembered happened. Thus, while historicity is a
> valuable criterion of reestablishing the validity of ancient historiogra-
> phy, it should not be the only criterion for determining whether a piece
> of writing belongs in the genre of historiography. Much of the present
> confusion in both sides of the debate about Israelite historiography is
> due to the fact that the term "historiography" is understood not as a

123. Ibid., 137.
124. Ibid., 123.
125. Ibid., 137–38.

genre classification, but rather as a sort of truth claim founded upon the assumption of equivocation between historical fact and truth.[126]

Second, there can be no doubt that, *if* the texts of the Hebrew Bible are evaluated on the basis of the conventionally assigned formal criteria of Greek historiography, they are *not* historiography. We find no explicit expressions of authorial intent as we do in Thucydides (and for that matter in the later Jewish and Christian historiographies of Josephus and Luke–Acts; see p. 108 above), just as there are no clear indications of sources' being weighed critically against each other, which is also a characteristic of Greek historiography. Thompson and Bolin may go too far by asserting that the authors were "scholarly bibliophiles" and that they were "concerned to preserve anything that smacked of antiquity," but if the classical definitions of the subgenres of "historiography" and "antiquarianism" are to be maintained, there can be no doubt that the allegedly historical texts of the Hebrew Bible in their overall outlook come closer to the latter than the former.

Furthermore, Thompson and Nielsen seem to go too far in their interpretation of authorial intent. The histories of Herodotus and Thucydides *may* be the yardstick for measuring what can and cannot be dubbed "historiography," and the label "antiquarianism" may be the best fit for the historical texts of the Hebrew Bible among conventional *Hellenistic* and *Classical* genre designations. But it does not follow that, because the historical texts of the Hebrew Bible lack the formal characteristics of Greek (and Roman) historiography, they also lack what these characteristics reveal—namely, a genuine historical consciousness and historical intent. This kind of argumentation (a) arrogantly sets up Greek historiography as the standard against which all other pieces of history-writing in the ancient world must be measured, and (b) precludes the possibility a priori that other ancient Near Eastern genres existed but employed different literary conventions and narrative strategies for the same purpose.[127] Even if, strictly speaking, we

---

126. Ibid., 123. Cf. also Marit Skjeggestad, "'Israels historie'. Litteratur *eller* historie? Eller: Historie *som* litteratur?" *NTT* 97 (1996) 207–8.

127. Though Bolin admittedly is more cautious about avoiding genre designations that are too rigid, he has the same tendency ("History, Historiography," 133) and comments that, "in this focus on the connection between the Hebrew Bible and antiquarian writing, the historical context has moved from the milieu of the ancient Near East to that of the Hellenistic Mediterranean. This shift is congruent with other lines of investigation which are beginning to look to the Hellenistic era as the intellectual background to the creation of the Hebrew Bible. It now remains to elaborate on some recurring features in the biblical texts which support the contention that it constitutes an attempt at

cannot talk about Israelite *historiography*, the historical texts in the Hebrew Bible may very well have historical intent.

Thompson may be correct in that the redactional techniques employed in writing, collecting, and editing the historical texts of the Hebrew Bible betray "antiquarian efforts" and that they reveal an intention that "is specifically inimical to that of historiography."[128] This would be primarily an observation on the formal differences between Greek historiography and Israelite history-writing, however, and not an argument against genuine historical consciousness and historical intent in the Israelite texts. Furthermore, it would only be true *if* historical consciousness and intent were inimical to or at least uninteresting to the subgenre "antiquarianism" (as the genre is generally understood) and, especially, *if* applying the genre designation "antiquarianism" to the texts of the Hebrew Bible were an adequate way of describing their narrative structure.

While it is probably true that an antiquarian's primary goal is not to give an accurate and reliable account of the past, Thompson has not, in my opinion, demonstrated that the redactional techniques used by the authors/editors of the Hebrew Bible are used to describe "worlds of story and fragmented tradition past" rather than "to give a presentation of what was perceived or traditionally held to be the real world of the past."[129] As argued above, we cannot tell from the representational or literary level whether the text's reference is real or imaginative. Even "genuine" historiography makes use of sophisticated literary devices, including those described by Thompson as characteristic of the biblical writers' redactional technique, and Thompson has not proved his assertion that redaction betrays a nonhistorical or nonreferential intent. Historical consciousness may not be explicitly stated and historical intent may be subordinated to other purposes and interests, but there is nothing on the representational level that in itself precludes the possibility that the biblical authors/editors *did* have such intentions. Consequently, the designation "antiquarianism" is highly problematic, even useless, in a description of ancient Israelite history-writing.

---

antiquarian writing rather than historiography, and to examine the lone biblical text which speaks about the Hebrew Bible as a corpus in order to see what light may be shed on this question by what the Bible says about its own composition."

128. Thompson, *Early History*, 377.
129. Ibid., 168.

We may add to the above arguments the fact that the tendency in current research is to avoid genre definitions that are too rigid. John Marincola is worth quoting at length. In his more general considera- tion of Greco-Roman historiography, he notes that certain types of historical information are often "relegated" to the category of "anti- quarianism" for no other reason than that they do not fit into the cate- gory of "historiography":

> The whole notion of "antiquarian" literature has recently been seen as problematic: Benedetto Bravo has demonstrated that Jacoby's category of "philologic-antiquarian" works does not correspond to ancient no- tions but is rather based on the modern separation of philology and history, while Schepens has shown the enormous practical problems raised by the imposition of modern categories onto ancient works. Nevertheless, we note that unlike historians, antiquarians did not usu- ally write in narrative form, but rather in analytic treatises. But the general assumption that there was little commerce between the two is true only up to a point: that history remained largely narrative and eschewed analysis. It can hardly be denied that much of the same ma- terial of interest to antiquarians—rituals, topography, monuments, origins—found its way into histories, even if it was treated differently within an historical narrative. . . . Attempts, therefore, to distinguish "annalists" from "historians" by pointing to subject matter fail be- cause they try to establish an artificial dividing line between what could and what could not be included in a history. . . . Given such a sit- uation, it seems best to abandon the traditional distinctions (i.e., seri- ous pragmatic history could not include marvels, portents, etc.), look instead at all the things included by a specific historian, and then in- terpret the individual work on its own terms. This must be done not to assign an historical work to one or another group, but rather as a first step to understanding what the historian sees as relevant to the por- trait of the past that he is attempting to create, and how the inclusion of such material in his work tries to mediate between that vision of the past and the present reality in which he finds himself. The form and content cannot be divorced from the context in which the work was produced, and the interplay of all of these factors must be considered in any evaluation an historiographical work. Such an approach, it seems to me, better reflects the way the ancients themselves viewed the materials and methods available for an inquiry into the past, and will make it much less likely that we force ancient works into modern categories.[130]

---

130. Marincola, "Greco-Roman Historiography," 307–8.

Thompson, Nielsen, and Bolin may all be correct in rejecting the label *historiography* as suitable for describing ancient Israelite history. But describing the texts as examples of "antiquarianism" seems to run counter to the more-cautious attitude taken by current genre research. The historical texts of the Hebrew Bible are not antiquarianism just because they are not historiography.

*   *   *   *   *

Much more could be said about the works we have reviewed. Each of them contains important contributions to our knowledge of the way that ancient Israelite history-writing was perceived by its ancient authors/readers and, consequently, how we should read it today. Halpern's outstanding contribution is his demonstration that nothing on the literary level prevents us from assigning a genuine historical consciousness and historical intent to the biblical author(s). The main thrust of Van Seters's work is his comparative approach. A comparison of the biblical texts with other pieces of ancient history-writing enables us to determine both the common features and the unique elements in the biblical. Thompson and Bolin, on the other hand, have argued convincingly that a close reading of the biblical texts makes it highly problematic to dub them "historiography," and though their own suggestion of "antiquarianism" may be problematic as well, they have nevertheless launched an important discussion about how to describe the texts on their own terms. Taken together, these approaches enable us to analyze *different aspects* of ancient Israelite history-writing and to formulate more *comprehensive* conclusions on their nature than before.

However, this review has also revealed certain flaws that need to be balanced with the insights previously mentioned from recent genre research. First, all of the works reviewed seem to fall prey to a too-rigid definition of genre. They need to be balanced by a more flexible approach. A promising suggestion by John Marincola is outlined below. Second, the same works seem to confuse or overstate the importance of different levels in the creation of a narrative as outlined in Ricoeur's model. Both Halpern and Thompson fail to pay enough attention to the limitations of the explanatory and representational levels in their arguments for and against genuine historical consciousness and historical intent. Though both acknowledge the importance of the documentary level for determining the character of referentiality, both seem to use arguments from the explanatory and representational levels as the driving force in their synthesis.

A New Approach

Having outlined the insights of modern genre research and de-scribed the benefits of recent studies on ancient Israelite history-writing, I will now seek to apply these insights to the books of Kings. Because both the length and scope of this study prevent a more com-prehensive and independent analysis, I shall limit myself to some rather preliminary observations and suggestions about the question of genre in the books of Kings. As might be expected and for reasons al-ready given, the analysis will be based on Ricoeur's three-tier model.

In order to counterbalance the approaches reviewed above, we will adopt a procedure suggested by John Marincola, namely, to reject too-rigid definitions and applications of the historiographical subgenres. Although he was writing specifically on Greco-Roman historiography, the procedure seems equally applicable to ancient Israelite historiog-raphy and will therefore be used in the following analysis of the ex-planatory/representational levels of the books of Kings.

By rejecting the conventional sharp distinctions between historio-graphical subgenres, Marincola is in full accord with modern genre research. While he does not abandon the existing taxonomy com-pletely, he does call for a new approach that takes into consideration the fact that the form of ancient historiography was "in a constant state of flux, of reaction and revision, of challenge and counter-challenge."[131] Instead of maintaining the conventional generic taxon-omy as the starting point of assigning genre labels to historical texts, he suggests that an analysis of historical works consider five criteria: whether they are *narrative or nonnarrative*, and what their *focalization*, *chronological limits*, *chronological arrangement*, and *subject matter* are. "These criteria can, and often are, interrelated, but we should be wary of automatically assuming that any particular one necessarily determines other aspects of the work. Rather, it is necessary to look at the totality of an historical work before forming conclusions about its nature and purpose."[132]

Narrative or Non-narrative

Obviously, one of the first decisions to be made by a historian, Marincola notes, is "whether he wishes to write an historical synchronic

---

131. Ibid., 130.
132. Ibid., 301–2.

narrative or whether he prefers a more diachronic descriptive method, or indeed some combination of the two."[133] Herman Strasburger, alternatively, suggests "kinetic" and "static" as the two identifiable types of historical-writing in ancient historical works, "kinetic" used for describing the history of wars and events and "static" for representations of culture and civilizations.[134] "Both," Marincola continues, "can be historical although pursuing different ends, and both can be concerned with causes and explanations."[135]

The books of Kings cannot be categorized as *either* narrative or non-narrative. It depends on whether one focuses on the whole or its parts, because it is a multigenre product. If narrative is defined broadly as anything told or recounted, the books of Kings as a whole undeniably qualify as narrative: they are a diachronic examination of the religious life in Israel united and divided, as exemplified by their kings and queens. Beneath the surface, however, the text is clearly a composite text, consisting of various text types ranging from plain narratives (e.g., the introductory narrative on the impotent King David) to annotated lists (e.g., the list of King Solomon's administrative officers in 1 Kings 4) and, not least, chronicle-like information. From 1 Kgs 14:21 onward, the well-known pattern

- In the nth year of King PN_1, PN_2 became king over Israel/Judah
- [Details from the reign of PN_2]
- He did what was pleasing/displeasing to the LORD
- All his actions are recorded in the Annals of the Kings of Israel/Judah
- PN_3 succeeded him as king

is only interrupted by the Elijah-Elisha narrative and supplemented with details where the author/editor found it appropriate and/or had access to additional information.

As for causes and explanations, the text—both as a whole and in its parts—clearly has narrational marks. When a king "walked in the ways of the Lord," he caused God to bless him and, through him, the people he represented. As long as David and Solomon obeyed the Lord, their kingdoms prospered. Conversely, when a king did "what was right in his own eyes" and thereby failed to comply with God's

---

133. Ibid., 302.

134. Hermann Strasburger, *Die Wesensbestimmung der Geschichte durch die antike Geschichtsschreibung* (Wiesbaden: Steiner, 1966) 972–73.

135. Marincola, "Greco-Roman Historiography," 302.

law, he caused him to impose punishment, if not immediately, then eventually. Both the fall of Samaria and the fall of Jerusalem are clearly described as this kind of final punishment by the author(s)/ editor(s), who thereby represents God as the supreme cause of all social and political events in the united and divided monarchies.

Thus, though not being what Marincola calls a "standard narrative history with its smooth connections and story-like structure of beginning, middle and end,"[136] the text nevertheless is a narrative in its own way. By using predominantly chronicle-like information—or, alternatively, casting the information available that way—a story-line is revealed that comprehensively sheds light on the religious ups and downs of Israel and Judah. And both are explained with recourse to Yahweh as the supreme cause of all that happens.

Focalization

Another important step in the examination of the explanatory/representational level is to determine the focus, that is, the orientation or point of view, taken by the narrator. "The possibilities that present themselves," Marincola notes, "range from that of an individual and his actions, one whom the author will argue determined events for his era (Philip, Alexander), to the deeds of a group (Xenophon's *Anabasis*, Caesar's *Gallic War*) to the nations of the whole known world (Diodorus, Pompeius Trogus) with increasing complexity as one treats more theaters and peoples."[137] At the same time, by choosing a particular focalization, the narrator naturally limits his perspective. This means, of course, that only events, persons, and so on that are *relevant* from this particular point of view are included, while others, however important they may be in other contexts, are omitted. This is what Postgate has in mind when he raises the question why the Sumerian King List fails to refer to the kings of Lagash: "It is irrelevant to accuse the King list of omitting things when we don't know why it was compiled and from which sources."[138]

Marincola proceeds by noting that, though the choice of a particular focalization does not ipso facto demand a certain *arrangement*, some types of focalization nevertheless seem to be naturally linked to a certain type of arrangement: "For example, a local history will most

---

136. Ibid., 302.
137. Ibid., 303.
138. Postgate, *Early Mesopotamia*, 32.

easily and appropriately be arranged according to the local magis-
trates, whereas an arrangement by Olympiads is conducive to a universal history."[139]

In the case of מלכים, the book of Kings, the main focus is on a group,
Israel and Judah, represented and personified by its kings and queens.
We need to say *main* focus, however, because, taken in isolation, the
Elijah/Elisha narratives clearly focus on "an individual and his actions, one whom the author will argue determined events for his era."
In the composite text, Elijah and Elisha have another function, however: adding to the picture of the larger group, Israel. This focalization
obviously limits the perspective, because the narrative focuses on Israel and Judah, and foreign rulers—however important their roles
may have been on the world scene—are only mentioned if their actions contribute to the narrative in question.

Chronological Limits

The author of a historical narrative must decide where to begin and
where to end his narrative. This decision is affected, of course, by his
choice of focalization. If the narrative focuses on Caesar as an individual, the chronological limitations are more or less determined. The
choice of chronological limits is also inextricably linked, however, to
the way a narrator casts his narrative. In his well-known work *Metahistory*, Hayden White suggests that all narratives (historical and
fictional) are emplotted in one of four patterns: comedy, tragedy, romance, or satire. White's categorization may very well be too rigid,
but, as argued in the introduction (see p. 12), I concur with Marincola
when he states that, "even if we disagree with the categories and their
exclusivity, nonetheless it cannot be denied that historians 'read' the
events of their history in a certain way, and if, for example, an historian sees his subject as glorious, he might begin and end differently
from one who saw the same events as comic or inglorious.... The
choice of chronological limits was important, therefore, not only for
the investigative work required of the historian, but also for the imposition of meaning and the emplotment of the narrative."[140]

Because the books of Kings focus on the kings of Israel and Judah—
united, divided and, finally, exiled—the chronological limits are more
or less a given. There is the possibility, of course, that the narrative is
part of a larger Deuteronomistic History and must therefore be con-

---

139. Marincola, "Greco-Roman Historiography," 303–4.
140. Ibid., 304–5.

sidered a continuation of the books of Samuel, but this is not the point here. Whatever relationship there may be between the individual books of the Former Prophets, the narrative, by choice of focalization, is clearly chronologically demarcated: from King David's last years (ca. 990 B.C.E.) to the last years of the exiled King Jehoiachin (ca. 560 B.C.E.).

The question of emplotment in the books of Kings is much more problematic: one major disagreement about the books of Kings is concerned with the tenor of the books. Do they begin gloriously and end with hope? Or is the beginning with the old, weak King David foreshadowing a tragic end? Or something in between? However, because it is not the purpose of this study to solve these hitherto unsolved questions, we will limit ourselves to pointing out the useful survey of scholarly research by Iain Provan (in his commentary).[141] The point to be made here is that the books of Kings, as is generally true of historical narratives, *do* have clear chronological demarcations, and these demarcations are closely linked to both focalization and emplotment.

Chronological Arrangement

A fourth element worth investigating in order to uncover historical intent on the explanatory/representational level is the method used to restructure the events underlying the work. Moses I. Finley, in a discussion of the differences between the epic of Homer and the history of Thucydides, notes that the former

> was not history. It was narrative, detailed and precise, with minute descriptions of fighting and sailing and feasting and burials and sacrifices, all very real and very vivid; it may even contain, buried away, some kernels of historical fact—but it was not history. Like all myth, it was timeless. Dates and coherent dating schemes are as essential to history as exact measurement is to physics. Myth also presented concrete facts, but these facts were completely detached: they were linked neither with what went before nor with what came after. . . . Historical husbands and wives grow old, but the plain fact is that neither Odysseus nor Penelope has changed one bit; they have neither developed nor deteriorated, nor does anyone else in the epic. Such men and women cannot be figures in history: they are too simple, too self-enclosed, too rigid and stable, too detached from their backgrounds. They are as timeless as the story itself.[142]

---

141. Provan, *1 & 2 Kings*; cf. idem, *1 and 2 Kings*.
142. Finley, "Myth, Memory, and History," 14, 16. Compare also the demonstration in Hornblower (*Greek Historiography*, 25) that Thucydides' occupation with chronological precision must be considered a trace of historical intention.

This is precisely what Marincola has in mind when he points to chronological arrangement as a key element in historical narratives. One example is the ordering of events according to the year in a more or less strict annalistic narrative. Another way of structuring narratives is to use kings or governors as chronological benchmarks. Following Finley and Marincola, we can state that the chronological system underlying a narrative is therefore an important indication that we *are* dealing with a historical narrative.

As was the case with chronological limitations, the chronological system is likewise linked to focalization. Marincola notes that the annalistic arrangement

> clearly worked well for histories with a single focalization. For large-scale histories, on the other hand, the arrangement by category, begun by Ephorus, was most useful. Using this system it was possible to treat events in one area in some detail and over several years, in order to assist the reader in understanding the events, before moving on to the next theater of action. Some chronological precision was sacrificed for greater comprehensibility.[143]

It is obvious that the books of Kings do have an underlying chronological system. The narrator chose to arrange his material according to the accession of the Israelite and Judean kings and queens, and despite occasional literary digressions (the Elijah/Elisha narratives, the prayer of Isaiah in 2 Kings 19) and regressions or "telescoping" (the account of the fall of Samaria in 2 Kings 17), the sections in question are clearly embedded in the overarching chronological structure mentioned above. The occurrence of an occupation with dates and chronological arrangement is suggestive. The narrative bears the clear marks of being a historical narrative, and these marks are most likely the traces of the author's historical intent.

Subject Matter

A final element to consider is subject matter. What is the narrative about? And what should it be about to be considered a historical narrative? There can be no doubt, as Marincola notes, that "history comprised a recognizable entity in antiquity." The problem comes when modern notions of history govern our assessment of which ancient texts can be regarded as history-writing. Marincola warns that

---

143. Marincola, "Greco-Roman Historiography," 306.

it is not uncommon in modern treatments, however, to find a marked preference for the deeds of war as the "proper" subject of history, such that historians of political and military events become the proper historians, and those who choose other subjects or treat them differently are relegated to an inferior status. The problem with this approach is that in an attempt to find precursors for primarily nineteenth-century notions of history, the vast variety of historiographical output in antiquity is overlooked and minimized. It might be argued that our "great" historians treated political and military history, and that this type thus has a legitimate right to be considered history *par excellence*. But as Guido Schepens has pointed out, this type of history is over-represented in surviving works, and there is plenty of evidence that many (and some of the most important non-surviving) historians saw their task as embracing many things other than wars and political upheavals.[144]

This is not just true for what must be considered the "old paradigm" in historical research, however. In the introduction, we noted the change in subject matter in modern history-writing (see the introduction, pp. 5ff.). Instead of focusing more or less exclusively on kings, emperors, and nations, current historiography tends to engage a number of disciplines in order to write a *histoire totale*. The focus has clearly shifted from political and military history to economic junctures, climatic changes, and sociological patterns in order to paint a much broader and more nuanced picture of a given historical period. This change, as we also noted, must be recommended.

At the same time, however, we need to be aware that the same pitfalls may afflict this approach as they did the "old." Whether we understand history-writing exclusively as treatments of war and politics or demand a multidisciplinary and critical approach to historical research, the danger is present of defining too narrowly what can be accepted as history-writing, ancient and modern alike. Marincola is very clear, therefore, in pointing out the need to counterbalance these "exclusive" tendencies of modern approaches to history-writing:

> So what must first be established is the variety of approaches possible towards the past, and the past must here be seen in its greatest extent and totality. That totality embraces many (and many different types of) subjects: they are, of course, political and military deeds, but they are also cultural events and activities; the religious life of a state and its people; the customs of a people, whether or not these are part of a

---

144. Marincola, "Greco-Roman Historiography," 306, with reference to G. Schepens, "Jacoby's *FGrHist*: Problems, Methods, Prospects," in *Collecting Fragments = Fragmente Sammeln* (Aporemata: Kritische Studien zur Philologiegeschichte 1; ed. Glenn W. Most; Göttingen: Vandenhoeck & Ruprecht, 1997) 146.

formal religion; and even the lives and characters of a state's leaders, particularly important when a state is ruled by a single man or woman. . . . The works of the Hellenistic historians, such as Megasthenes, Berossus of Babylon, Manetho, Timaeus, and Posidonius, clearly included a large amount of material that did not concern itself with political and military affairs. The usual relegation of most of these writers to the category of "ethnography" is a *petitio principii*, and an assumption that such material is something different from and alien to history. Also to be avoided is the relegation of certain types of information to the category of "antiquarianism."[145]

The books of Kings *are* about politics and wars. Consider the delicate maneuvers of David in handing over the throne to Solomon (1 Kings 1–2) or Solomon's diplomacy with Hiram of Tyre when building his palace and temple (1 Kings 5) or Israel's frequent wars with the Arameans (1 Kings 20; 22; 2 Kings 6–7). But however important, interesting, entertaining, and spectacular these passages are, the primary subject of the narrative is *not* the political and military endeavors of the Israelite and Judean kings. The books of Kings is first and foremost about "the religious life of a state and its people." This "layered" approach to the books of Kings has been acknowledged by many commentators but perhaps finds its clearest expression in Iain Provan's guide to the books of Kings.[146]

Thus, following Marincola's rejection of rigid genre distinctions and acknowledgment of the variety of approaches in antiquity that must be appreciated as history-writing, we can conclude that the books of Kings—at least as far as subject matter is concerned—clearly qualify as history-writing.

Synthesis

Where does this cursory analysis of the explanatory/representational level of the narrative lead us? Do the considerations of narrative, focalization, chronology, and subject matter (despite the absence of explicitly-stated authorial intent, whether this reflects a conscious choice or an accidental omission) provide any clues?

Based on our analysis, we can conclude (a) that the book of Kings is a narrative; (b) that by choosing a religious history of the kings of Israel and Judah, the narrator was bound to a close relationship between focalization, chronological limitations, and arrangement; and (c) that

---

145. Marincola, "Greco-Roman Historiography," 306–7.
146. Provan, *1 & 2 Kings*.

because its theme is the religious life of Israel and Judah as represented by their kings and queens, the narrative qualifies as history-writing. In all aspects of the explanatory and representational levels analyzed, therefore, the books of Kings are history-writing and there is nothing to prevent us from ascribing historical intent to the author(s)/editor(s) responsible for the creation/collection of the narrative.

Three points, however, qualify this otherwise clear-cut conclusion. In the presentation of Marincola's procedure for analyzing the explanatory/representational levels of a (potentially) historical narrative, he warned that "these criteria can, and often are, interrelated, but we should be wary of automatically assuming that any particular one necessarily determines other aspects of the work. Rather, it is necessary to look at the totality of an historical work before forming conclusions about its nature and purpose."[147] Only taken together, therefore, are the results conclusive. A second moderating point is that we have not in any way *proved* that the author(s)/editor(s) of the books of Kings had historical intent, let alone that they succeeded in doing what they intended to do, which was to write reliable history. We have only demonstrated that nothing speaks against it. Or, put a little more positively and optimistically, the books bear all the marks of being a historical narrative. Third, we must keep in mind that we have so far only discussed the explanatory and representational levels. And, as Ricoeur's model reminds us, the most decisive arguments are not to be found on these levels but on the documentary level.

Despite the reservations outlined, the results seem to contradict what some scholars have argued. Thomas Thompson is right, for example, in pointing out the need for a comparison on the documentary level with external evidence in an assessment of the text's *epistemic* value, but he also seems to confuse historical *truth* with historical *intent*. Besides leading to confusion, this also leads to a much too-skeptical analysis on the explanatory/representational levels: "Yet, the narration is so unhistorical in both its interests and its goals that we have no way of distinguishing what is historical from the account itself. While reliable history needs confirmation and support from dependable sources, from inscriptions and from records, in this case we shall see that such sources are very hard to come by."[148] Even if a given piece of information is not "true" or "reliable," it does *not* necessarily follow that the author did not have genuine historical intention in writing what he did.

147. Marincola, "Greco-Roman Historiography," 301–2.
148. Thompson, *The Bible in History*, 189–90.

When Robert P. Carroll reminds us of the general possibility that the biblical authors *may* have been rather like James Macpherson (who is alleged to have invented the Celtic poet Ossian) or Shakespeare (who recontextualized historical figures in fictional works), he fails to explain why this possibility leads to a general presumption against reading the Bible as historical.[149]

Because nothing on the explanatory/representational levels prevents us from viewing the narrative as intended history-writing, it would be only natural for us to follow the suggestion of V. Philips Long that, "where the text offers no such clues (another distinct genre such as fable), and where the evidence of the larger context and the flow of the narrative generally suggest a historiographical purpose, this should be the interpreter's working assumption."[150] Having demonstrated the *possibility* or even the *likelihood* of historical intent on the explanatory/representational levels, we can justifiably proceed to a discussion on the documentary level, with this working hypothesis in our minds.

The Documentary Level

By basing arguments for and against factuality and fiction on the explanatory (authorial intention) and especially the documentary (testimony) levels, Ricoeur has given voice to the consensus of contemporary historical theory and epistemology. Because historians (whether they have expressed their historical intent explicitly or not), in contrast to authors of fictional texts, claim accuracy with regard to their subjects, an obvious way of establishing and/or checking their intent is to compare their claims against their alleged referents in the real world.

Ricoeur's model has clear limitations. As Ricoeur himself notes, "the whole structure of the linguistic community to which I belong" relies on whether the truth-claim of a given testimony is trusted or not.[151] Furthermore, because we never face a text that can be verified in its totality, it is only a limited amount of information that can be cross-checked. There will always be a percentage of claims, argu-

---

149. R. P. Carroll, "Madonna."

150. V. Philips Long, "Old Testament History: A Hermeneutical Perspective," *NIDOTTE* (ed. Willem A. VanGemeren; Carlisle: Paternoster, 1997) 89; idem, *The Art of Biblical History* (Grand Rapids: Zondervan, 1994).

151. Ricoeur, "Humanities between Science and Art," 7.

ments, and information whose factuality can only be assessed as a nonverifiable part of a verifiable context. Another warning we need to repeat is that the fusion of fact and fiction—that is, what we see as the blending of genres—sometimes makes it impossible or at least extremely difficult to distinguish between referential and nonreferential claims or information. The problem is surmountable when there is a clear indication of authorial intent on the explanatory level and/or when we find available data on the documentary level to verify or falsify information. It is much more difficult to determine the epistemic value when there is an intentional/unintentional blending of genres.

Because the relationship between the documentary level and the alleged referents in the real world can only be evaluated with recourse to the results of chap. 4, a brief summary of this chapter's conclusions is appropriate. In chap. 4, we compared the books of Kings with external, that is, extrabiblical material from the period it purports to describe. The goal was to determine whether or not the historical information given in the books of Kings either wholly or partly was in line with the information provided by contemporary extrabiblical sources. A number of cases were reviewed, and the conclusion was that, wherever information could be checked against the comparative material, it has proved reliable and "correct." Because a representative number of cases have already been discussed, there is no need to add more. Suffice it to say that due attention must be given to the above-mentioned "wherever." In other words, although a considerable amount of information in the books of Kings *can* be cross-checked against external evidence, there are also a considerable number of "claims, arguments and information, whose factuality only can be assessed as part of a verifiable context."

Where does this take us? Because it is extremely easy to confuse authorial intent with authorial "success," we need to emphasize again that, while the issue of chap. 4 was historical *reliability*, the purpose of the present chapter is *intentionality*. In other words, the purpose here is not to decide whether the author(s) of the books of Kings *succeeded* in writing a historically reliable history but whether he (they) *intended* to do so. What *can* be said, however, on the basis of the documentary level, is that the analysis in chap. 4 *did* find agreement between "real" information (on the documentary level of Ricoeur's model) and the information given in the text, which suggests therefore that the authorial intent was to write reliable history.

Concluding Remarks

At the beginning of this chapter, we demonstrated that a clear trend in current genre research is to avoid rigid genre definitions and to acknowledge genres' nonstatic character. Genres are more like pigeons than pigeonholes! We found Ricoeur's three-tier model especially useful with regard to referentiality. Ricoeur, on the one hand, acknowledges the fact that factual texts employ precisely the same literary devices as a number of fictional genres but, on the other hand, provides historians with a tool that enables them to analyze a given text for authorial intent and the character of referentiality. Although there are no doubt a variety of ways in which a text's explanatory and representational levels can be analyzed, we chose to use a procedure suggested by Marincola. Being aware of the latest developments in genre research and taking into consideration a number of literary features, I find his method to be one of the most up-to-date and relevant approaches for determining whether a given ancient text should be considered history-writing or not.

In my review of previous works on genre in the so-called historical books of the Hebrew Bible, I pointed out a number of important insights. Both Van Seters and Halpern have (each in his own way) demonstrated that a number of literary features display clear historical consciousness and intent on the part of the author. Taken together, their methods constitute an important tool for analyzing the explanatory and representational levels of the biblical texts. Thompson, Nielsen, and Bolin, on the other hand, have just as clearly demonstrated that, no matter what the authorial intent may have been, it was not "historiographical," at least not when this term is reserved for the historical genre that was "defined" in this way by the Greek historians.

In my comparative review of current genre research, I also demonstrated a number of shortcomings. All the studies discussed (with the possible exception of Bolin) seem to base their analysis on an outdated understanding of the nature of genre. While Van Seters exaggerates the importance of elements in Greek historiography for determining the genre of the Deuteronomistic History, Halpern seems to overstate the importance of the explanatory/representational level for determining authorial intent for the biblical texts in question.

There are many ways in which the insights of current genre research can be applied to the allegedly historical books of the Hebrew Bible, and I find Ricoeur's and Marincola's especially promising. In my cursory analysis of the explanatory and representational levels of the books of Kings, I find that in all respects they conform to literary patterns that would be expected of a text referring to the real world—that is, history-writing. Or, put differently, there is nothing on the explanatory and representational levels that prevents us from regarding them as history-writing. This result is in no way compromised by the analysis on the documentary level. The comparison in chap. 5 of a considerable amount of information with external evidence demonstrated that, wherever we can check information with external sources, the texts seem to refer to real-time events, persons, and places.

Thus, although we have not proved the author's historical intent, both the literary features investigated on the explanatory/representational levels *and* the coherence between information on the documentary level and external sources are suggestive of historical intent, at least for the relevant parts. While remaining aware of the danger of confusing parts for the whole, I suggest that, based on the considerable amount of literary features and documentary information, the books of Kings should be recognized as intended history-writing. Although the narratives clearly share features characteristic of Greek historiography, we are, nevertheless, dealing with a different configuration of literary elements characteristic of historical texts, and a more-detailed and precise designation for the genre of ancient Israelite history-writing (e.g., the books of Kings) must await further research.

Further Research

The methodological approach of this book has been chosen deliberately. It is my contention that matters of method and presupposition have been largely overlooked in the debate over the epistemological and historiographical value of the biblical texts, and I have therefore preferred a methodological approach here over an analytical approach. This means, however, that this study cannot stand alone. The thesis cannot be further substantiated until case studies and analytically-oriented research have been done. We need new methodologically-conscious case studies on the books of Kings and other apparently historical books of the Hebrew Bible.

Another area ripe for future research is, as suggested above, comparative historiography. The genre of the apparently historiographical texts in the Hebrew Bible has so far largely been determined on the basis of foreign (i.e., Greek) standards, and further research is necessary before it can be valued on its own terms. The conclusion to this study, therefore, is actually an introduction to future research.

Works Cited

Abegg Jr., M., P. Flint, and E. Ulrich (eds.). *The Dead Sea Scrolls Bible*. New York: HarperCollins, 1999.

Abou-Assaf, A., P. Bordreuil, and A. R. Millard. *La statue de Tell Fekherye et son inscription bilingue assyro-araméenne*. Études assyriologiques. Cahier/Éditions Recherche sur les civilisations 7. Paris: Éditions Recherche sur les civilisations, 1982.

Achtemeier, P. J. "Omne Verbum Sonat: The New Testament and the Oral Environment of Late Western Antiquity." *JBL* 109 (1990) 3–27.

Ackroyd, P. R. "Continuity and Discontinuity: Rehabilitation and Authentication." Pp. 215–34 in *Tradition and Theology in the Old Testament*. Edited by D. A. Knight. Sheffield: JSOT Press, 1990.

Adams, W. J., Jr. *An Investigation into the Diachronic Distribution of Morphological Forms and Semantic Features of Extra-Biblical Hebrew Sources*. Ph.D. dissertation, University of Utah, 1987.

Alexander, P. S. "Orality in Pharisaic-Rabbinic Judaism at the Turn of the Eras." Pp. 158–84 in *Jesus and the Oral Gospel Tradition*. Edited by H. Wansbrough. Sheffield: Sheffield Academic Press, 1991.

Alinei, M. "The Problem of Dating in Historical Linguistics." *Folia Linguistica Historica* 12 (1991) 107–26.

Alter, R. *The Art of Biblical Narrative*. New York: Basic, 1981.

Andersen, F. I. "The Dedicatory Philistine Inscription from Eqron." *Buried History: Quarterly Journal of the Australian Institute of Archaeology* 35 (1999) 7–22

Andersen, F. I., and D. A. Forbes. *Spelling in the Hebrew Bible*. Rome: Pontifical Biblical Institute, 1986.

Ankersmit, F. "Historical Representation." *History and Theory* 27 (1988) 205–13.

Appleby, J., Lynn Hunt, and Margaret Jacob. *Telling the Truth about History*. New York: Norton, 1994.

Ap-Thomas, D. R. "The Phoenicians." Pp. 259–86 in *Peoples of Old Testament Times*. Edited by D. J. Wiseman. Oxford: Clarendon, 1973.

Arnold, P. D. "Book Reviews. Van Seters, John. *In Search of History: Historiography in the Ancient World and the Origins of the Biblical History*. New Haven: Yale University Press, 1983." *CBQ* 52 (1990) 713–14.

Aronowicz, A. "The Secret of the Man of Forty." *History and Theory* 32 (1993) 101–18.

Assmann, J. *Das kulturelle Gedächtnis: Schrift, Erinnerung und politische Identität in frühen Hochkulturen*. Munich: Beck, 1997.

Attridge, H. *Qumran Cave 4, VIII: Parabiblical Texts, Part 1*. DJD 13. Oxford: Clarendon, 1994.

Aune, D. E. "Oral Tradition in the Hellenistic World." Pp. 59–106 in *Jesus and the Oral Gospel Tradition*. Edited by H. Wansbrough. JSNTSup 64. Sheffield: Sheffield Academic Press, 1991.

Avigad, N., and B. Sass. *Corpus of West Semitic Stamp Seals.* Jerusalem: Israel Academy, 1997.

Bagnall, R. S. *Reading Papyri, Writing Ancient History.* London: Routledge, 1995.

Bailey, K. E. "Informal Controlled Oral Tradition and the Synoptic Gospels." *Asia Journal of Theology* 5 (1991) 34–54.

_____. "Informal Controlled Oral Tradition and the Synoptic Gospels." *Themelios* 20/2 (1991) 4–11.

_____. "Middle Eastern Oral Tradition and the Synoptic Gospels." *Expository Times* 106 (1995) 363–67.

Baillet, M., J. T. Milik, and R. de Vaux. *Les 'Petites Grottes' de Qumran: Exploration de la falaise. Les grottes 2Q, 3Q, 5Q, 6Q, 7Q á 10Q. Le rouleau de cuivre.* DJD 3. Oxford: Clarendon, 1962.

Balentine, S. E. " 'You Can't Pray a Lie': Truth *and* Fiction in the Prayers of Chronicles." Pp. 246–67 in *The Chronicler as Historian.* Edited by M. P. Graham, K. G. Hoglund, and S. L. McKenzie. Sheffield: Sheffield Academic Press, 1997.

Barr, J. "Philo of Byblos and His 'Phoenician History.'" *BJRL* 57 (1974) 17–68.

_____. *The Scope and Authority of the Bible.* London: SCM, 1980.

_____. "Story and History in Biblical Theology." *Journal of Religion* 56 (1976) 1–17.

_____. *The Variable Spellings of the Hebrew Bible.* Oxford: Oxford University Press, 1986.

Barré, L. M. *The Rhetoric of Political Persuasion: The Narrative Artistry and Political Intentions of 2 Kings 9–11.* Catholic Biblical Quarterly Monograph Series. Washington, D.C.: Catholic Biblical Association, 1988.

Barstad, H. M. "History and the Hebrew Bible." Pp. 37–64 in *Can a "History of Israel" Be Written?* Edited by L. L. Grabbe. JSOTSup 245. Sheffield: Sheffield Academic Press, 1997.

_____. *The Myth of the Empty Land: A Study in the History and Archaeology of Judah during the "Exilic" Period.* Oslo: Oslo University Press, 1996.

Bartholdy, H. "Syntactical Criteria for Determining Late Biblical Hebrew—and an Appendix on Esther." Paper submitted to Dr. Robert Hubbard at Trinity Evangelical Divinity School, 1997.

_____. "Syntaktiske kriterier til bestemmelse af sent bibelsk hebraisk—med et appendiks om Ester." *Nemalah* 16 (1997) 96–112.

Barton, G. A. "The Cruciform Monument of Maništušu." Pp. 130–35 in *The Royal Inscriptions of Sumer and Akkad.* New Haven: Yale University Press, 1929.

Bauer, B., and Waltraud Strickhausen. "Autobiographie oder Fiktion? Zum Fall Binjamin Wilkomirski." Zum Program der Tagung "Für ein Kind war das anders," 2001. http://staff-www.uni-marburg.de/tatbauerb/text_wilkom.html (July 30, 2001).

Bauer, H., and P. Leander. *Historische Grammatik der hebräischen Sprache des Alten Testaments.* Halle, 1922.

Bauer, U. F. "Anti-Jewish Interpretations of Psalm 1 in Luther and in Modern German Protestantism. " *JHS* 2 (1998). http://www.arts.ualberta.ca/JHS/Articles/article8.pdf (May 14, 2003).

Bebbington, D. *Patterns in History: A Christian Perspective on Historical Thought.* Leicester: Apollos, 1992.

Beebee, T. O. *The Ideology of Genre.* University Park: Pennsylvania State University Press, 1994.

Benzinger, I. *Die Bücher der Könige.* Kurzer Hand-Commentar zum Alten Testament. Freiburg i.B.: Mohr, 1899.

Ben-Zvi, E. "Who Wrote the Speech of Rabshakeh and When?" *JBL* 109 (1990) 79–92.

Bergey, R. L. "Late Linguistic Features in Esther." *JQR* 75 (1984) 66–78.

Berkhofer, R. F., Jr. *Beyond the Great Story: History as Text and Discourse.* Cambridge, Massachusetts: Belknap, 1995.

Bintliff, J. "The Contribution of an *Annaliste*/Structural History Approach to Archaeology." Pp. 1–33 in *The Annales School and Archaeology.* Edited by J. Bintliff. London: Leicester University Press, 1995.

Birkeland, H. *Zum hebräischen Traditionswesen: Die Komposition der prophetischen Bücher des Alten Testaments.* ANVAO 1938. Oslo: Det norske videnskapsakademi, 1938.

Blenkinsopp, J. "An Assessment of the Alleged Pre-exilic Date of the Priestly Material in the Pentateuch." *ZAW* 108.4 (1996) 495–518.

_____. "Memory, Tradition, and the Construction of the Past in Ancient Israel." *Biblical Theology Bulletin* 27 (1997) 76–82.

Bloch, Maurice. "Literacy and Enlightenment." Pp. 15–37 in *Literacy and Society.* Edited by Karen Schousboe and Mogens Trolle Larsen. Copenhagen: Akademisk, 1989.

Bolin, T. "History, Historiography, and the Use of the Past in the Hebrew Bible." Pp. 113–40 in *The Limits of Historiography: Genre and Narrative in Ancient Historical Texts.* Edited by C. S. Kraus. Leiden: Brill, 1999.

_____. "When the End Is the Beginning: The Persian Period and the Origins of the Biblical Tradition." *SJOT* 19 (1996) 3–15.

Borger, R. *Babylonish-Assyrische Lesestücke.* Rome: Pontifical Biblical Institute, 1963.

Braudel, F. *The Mediterranean and the Mediterranean World in the Age of Philip II.* Vols. 1–2. London: Collins, 1972.

_____. *On History.* Chicago: University of Chicago Press, 1980.

Braun, R. L. "1 Chronicles 1–9 and the Reconstruction of the History of Israel: Thoughts on the Use of Genealogical data in Chronicles in the Reconstruction of the History of Israel." Pp. 92–105 in *The Chronicler as Historian.* Edited by M. P. Graham, K. G. Hoglund, and S. L. McKenzie. Sheffield: Sheffield Academic Press, 1997.

Brettler, M. Z. "Book Reviews. Van Seters, John. *In Search of History: Historiography in the Ancient World and the Origins of the Biblical History.* New Haven: Yale University Press, 1983." *Journal of Religion* 70 (1990) 83–84.

_____. *The Creation of History in Ancient Israel.* London: Routledge, 1998.

Bright, J. *A History of Israel.* Philadelphia: Westminster, 1981.

Budge, E. A. W. (trans.). *The Queen of Sheba and Her Only Son Menylek: Being the History of the Departure of God and His Ark of the Covenant from Jerusalem to Ethiopia, and the Establishment of the Religion of the Hebrews and the Solomonic Line of Kings in That Country.* London: Medici Society, 1922.

Bull, L. "Ancient Egypt." Pp. 3–34 in *The Idea of History in the Ancient Near East.* Edited by R. C. Dentan. New Haven, Connecticut: American Oriental Society, 1983.

Bunnens, G. "L'histoire événementielle partim Orient." Pp. 222–36 in *La civilisation phénicienne et punique*. Edited by V. Krings. HdO 20. Leiden: Brill, 1995.

Burke, P. *The French Historical Revolution: The Annales School, 1929–89*. Cambridge: Polity, 1990.

Burney, C. F. *Notes on the Hebrew Text of the Book of Kings*. Oxford: Clarendon, 1903.

Bush, F. *Ruth/Esther*. WBC 9. Dallas: Word, 1996.

Byrskog, S. *Jesus the Only Teacher: Didactic Authority and Transmission in Ancient Israel, Ancient Judaism and the Matthean Community*. Coniectanea Biblica. New Testament Series 24. Stockholm: Almquist & Wiksell, 1994.

Cameron, A. "Introduction." Pp. 1–10 in *History as Text: The Writing of Ancient History*. Edited by A. Cameron. London: Duckworth, 1989.

Cancik, H. "The History of Culture, Religion, and Institutions in Ancient Historiography: Philological Observations concerning Luke's History." *JBL* 116 (1997) 673–95.

Carr, E. *What Is History?* London: Penguin, 1987.

Carroll, L. *The Annotated Alice: Alice's Adventures in Wonderland and Through the Looking Glass*. New York: Wings, 1995.

Carroll, R. P. "Madonna of Silences: Clio and the Bible." Pp. 84–103 in *Can a 'History of Israel' Be Written?* Edited by L. L. Grabbe. JSOTSup 245. Sheffield: Sheffield Academic Press, 1997.

Carruthers, M. J. *The Book of Memory*. Cambridge: Cambridge University Press, 1990.

Cavigneaux, A., and B. K. Ismail. "Die Statthalter von Suhu und Mari im 8. Jh. v. Chr." *Baghdader Mitteilungen* 21 (1990) 321–456.

Cazelles, H. "Biblical and Prebiblical Historiography." Pp. 98–128 in *Israel's Past in Present Research*. Edited by V. P. Long. Sources for Biblical and Theological Study 7. Winona Lake, Indiana: Eisenbrauns, 1999.

_____. "Historiographies bibliques et prébibliques." *Revue Biblique* 98 (1991) 481–512.

Chavalas, M. W. "Genealogical History as 'Charter.'" Pp. 103–28 in *Faith, Tradition, and History: Old Testament Historiography in Its Near Eastern Context*. Edited by A. R. Millard, J. K. Hoffmeier, and D. W. Baker. Winona Lake, Indiana: Eisenbrauns, 1994.

Childs, H. *The Myth of the Historical Jesus and the Evolution of Consciousness: John Dominic Crossan's Quest in Psychological Perspective*. Paper read at the SBL 2000 Annual Meeting's Psychology and Biblical Studies Section in Orlando, 2000. http://f2.grp.yahoofs.com/v1/8CKuPvfztap5YwPOPCPbbI5DoDChkVslULc-w5dkQcMTx94Q4Nz6A3YOMKWHoD0V4aUMUNxG9eanxEf/Articles%20for-%20Review/ChildsCrossanExchange.htm (April 30, 2003).

Christiansen, B. S. "Palæstinahistorien i skolen." *Palæstina Orientering* 1 (1994)

Coady, C. *Testimony: A Philosophical Study*. Oxford: Clarendon, 1992.

Cockburn, C. *Crossing the Line*. London: MacGibbon & Lee, 1958.

Cohen, C. "Neo-Assyrian Elements in the First Speech of the Biblical Rab-Šaqê." *Israel Oriental Studies* 9 (1979) 32–48.

Cohen, Ralph. "History and Genre." *New Literary Theory* 27 (1986) 203–18.

Cohen, S. J. D. "Book Reviews. Van Seters, John. *In Search of History: Historiography in the Ancient World and the Origins of the Biblical History*. New Haven: Yale University Press, 1983." *American Historical Review* 95 (1990) 1500–1501.

_____. "History and Historiography in the *Against Apion* of Josephus." *History and Theory* Beiheft 27 (1988) 1–11.

_____. *Josephus in Galilee and Rome: His Vita and Development as a Historian.* Columbia Studies in the Classical Tradition 8. Leiden: Brill, 1979.

Collin, F., and B. Jacobsen. "Kritisk rationalisme og paradigmer." Pp. 87–108 in *Humanistisk videnskabsteori.* Edited by F. Collin and B. Jacobsen. Copenhagen: Danmarks Radio Forlaget, 1995.

Connerton, P. *How Societies Remember.* Cambridge: Cambridge University Press, 1989.

Conte, G. B. *Genres and Readers: Lucretius, Love Elegy, Pliny's Encyclopedia.* Baltimore: Johns Hopkins University Press, 1994.

Coote, R. *Early Israel: A New Horizon.* Minneapolis: Fortress, 1990.

Cornell, T. J. *The Beginnings of Rome: Italy and Rome from the Bronze Age to the Punic Wars (c. 1000–264 BC).* London: Routledge, 1995.

Cross, F. M., and D. N. Freedman. *Early Hebrew Orthography: A Study of the Epigraphic Evidence.* New Haven, Connecticut: American Oriental Society, 1952.

Cryer, F. "The Problem of Dating Biblical Hebrew and the Hebrew of Daniel." Pp. 185–98 in *In the Last Days: On Jewish and Christian Apocalyptic and Its Period.* Edited by K. Jeppesen et al. Århus: Århus University Press, 1994.

Culley, R. C. "Oral Tradition and the OT: Some Recent Discussion." Pp. 1–33 in *Oral Tradition and Old Testament Research.* Edited by R. C. Culley. Missoula, Montana: Scholars Press, 1976.

Culley, R. C. (ed.). *Oral Tradition and Old Testament Research.* Missoula, Montana: Scholars Press, 1976.

Danto, A. C. *Narration and Knowledge.* New York: Columbia University Press, 1985.

Davies, G. I. *Hosea.* New Century Bible Commentary. Grand Rapids, Michigan: Eerdmans, 1992.

Davies, P. R. *In Search of Ancient Israel.* Sheffield: JSOT Press, 1992.

_____. "Method and Madness: Some Remarks on Doing History with the Bible." *JBL* 114 (1995) 699–705.

_____. *Scribes and Schools: The Canonization of the Hebrew Scriptures.* Louisville: Westminster, John Knox, 1998.

_____. "Whose History? Whose Israel? Whose Bible? Biblical Histories, Ancient and Modern." Pp. 104–22 in *Can a 'History of Israel' Be Written?* Edited by L. L. Grabbe. JSOTSup 245. ESHM 1. Sheffield: Sheffield Academic Press, 1997.

DeCaen, V. "Hebrew Linguistics and Biblical Criticism: A Minimalist Programme." *JHS* 3 (2001). http://www.arts.ualberta.ca/JHS/Articles/article_18.pdf (May 14, 2003).

Dever, W. G. "Archaeology, Ideology, and the Quest for an 'Ancient' or 'Biblical' Israel." *NEA* 61 (1998) 39–52.

_____. "Histories and Nonhistories of Ancient Israel." *BASOR* 316 (1999) 89–105.

_____. "The Identity of Early Israel: A Rejoinder to Keith W. Whitelam." *JSOT* 72 (1996) 3–24.

_____. *What Did the Biblical Writers Know, and When Did They Know It? What Archaeology Can Tell Us about the Reality of Ancient Israel.* Grand Rapids, Michigan: Eerdmans, 2001.

Dimant, D. "Apocalyptic Texts at Qumran." Pp. 175–91 in *The Community of the Renewed Covenant: The Notre Dame Symposium of the Dead Sea Scrolls.* Edited by

E. Ulrich and J. C. VanderKam. Notre Dame, Indiana: University of Notre Dame Press, 1994.

Dobbs-Allsopp, F. W. "Linguistic Evidence for the Date of Lamentations." *JANES* 26 (1998) 1–36.

Driver, S. R. *An introduction to the Literature of the Old Testament.* New York: Scribner's, 1913.

Dubrow, H. *Genre.* London: Methuen, 1982.

Ehrensvärd, M. "Once Again: The Problem of Dating Biblical Hebrew." *SJOT* 11 (1997) 29–43.

_____. *Studies in the Syntax and the Dating of Biblical Hebrew.* Ph.D. diss., University of Århus, 2002.

Einarsdóttir, Ó. "Om samtidssagaens kildeværdi belyst ved *Hákonar saga Hákonarsonar.*" *Alvíssmál* 5 (1995) 29–80.

Elliger, K., and W. Rudolph (eds) *Biblia Hebraica Stuttgartensia.* Stuttgart: Deutsche Bibelgesellschaft, 1967.

Engnell, I. "Methodological Aspects of Old Testament Study." In *Congress Volume: Oxford, 1959.* VTSup 7. Leiden: Brill, 1960.

Eph'al, I., and J. Naveh. "Remarks on the Recently Published Moussaieff Ostraca." *IEJ* 48 (1998) 269–73.

Erslev, K. *Historisk Teknik: Den historiske undersøgelse fremstillet i sine grundlinier.* Copenhagen: Gyldendal, 1972.

Eskhult, M. *Studies in Verbal Aspect and Narrative Technique in Biblical Hebrew Prose.* Uppsala: Almqvist & Wiksell, 1990.

Fales, F. M. *Aramaic Epigraphs on Clay Tablets of the Neo-Assyrian Period.* Studi semitici n.s. 2. Rome: Università degli studi "La Sapienza," 1986.

Falkenstein, A., and W. von Soden. *Sumerische und Akkadische Hymnen und Gebete.* Zurich: Artemis, 1953.

Finkelstein, I. "The Rise of Early Israel: Achaeology and Long-Term History." Pp. 7–39 in *The Origin of Early Israel—Current Debate: Biblical, Historical and Archaeological Perspectives. Irene Levi-Sala Seminar, 1997.* Be'er Sheva 12. Edited by Shmuel Aḥituv and Eliezer D. Oren. London: Institute of Archaeology and Institute of Jewish Studies, University College, 1998.

Finkelstein, J. J. "Mesopotamian Historiography." *Proceedings of the American Philosphical Society* 107 (1963) 461–72.

Finley, M. I. "Myth, Memory, and History." *History and Theory* 4 (1965) 281–302.

_____. "Myth, Memory, and History." Pp. 9–28 in *Geschichtsbild und Geschichtsdenken im Altertum.* Edited by J. M. Alonso-Nunez. Wege der Forschung 631. Darmstadt: Wissenschaftlicher Buchgesellschaft, 1991.

Fishbane, M. "Torah and Tradition." Pp. 275–300 in *Tradition and Theology in the Old Testament.* Edited by D. A. Knight. Sheffield: JSOT Press, 1990.

Fleischman, R. *Divergent Streams of Accounting History: A Review and Call for Confluence.* Sixth Interdisciplinary Perspectives on Accounting Conference. Manchester, 2000.

Floto, I. *Historie i nyere og nyeste tid.* Copenhagen: Gyldendal, 1985.

Forster, E. M. *Aspects of the Novel.* London: Penguin, 1970.

Foster, B. R. *From Distant Days: Myths, Tales, and Poetry of Ancient Mesopotamia.* Bethesda, Maryland: CDL, 1999.

Fowler, A. *Kinds of Literature: An Introduction to the Theory of Genres and Modes*. Oxford: Clarendon, 1991.

Frahm, E. "Nabû-zuqup-kēnu, das Gilgameš-Epos und der Tod Sargons II." *JCS* 51 (1999) 73–90.

Frederick, M. G. "Doing Justice in History: Using narrative Frames Responsibly." Pp. 220–34 in *History and the Christian Historian*. Edited by R. A. Wells. Grand Rapids, Michigan: Eerdmans, 1998.

Fredericks, D. C. "A North Israelite Dialect in the Hebrew Bible? Questions of Methodology." *Hebrew Studies* 37 (1996) 7–20.

Freedman, D. N., A. D. Forbes, and F. I. Andersen. *Studies in Hebrew and Aramaic Orthography*. Biblical and Judaic Studies from the University of California, San Diego 2. Winona Lake, Indiana: Eisenbrauns, 1992.

Fritz, V. "Temple Architecture: What Can Archaeology Tell Us about Solomon's Temple." Pp. 116–28 in *Essential Papers on Israel and the Ancient Near East*. Edited by F. Greenspahn. Essential Papers on Jewish Studies. New York: New York University Press, 1991.

Galan, F. W. "Literary System and Systemic Change: The Prague School Theory of Literary History 1928–48." *PMLA* 94 (March 1979) 275–85.

Garbini, G. *History and Ideology in Ancient Israel*. New York: Crossroad, 1988.

Garr, W. R. *Dialect Geography of Syria–Palestine, 1000–586 B.C.E.* Philadelphia: University of Pennsylvania Press, 1985. Reprinted, Winona Lake, Indiana: Eisenbrauns, 2004.

Gelb, I. J. "The Date of the Cruciform Monument of Maništušu." *JNES* 8 (1949) 346–48.

George, A. R. *The Epic of Gilgamesh*. London: Penguin, 1999.

Gerhardsson, B. *Memory and Manuscript*. Lund: C.W.K. Gleerup, 1961.

Ginzberg, L., and H. Szold. *The Legends of the Jews*. Vol. 4. Philadelphia: Jewish Publication Society, 1913.

Givón, T. "The Drift from VSO to SVO in Biblical Hebrew: The Pragmatics of Tense-Aspect." Pp. 181–254 in *Symposium on the Mechanisms of Syntactic Change*. Edited by C. Li. Austin: University of Texas Press, 1977.

Gogel, S. L. *A Grammar of Epigraphic Hebrew*. SBL Resources for Biblical Study 23. Atlanta: Society of Biblical Literature, 1998.

Gordon, Robert P. "Who Made the Kingmaker? Reflections on Samuel and the Institution of the Monarchy." Pp. 255–69 in *Faith, Tradition, and History: Old Testament Historiography in Its Near Eastern Context*. Edited by A. R. Millard, J. K. Hoffmeier, and D. W. Baker. Winona Lake, Indiana: Eisenbrauns, 1994.

Goyon, J. C. "Une parallèle tardif d'une formule des inscriptions de la statue prophylactique de Ramsès III au Musée du Caire (Papyrus Brooklyn 47.218.138, col. X+13, 9 à 15)." *JEA* 57 (1971) 154–59.

Grabbe, L. L. "Fellow Creatures—or Different Animals?" Pp. 19–36 in *Can a "History of Israel" Be Written?* Edited by L. L. Grabbe. JSOTSup 245. ESHM 1. Sheffield: Sheffield Academic Press, 1997.

_____. "Hat die Bibel doch Recht? A Review of T. L. Thompson's *The Bible in History*." *SJOT* 14 (2000) 117–39.

Grabbe, L. L. (ed.). *Can a "History of Israel" Be Written?* JSOTSup 245. ESHM 1. Sheffield: Sheffield Academic Press, 1997.

_____. *Did Moses Speak Attic? Jewish Historiography and Scripture in the Hellenistic Period*. JSOTSup 317. ESHM 3. Sheffield: Sheffield Academic Press, 2001.

_____ *Leading Captivity Captive: 'The Exile' as History and Ideology*. JSOTSup 278. ESHM 2. Sheffield: Sheffield Academic Press, 1998.

Gray, J. *I and II Kings*. OTL. London: SCM, 1964.

Grayson, A. K. *Assyrian and Babylonian Chronicles*. Texts from Cuneiform Sources 5. New York: Augustin, 1975. Reprinted, Winona Lake, Indiana: Eisenbrauns, 2000.

Greenfield, J. C. "Of Scribes, Scripts and Languages." Pp. 173–85 in *Phoinikeia grammata. Lire et écrire en Méditerranée: Actes du Colloque de Liège, 15–18 novembre 1989*. Edited by V. Krings, C. Bonnet, and Baurain Claude. Namur: Société des Études Classiques, 1991.

Goody, Jack. *The Domestication of the Savage Mind*. Cambridge: Cambridge University Press, 1977.

_____. *Literacy in Traditional Societies*. Cambridge: Cambridge University Press, 1968.

_____. *The Logic of Writing and the Organization of Society*. Cambridge: Cambridge University Press, 1986.

Güterbock, H. G. "Die historische Tradition und ihre literarische Gestaltung bei Babyloniern und Hethitern bis 1200." *ZA* 42 (1934) 1–91; 44 (1938) 45–149.

_____. "Hittite Historiography: A Survey." Pp. 21–35 in *History, Historiography and Interpretation: Studies in Biblical and Cuneiform Literatures*. Edited by H. Tadmor and M. Weinfeld. Jerusalem: Magnes, 1984.

Gunkel, H. *Genesis*. 3rd ed. Göttinger Handkommentar zum Alten Testament 1. Göttingen: Vandenhoeck & Ruprecht, 1922.

Gunn, D. M. *The Story of King David: Genre and Interpretation*. Sheffield: Sheffield Academic Press, 1978.

Halliday, M. A. K. "Anti-languages." *American Anthropologist* 78 (1976) 570–84.

Hallo, W. W. "Biblical History in Its Near Eastern Setting: The Contextual Approach." Pp. 1–26 in *Scripture in Context: Essays on the Comparative Method*. Edited by C. D. Evans, William W. Hallo, and John B. White. PThMS 34. Pittsburgh: Pickwick, 1980.

_____. The Limits of Skepticism. *JAOS* 110 (1990) 187–99.

_____. "Sumerian Historiography." Pp. 9–20 in *History, Historiography and Interpretation*. Edited by H. Tadmor and M. Weinfeld. Jerusalem: Magnes, 1984.

Hallo, W. W., and K. L. Younger, Jr. (eds.). *Canonical Compositions from the Biblical World*. Vol. 1 of *The Context of Scripture*. Leiden: Brill, 1997.

_____. *Monumental Inscriptions from the Biblical World*. Vol. 2 of *The Context of Scripture*. Leiden: Brill, 1997.

Halpern, Baruch. "The Construction of the Davidic State." Pp. 44–75 in *The Origins of the Ancient Israelite States*. Edited by V. Fritz and P. R. Davies. Sheffield: Sheffield Academic Press, 1996.

_____. *David's Secret Demons: Messiah, Murderer, Traitor, King*. Grand Rapids, Michigan: Eerdmans, 2001.

_____. "Erasing History: The Minimalist Assault on Ancient Israel." *Bible Review* 11/6 (1995) 26–35, 47.

_____. "Erasing History: The Minimalist Assault on Ancient Israel." Pp. 415–26 in *Israel's Past in Present Research*. Edited by V. P. Long. Sources for Biblical and Theological Study 7. Winona Lake, Indiana: Eisenbrauns, 1999.

_____. *The First Historians: The Hebrew Bible and History*. San Francisco: Harper, 1988.

Haran, M. "Book-Scrolls at the Beginning of the Second Temple Period: The Transition from Papyrus to Skins." *HUCA* 54 (1983) 111–22.

Harris, William V. *Ancient Literacy*. Cambridge: Harvard University Press, 1989.

Havelock, Eric A. "The Alphabetization of Homer." Pp. 3–21 in *Communication Arts in the Ancient World*. Edited by Eric A. Havelock and Jackson P. Hershbell. New York: Hastings, 1978.

_____. *The Literate Revolution in Greece and Its Cultural Consequences*. Princeton: Princeton University Press, 1982.

_____. *The Muse Learns to Write: Reflections on Orality and Literacy from Antiquity to the Present*. New Haven: Yale University Press, 1986.

_____. *Origins of Western Literacy*. Toronto: Ontario Institute for Studies in Education, 1976.

_____. *Preface to Plato*. Oxford: Blackwell, 1963.

Hayes, J. H., and J. M. Miller. *Israelite and Judaean History*. Edited by J. H. Hayes. OTL. London: SCM, 1977.

Head, P. M. "The Role of Eyewitnesses in the Formation of the Gospel Tradition: A Review Article of Samuel Byrskog, *Story as History—History as Story*." *TynBul* 52 (2001) 275–94.

Heehs, P. "Myth, History, and Theory." *History and Theory* 33 (1994) 1–19.

Heelan, P. A. "An Anti-Epistemological or Ontological Interpretation of the Quantum Theory and Theories like It." Pp. 55–68 in *Continental and Postmodern Perpectives in the Philosophy of Science*. Edited by I. Babich and E. Babette. Aldershot, Hampshire: Avebury, 1995.

Hess, Rick. "Literacy in Iron Age Israel." Pp. 82–102 in *Windows into Old Testament History: Evidence, Argument, and the Crisis of "Biblical Israel."* Edited by V. P. Long, David W. Baker, and Gordon J. Wenham. Grand Rapids, Michigan: Eerdmans, 2002.

Hirsch, E. D. *Validity in Interpretation*. New Haven: Yale University Press, 1967.

Hitchcock, L. "One Cannot Export a Palace on Board a Ship." *Backdirt* Fall/Winter (2000). http://www.sscnet.ucla.edu/ioa/backdirt/Fallwinter00/cypriot.html (November 17, 2004).

Hjelm, I. *The Samaritans in Early Judaism: A Literary Analysis*. CIS 7. Sheffield: Sheffield Academic Press, 2000).

Hoffmann, P. *Nattetanker i arken*. Copenhagen: Frimodt, 1966.

Hoffmeier, J. K. "The Evangelical Contribution to Understanding the (Early) History of Ancient Israel in Recent Scholarship." *BBR* 7 (1997) 77–90.

_____. "The Problem of 'History' in Egyptian Royal Inscriptions." Pp. 291–99 in vol. 1 of *VI Congresso Internazionale di Egittologia Atti*. Edited by S. Curto. Turin, 1992.

Hoffner, H. A. "Histories and Historians of the Ancient Near East: The Hittites." *Orientalia* 49 (1980) 283–332.

Hoftijzer, J., and G. van der Kooij. *The Balaam Text from Deir 'Alla Re-evaluated*. Leiden: Brill, 1991.

Holloway, S. W. "Book of 1–2 Kings." Pp. 69–83 in vol. 4 of *ABD.* Edited D. N. Freedman. New York: Doubleday, 1992.

Hornblower, S. (ed.). *Greek Historiography.* Oxford: Clarendon, 1994.

Horsnell, M. "False Witness." *The Times,* Wednesday. April 12.2 (2000) 2–4 .

Huehnergard, J. *A Grammar of Akkadian.* HSS 45. Atlanta: Scholars Press, 1997.

Huizinga, J. "A Definition of the Concept of History." Pp. 1–10 in *Philosophy and History: Essays Presented to Ernst Cassirer.* Edited by R. Klibansky and H. Paton. Oxford: Clarendon, 1936.

Hurowitz, V. *I Have Built You an Exalted House: Temple Building in the Bible in Light of Mesopotamian and Northwest Semitic Writings.* JSOTSup 115. ASOR Monograph Series 5. Sheffield: Sheffield Academic Press, 1992.

Hurvitz, A. "Can Biblical Texts Be Dated Linguistically? Chronological Perspectives in the Historical Study of Biblical Hebrew." Pp. 143–60 in *IOSOT Congress Volume: Oslo, 1998.* Edited by A. Lemaire and M. Sæbø. Leiden: Brill, 2000.

_____. "The Chronological Significance of 'Aramaisms' in Biblical Hebrew." *IEJ* 18 (1968) 234–40.

_____. "The Historical Quest for 'Ancient Israel' and the Linguistic Evidence of the Hebrew Bible: Some Methodological Observations." *VT* 47 (1997) 301–15.

_____. "Linguistic Criteria for Dating Problematic Biblical Texts." *Hebrew Abstracts* 14 (1973) 74–79.

_____. *A Linguistic Study of the Relationship between the Priestly Source and the Book of Ezekiel.* Paris: Gabalda, 1982.

_____. "Once Again: The Linguistic Profile of the Priestly Material in the Pentateuch and Its Historical Age. A Response to J. Blenkinsopp." *ZAW* 112 (2000) 180–91.

_____. "The Origins and Development of the Expression מְגִלַּת סֵפֶר: A Study in the History of Writing-Related Terminology in Biblical Times." Pp. 37*–46* in *Texts, Temples, and Traditions: A Tribute to Menahem Haran.* Edited by M. V. Fox et al. Winona Lake, Indiana: Eisenbrauns, 1996. [Hebrew]

_____. "The Relevance of Biblical Hebrew Linguistics for the Historical Study of Ancient Israel." Pp. 21–33 in *Proceedings of the Twelfth World Congress of Jewish Studies.* Jerusalem, 1999.

_____. *The Transition Period in Biblical Hebrew: A Study in Post-exilic Hebrew and Its Implications for the Dating of Psalms.* Jerusalem: Magnes, 1972. [Hebrew]

Husser, J.-M. *Dreams and Dream Narratives in the Biblical World.* Biblical Seminar 63. Sheffield: Sheffield Academic Press, 1999.

Hutton, P. H. "The Role of Memory in the Historiography of the French Revolution." *History and Theory* 30 (1989) 56–69.

Iggers, G. *New Directions in European Historiography.* Middletown, Connecticut: Wesleyan University Press, 1984.

Irvine, Judith T. "When Is Genealogy History? Wolof Genealogies in Comparative Perspective." *American Ethnologist* 5 (1978) 651–74.

Irwin, W. A. "The Orientalist as Historian." *JNES* 8 (1949) 298–309.

Isserlin, B. S. J. "Language, Writing and Texts." Pp. 204–33 in *The Israelites.* Edited by B. S. J. Isserlin. London: Thames & Hudson, 1998.

Jamieson-Drake, D. W. *Scribes and Schools in Monarchic Judah: A Socio-archaeological Approach.* JSOTSup 109. Sheffield: Sheffield Academic Press, 1991.

Jellicoe, S. *The Septuagint and Modern Study.* Oxford: Clarendon, 1968.

Jensen, B. E. "Historie- og tidsbevidsthed som forskningsfelt: Begrebsanalytiske og socialhistoriske overvejelser." Pp. 39–76 in *Tidsopfattelse og historiebevidsthed*. Studier i historisk metode 18. Århus: Antikva, 1985.

_____. "Historisme." Pp. 140–57 in *Humanistisk Videnskabsteori*. Edited by F. Collin and B. Jacobsen. Copenhagen: Danmarks Radio Forlaget, 1995.

Jensen, H. J. L. "Efterskrift: Litterære læsninger. En videnskabshistorisk skitse." Pp. 144–55 in *Sola Scriptura*. Edited by K. M. Andersen, E. Hviid, and H. J. L. Jensen. Copenhagen: Anis, 1993.

Jensen, J. J. "Vergil ifølge ham selv." *Weekendavisen. Bøger* (April 9, 1999) 7.

Jeppesen, K. *Græder ikke saa saare: Studier i Mikabogens sigte*. Vol. 1. Århus: Århus Universitetsforlag, 1987.

Jeppesen, K., and B. Otzen (eds.). *The Productions of Time: Tradition Hsitory in Old Testament Scholarship*. Sheffield: Almond, 1984.

Joachimsen, K. "Diakron og synkron, historisk eller litterær? Knut Holters *Second Isaiah's Idol-Fabrication Passages* og nye trender i deutero-jesajansk eksegese." *NTT* 97 (1996) 246–51.

Josephus. *Jewish Antiquities*. Translated by H. St. J. Thackeray. Loeb Classical Library. Cambridge: Harvard University Press, 1998.

Joüon, P. *Grammaire de l'hébreu biblique*. Rome: Pontifical Biblical Institute, 1923.

Kallai, Z. "Biblical Historiography and Literary History: A Programmatic Survey." *VT* 49 (1999) 338–50.

_____. "The Patriarchal Boundaries, Canaan and the Land of Israel: Patterns and Application in Biblical Historiography." *IEJ* 47 (1997) 69–82.

Kapelrud, A. S. "The Traditio-historical Study of the Prophets." Pp. 53–66 in *The Productions of Time: Tradition History in Old Testament Scholarship*. Edited by K. Jeppesen and B. Otzen. Sheffield: Almond, 1984.

Kaplan, S. *The Beta Israel (Falasha) in Ethiopia: From Earliest Times to the Twentieth Century*. New York: New York University Press, 1992.

Kautzsch, E. *Die Aramaismen im AT*. Halle, 1902.

Kelber, W. H. *The Oral and the Written Gospel*. Philadelphia: Fortress, 1983.

Kenyon, F. G. *The Text of the Greek Bible*. Revised by A. W. Adams. London: Duckworth, 1975.

King, L. W. "The Cruciform Monument of Manishtusu." *Revue d'Assyriologie et d'Archeologie Orientale* 9/3 (1912) 91–105.

Kirkpatrick, P. G. *The Old Testament and Folklore Study*. JSOTSup 62. Sheffield: JSOT Press, 1988.

Kitchen, K. A. *Documentation for Ancient Arabia, Part 1*. The World of Ancient Arabia Series. Liverpool: Liverpool University Press, 1994.

_____. *Documentation for Ancient Arabia, Part 2*. The World of Ancient Arabia Series. Liverpool: Liverpool University Press, 1999.

_____. "Egytians and Hebrews, from Ra'amses to Jericho." Pp. 65–131 in *The Origin of Early Israel—Current Debate: Biblical, Historical and Archaeological Perspectives. Irene Levi-Sala Seminar, 1997*. Edited by Shmuel Aḥituv and Eliezer D. Oren. Be'er Sheva 12. London: Institute of Archaeology and Institute of Jewish Studies, University College, 1998.

_____. "The King List of Ugarit." *UF* 9 (1977) 131–42.

_____. *Poetry of Ancient Egypt*. Documenta Mundi: Aegyptiaca 1. Jonsered: Åströms, 1999.

_____. *Ramesside Inscriptions: Translated and Annotated. Notes and Comments.* 2 vols. Oxford: Blackwell, 1994–1999.

_____. *Ramesside Inscriptions: Translated and Annotated. Translations.* 3 vols. Oxford: Blackwell, 1993–2000.

_____. "Sheba and Arabia." Pp. 127–53 in *The Age of Solomon: Scholarship at the Turn of the Millennium.* Edited by L. K. Handy. Leiden: Brill, 1997.

_____. "Two Notes on the Subsidiary Rooms of Solomon's Temple." *Eretz-Israel* 20 (Yadin Volume; 1989) 107*–112*. [Hebrew]

Kjeldstadli, K. *Fortida er ikke hva den en gang var—en innføring i historiefaget.* Oslo, 1994.

Klein, J. *The Royal Hymns of Shulgi King of Ur: Man's Quest for Immortal Fame.* TAPS 71/7. Philadelphia: American Philosophical Society, 1981.

Knauf, E. A. "From History to Interpretation." Pp. 26–64 in *The Fabric of History: Text, Artifact and Israel's Past.* Edited by D. Edelman. JSOTSup 127. Sheffield: Sheffield Academic Press, 1991.

_____. "War 'Biblisch-Hebräisch' eine Sprache?" *ZAH* 3 (1990) 11–23.

Knight, D. A. (ed.). *Tradition and Theology in the Old Testament.* Sheffield: JSOT Press, 1990.

Knoppers, G. N. "History and Historiography: The Royal Reforms." Pp. 178–203 in *The Chronicler as Historian.* Edited by M. P. Graham, K. G. Hoglund, and S. L. McKenzie. Sheffield: Sheffield Academic Press, 1997.

Kofoed, J. B. "Epistemology, Historiography, and the 'Copenhagen School.'" Pp. 23–43 in *Windows into Old Testament History: Evidence, Argument, and the Crisis of "Biblical Israel."* Edited by V. P. Long, David W. Baker, and Gordon J. Wenham. Grand Rapids, Michigan: Eerdmans, 2002.

_____. *Israels historie som teologisk disciplin.* Copenhagen: Dansk Bibel-Institut, 1998.

Kovacs, M. G. *The Epic of Gilgamesh.* Stanford: Stanford University Press, 1989.

Kropat, A. *Die Syntax des Autors der Chronik.* BZAW 16. Giessen: Alfred Töpelmann, 1909.

Kuhn, T. S. *The Structure of Scientific Revolutions.* Chicago: The University of Chicago Press, 1970.

Kuhrt, A. *The Ancient Near East c. 3000–330 BC.* 2 vols. London: Routledge, 1995.

Kutscher, E. Y. *A History of the Hebrew Language.* Jerusalem: Magnes/ Leiden: Brill, 1982.

_____. *The Language and Linguistic Background of the Isaiah Scroll (1QIsᵃ).* Leiden: Brill, 1974.

Kvanvig, H. S. "Den hebraiske fortelling. Narrativ lesning av bibeltekster." *NTT* 97 (1996) 219–34.

_____. *Historisk bibel og bibelsk historie.* Kristianssand: Høyskoleforlaget, 1999.

Lapointe, R. "Tradition and Language: The Import of Oral Expression." Pp. 125–42 in *Tradition and Theology in the Old Testament.* Edited by D. A. Knight. Sheffield: JSOT Press, 1990.

Larsen, Mogens Trolle. *Literay and Society.* Copenhagen: Akademisk Forlag, 1989.

Larsson, G. "Chronology as a Structural Element in the Old Testament." *SJOT* 14 (2000) 207–18.

Lass, R. *Historical Linguistics and Language Change.* Cambridge Studies in Linguistics 81. Cambridge: Cambridge University Press, 1997.

Lassner, J. " 'Doing' Early Islamic History: Brooklyn Baseball, Arabic Historiography, and Historical Memory." *JAOS* 114 (1994) 1–10.

Lehman, G., and T. Schneider. "Tell el-Far'ah (South), 1999 and 2000." *IEJ* 50 (2000) 258–61.

Lehmkühler, K. " 'Geschichte durch Geschichte überwinden': Zur verwendung eines Zitates." *Jahrbuch für Evangelikale Theologie* (1998–99) 115–37.

Lemaire, A. *Les écoles et la formation de la Bible dans l'ancien Israël.* Fribourg: Éditions Universitaires / Göttingen: Vandenhoeck & Ruprecht, 1981.

―――. "Review of *Scribes and Schools in Monarchich Judah: A Socio-archeological Approach* by D. W. Jamieson-Drake." *JAOS* 112 (1992) 707–8.

Lemche, N. P. *The Canaanites and Their Land.* Sheffield: Sheffield Academic Press, 1991.

―――. "Clio Is Also among the Muses. Keith W. Whitelam and the History of Palestine: A Review and a Commentary." *SJOT* 10 (1996) 88–114.

―――. *The Israelites in History and Tradition.* Library of Ancient Israel. London: SPCK / Louisville: Westminster John Knox, 1998.

―――. "Om historisk erindring i Det Gamle Testamentes historiefortællinger." Pp. 11–28 in *Bibel og historieskrivning.* Edited by Geert Hallbäck and John Strange. Forum for Bibelsk Eksegese 10. Copenhagen: Museum Tusculanum, 1999.

―――. "On the Problem of Reconstructing Pre-Hellenistic Israelite (Palestinian) History." *JHS* 3 (2000) 1–14.

―――. "The Origin of the Israelite State: A Copenhagen Perspective on the Emergence of Critical Historical Studies of Ancient Israel in Recent Times." *SJOT* 12 (1998) 44–63.

―――. *Die Vorgeschichte Israels: Von den Anfängen bis zum Ausgang des 13. Jahrhunderts v.Chr.* Biblische Enzyklopädie. Stuttgart: Kohlhammer, 1996.

Lemche, N. P., and T. L. Thompson. "Did Biran Kill David? The Bible in the Light of Archaeology." *JSOT* 64 (1994) 3–22.

Levy, T. (ed.). *The Archaeology of Society in the Holy Land.* New York: Facts On File, 1995.

Lewis, B. *The Sargon Legend.* ASOR Dissertation Series 4. Cambridge, Massachusetts: American School of Oriental Research, 1980.

Liverani, M. "Early Caravan Trade between South-Arabia and Mesopotamia." *Yemen* 1 (1992) 111–15.

―――. "Memorandum on the Approach to Historiographic Texts." Pp. 178–94 in *Approaches to the Study of the Ancient Near East: A Volume of Studies Offered to Ignace Jay Gelb on the Occasion of His 65th Birthday.* Edited by G. Buccellati. Rome: Pontifical Biblical Institute / Los Angeles: Undena, 1973.

―――. "Model and Actualization: The Kings of Akkad in the Historical Tradition." Pp. 41–67 in *Akkad. The First World Empire: Structure, Ideology, Traditions.* Edited by M. Liverani. HANES 5. Padua: Sargon, 1993.

Long, B. O. *Planting and Reaping Albright: Politics, Ideology, and Interpreting the Bible.* University Park: Pennsylvania State University Press, 1997.

Long, G. "The Written Story: Toward Understanding Text as Representation and Function." *VT* 49 (1999) 165–85.

Long, V. Philips. *The Art of Biblical History.* Grand Rapids, Michigan: Zondervan, 1994.

_____. "How Reliable Are Biblical Reports? Repeating Lester Grabbe's Comparative Experiment." *VT* 52 (2002) 367–84.

_____. "Old Testament History: A Hermeneutical Perspective." Pp. 86–102 in *NIDOTTE*. Edited by W. A. VanGemeren. Carlisle: Paternoster, 1997.

Long, V. Philips (ed.). *Israel's Past in Present Research.* Studies in Biblical and Theological Study 7. Winona Lake, Indiana: Eisenbrauns, 1999.

Longacre, R. E. *Joseph, A Story of Divine Providence: A Text Theoretical and Textlinguistic Analysis of Genesis 37 and 39–48.* Winona Lake; Indiana: Eisenbrauns, 1989.

Longman III, T. *Fictional Akkadian Autobiography: A Generic and Comparative Study.* Winona Lake, Indiana: Eisenbrauns, 1991.

Lord, A. B. *The Singer of Tales.* Harvard Studies in Comparative Literature 24. Cambridge: Harvard University Press, 1960.

Lourié, Basil. "From Jerusalem to Aksum through the Temple of Solomon: Archaic Traditions Related to the Ark of Covenant and Sion in the Kebra Nagast and Their Translation through Constantinople." *Xristianskij Vostok* 2 [2001] 137–207.

MacDonald, M. C. A. "North Arabia in the First Millennium B.C.E." Pp. 1355–69 in vol. 2 of *Civilizations of the Ancient Near East.* Edited by J. M. Sasson. New York: Scribner, 1995.

Machinist, P. "Assyria and Its Image in the First Isaiah." *JAOS* 103 (1983) 719–37.

Macintosh, A. A. *A Critical and Exegetical Commentary on Hosea.* Edinburgh: T. & T. Clark, 1997.

Malamat, A. "The Aramaeans." Pp. 134–55 in *Peoples of Old Testament Times.* Edited by D. Wiseman. Oxford: Clarendon, 1973.

_____. "The Proto-history of Israel: A Study in Method." Pp. 303–13 in *The Word of the Lord Shall Go Forth: Essays in Honor of David Noel Freedman in Celebration of His Sixtieth Birthday.* Edited by C. L. Meyers and M. O'Connor. Winona Lake, Indiana: Eisenbrauns, 1983.

Malul, M. *The Comparative Method in Ancient Near Eastern and Biblical Legal Studies.* Neukirchen-Vluyn: Neukirchener Verlag, 1990.

Marincola, J. "Genre, Convention, and Innovation in Greco-Roman Historiography." Pp. 281–324 in *The Limits of Historiography: Genre and Narrative in Ancient Historical Texts.* Edited by C. S. Kraus. Leiden: Brill, 1999.

Martin, W. J. "The Hebrew of Daniel." Pp. 28–30 in *Notes on Some Problems in the Book of Daniel.* Edited by D. J. Wiseman et al. London: Tyndale, 1965.

McCann, J. C. (ed.). *The Shape and Shaping of the Psalter.* JSOTSup 159. Sheffield: JSOT Press, 1993.

McNutt, P. M. "Interpreting Israel's 'Folk Traditions.'" *JSOT* 39 (1987) 44–52.

Megill, A. "Jörn Rüsen's Theory of Historiography between Modernism and Rhetoric of Inquiry." *History and Theory* 33 (1994) 39–60.

Melrose, S. *A Semiotics of the Dramatic Text.* New Directions in Theatre. New York: St. Martin's, 1994.

Mendels, D. *Identity, Religion and Historiography.* JSPSup 24. Sheffield: Sheffield Academic Press, 1998.

Merrill, E. H. "Remembering: A Central Theme in Biblical Worship." *JETS* 43 (2000) 27–36.

Meyer, B. F. "Some Consequences of Birger Gerhardsson's Account of the Origins of the Gospel Tradition." Pp. 424–40 in *Jesus and the Oral Gospel Tradition.* Edited by H. Wansbrough. JSNTSup 64. Sheffield: Sheffield Academic Press, 1991.

Meyer, E. *Geschichte des Altertums*. Vol. 2. 2nd ed. Berlin, 1928.

Meyer, R. "Bemerkungen zu den hebräischen Aussprachetraditionen von Chirbet Qumrân." *ZAW* 70 (1958) 39–48.

_____. "Das Problem der Dialektmischung in den hebräischen Texten von Chirbet Qumrân." *VT* 7 (1957) 139–48.

Michalowski, P. "Commemoration, Writing, and Genre in Ancient Mesopotamia." Pp. 69–90 in *The Limits of Historiography: Genre and Narrative in Ancient Historical Texts*. Edited by C. S. Kraus. Leiden: Brill, 1999.

Mieroop, M. van de. "On Writing a History of Ancient Near East." *BiOr* 54 (1997) 285–305.

Millard, A. R. "Assyrian Royal Names in Biblical Hebrew." *JSS* 21 (1976) 1–14.

_____. "Back to the Iron Bed: Og's or Procrustes?" Pp. 193–203 in *Congress Volume: Paris, 1992*. Edited by J. Emerton. VTSup 61. Leiden: Brill, 1995.

_____. "Books in the Late Bronze Age in the Levant." Pp. 171–81 in *Israel Oriental Studies* 18. Edited by S. Izre'el, I. Singer, and R. Zadok. Winona Lake, Indiana: Eisenbrauns, 1998.

_____. "*The Corpus of West Semitic Stamp Seals*: Review Article." *IEJ* 51 (2001) 76–87.

_____. "The Doorways of Solomon's Temple." *Eretz-Israel* 20 (Yadin Volume; 1989) 135*–39*.

_____. "Epigraphic Notes, Aramaic and Hebrew." *PEQ* 110 (1978) 23–26.

_____. "History and Legend in Early Babylonia." Pp. 103–10 in *Windows into Old Testament History: Evidence, Argument, and the Crisis of "Biblical Israel."* Edited by V. P. Long, David W. Baker, and Gordon J. Wenham. Grand Rapids, Michigan: Eerdmans, 2002.

_____. "How Reliable Is Exodus?" *BAR* 26/4 (1999) 51–57.

_____. "Israelite and Aramean History in the Light of Inscriptions." *TynBul* 41 (1990) 261–75.

_____. "Judith, Tobit, Ahiqar and History." Pp. 195–203 in *New Heaven and New Earth: Prophecy and the Millenium*. Edited by P. Harland and C. Hayward. Leiden: Brill, 1999.

_____. "King Solomon in His Ancient Context." Pp. 30–53 in *The Age of Solomon: Scholarship at the Turn of the Millennium*. Edited by L. K. Handy. Leiden: Brill, 1997.

_____. "The Knowledge of Writing in Iron Age Palestine." *TynBul* 46 (1995) 207–17.

_____. "The Knowledge of Writing in Late Bronze Age Palestine." Pp. 317–26 in *Languages and Cultures in Contact: At the Crossroads of Civilizations in the Syro-Mesopotamian Realm. Proceedings of the 42th RAI*. Edited by K. v. Lerberghe and G. Voet. Orientalia Lovaniensia Analecta 96. Leuven: Peeters, 2001.

_____. "A Lexical Illusion." *JSS* 31 (Spring 1986) 1–3.

_____. "Please Speak Aramaic." *Buried History* 25 (1989) 67–73.

_____. "La Prophétie et l'écriture: Israël, Aram, Assyrie." *Revue de l'Histoire des Religions* 202 (1985) 125–44.

_____. "Review of James Barr, *The Variable Spellings of the Hebrew Bible*." *JTS* 41 (1990) 571–75.

_____. "Review. Niditch, *Oral World and Written Word: Orality and Literacy in Ancient Israel*." *JTS* 49 (1998) 699–705.

_____. "Story, History, and Theology." Pp. 37–64 in *Faith, Tradition, and History: Old Testament Historiography in Its Near Eastern Context.* Edited by A. R. Millard, J. K. Hoffmeier, and D. W. Baker. Winona Lake, Indiana: Eisenbrauns, 1994.

_____. "Text and Comment." Pp. 245–52 in *Biblical and Near Eastern Studies in Honour of William Sanford LaSor.* Edited by Gary A. Tuttle. Grand Rapids, Michigan: Eerdmans, 1978.

_____. "The Uses of the Early Alphabets." Pp. 101–14 in *Phoinikeia grammata. Lire et écrire en Méditerranée: Actes du Colloque de Liège, 15–18 novembre 1989.* Edited by V. Krings, C. Bonnet, and Baurain Claude. Namur: Société des Études Classiques, 1991.

_____. "Variable Spelling in Hebrew and Other Ancient Texts." *JTS* 41 (1991) 106–15.

_____. "Writing." Pp. 1286–95 in *NIDOTTE.* Edited by W. A. VanGemeren. Grand Rapids: Zondervan, 1997.

_____. "*YW* and *YHW* Names." *VT* 30 (1980) 208–12.

Miller, David L. *Introduction to Collective Behavior and Collective Action.* Prospect Heights, Illinois: Waveland, 2000.

Miller, J. M. "Is It Possible to Write a History of Israel without Relying on the Hebrew Bible?" Pp. 93–102 in *The Fabric of History.* Edited by Diana V. Edelman. JSOTSup 127. Sheffield: Sheffield Academic Press, 1991.

Momigliano, A. *Studies in Historiography.* London: Weidenfeld & Nicolson, 1966.

Monson, J. "The New ʿAin Dara Temple: Closest Solomonic Parallel." *BAR* 26/3 (2000) 20–35, 67.

Montgomery, J. A. *A Critical and Exegetical Commentary on the Books of Kings.* ICC. Edinburgh: T. & T. Clark, 1967.

Morag, S. "Review: *Die Lexikalischen und Grammatikalischen Aramaismen im Alttestamentlichen hebräisch.*" *JAOS* 92 (1972) 298–300.

Müller, H.-P. "ʿTodʾ des alttestamentlichen Geschichtsgottes?" *NZSTh* 41 (1999) 1–21.

Müller, M. *The First Bible of the Church.* Sheffield: Sheffield Academic Press, 1996.

Muilenburg, J. "Form Criticism and Beyond." *JBL* 88 (1969) 1–18.

Mullen, S. A. "Between ʿRomanceʾ and ʿTrue Historyʾ: Historical Narrative and Truth Telling in a Postmodern Age." Pp. 23–40 in *History and the Christian Historian.* Edited by R. A. Wells. Grand Rapids, Michigan: Eerdmans, 1998.

Murray, D. "Review of Flemming A. J. Nielsen, ʿTragedy in History.ʾ" *JTS* 50 (1999) 183–87.

Muscarella, O. W. *The Lie Became Great: The Forgery of Ancient Near Eastern Cultures.* Groningen: Styx, 2000.

Naʾaman, N. "The Contribution of Royal Inscriptions for a Re-evaluation of the Book of Kings as a Historical Source." *JSOT* 82 (1999) 3–17.

_____. "Royal Inscriptions and the Histories of Joash and Ahaz, Kings of Judah." *VT* 48 (1998) 333–49.

_____. "Sources and Composition in the History of David." Pp. 170–86 in *The Origins of the Ancient Israelite States.* Edited by V. Fritz and P. R. Davies. Sheffield: Sheffield Academic Press, 1996.

_____. "Sources and Composition in the History of Solomon." Pp. 57–80 in *The Age of Solomon: Scholarship at the Turn of the Millennium.* Edited by L. K. Handy. Leiden: Brill, 1997.

New York Times. "Radio Listeners in Panic: Taking War Drama as Fact." *New York Times* (October 31, 1938) 1–2.

Niditch, S. *Oral World and Written Word*. Louisville: Westminster John Knox, 1996.

Niehr, H. "Some Aspects of Working with the Textual Sources." Pp. 156–65 in *Can a "History of Israel" Be Written?* Edited by L. L. Grabbe. Sheffield: Sheffield Academic Press, 1997.

Nielsen, E. *Oral Tradition*. Studies in Biblical Theology 11. London: SCM, 1955.

_____. "The Traditio-historical Study of the Pentateuch." Pp. 11–28 in *The Productions of Time: Tradition History in the Old Testament*. Edited by K. Jeppesen and B. Otzen. Sheffield: Almond, 1984.

Nielsen, Flemming A. *The Tragedy in History: Herodotus and the Deuteronomistic History*. JSOTSup 251. CIS 4. Sheffield: Sheffield Academic Press, 1997.

Niemann, H. M. *Herrschaft, Königtum und Staat: Skizzen zur soziokulturellen Entwicklung im monarchischen Israel*. Forschungen zum Alten Testament. Tübingen: Mohr, 1993.

Noll, K. "Is There a Text in This Tradition? Readers' Response and the Taming of Samuel's God." *JSOT* 83 (1999) 31–51.

Norin, S. "*Jô-*Namen und *Jehô-*Namen." *VT* 29 (1979) 87–97.

_____. "Onomastik zwischen Linguistik und Geschichte." Pp. 161–78 in *International Organization for the Study of the Old Testament, Congress Volume: Oslo, 1998*. Edited by A. Lemaire and M. Sæbø. Leiden: Brill, 2000.

Norman, A. P. "Telling It like It Was: Historical Narratives on Their Own Terms." *History and Theory* 30 (1989) 119–35.

North, R. "Could Hebrew Have Been a Cultic Esperanto?" *Zeitschrift für Althebraistik* 12 (1999) 202–16.

Noth, M. *The Deuteronomistic History*. JSOTSup 15. Sheffield: JSOT Press, 1981.

_____. *Überlieferungsgeschichtliche Studien*. Halle (Saale): Max Niemeyer, 1943.

Novick, P. *That Noble Dream: The Objectivity Question and the American Historical Profession*. Ideas in Context. Cambridge: Cambridge University Press, 1988.

Nyberg, H. S. *Studien zum Hoseabuche: Zugleich ein Beitrag zur Klärung des Problems des alttestamentlichen Textkritik*. UUÅ 6. Uppsala: Almqvist & Wiksells, 1935.

Olafsson, S. "Late Biblical Hebrew: Fact or Fiction?" Pp. 135–47 in *Intertestamental Essays in Honour of Jozef Tadeusz Milik*. Edited by J. Zdzislaw Kapera. Cracow: Enigma, 1992.

Olmstead, A. T. *History of Palestine and Syria to the Macedonian Conquest*. New York: Scribner's, 1931.

Ong, W. J. *Interfaces of the Word: Studies in the Evolution of Consciousness and Culture*. Ithaca, New York: Cornell University Press, 1977.

_____. "Literacy and Orality in Our Times." Pp. 8–20 in *Oral and Traditional Literatures*. Edited by Norman Simms. Hamilton: Outrigger, 1982.

_____. *Orality and Literacy: The Technologizing of the Word*. London: Methuen, 1982.

Pardee, D. *Handbook of Ancient Hebrew Letters*. Chico, California: Scholars Press, 1982.

_____. "Review of *Linguistic Evidence for the Northern Origin of Selected Psalms* by Gary A. Rendsburg." *JAOS* 112 (1992) 702–4.

Parpola, S. *Letters from Assyrian Scholars to the Kings Esarhaddon and Assurbanipal*. AOAT 5/1. Neukirchen-Vluyn: Neukirchener Verlag, 1970.

Pasto, J. "When the End Is the Beginning? Or When the Biblical Past Is the Political Present: Some Thoughts on Ancient Israel, 'Post-Exilic Judaism,' and the Politics of Biblical Scholarship." *SJOT* 12 (1998) 157–202.

Pelling, C. "Epilogue." Pp. 325–57 in *The Limits of Historiography: Genre and Narrative in Ancient Historical Texts.* Edited by C. S. Kraus. Leiden: Brill, 1999.

Phillips, M. S. "Reconsiderations on History and Antiquarianism: Arnaldo Momigliano and the Historiography of Eighteenth-Century Britain." *Journal of the History of Ideas* 57 (1996) 297–316.

Polak, F. H. "The Oral and the Written: Syntax, Stylistics and the Development of Biblical Prose Narrative." *JANES* 26 (1998) 59–105.

Polanyi, M. *Personal Knowledge: Towards a Post-critical Philosophy.* Chicago: University of Chicago Press, 1962.

Polzin, R. *Late Biblical Hebrew: Toward an Historical Typology of Biblical Hebrew Prose.* HSM 12. Missoula, Montana: Scholars Press, 1976.

Postgate, J. N. *Early Mesopotamia: Society and Economy at the Dawn of History.* London: Routledge, 1992.

Prince, J. D. "An Akkadian Cruciform Monument." *AJSL* 29 (1912–13) 95–110.

Pritchard, J. B. (ed.). *Ancient Near Eastern Texts.* 3rd ed. Princeton: Princeton University Press, 1969.

Provan, I. W. *1 and 2 Kings.* NIBC. Peabody, Massachusetts: Hendrickson, 1995.

————. *1 & 2 Kings.* Old Testament Guides. Sheffield: Sheffield Academic Press, 1997.

————. "Ideologies, Literary and Critical: Reflections on Recent Writing on the History of Israel." *JBL* 114 (1995) 585–606.

————. "In the Stable with the Dwarves: Testimony, Interpretation, Faith and the History of Israel." Pp. 281–319 in *International Organization for the Study of the Old Testament, Congress Volume: Oslo, 1998.* Edited by A. Lemaire and M. Sæbø. VTSup 80. Leiden: Brill, 1998.

Qimron, E. *The Hebrew of the Dead Sea Scrolls.* HSS 29. Atlanta: Scholars Press, 1986.

————. "Observations on the History of Early Hebrew (1000 B.C.E.–200 C.E.) in the Light of the Dead Sea Documents." Pp. 349–61 in *The Dead Sea Scrolls: Forty Years of Research.* Edited by D. Dimant and U. Rappaport. Studies on the Texts of the Desert of Judah 10. Leiden: Brill, 1992.

Rad, Gerhard von. "The Beginning of Historical Writing in Ancient Israel." Pp. 166–204 in *The Problem of the Hexateuch and Other Essays.* Translated by E. W. Trueman Dicken. Edinburgh: Oliver & Boyd, 1966.

————. *Old Testament Theology.* Vol. 1. Translated by D. M. G. Stalker. Edinburgh: Oliver & Boyd, 1962.

Ranke, Leopold von. *Geschichten der romanischen und germanischen Völker von 1494 bis 1514.* Leipzig: Duncker & Humblot, 1874.

Rawson, E. *Intellectual Life in the Late Roman Republic.* London: Duckworth, 1985.

Reiner, E., and H. G. Güterbock. "The Great Prayer to Ishtar and Its Two Versions from Boğazköy." *JCS* 21 (1967) 255–66.

Rendsburg, G. A. *Diglossia in Ancient Hebrew.* New Haven, Connecticut: American Oriental Society, 1990.

————. *Israelian Hebrew in the Book of Kings.* OPDNESPJSCU 5. Bethesda, Maryland: CDL, 2002.

————. "Late Biblical Hebrew and the Date of 'P.'" *JANES* 12 (1980) 5–80.

_____. *Linguistic Evidence for the Northern Origin of Selected Psalms*. Atlanta: Scholars Press, 1990.

_____. "Notes on Israelian Hebrew (I)." Pp. 255–58 in *Michael: Historical, Epigraphical and Biblical Studies in Honor of Prof. Michael Heltzer*. Edited by Y. Avishur and R. Deutsch. Tel-Aviv: Archaeological Center Publications, 1999.

_____. "Notes on Israelian Hebrew (II)." *JNSL* 26 (2000) 33–45.

Rendtorff, R. "The Paradigm Is Changing: Hopes—and Fears." *Biblical Interpretation* 1 (1993) 34–53.

_____. *Das überlieferungsgeschichtliche Problem des Pentateuch*. BZAW 147. Berlin: de Gruyter, 1977.

Renz, J. "Dokumentation neuer Texte." *ZAH* 13 (2000) 106–20.

Renz, J., and W. Röllig. *Handbuch der althebräischen Epigraphik I*. Darmstadt: Wissenschaftliche, 1995.

Ribichini, S. "Taautos et l'invention de l'écriture chez Philon de Byblos." Pp. 201–13 in *Phoinikeia grammata. Lire et écrire en Méditerranée: Actes du Colloque de Liège, 15–18 novembre 1989*. Edited by V. Krings, C. Bonnet, and Baurain Claude. Liège-Namur: Société des Études Classiques, 1991.

Ricoeur, P. "Humanities between Science and Art." Transcript of Paul Ricoeur's speech at the opening ceremony of the *Humanities at the Turn of the Millennium* Conferences, University of Århus, Denmark, June 4, 1999. Transcription by Eline Busck. http://www.hum.au.dk/ckulturf/pages/publications/pr/hbsa.htm. (November 22, 1999).

_____. *Time and Narrative*. Chicago: University of Chicago Press, 1984.

Riesenfeld, H. *The Gospel Tradition Essays*. Philadelphia: Fortress, 1970.

Riesner, R. "Jesus as Preacher and Teacher." Pp. 185–210 in *Jesus and the Oral Gospel Tradition*. Edited by H. Wansbrough. JSNTSup 64. Sheffield: Sheffield Academic Press, 1991.

Rooker, M. F. *Biblical Hebrew in Transition: The Language of the Book of Ezekiel*. JSOTSup 90. Sheffield: JSOT Press, 1990.

_____. "Dating Isaiah 40–66: What Does the Linguistic Evidence Say?" *WTJ* 58 (1996) 303–12.

_____. "The Diachronic Study of Biblical Hebrew." *JNSL* 14 (1988) 199–214.

Roth, M. T. *Law Collections from Mesopotamia and Asia Minor*. SBL Writings from the Ancient World 6. Atlanta: Scholars Press, 1997.

Rüger, H.-P. "Oral Tradition in the Old Testament." Pp. 107–20 in *Jesus and the Oral Gospel Tradition*. Edited by H. Wansbrough. JSNTSup 64. Sheffield: Sheffield Academic Press, 1991.

Sacks, K. S. "Diodorus and His Sources: Conformity and Creativity." Pp. 213–32 in *Greek Historiography*. Edited by S. Hornblower. Oxford: Clarendon, 1994.

Sáenz-Badillos, A. *A History of the Hebrew Language*. Cambridge: Cambridge University Press, 1993.

Sancisi-Weerdenburg, H. "The Persian Kings and History." Pp. 91–112 in *The Limits of Historiography: Genre and Narrative in Ancient Historical Texts*. Edited by Christina Shuttleworth Kraus. Leiden: Brill, 1999.

Sarfatti, G. B. "Hebrew Inscriptions of the First Temple Period: A Survey and Some Linguistic Comments." *Maarav* 3 (1982) 55–83.

Sasson, J. "On Choosing Models for Recreating Israelite Pre-monarchic History." *JSOT* 21 (1984) 3–24.

Schepens, G. "Jacoby's *FGrHist*: Problems, Methods, Prospects." Pp. 144–72 in *Collecting Fragments = Fragmente sammeln*. Edited by G. W. Most. Aporemata: Kritische Studien zur Philologiegeschichte 1. Göttingen: Vandenhoeck & Ruprecht, 1997.

Schmid, H. H. *Der sogenannte Jahwist: Beobachtungen und Fragen zur Pentateuchforschung*. Zurich: Theologischer Verlag, 1976.

Schmidt, B. "A Re-evaluation of the Ugaritic King List." Pp. 289–304 in *Ugarit, Religion, and Culture*. Edited by N. Wyatt, W. Watson, and J. Lloyd. Münster: Ugarit-Verlag, 1996.

Schniedewind, W. M. "Qumran Hebrew as an Antilanguage." *JBL* 118 (1999) 235–52.

Schüle, A. *Die Syntax der althebräischen Inschriften: Ein Beitrag zur historischen Grammatik des Hebräischen*. Münster: Ugarit-Verlag, 2000.

Schwarz, M. "Can We Rely on Later Authorities for the Views of Earlier Thinkers?" *Israel Oriental Studies* 1 (1971) 241–48.

Shahid, Irfan. "The Martyrs of Najrân: New Documents." *Subsidia Hagiographica* 49 (1971) 53–60.

Shapin, S. *A Social History of Truth: Civility and Science in Seventeenth-Century England*. Chicago: University of Chicago Press, 1994.

Shryock, Andrew. *Nationalism and the Genealogical Imagination: Oral History and Textual Authority in Tribal Jordan*. Berkeley: University of California Press, 1997.

Silberman, N. "Power, Politics and the Past: The Social Construction of Antiquity in the Holy Land." Pp. 8–23 in *The Archaeology of Society in the Holy Land*. Edited by Thomas E. Levy. New York: Facts On File, 1995.

Silberman, N., and and D. B. Small (eds.). *The Archaeology of Israel: Constructing the Past, Interpreting the Present*. JSOTSup 237. Sheffield: Sheffield Academic Press, 1997.

Silver, M. *Prophets and Markets: The Political Economy of Ancient Israel*. Social Dimensions of Economics. Boston: Kluwer-Nijhoff, 1983.

Singer, I. "A Political History of Ugarit." Pp. 601–733 in *Handbook of Ugaritic Studies*. Edited by W. G. Watson and N. Wyatt. Leiden: Brill, 1999.

Sivan, D. *A Grammar of the Ugaritic Language*. Leiden: Brill, 1997.

Skjeggestad, M. *Facts in the Ground: Biblical History in Archaeological Interpretation of the Iron Age in Palestine*. Acta Theologica 3. Oslo: Unipub, 2001.

_____. " 'Israels historie': Litteratur *eller* historie? Eller: Historie *som* litteratur?" *NTT* 97 (1996) 203–18.

Smelik, K. *Converting the Past: Studies in Ancient Israelite and Moabite Historiography.* Oudtestamentische Studien. Leiden: Brill, 1992.

Smith, M. "A Comparison of Early Christian and Early Rabbinic Tradition." *JBL* 82 (1963) 176–79.

_____. *Palestinian Parties and Politics That Shaped the Old Testament*. London: SCM, 1987

_____. *Studies in the Cult of Yahweh*. Edited by S. J. D. Cohen. Religions in the Graeco-Roman World 130. Leiden: Brill, 1996.

Soggin, J. A. "The History of Ancient Israel: A Study in Some Questions of Method." *Eretz-Israel* 14 (Ginsberg Volume; 1978) *44–*51.

Sollberger, E. "The Cruciform Monument." *JEOL* 20 (1968) 50–70.

Spivak, G. "Identity and Alterity: An interview." *Arena* (1991) 65–76.

Stade, B. *Geschichte des Volkes Israels*. 2 vols. Berlin: G. Grote, 1887–88.

Steenstrup, J. *Historieskrivningen*. Copenhagen: Hagerups, 1915.

Sternberg, M. *The Poetics of Biblical Narrative: Ideological Literature and the Drama of Reading*. Bloomington: Indiana University Press, 1985.

Stock, B. *Listening to the Text: On the Uses of the Past*. Baltimore: Johns Hopkins University Press, 1990.

Strange, J. "Arkæologisk syntese og historieskrivning." Pp. 43–57 in *Bibel of Historieskrivning*. Edited by Geert Hallbäck and John Strange. Forum for Bibelsk Eksegese 10. Copenhagen: Museum Tusculanum, 1999.

Strasburger, H. *Die Wesensbestimmung der Geschichte durch die antike Geschichtsschreibung*. Wiesbaden: Steiner, 1996.

Summers, J. L. "Teaching History, the Gospel, and the Postmodern Self." Pp. 205–19 in *History and the Christian Historian*. Edited by R. A. Wells. Grand Rapids, Michigan: Eerdmans, 1998.

Swierenga, R. P. "Social Science History: An Appreciative Critique." In *History and Historical Understanding*. Edited by C. McIntyre and R. A. Wells. Grand Rapids, Michigan: Eerdmans, 1984.

Talmon, S. "Oral Tradition and Written Transmission, Or the Heard and the Seen Word in Judaism of the Second Temple Period." Pp. 121–58 in *Jesus and the Oral Gospel Tradition*. Edited by H. Wansbrough. JSNTSup 64. Sheffield: Sheffield Academic Press, 1991.

Talshir, Z. "The Three Deaths of Josiah and the Strata of Biblical Historiography (2 Kings XXIII 28–30; 2 Chronicles XXXV 20–5; 1 Esdras I 23–31)." *VT* 46 (1996) 213–36.

Thompson, H. O. *Biblical Archaeology*. New York: Paragon, 1987.

Thompson, T. L. *The Bible in History: How Writers Create a Past*. London: Cape, 1999.

_____. "Defining History and Ethnicity in the South Levant." Pp. 166–87 in *Can a "History of Israel" Be Written?* Edited by Lester L. Grabbe. JSOTSup 245. ESHM 1. Sheffield: Sheffield Academic Press, 1997.

_____. *Early History of the Israelite People from the Written and Archaeological Sources*. Studies in the history of the Ancient Near East. Leiden: Brill, 1992.

_____. "4QTestimonia og Bibelens affattelse: En københavnsk legohypotese." Pp. 233–41 in *Dodehavsteksterne og Bibelen*. Edited by Niels Hyldahl and Thomas L. Thompson. Copenhagen: Museum Tusculanum, 1996.

_____. *The Historicity of the Patriarchal Narratives: The Quest for the Historical Abraham*. BZAW 133. Berlin: de Gruyter, 1974.

_____. "Historiography (Israelite)." Pp. 206–12 in vol. 3 of *ABD*. Edited by D. N. Freedman. New York: Doubleday, 1992

_____. "How Yahweh Became God: Exodus 3 and 6 and the Heart of the Pentateuch." *JSOT* 68 (1995) 57–74.

_____. "The Intellectual Matrix of Early Biblical Narrative: Inclusive Monotheism in Persian Period Palestine." Pp. 107–24 in *The Triumph of Elohim*. Edited by D. V. Edelman. Kampen: Kok Pharos, 1995.

_____. "Lester Grabbe and Historiography: An *Apologia*." *SJOT* 14 (2000) 140–61.

_____. "A Neo-Albrightean School in History and Biblical Scholarship?" *JBL* 114 (1995) 683–98.

_____. *The Origin Tradition of Ancient Israel: The Literary Formation of Genesis and Exodus 1–23*. JSOTSup 55. Sheffield: JSOT Press, 1987.

_____. "Some Exegetical and Theological Implications of Understanding Exodus as a Collected Tradition." Pp. 233–42 in *Fra dybet*. Edited by Niels Peter Lemche and Mogens Müller. Copenhagen: Museum Tusculanum, 1994.

_____. "Text, Context and Referent in Israelite Historiography." Pp. 65–82 in *The Fabric of History*. Edited by D. V. Edelman. JSOTSup 127. Sheffield: Sheffield Academic Press, 1991.

Tigay, J. H. *The Evolution of the Gilgamesh Epic*. Philadelphia: University of Pennsylvania Press, 1982.

Tinney, S. "Ur-Namma the Canal-Digger: Context, Continuity and Change in Sumerian Literature." *JCS* 51 (1999) 31–54.

Tinniswood, R. "Choirboy Raised by Monkeys." *Liverpool Echo* (Thursday, October 7, 1999) 9.

Toorn, Karel van der. "In the Lions' Den: The Babylonian Background of a Biblical Motif." *CBQ* 60 (1998) 626–40.

Tov, E. *Textual Criticism of the Hebrew Bible*. Minneapolis: Fortress / Assen: Van Gorcum, 1992.

Trebolle Barrera, J. "A 'Canon within a Canon': Two Series of Old Testament Books Differently Transmitted, Interpreted and Authorized." *Revue de Qumran* 19 (2000) 383–99.

_____. "Edition préliminaire de 4QChroniques." *Revue de Qumran* 15 (1992) 523–29.

Uchitel, A. "Local versus General History in Old Hittite Historiography." Pp. 55–68 in *The Limits of Historiography: Genre and Narrative in Ancient Historical Texts*. Edited by Christina Shuttleworth Kraus. Leiden: Brill, 1999.

Ullendorf, E. *Ethiopia and the Bible*. Schweich Lectures. London: Oxford University Press, 1968.

_____. *The Ethiopians: An Introduction to Country and People*. London: Oxford University Press, 1973.

_____. "Is Biblical Hebrew a Language?" *BSOAS* 34 (1971) 241–55.

Ulrich, E. C. *The Qumran Text of Samuel and Josephus*. HSM 19. Missoula, Montana: Scholars Press, 1978.

Ulrich, E. C., and F. M. Cross. *Qumran Cave 4, IX: Deuteronomy, Joshua, Judges, Kings*. DJD 14. Oxford: Clarendon, 1995.

VanderKam, J. C. "Book Reviews. Van Seters, John. *In Search of History: Historiography in the Ancient World and the Origins of the Biblical History*. New Haven: Yale University Press, 1983." *Interpretation* 44 (1990) 293–95.

Vanhoozer, K. J. *Biblical Narrative in the Philosophy of Paul Ricoeur: A Study in Hermeneutics and Theology*. Cambridge: Cambridge University Press, 1990.

_____. "Introduction: Hermeneutics, Text, and Biblical Theology." Pp. 14–50 in *NIDOTTE*. Edited by W. A. VanGemeren. Carlisle: Paternoster, 1997.

_____. *Is There a Meaning in This Text?* Leicester: Apollos, 1998.

Van Seters, J. *Abraham in History and Tradition*. New Haven: Yale University Press, 1975.

_____. *In Search of History: Historiography in the Ancient World and the Origins of Biblical History*. New Haven: Yale University Press, 1983. Reprinted, Winona Lake, Indiana: Eisenbrauns, 1997.

_____. *The Life of Moses: The Yahwist as Historian in Exodus–Numbers*. Louisville: Westminster John Knox, 1994.

_____. *Prologue to History: The Yahwist as Historian in Genesis.* Louisville: Westminster John Knox, 1992.

_____. "Solomon's Temple: Fact and Ideology in Biblical and Near Eastern Historiography." *CBQ* 59 (1997) 45–57.

Vansina, J. *Oral Tradition as History.* London: James Currey / Nairobi: Heinemann Kenya, 1985.

_____. *Oral Tradition: A Study in Historical Methodology.* Chicago: Aldine, 1965.

Vanstiphout, H. "Memory and Literacy in Ancient Western Asia." Pp. 2181–96 in vol. 4 of *Civilizations of the Ancient Near East.* Edited by J. M. Sasson, J. Baines, and G. Beckman. New York: Scribner's, 1995.

Vanutelli, P. *Libri synoptici Veteris Testamenti seu librorum Regum et Chronicorum loci paralleli.* 2 vols. Rome: Pontifical Biblical Institute, 1931.

Veldhuis, N. "TIN.TIR = Babylon, the Question of Canonization, and the Production of Meaning." *JCS* 50 (1998) 67–76.

Verheij, A. J. C. *Verbs and Numbers: A Study of the Frequencies of the Hebrew Verbal Tense Forms in the Books of Samuel, Kings, and Chronicles.* Assen: Van Gorcum, 1990.

Vernes, M. *Précis d'histoire juive depuis les origines jusqu'à l'époque persane.* Paris: Hachette, 1889.

Wagner, M. *Die lexikalischen und grammatikalischen Aramaismen im alttestamentlichen Hebräisch.* BZAW 96. Berlin: de Gruyter, 1966.

Waltke, B. K., and M. O'Connor. *An Introduction to Biblical Hebrew Syntax.* Winona Lake, Indiana: Eisenbrauns, 1990.

Wansbrough, H. (ed.). *Jesus and the Oral Gospel Tradition.* JSNTSup 64. Sheffield: Sheffield Academic Press, 1991.

Weinfeld, M. *Getting at the Roots of Wellhausen's Understanding of the Law of Israel on the 100th Anniversary of the Prolegomena.* Report No. 14. Jerusalem: Hebrew University of Jerusalem, 1979.

Weippert, H. "Book Reviews. Van Seters, John. *In Search of History: Historiography in the Ancient World and the Origins of the Biblical History.* New Haven: Yale University Press, 1983." *Journal of Religion* (1987) 530–31.

Wellhausen, J. *Die Composition des Hexateuchs und der historischen Bücher des Alten Testaments.* Berlin: Reimer, 1899.

Westenholz, J. G. *Legends of the Kings of Akkade: The Texts.* Mesopotamian Civilizations 7. Winona Lake, Indiana: Eisenbrauns, 1997.

_____. "Relations between Mesopotamia and Anatolia in the Age of the Sargonic Kings." Pp. 5–22 in *XXXIV^{éme} Rencontre Assyriologique Internationale 6–10/ VII/1987—Istanbul.* Ankara: Türk Tarih Kurumu Basimevi, 1998.

White, H. "Historicism, History, and the Figurative Imagination." *History and Theory* Beiheft 14 (1975) 48–67.

_____. *Metahistory: The Historical Imagination in Nineteenth-Century Europe.* Baltimore: Johns Hopkins University Press, 1973.

_____. "The Question of Narrative in Contemporary Historical Theory." *History and Theory* 23 (1984) 1–33.

Whitelam, K. W. "The Search for Early Israel: Historical Perspective." Pp. 41–64 in *The Origin of Early Israel—Current Debate: Biblical, Historical and Archaeological Perspectives. Irene Levi-Sala Seminar, 1997.* Edited by Shmuel Ahituv and Eliezer

D. Oren. Beʾer Sheva 12. London: Institute of Archaeology and Institute of Jewish Studies, University College, 1998.

Williams, J. G. *The Times and Life of Edward Robinson: Connecticut Yankee in King Solomon's Court.* SBL Biblical Scholarship in North America 19. Atlanta: Scholars Press, 1999.

Wind, E. "Some Points of Contact between History and Natural Science." Pp. 255–64 in *Philosophy and History.* Edited by R. Klibansky and H. Paton. Oxford: Clarendon, 1936.

Winternitz, M. *Geschichte der indischen Litteratur.* Die Litteraturen des Ostens 9. Leipzig: Amelang, 1909.

Winther-Nielsen, N. "Fact, Fiction and Language Use: Can Modern Pragmatics Improve on Halpern's Case for History in Judges?" Pp. 44–81 in *Windows into Old Testament History: Evidence, Argument, and the Crisis of Biblical Israel.* Edited by V. Philips Long, David W. Baker, and Gordon J. Wenham. Grand Rapids: Eerdmans, 2001.

_____. "Tracking the World of Judges: The Use of Contextual Resources in Narration and Conversation." Forthcoming in *Hiphil* at http://www.see-j.net.

Yamauchi, E. "The Current State of Old Testament Historiography." Pp. 1–36 in *Faith, Tradition, and History: Old Testament Historiography in Its Near Eastern Context.* Edited by A. R. Millard, J. K. Hoffmeier, and D. W. Baker. Winona Lake, Indiana: Eisenbrauns, 1994.

Yeivin, S. "The Juridical Petition from Mezad Hashavyahu." *BO* 19 (1962) 3–10.

Young, I. M. *Diversity in Pre-exilic Hebrew.* Forschungen zum Alten Testament 5. Tübingen: Mohr (Siebeck), 1993.

_____. "Israelite Literacy: Interpreting the Evidence. Part I." *VT* 48 (1998) 239–53.

_____. "Israelite Literacy: Interpreting the Evidence. Part II." *VT* 48 (1998) 408–22.

Younger, K. L. *Ancient Conquest Accounts: A Study in Ancient Near Eastern and Biblical History Writing.* JSOTSup 98. Sheffield: Sheffield Academic Press, 1990.

_____. "Book Review. Van Seters, John. *In Search of History: Historiography in the Ancient World and the Origins of BIblical History.* New Haven and London: Yale University Press, 1983." *JSOT* 40 (1988) 110–17.

Zadok, R. *Geographical Names according to New- and Late-Babylonian Texts.* Répertoire Géographique des Texts Cunéiforms 8. Beihefte zum Tübinger Atlas des Vorderen Orients 7/8. Wiesbaden: Reichert, 1985.

Zevit, Z. 1980. "Clio, I Presume." *BASOR* 260 (1985) 71–82.

_____. *Matres Lectionis in Ancient Hebrew Epigraphs.* ASOR Monograph Series 2. Cambridge, Massachusetts: ASOR, 1980.

Zimmerli, W. "Prophetic Proclamation and Reinterpretation." Pp. 69–100 in *Tradition and Theology in the Old Testament.* Edited by D. A. Knight. Sheffield: JSOT Press, 1990.

Indexes

Index of Authors

Index of Scripture

New Testament

Deuterocanonical Literature

Index of Topics

Hebrew, Biblical (*cont.*)
  dialects of 129
  linguistic variation 129
  morphology of 129, 135
  orthography 129, 135
  syntax 149
  vocabulary 129
  inscriptions 126, 150
  Israelite 114, 132
  Mishnaic 114, 117, 136, 152–153, 159–161
    contrast with Biblical Hebrew 153
    vocabulary 119
    word order 119
  Modern 122, 149
  orthography 154
  paleography 176
  Qumran 114, 136, 140, 151
    orthography 136, 140
    paleography 136
    spelling 136
    syntax 140
    vocabulary 136
  Rabbinic 114
  verb forms of 148–149
Hebrew Bible *see* Bible, Hebrew
Hecataeus 103
Heliopolis 91
Hellenica 197, 220
Hellenistic culture 107
Hellenistic historians 175, 227
Hellenistic Period 3, 24, 33, 51, 59, 78, 99–100, 108, 119, 133, 141, 167, 170, 184–185, 188, 231
  pan-Hellenistic consciousness 66
hermeneutics 10, 13, 15
  hermeneutic of suspicion 3
Herodotus 11, 15, 22, 66, 164, 197, 207, 213, 216–217, 220, 222, 225, 231
  Histories 221
Hesiod 66
  Theogony 222
Hezekiah 154, 169–171, 176
Hindanu 182
Hiram 46, 242
histoire totale 5, 241
historians 9–10, 12, 15, 19, 26, 40–41, 56, 78, 95, 103, 109, 204–205, 211, 214, 227, 233, 238, 241, 244, 246
  American 5
  ancient 226
  ancient Near Eastern 216–217

historians (*cont.*)
  and bias 11
  biblical 3, 78, 186
  Classical 47, 214
  consensus of 111
  contrasted with "chroniclers" 8
  and emplotment 12
  Greek 92, 222
  Hellenistic 175, 215, 242
  and impartiality 11
  of Israel 26, 53
  Israelite 218, 221
  medieval 57
  methodological assumptions of 4
  modern 39–40, 57, 59, 213
  pre-Hellenistic 216–217
  revisionist 203, 211
  Roman 47, 215
historical change 6
historical consciousness 79, 203, 221, 231, 234, 246
  in the Deuteronomist 223
historical-critical research 3, 24
historical intent 30, 220–221, 223, 232, 234, 243
historical linguistics 158
historical narrative 11–14
  and epistemic value 13
  and truth-claims 13–15
historical reconstruction *see* reconstruction, historical
historical theory 5, 10, 41, 204, 244
  and hermeneutics 11
  and linguistics 11
  and literary theory 11
historicism 5, 9, 27, 219
historicity 15, 33, 45, 51, 56, 64, 66–68, 70, 75, 96, 98, 100, 103, 107, 166, 179–180, 219, 223, 227–228, 230, 245
historiography 1, 5, 9–10, 18–19, 23, 25, 30–31, 54, 95, 106–107, 112, 180, 186, 190, 193, 197–198, 202–204, 207, 212–216, 218–220, 224–235, 240–244, 246–247
  ancient 25, 206, 220, 231
  ancient Near Eastern 184, 216
  and biases 43
  biblical 26, 112
  Christian 214
    authorial intent in 231
  and climate change 5
  definition of 219

inscriptions (*cont.*)
  Khirbet el-Kom 124
  Meṣad Ḥashavyahu 124–125
  monumental 138, 149
  Neo-Assyrian 172
  preexilic Hebrew 151, 162–163
  Ramesside inscriptions 21
  votive 104
Institute of Palestinian Archaeology 20
instruction, oral 80
interpretation 1, 11, 100
  ancient 106
  of artifactual data 27
  biblical 22
  epistemological 12
  and genre 196
  and historical research 18, 26
  and metastory 11
  ontological 12
Iron Age 19, 26–28, 33, 37–38, 48, 52–53, 79, 98
  paucity of evidence from 26
Isaiah Scroll 156
  see also Dead Sea Scrolls
Isaiah, book of 118, 172, 174
Isaiah, prophet 156–157, 171
Isin 93
Islam 76
Islamic civilization 57
Islamic history 15
Israel 2, 18, 20–21, 24–25, 37, 59, 62, 76–80, 86, 88, 92, 99, 102, 133, 177–178, 180, 183, 209, 215, 236–238
  archaeology of 53, 110
  as ancient state 3
  early 2
  epigraphic remains from 53, 147
  historiography in 216
  history of 4, 19, 25–26, 41, 48, 58, 89, 107
    political history 2
  history-writing in 214–216
  Iron Age 33, 48, 58, 79, 111, 123, 193
  kingdom of 98
  kings of 98
  literacy in 84–86
  Northern Kingdom 133
  oral tradition in 63, 68, 75, 77, 82, 84, 88, 92
  origins of 2, 5
  preexilic 63, 77

Israel (*cont.*)
  religious life in 236
  storytellers in 76
  writing in 87
Israeli-Palestinian conflict 20
Israelite(s) 3, 19, 44, 51, 85, 97, 120, 130, 171–172, 183
  as ethnic designation 3
  and literature 30
  settlement 19
  traditions of 98, 100
Ištar, Great Prayer to 121
Italian, and Latin 44

Jason of Cyrene 227
Jehoahaz 168
Jehoash 168
Jehoash Inscription 124
Jehoiachin 169, 239
Jehoiakim 82
Jehu 168, 185
Jeremiah, book of 118, 126, 175
Jeremiah, prophet 81–82, 126, 156
Jerusalem 3, 107, 110, 116, 125, 130, 133, 171, 186
  destruction of 78, 81, 150, 237
Jerusalem Jar 125
Jesus 12, 73–75
  oral traditions 70
  search for historical 1, 69
  as teacher 69–71
  traditions about 70
Jews 20, 29, 108
  Egyptian 36
  of Hellenistic Period 100
  identity contrasted with Hebrews 20
  Palestinian 36
Joah 130, 171
Job, book of 115–116, 137
  language 137
Jonah, book of 160
Joppa 208
Josephus 36, 46, 179, 187–188, 231
  Jewish Antiquities 108
Joshua, book of 3, 217
Josiah, reform of 176
Judah, Judea 3, 78–79, 92, 110, 116–117, 120, 130, 133, 166, 171, 236–238
  administration of 99
  customs of 171
  Iron Age 58, 79
  kingdom of 98